T0295856

The Handbook
of Credit Risk
Management

The Handbook of Credit Risk Management

Originating, Assessing, and Managing Credit Exposures

Second Edition

SYLVAIN BOUTEILLÉ
DIANE COOGAN-PUSHNER

WILEY

Library of Congress Cataloging-in-Publication Data

Names: Bouteillé, Sylvain, author. | Coogan-Pushner, Diane, author.
Title: The handbook of credit risk management : originating, assessing, and
    managing credit exposures / Sylvain Bouteillé, Diane Coogan-Pushner.
Description: Second edition. | Hoboken, New Jersey : Wiley, [2022] |
    Series: Wiley finance | Includes index.
Identifiers: LCCN 2021042739 (print) | LCCN 2021042740 (ebook) | ISBN
    9781119835639 (hardback) | ISBN 9781119835653 (adobe pdf) | ISBN
    9781119835646 (epub)
Subjects: LCSH: Credit—Management. | Risk management.
Classification: LCC HG3751 .B68 2022 (print) | LCC HG3751 (ebook) | DDC
    658.8/8—dc23
LC record available at https://lccn.loc.gov/2021042739
LC ebook record available at https://lccn.loc.gov/2021042740

Cover Design: Wiley
Cover Image: © By Piotr Zajc

SKY10030235_111121

To my wife, Setsuko; my sons Pierre and François
and my parents.

—Sylvain Bouteillé

To George, James, Bonnie and Adam.

—Diane Coogan-Pushner

Contents

PART TWO

Credit Assessment

CHAPTER 4
Measurement of Credit Risk   47

CHAPTER 5
Dynamic Credit Exposure   67

CHAPTER 6
Fundamental Credit Analysis   81

CHAPTER 7
Alternative Estimations of Credit Quality   107

Preface

The first edition of *The Handbook of Credit Risk Management: Originating, Assessing, and Managing Credit Exposures* was published at the end of 2012 at a time when the global economy had just started to recover after one of the worst financial crises of modern history (which we refer to as the "2007 crisis" because in 2007, delinquencies on mortgages began occurring on a large scale). The expectation was that leadership teams of financial institutions, risk management professionals, investors, governments, and regulators would reflect on what had gone wrong in the buildup to the crisis and make all necessary changes so that it would not happen again.

As risk professionals, we have been very satisfied by what happened for the most part. We originally wondered how good intentions would translate into concrete actions and changes of behaviors. Then we were skeptical that the changes would last long and feared that, after a while, memories of the 2007 crisis would fade away, regulators would gradually relax their rules and financial institutions and investors would start again making big bets.

It did not happen and we can now clearly see that the financial system is more resilient than it used to be. No major crisis occurred in the last decade although risk management principles were tested by unprecedented events such as a global pandemic, a negative oil price, or a short squeeze of stocks organized by a new breed of investors in their 20s.

Overall, the last decade reinforced the role that credit risk management (CRM) teams play in the world economy. Resources allocated to CRM have increased in many institutions. The opinions of credit risk managers are taken more seriously into account than ever and their voices are heard louder when they ask to improve the structure of a new transaction or to strengthen internal processes.

Since the publication of the first edition of *The Handbook of Credit Risk Management*, we received numerous testimonials from readers who acknowledged that the book had helped them improve their knowledge of the topics covered and contributed to their professional success. We have also been humbled by the number of universities and companies who used our book to support the education of their students and employees.

The support we received encouraged us to write a second edition. So many things changed since 2012 that we thought that the time was right to publish a completely updated version. What's new? Financial markets are constantly evolving so we updated many concepts and market practices with the latest industry standards. We also updated all data and provided many new examples to illustrate the topics we present. We also did not hesitate to delete entire sections when the content of the first edition was no longer relevant. One example is the ABS CDO market, which was as big as $500 billion prior to the 2007 crisis and which has completely disappeared today and is unlikely to reemerge in the foreseeable future.

Finally, we wrote three completely new chapters we thought would be of interest to our readers. They cover consumer finance, state and local government credit, and sovereign credit risk.

We are still of the opinion that too often credit risk management is viewed only as the art of assessing single name counterparties and individual transactions. For us, CRM remains more than that. The management of a credit risk portfolio involves four sequential steps:

1. Origination
2. Credit assessment
3. Portfolio management
4. Mitigation and transfer

Each one must be individually well understood, but, also, the way they interact together must be mastered. It is only by fully comprehending the entire chain of steps that risk professionals can properly fulfill their task of protecting the balance sheet of the firms employing them.

We provide a comprehensive framework to manage credit risk, introducing one of the four essential steps in each part of the book. This book is based on our professional experience and also on our experience with teaching CRM to graduate students and finance professionals.

We hope that you will find the second edition of *The Handbook of Credit Risk Management* valuable, whether you are a student, someone new in the field of risk management, or a professional interested in learning more about this important topic.

Next, we provide an overview of each part.

PART ONE: ORIGINATION

Part One focuses on the description of credit risk and on the credit risk taking process in any organization involved in credit products. We also provide a simple checklist to analyze new transactions.

In Chapter 1 ("Fundamentals of Credit Risk"), we define credit risk and present the major families of transactions that generate credit risk for industrial companies and financial institutions. We conclude with the main reasons why properly managing a portfolio of credit exposures is essential to generate profits, produce an adequate return on equity, or simply survive.

In Chapter 2 ("Governance"), we present the strict rules that must be in place within all institutions taking credit risk. It all starts with clear and understandable credit policies or guidelines. Then, in order to control accumulation, we discuss the role of limits on similar exposures. We also provide a concrete framework to approve new transactions. To finish, we discuss the human factor: how a risk management unit must be staffed and where it must be located inside an organization.

In Chapter 3 ("Checklist for Origination"), we introduce nine key questions that must be answered before accepting any transaction generating credit risk. It may sound trivial, but the best way to avoid credit losses is to not originate bad transactions. All professionals involved in risk taking must, therefore, ask themselves essential questions such as: Does the transaction fit the strategy? Does it fit into the existing portfolio? Is the nature of the credit risk well understood? Is the deal priced adequately or is there an exit strategy?

PART TWO: CREDIT ASSESSMENT

Part Two introduces the methods to estimate the amount of exposure generated by transactions of various natures before detailing how to analyze the creditworthiness of a company, government, or of a structured credit product.

The focus of Chapter 4 ("Measurement of Credit Risk") is on the quantification of credit risk for individual transactions. We present the three main drivers influencing the expected loss of a transaction: the exposure, the probability of default, and the recovery rate. The exposure is the evaluation of the amount of money that may be lost in case of default of the counterparty. The probability of default is a statistical measure that aims at forecasting the likelihood that an entity will default on its financial obligations. We introduce a two-step approach to derive a default probability: the assignment of a rating followed by the use of historical data. Finally, there are few transactions that generate a complete loss when an entity defaults. Creditors are usually able to receive some money back. The amount is summarized by the recovery rate. The expected loss is the multiplication of the three parameters presented above.

Chapter 5 ("Dynamic Credit Exposure") is dedicated to the measurement of exposures that are not fixed but change with the changes of financial market values. We present, with examples, two main families of transactions generating a dynamic credit exposure: long-term supply/purchase agreements of physical commodities and derivatives trades involving, for instance, interest rates, foreign exchange, or commodities. We explain that at any given time, the credit exposure of such transactions is the replacement cost of the counterparty and is measured with the concept of mark-to-market (MTM) valuation. We conclude by introducing the concept of value at risk (VaR), which provides a statistical measurement of credit risk for a given time horizon and within a certain confidence interval. One of the key things to remember is that VaR is a useful method, but it does not represent the worst-case scenario. In the real world, actual losses can and have exceeded VaR.

The cornerstone of all credit risk management processes is assessing the credit risk of counterparties. In Chapter 6 ("Fundamental Credit Analysis"), we present the most common method of analysis, which is a quantitative-based review of the counterparty's financial data, and we also present a qualitative-based review of the firm's operations and economic environment in which it operates. We start the analysis by covering basic principles of accounting and the salient features of a company's balance sheet, income statement, and cash flow statement. We then describe the key ratios summarizing the financial health of a company.

We introduce the concept that the interests of the shareholders and of the creditors are not aligned. This is known as an agency conflict. In essence, creditors are not in a position to influence decisions impacting the fate of the money they invest in a company. This is the prerogative of management, appointed by shareholders. We conclude Chapter 6 by outlining a model building of the shareholders-versus-creditors relationship, developed in the 1970s by the Nobel Prize Laureate Robert Merton.

Besides fundamental credit analysis, there are alternative ways for estimating the creditworthiness of a company, including its probability of default. We present the most common alternative ways in Chapter 7 ("Alternative Estimations of Credit Quality"). The most popular is based on the Merton Model presented in Chapter 6. Several companies offer commercial applications of the model, such as Moody's Analytics Expected Default Frequency (EDF™). We introduce the basics of the methodology behind the EDF™ and also its pros and cons. We explain that useful indications of credit quality can be extracted from the capital markets, notably the prices of credit default swaps and of corporate bonds. The limitations of these alternative sources are fully explained.

Individuals are important sources of credit risk for many financial institutions like credit card companies, mortgage lenders, or student loan providers. The new Chapter 8 ("Consumer Finance)" reviews major consumer finance products generating credit risk and techniques used to analyze the credit worthiness of individuals when deciding whether or not to approve a loan request. We conclude with a brief introduction to the regulatory framework.

Chapter 9 ("State and Local Government Credit") is a new chapter that covers state and local government finance. Our focus is solely on state and local governments, not on the entirety of the public finance category, and we look at the risks associated with the bonds they issue and of other obligations, such as retirement benefits.

Chapter 10 ("Sovereign Credit Risk") is also a new chapter that covers sovereign credit risk and describes important risk characteristics of this sector including how recoveries are handled.

Earlier chapters focus on types of obligors, such as corporates, financial institutions, and governments, but in Chapter 11 ("Securitization") we introduce the basics of structured credit products, primarily asset-backed securities or ABSs. Banks developed asset securitization in the 1970s as a way to originate mortgages without keeping them and their associated credit risk on their balance sheet. We discuss the three building blocks of any securitization scheme: the collateral (i.e., the assets sold by the originator), the issuer of the ABS (which is an entity created for the sole purpose of making a transaction possible and is called a special purpose vehicle or SPV), and the securities sold to investors. We present the main families of ABS that are primarily supported by consumer assets like mortgages, auto loans, and credit-card receivables.

We start Chapter 12 ("Collateral Loan Obligations [CLOs]") by reviewing the three main families of corporate borrowers and the way corporate loans are funded, which includes collateralized loan obligations (CLOs), a form of securitization detailed in Chapter 11. We distinguish between the CLOs structured to fund leveraged loans (*arbitrage cash* CLOs) and CLOs used by banks only to transfer the credit risk attached to loans (*synthetic balance sheet CLOs*). We provide a framework to analyze CLOs for entities investing in them.

PART THREE: PORTFOLIO MANAGEMENT

Part Three is primarily dedicated to the management of a portfolio of credit exposures with a focus on capital requirements. We also present how regulators all over the world impose strict conditions on financial institutions in order to limit their risk taking and maintain their capital levels, as the regulators' mandate is to protect the public and maintain the financial stability of the world economy. We finish with a description of the main accounting implications associated with the major credit products.

Assessing individual transactions is not enough to protect a firm's balance sheet. In Chapter 13 ("Credit Portfolio Management"), we introduce the fundamentals of credit portfolio management (CPM), which consists of analyzing the totality of the exposures owned by a firm. The main goals of CPM are to avoid accumulation of some companies or industry sectors, to prevent losses by acting when the financial situation of a counterparty deteriorates, and to estimate and minimize the amount of capital necessary to support a credit portfolio. For companies with a small portfolio, CPM can be intuitive and performed with simple methods. For institutions with a large portfolio and complex exposures, CPM requires the use of analytical models. We explain why it is crucial to adapt the sophistication of CPM activities to the real needs of an entity. As such, we present three different complexity levels that we recommend any firm adopt based on its own needs and resources.

Chapter 14 ("Economic Capital and Credit Value at Risk [CVaR]") is dedicated to the description of the analytical concepts used to evaluate the amount of capital necessary to support a credit portfolio. We introduce the concept of a loss distribution, which associates an amount of money that can be lost with a corresponding probability. The shape of the distribution is influenced by the correlation between the assets, that is, the chance that the financial condition of distinct entities deteriorates at the same time, usually as a result of the same economic conditions. A credit loss distribution is not a normal bell-shaped distribution, but, rather, it is heavily skewed. This reveals that there is a high probability of losing a small amount of money (summarized by the expected loss of the portfolio) and a low probability of losing a lot of money. To survive under the latter scenario, firms need to set aside capital. We explain that the amount of capital is determined by the concept of VaR due to credit exposure (or credit VaR, i.e., CVaR) applied to the entire portfolio. Active portfolio management aims at reducing the amount of capital by executing rebalancing transactions.

Chapter 15 ("Regulation") outlines the myriad of regulators and their respective domains as it relates to assuming or being exposed to credit risk. We present the reach of the regulators from the perspective of a credit originating business that does business with a regulated entity, since the regulation itself will materially influence the credit profile of the obligor. We also present the reach of the regulators from the perspective of the regulated entity, which are primarily financial institutions, as it relates to taking on credit risk. Regulators and their regulations are numerous, and the global efforts underway have succeeded to a large extent in the harmonization of both the regulatory agencies and their regulations and in removing the loopholes that exist. We attempt to give readers a sense for these new regulatory directives, including their mandates, scope, and timelines.

In Chapter 16 ("Accounting Implications of Credit Risk"), we outline for readers the accounting treatment related to recognition, disclosure, and valuation, under both U.S. GAAP and IFRS, of instruments that involve credit risk. This includes the accounting for loans, for other credit instruments such as bonds, and impairment. We outline the rules relating to de-recognition and consolidation of assets, counterparty netting agreements, and the credit and debit valuation adjustments used in derivatives accounting. Although accounting should never drive risk management decisions, all risk professionals should understand the basic accounting implications associated with originating, holding, and unwinding exposures.

PART FOUR: MITIGATION AND TRANSFER

Because there is always a risk that the financial situation of a counterparty deteriorates after the conclusion of a transaction, it is common to put safeguards in the legal documentation. If properly designed, the safeguards in place can reduce the risk of default or improve the amount recovered after a default. We describe the most common safeguards at the beginning of Part Four. We then introduce techniques available to risk managers to either transfer the credit risk they hold to a third party, or to neutralize it with an offsetting position, both tactics known as hedging.

For derivative transactions, in order to reduce the losses in case of the default of one's counterparty, financial institutions utilize standard principles that we describe in Chapter 17 ("Mitigating Derivative Counterparty Credit Risk"). The implementation of these principles provides confidence to market participants and promotes large scale trading or liquidity. One standard principle to limit credit exposure is to have counterparties post collateral, that is, transfer cash or easily sellable assets whenever their trading losses, measured by the mark-to-market value of all the transactions, exceed a pre-agreed threshold. By setting very low thresholds, the uncollateralized exposure and, therefore, the potential loss are always low. We explain the key principles of a robust collateral posting mechanism. After the 2007 crisis, regulators vowed to impose even stronger rules for derivatives markets participants. We explain how bilateral trades between financial institutions are gradually being replaced by the involvement of central counterparties or clearinghouses.

Chapter 18 ("Structural Mitigation") is dedicated to techniques and conditions imposed on a counterparty during the lifetime of a transaction. Their objectives are either to maintain the creditworthiness of the counterparty after the inception of a transaction, or to trigger immediate repayments in case of deterioration. We start by outlining the standard techniques used in bank loans. Conditions imposed on borrowers are called covenants and we present the two main types, negative and affirmative. They do not improve the recovery expectations but prevent or delay defaults. We also describe the differences between secured and unsecured loans. In the second part we focus on the various techniques used to strengthen securitization schemes.

In Chapter 19 ("Credit Insurance, Surety Bonds, and Letters of Credit"), we introduce three traditional methods used to transfer the credit risk that an entity faces to a third party. Credit insurance applies primarily to trade receivables, that is, invoices sent to customers after a sale. It is offered by insurance companies and indemnifies the policyholder if a client does not pay. Insurance companies also offer surety bonds. Their role is to provide a payment if a counterparty fails to perform a contractual, legal, or tax obligation. We present the main two applications of surety: contract bonds in the construction industry and commercial bonds in many industrial sectors. We conclude by introducing letters of credit (LoCs) offered by banks to support transactions entered into by their clients. If a counterparty does not perform on its obligations, the letter of credit is drawn, that is, the issuing bank pays on behalf of its client, thereby reducing the losses.

Credit derivatives are another technique employed to reduce a credit exposure and are explained in detail in Chapter 20 ("Credit Derivatives"). We first present the concept of the product before explaining how a firm purchasing a credit derivative is protected in case of default of a third-party entity. We then present the various uses of credit derivatives. First, a credit derivative provides a simple way to hedge a credit exposure. This was the original purpose of these instruments. Second, it can be a relatively simple way to gain credit exposure to an entity, without having to fund an investment and without having to assume interest rate exposure. Third, it can be used to speculate on the demise of an entity. We terminate by providing an overview of the limitations of credit derivatives as a hedging instrument and by presenting products based on credit derivatives exchanged in the marketplace.

Chapter 21 ("Bankruptcy") is dedicated to financial distress and bankruptcy. We start by defining bankruptcy and its legal context. We provide patterns of companies that have defaulted, which serve as early warning for credit analysts. In order to be concrete, we present the cases of two U.S. companies that defaulted: Eastman Kodak and MF Global Holdings.

Acknowledgments

We would like to acknowledge James Galasso for his valuable research assistance. We also thank the professionals at Wiley who guided the writing of this book start to finish: Bill Falloon, Hemalatha Thirunavukkarasu, Jayaprakash Unni, Purvi Patel, Samantha Enders and Samantha Wu. Of course, all mistakes are ours. The opinions expressed in this book are those of Mr. Bouteillé and of Ms. Coogan-Pushner, and they do not reflect in any way those of the institutions to which they are or have been affiliated.

About the Companion Website

This book is accompanied by a companion website for instructors:
www.wiley.com\go\bouteille\handbookcreditriskmanagement
   The website includes:

- Slide decks by chapter
- Cases studies to illustrate the concepts covered in the Handbook and in classes
- Test bank with various quizzes
- Merton-Model to assess a default probability

One

Origination

CHAPTER 1

Fundamentals of Credit Risk

WHAT IS CREDIT RISK?

Credit risk is the possibility of losing money due to the inability, unwillingness, or nontimeliness of a counterparty to honor a financial obligation. Whenever there is a chance that a counterparty will not pay an amount of money owed, live up to a financial commitment, or honor a claim, there is credit risk.

Counterparties that have the responsibility of making good on an obligation are called "obligors." The obligations themselves often represent a legal liability in the form of a contract between counterparties to pay or perform. Note, however, that, from a legal standpoint, a contract may not be limited to the written word. Contracts that are made orally can be legally binding.

We distinguish among three concepts associated with the inability to pay. First is insolvency, which describes the financial state of an obligor whose liabilities exceed its assets. Note that it is common to use insolvency as a synonym for bankruptcy but these are different events. Second is default, which is failure to meet a contractual obligation, such as through nonpayment. Default is usually—but not always—due either to insolvency or illiquidity. Third is bankruptcy, which occurs when a court steps in upon default after a company files for protection under either Chapter 11 or Chapter 7 of the bankruptcy laws (in the United States). The court reviews the financial situation of the defaulted entity and negotiates with its management, creditors, and sometimes equity owners. Whenever possible, the court tries to keep the entity in business by selling assets and/or renegotiating financing arrangements with lenders. Bankruptcy proceedings may end in either a restructuring of the obligor's business or in its dissolution if the business cannot be restructured.

In most cases, losses from credit risk involve an obligor's inability to pay a financial obligation. In a typical scenario, a company funds a rapid expansion plan by borrowing and later finds itself with insufficient cash flows from operations to repay the lender. Other common cases include businesses whose products or services become obsolete or whose revenues simply no longer cover operating and financing costs. When the scheduled payment becomes due and the company does not have enough funds available, it defaults and may generate a credit loss for the lenders and all other counterparties. There are also more and more cases where the inability to pay follows an unexpected and uninsured event that destroys an entity in a short time. Just think of all the small and medium-sized companies that disappeared in 2020 after the COVID-19 pandemic or the wildfires in California.

Credit losses can also stem from the unwillingness of an obligor to pay. This is less common, but can lead to the same consequences for the creditors. The most frequent cases are commercial disputes over the validity of a contract. In instances in which unwillingness is at issue, if the dispute ends up in litigation and the lender prevails, there is recovery of the amount owed, and ultimate losses are lessened or even avoided entirely because the borrower has the ability to pay.

Frequently, credit losses can arise in the form of timing. For example, if monies are not repaid on a timely basis, there can be either interest income foregone or working capital finance charges incurred by the lender or trade creditor, so time value of money is at stake.

Credit risk can be coupled with political risk. Obligors doing business in different countries may have both the ability and willingness to repay, but their governments may, without much warning, force currency conversion of foreign-currency denominated accounts. This happened in 2002 in Argentina with the "pesification," in which the government of Argentina forced banks to convert their dollar-denominated accounts and debts to Argentine pesos. Companies doing business in Argentina saw their U.S. dollar-denominated bank deposits shrink in value, and their loans and trade credits shrink even more, since the conversion rate was even more egregious for loans than deposits.

A common feature of all credit exposures is that the longer the term of a contract, the riskier that contract is, because every additional day increases the possibility of an obligor's inability, unwillingness, or nontimeliness of repayment or making good on an obligation. Time is risk, which is a concept that we will explore further throughout the book.

For each transaction generating credit risk, we will address three fundamental questions in the forthcoming chapters:

1. What is the amount of credit risk? How much can be lost or what is the total cost if the obligor fails to repay or perform?
2. What is the probability of default of the counterparty? What is the likelihood that the obligor fails to pay or perform?

3. How much can be recovered in case of bankruptcy? In the case of non-payment or nonperformance, what is the remedy and how much can be recovered, in what time frame, and at what expense?

TYPES OF TRANSACTIONS THAT CREATE CREDIT RISK

Managing credit risk requires first identifying all situations that can lead to a financial loss due to the default of a counterparty. Long gone are the days when it was an easy task. Today, there are many different types of financial transactions, sometimes very sophisticated, that generate credit risk.

Traditionally, credit risk was actively managed in bank lending and trade receivables transactions. A rule of thumb for identifying credit risk was to look for an exchange of cash or products at the beginning of a commercial agreement. The risk was that the money would not be repaid or the products not paid for. Recently, however, the development of modern banking products led to transactions generating large credit exposures without lending money or selling a product, as we explain in Chapter 5, which is dedicated to dynamic credit exposures mostly generated by derivatives transactions.

Credit risk is present in many types of transactions. Some are unique but some are rather common. In the following paragraphs, we will describe seven common business arrangements that generate credit risk.

Lending is the most obvious area. There is a cash outflow up front, from the lender to the borrower, with a promise of later repayment at a scheduled time. A second transaction type involves leases, when a piece of equipment or a building is made available by an entity (the lessor) to another entity (the lessee) that commits to make regular payments in the future. The lessor typically borrows money to finance the asset it is leasing and expects the future cash flow from the lessee to service the debt it contracted. The third type is the sale of a product or a service without immediate cash payment. The seller sends an invoice to the buyer after the product has been shipped or the service performed, and the buyer has a few weeks to pay. This is known as an account receivable.

Prepayment of goods and services is a fourth type of transaction that involves credit risk. Delivery is expected at a certain time and of a certain quality and/or performance, and the failure of the counterparty may lead to the loss of the advanced payments and also generates business interruption costs. A fifth type of transaction that creates credit risk involves a party's claim on an asset in the custody of or under the management of another party, such as a bank deposit. Most individuals choose their bank more for the services they offer or the proximity to their home rather than after a detailed analysis of its financial conditions. Large corporates think differently because they have large amounts of cash available. They worry that the banks with their deposits may default. Before trusting a financial institution, they review its creditworthiness. They also spread their assets among many banks to avoid a risk concentration, as the Federal Deposit Insurance Corporation's (FDIC) coverage limit of $250,000 per account is insufficient to cover most deposits of large corporations. The bankruptcy of MF Global in 2011 reminded many individuals and businesses to think twice about cash left in brokerage accounts and to carefully evaluate limits under the Securities Investor Protection Corporation (SIPC) or, outside the United States, its equivalent.

A sixth type of transaction is a special case of a claim on an asset—a contingent claim. The claim is contingent on certain events occurring, such as a loss covered by an insurance policy. At policy inception, the policyholder has no claim on the insurer. However, once the insured suffers a covered loss, the insured has a claim. If the insurer fails to pay the claim, this would constitute a credit loss. Another example of a contingent claim would be a pension fund that has a claim on the assets of its sponsor, should the fund's liabilities exceed its assets. Nothing has been prepaid and no funds were lent, but there is credit risk borne by the pension participants in the event that the sponsor cannot honor the fund's liabilities.

Finally, a seventh type of transaction involves not a direct exposure but a derivative exposure. It arises from derivatives transactions like interest-rate swaps or foreign-exchange futures. Both parties commit to make future payments, the amounts of which are dependent on the market value of an underlying product, for example, the exchange rate between the U.S. dollar and the Japanese yen. In Chapter 5 we explain how to calculate the amount of credit risk in these types of transactions. Although there is no up-front cash outflow as there is in a loan, the counterparty's financial distress results in the same outcome—loss of money. Other examples of credit risk stemming from changes in the value of an underlying financial asset include repurchase agreements, options, and short-selling of shares.

These transactions groupings, as described in Table 1.1, are general categories. Further breakdowns are possible that map to particular credit instruments frequently used in these transactions. For example, loaned money can take the instrument form of a corporate bond, a bank loan, a consumer loan, asset-based lending, and commercial paper, among others.

Figure 1.1 displays credit risk exposure associated with borrowing instruments as of September 30, 2020, for the United States. The predominant source of credit exposure in the United States is corporate obligations. Although there is roughly $55.5 trillion of debt outstanding in U.S. debt markets, these include noncredit risky instruments such as U.S. Treasury obligations, government-sponsored enterprise (GSE, or "agency") obligations, and agency-backed mortgage obligations. Of instruments that have credit risk, the majority is issued by the corporate sector in the form of corporate bonds, bank loans, and commercial paper.

TABLE 1.1 Types of Transactions That Create Credit Risk

Credit Type	Losses Result From	Loss Type
Loaned money	Nonrepayment	Face amount, interest
	Slow repayment	Time value of money
	Dispute/enforcement	Frictional costs
Lease obligation	Nonpayment	Recovery of asset, remarketing costs, difference in conditions
Receivables	Nonpayment of goods delivered or service performed	Face amount
Prepayment for goods or services	Nondelivery	Replacement cost
	Performance on delivery not as contracted	Incremental operating cost
	Slow delivery	Time value of money
	Dispute/enforcement	Frictional costs
Deposits	Nonrepayment	Face amount
		Time value of money
Claim or contingent claim on asset	Nonrepayment/Noncollection	Face amount
	Slow repayment/Slow collection	Time value of money
	Dispute/enforcement	Frictional costs
Derivative	Default of third party	Replacement cost (mark-to-market value)

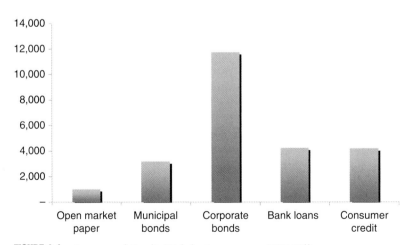

FIGURE 1.1 Sources of Credit Risk by Instrument, USD Billions
Source: Federal Reserve Board of Governors, "Z.1. Financial Accounts of the United States," September 30, 2020, Tables L.208, L.212, L.213, and L.214.

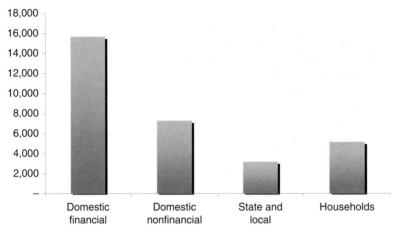

FIGURE 1.2   Sources of Credit Risk by Entity Type, USD Billions
Source: Federal Reserve Board of Governors, "Z.1. Financial Accounts of the United States," September 30, 2020, Tables L.208, D.3., and B101.h. Note that deposits are not counted in the Federal Reserve's definition of credit market debt.

Figure 1.2 displays the source of credit risk exposure by entity. Note that financial corporations are a far larger source of credit exposure than are both nonfinancial corporations and households. Again, we choose not to include federal government debt or household-mortgage debt (the majority of which is agency backed), since one could argue that these forms of borrowing have no associated credit risk exposure, a topic that we will explore further in Chapter 10, "Sovereign Credit Risk."

In the United States alone, over $5 trillion of trade receivables are on the books of all corporations, and this figure represents 89% percent of all trade receivables as of September 2020.[1]

Finally, the potential notional credit exposure arising from derivative transactions as of June 2020 is estimated to be in excess of $600 trillion on a global basis. Nearly all of this exposure arises from over-the-counter (OTC) interest-rate derivative contracts, with the remaining roughly $30 billion, trading on exchanges. Figure 1.3 shows the relative sizing of counterparty credit risk exposure by derivative type, based on the notional value of the contracts for OTC transactions. Note that the notional value corresponds to gross credit exposure, which we discuss in Chapter 4 and which is the most conservative measure of credit risk.

---

[1]U.S. Federal Reserve Board of Governors, "Flow of Funds," Table L.225, "Trade Credit."

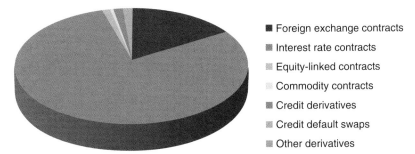

- Foreign exchange contracts
- Interest rate contracts
- Equity-linked contracts
- Commodity contracts
- Credit derivatives
- Credit default swaps
- Other derivatives

FIGURE 1.3 Notional Value of Counterparty Credit Risk Exposure for OTC and Exchange-Traded Derivatives, End-June 2020, USD Billions
Source: Bank of International Settlements, Statistical Release, Tables D5.1 and D5.2, June 2020: "Notional Amounts Outstanding of Over-the-Counter (OTC) Derivatives."

WHO IS EXPOSED TO CREDIT RISK?

All institutions and individuals are exposed to credit risk, either willingly or unwillingly. However, not all exposure to credit risk is inherently detrimental; banks and hedge funds exist and profit from their ability to originate and manage credit risk. Individuals choose to invest in fixed income bond funds to capture extra return relative to holding U.S. Treasury bonds. For others, like industrial corporations or service companies, because they sell goods or services without prepayments, credit risk is a necessary by-product of their main activities.

In Figure 1.4, we can see who bears the exposure to debt securities issued by corporates and other entities. We see that financial institutions, including public and private pension funds, mutual funds, banks, insurance companies, and others, have the largest exposure, followed by households and nonprofits, foreign entities, and the government sector (federal, state, and local). Governments and nonfinancial corporations are not in business to invest in debt instruments or to assume credit risk as a primary business endeavor so it is reasonable that they have the smallest holdings.

Figure 1.5 shows the breakdown of the financial sector in terms of who holds the exposure to these debt instruments. Within the financial sector, depository institutions and mutual funds have the most exposure (almost $12 and $10 trillion, respectively), with insurers, pension plans, and finance companies each having about half as much. This figure paints a high-level picture of why some institutions, primarily financial institutions, employ large teams of credit risk managers, since so much is at stake.

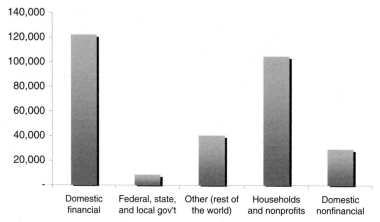

FIGURE 1.4   Exposure to Credit Market Instruments by Entity, USD Billions
Source: Federal Reserve Board of Governors, "Z.1. Financial Accounts of the United States," September 30, 2020, Tables L.101, L.102, L.105, L.108, and L.133.

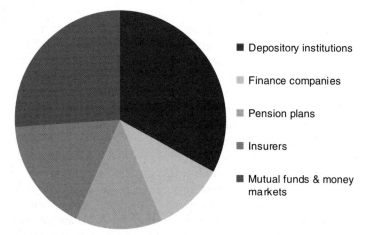

FIGURE 1.5   Financial Institutions' Exposure to Credit Market Instruments, USD Billions
Source: Federal Reserve Board of Governors, "Z.1. Financial Accounts of the United States," September 30, 2020, Tables L.208 and L.214.

Financial Institutions

Since financial institutions face the most credit risk exposure, we will naturally focus on these entities throughout this book. In the following subsections, we briefly describe how each of these financial institutions is exposed.

Banks Because they are in business to extend credit, banks have the largest credit portfolios and possess the most sophisticated risk management organizations. Interestingly enough, their appetite for credit risk has declined over the years, as margins are low and regulatory capital requirements high. The recent activities of regulators across the globe to strengthen the financial system will lead to further reluctance to take on credit risk.

The focus for large banks has shifted toward fee-generating services such as mergers-and-acquisitions advisory services or debt and equity issuance. However, loans and lines of credit still constitute the largest sources of credit risk for a bank. For corporate clients, they are offered as a way to develop a relationship, and often would not produce a sufficient return on capital on a stand-alone basis. However, because the loans and lines of credit represent the potential for large losses, banks employ teams of risk managers who do nothing but analyze the credit risk of borrowers and review the loans' legal documents. In order to further reduce the credit risk exposure that these loans present, banks are increasingly turning to the capital markets to hedge the exposure created in extending the credit.

Loans include asset-based lending like repurchase agreements ("repos") and securities lending. In short, banks lend money or securities against the provision of collateral such as Treasury bonds or equity. If the borrower cannot repay or give back the securities, the lender can sell the collateral, thus reducing or eliminating losses. In theory, the collateral held is sufficient to cover the amount of borrowed money or the value of the securities in case the counterparty defaults. When the financial markets are volatile, though, the value of the collateral can decline quickly, just at the time when the counterparty defaults. Banks, therefore, manage their exposures carefully. We introduce repos in more detail in Chapter 17.

After loans, the derivatives business generates the largest credit risk exposure for banks and comes from many directions. We will explain in Chapter 5 why derivatives generate a form of credit risk known as "derivative counterparty" exposure. For JPMorgan Chase & Co., the derivative receivables counterparty credit risk exposure on a fair-value basis at the end of 2020 was $707 billion, comprised of interest-rate contracts, followed by foreign exchange contracts, credit derivatives, equity contracts, and commodity contracts. Net of cash and liquid security collateral, the derivative receivables exposure was approximately $80 billion, which compares to its equity base of almost $280 billion. Although the ratio appears large, the exposure metric represents what would be lost if all counterparties defaulted on the exposure valuation date.

Most of the examples used in this book relate to banks' exposures.

Asset Managers The asset management business consists of collecting money from individuals and institutions and investing it in order to meet the investors' risk and return objectives. For instance, cautious investors anxious to protect their principal prefer money-market funds, primarily invested in short-term and high-quality debt. Investors with more appetite for risk may favor mutual funds focusing on equities or emerging markets debt and equity.

Asset management is a huge business worldwide. In the United States, companies such as Blackrock or Vanguard Group manage more than $5 trillion of third-party money. The result is that asset managers, with huge amounts of money to invest, face credit risk exposures on behalf of their clients, whose management is integral to their business model. When managers select their investments, they pay very close attention to the creditworthiness of a corporate or of a sovereign borrower that has the potential to reduce the performance of their fund, including causing losses to their clients. Whereas portfolio managers may be tempted to make investments that promise high returns, the funds' risk managers will discourage the portfolio managers from doing so due to the real possibility that the money may not be repaid.

Hedge Funds Hedge funds also have vast amounts of funds to invest daily and have a correspondingly large amount of credit exposure. Their investors have a greater risk appetite, but demand high returns to compensate for this risk. They are, therefore, more aggressive than typical investors, and they invest in riskier financial instruments, many of which traditional asset managers do not have access to. Their participation in financial markets has made many business transactions possible that otherwise would not have occurred by allowing risk to be transferred. For example, they may purchase distressed loans, sell protection against a decline in a borrower's creditworthiness, or assume the riskiest positions in commercial real estate financing, all of which allow for the necessary transfer of risk to make a transaction possible. In many corporate restructurings, hedge funds play a proactive role to maximize their recoveries, as a result of their investment in risky debt.

What is unique though is that some hedge funds also view the possibility of an entity defaulting as an opportunity to deploy capital. In contrast to traditional financial institutions that hire credit risk managers to avoid the default of their counterparties and protect shareholders' money, hedge funds employ resources to identify entities that may default. They enter into transactions like short-selling or writing of options that make, not lose, money, in cases of financial distress.

Whereas a bank that has a credit exposure may want to hedge the exposure and collect if a credit loss occurs, a hedge fund may profit from the financial distress of an obligor even if it has no direct exposure to that obligor. The growth in derivatives products has made the execution of such strategy relatively easy. We describe in Chapter 20 how credit default swaps (CDSs) work and how they can be used to "short" credit, that is, to make money when the financial situation of a company or a country deteriorates.

CDS and short-selling transactions involve a lot of risk for both fundamental and technical reasons. On the fundamental side, a turnaround by a new management team may be successful. Or, on the technical side, the current supply and demand conditions in the market may lead to severe financial stress.

One example of financial distress caused by short-selling of shares is what happened to the hedge fund Melvin Capital in January 2021. Thinking that the financial situation of GameStop, a video game and consumer electronics retailer, would deteriorate and their share price decline, Melvin entered into short-selling transactions on a big scale: they borrowed shares from investors, with a promise to give them back at a scheduled time, and sold them to other investors at the prevailing market price, which was between $10 and $15. They expected that GameStop's share price would keep declining and that they would be able to buy shares in the open market, give them back to original investors, and make a profit. However, some individual investors realized that companies like Melvin would have to buy large amounts of shares to cover their borrowings and started purchasing shares. As a result, instead of declining, the share price increased. At one point, GameStop's shares reached close to $350. The bigger the increase, the higher the losses for Melvin. When they decided to close their positions, they paid a few hundred dollars per share and recorded a financial loss of several billion dollars. They had to be bailed out by two other hedge funds, Citadel and Point72, without which they would have likely defaulted.

Insurance Companies   Insurance companies are exposed to credit risk in three main areas: underwriting activities, the investment portfolio, and reinsurance recoverables.

Certain insurers offer to protect their clients' credit exposures with trade credit insurance on receivables and with surety bonds, which are reviewed in Chapter 19. As a consequence, insurers and reinsurers may suffer significant losses due to the default of a company they provide coverage on.

One example is the bankruptcy of the British travel agency Thomas Cook in 2019, which cost the (re)insurance industry hundreds of millions of dollars.

The insurance business is similar to asset management in that the company has vast amounts of cash to invest. It collects premiums from policyholders, invests the money, and later pays claims when losses occur. It is not unusual for an insurance company to show losses on its core underwriting operations (i.e., claims paid plus operating expenses exceed premiums collected for a block of policies) yet record profits, thanks to the float on the assets they hold prior to paying claims. Every year, in his annual letter to Berkshire Hathaway shareholders, Warren Buffett, who owns several insurance companies including GEICO, spends pages explaining why he likes a business that provides him with cash flow and the means to do what he likes and does best: invest.

An insurance company's balance sheet is, therefore, characterized by large amounts of claims reserves and equity on the liability and equity side, respectively, and corresponding investment positions on the asset side. The liability reserves are established to pay policyholder claims. If all claims are satisfied, then any remaining assets belong to shareholders. One of the largest U.S. life insurance group, MetLife, Inc., has $480 billion of general account (reserves and equity) assets on its balance sheet as of the fourth quarter of 2020.

As a result, insurance companies are among the largest and most active institutional investors. With each dollar invested comes the possibility not to be paid back. In the insurer's strategic asset allocation process, one of the most important criteria is credit risk. Management of this risk is key since there is a trade-off between expected return, which favors shareholders, and maintaining a low risk profile, which favors policyholders (note that this dichotomy of interests is not present for a mutually owned insurer in which the company is owned by the policyholders). Their portfolio will include large proportions of safe Treasury bonds, which require little to no credit analysis, as well as riskier and higher returning debt issued by commercial real estate vehicles or even leveraged equity investments in hedge funds. Insurance companies have large dedicated teams of professionals in charge of managing all credit positions they hold, even when these positions are managed on a day-to-day basis by a third-party asset manager.

In addition, life insurance companies manage money on behalf of their policyholders in separate accounts. These assets will never belong to MetLife shareholders, even after all claims are paid. These funds are more akin to the assets of an asset manager who has a fiduciary duty to their clients. For MetLife, separate account assets totaled an additional $162 billion in 2020. While in most instances MetLife's shareholders are not directly impacted by credit losses in separate accounts, the insurer may suffer damage to its reputation and jeopardize future business opportunities. Finally, the insurer may offer a product to its clients that guarantees minimum investment returns. In these instances, if credit losses are severe enough, the insurers may only be able to make good on its guarantee by depleting its own capital base, which could lead to insolvency.

The third area of credit risk faced by the insurer relates to their reinsurance activities. Insurers first originate policies that carry the risk of claims becoming far larger than premiums collected. If so, reserves set aside will be inadequate to cover losses, and insurers' capital would be tapped. Thus, behind the scenes, insurance companies all over the world transfer some of the risks they originate to reinsurers. The reinsurance business is dominated by a handful of large, primarily European companies like Swiss Re (Switzerland) or Munich Re (Germany).

The transfer of the risk from primary insurers to reinsurers happens via reinsurance contracts. The model is straightforward: Insurers who originate policies and collect policyholder premiums transfer part of the risk by buying a policy and paying a premium. Once a policyholder reports a claim to the insurer, the insurer reports part of this claim to the reinsurer. The insurer's claim then becomes a reinsurance receivable and it has to be paid within a few weeks. During this period, reinsurers verify and sometimes question the validity of the claims. For small and frequent losses, the credit risk stems essentially from this time lag. The amount of premium paid equates more or less to the amount of losses to be claimed, with the risk being that the reinsurer has disappeared in the intervening time period. For catastrophic losses, the credit risk is much larger. When an earthquake or a hurricane occurs, reinsurers may have inadequate resources to make payments. Thus, primary insurers must carefully choose their reinsurance partners and try to avoid "putting all their eggs in one basket"; that is, they distribute risks among many reinsurers, which is not an easy task because the industry is highly concentrated.

Another form of credit risk associated with reinsurance is the contingent claim that the insurer has on the reinsurer. In the preceding example for receivables, the primary insurer knows its losses and submits its claim to the reinsurer. However, in the case of some liability policies, there can be decades between collecting premiums and the policyholder's report and ultimate settlement of a claim. The insurer must estimate what these claims might be, and these estimates generate a contingent claim on the reinsurer, that is, an asset on its balance sheet contingent on the event that it ultimately pays those estimated losses to policyholders. This asset is called a reinsurance recoverable, and it represents an even larger item on an insurer's balance sheet than receivables on paid losses. For the typical insurer, it is usually the largest single item on the asset side of the balance sheet after invested assets.

The reinsurance business is more than 150 years old, and for a long time the only market participants were well-established reinsurance companies. However, in the past 20 years an alternative market developed, as investors appreciate the solid returns (absent natural catastrophes) and the absence of correlation with other investment asset classes. Out of $600 billion of capital deployed to the reinsurance industry, close to $100 billion was provided by alternative capital at the end of 2020. However, insurers do not want to take the credit risk of these investors so their participation is typically fully collateralized, which means that investors must provide cash in advance to the same amount of the maximum liability they accept in their reinsurance contracts. The credit risk is therefore eliminated.

Pension Funds   Similar to a life insurer that invests monies on behalf of a policyholder, a pension fund sponsor (e.g., corporate employer) invests funds on behalf of pension plan members. As of September 2020, corporations and the private sector had $3.5 trillion of defined benefit pension assets. For public plans under U.S. state and local government plans, sponsors had $9 trillion in assets, and those in U.S. federal government sponsored plans totaled $3.8 trillion.[2] A significant portion of these funds is invested in credit risky assets. Private pension funds must abide by ERISA (Employee Retirement Income Security Act of 1974) prudent-investor rules, and public funds have similar standards; as such, both must be active managers of credit risk even if the asset management of the funds is outsourced to third-party managers.

Corporates

Corporates do not like credit risk but cannot avoid it. It is a by-product of their operations, and their position is not enviable. Investors, rating agencies, and other stakeholders have little tolerance for credit losses, and yet credit risk management is outside of their core competency. To make matters worse, when the customer of a corporation files for bankruptcy, a list of the customer's creditors is published and often relayed by the mass media. The bankruptcy of a customer creates negative publicity and can have a negative effect on the corporation's stock price performance and raise questions about the quality of its operations. Examples include the many retailers that filed for bankruptcy protection in the late 2010s due to the change of consumers' habits and the competition of online shopping. For example, when high-end retailer Neiman Marcus filed for bankruptcy in May 2020, many luxury brands like Chanel, Gucci, or Prada were on the list of creditors with millions of dollars of unpaid invoices.

---

[2]Federal Reserve Bank Flow of Funds Financial Accounts Z.1, tables L.118, L.119, and L.120

The biggest source of credit risk for a corporate is account receivables. Sales are generally not paid in advance, and, thus, corporates have effectively extended short-term credit to their customers. The stronger the customer, the longer and more favorable the terms of payment are for that customer. Well-known examples in the retail industry of a company's ability to extract long and favorable terms from suppliers are Walmart in the United States and Carrefour in France.

Assessing the credit quality of a customer can be very challenging. Most corporates have a few large clients for whom public information is current and easily available. However, the majority of a company's business customers are often small firms for which reliable financial data are more difficult to obtain. In the past 20 years in developed economies, progress has been made toward making the publication of updated statements compulsory, but there is still a long way to go.

Risk managers working in corporations have to make credit decisions based on spotty information. They are helped by specialized companies that have developed databases with millions of records related to financial information and payment patterns. A credit score that summarizes the most relevant criteria to assess the probability of getting paid can complement raw data. The most well-known vendor in the United States is Dun & Bradstreet; in Europe, Bureau Van Dijk (acquired in 2017 by Moody's Corporation); and in Japan, Teikoku Databank.

Faced with the decision of whether to sell to a customer, corporates have options to mitigate this credit risk exposure:

- They can buy insurance on their receivables and an insurer indemnifies them in the event they are not paid.
- They can sell their receivables to factoring companies, which provide cash and credit insurance at the same time.
- Foreign transactions can be secured by documentary credit.

These mitigation tools are explored in Chapter 18.

The second source of credit risk for corporates stems from the circumstance in which they have significant amounts of cash to invest. When investor demand for long-dated bonds is high and yields are low, large corporates take advantage of the market conditions to draw on their credit lines or they issue large amounts of bonds even though they have no immediate funding needs. They build war chests that they can use when acquisition and other business opportunities arise. Yet, due to the dearth of investment opportunities, the cash is not always deployed into the business but instead is deposited in banks and invested in short-term securities, both of which bear credit risk.

Generally speaking, corporates are prudent and favor safe investments like cash and cash-equivalent products, thereby limiting the amount of credit risk they are taking. Certainly, it makes little sense for bondholders to hand over cash for the corporate to buy securities or deposit in banks, since the bondholders could do that directly. However, as we saw during the 2007 crisis, even cash is not safe. To reduce the risk of losing money on their investments, corporates evaluate creditworthiness of their banks and then diversify their deposits across banks, knowing that, ultimately, no bank is "too big to fail."

For certain industry sectors, the third source of credit risk is—by choice or by obligation—derivative trading activities such as the trading of commodity futures. Given the volatility of the price of commodities, corporates that need these raw materials usually enter into long-term, fixed-price contracts. Examples include food companies, which buy agricultural futures, and utilities, which buy combustible product futures to lock in the cost of running their power plants.

Inherent in these trades is a counterparty's inability to make or take delivery of the commodity, and both parties in the trade are exposed to each other's credit risk—the seller who must make delivery and the futures buyer who must make a payment. In the past two decades, the futures markets have become adept at mitigating these inherent sources of credit risk with the clearinghouses requiring margins, or collateral, which vary with the price of the commodity, and providing a backstop to these transactions in the event that the margin proves insufficient. However, many corporates are engaged in the buying and selling of commodities for delivery at a future date that does not happen on an organized exchange, that is, using forward contracts, and in these cases the credit risk exposure is large on both sides. The counterparty can default on its obligation, forcing the corporate to buy or sell in the spot market at prevailing conditions, which can result in a mismatch of costs and revenues with the potential for significant losses. In Chapter 5, we review examples of contracts that create large credit exposures, especially compared to the company's income and capital bases. Corporates engaged in these industries—agriculture, food, energy, and utilities—generally have the most well-developed credit management teams.

Some large corporates that produce expensive equipment have financing arms to help their clients acquire or lease their products. This activity is known as vendor financing. IBM Global Financing (technology), Caterpillar Financial Services (heavy equipment), or Ford Motor Credit Company (automobile) are good examples. They work exclusively for their parent company's clients, and they function like nondepository banks. The business model is to buy equipment from their parents with borrowed money (bank debt and capital markets) and to rent or lease the equipment to customers.

The risk is that customers may default on their repayments and leave the lenders with credit losses.

Finally, an emerging source of credit risk for corporates comes from their supply chain. Manufacturing companies and service companies like retailers are dependent on their suppliers. Bankruptcy of a major or unique supplier can have devastating consequences and lead to a financial loss. It is therefore a credit risk. One example is Apple, which a few years ago had only one supplier for screens used in some Apple Watches. Liquidation of GT Advanced Technologies would have led to a major issue for Apple, so they kept providing capital to keep it afloat. Similarly, when the South Korean shipping company Hanjin defaulted in 2016, ports did not allow them to dock unless they paid the fees they owed and containers filled with valuable products stayed offshore for a long time, disrupting the supply chains of manufacturing companies and retailers. Media reported that containers stranded at sea carried $14 billion worth of products. This is the reason why corporates pay more and more attention to the credit quality of the companies involved in their "ecosystems" and try to diversify their partners.

Individuals

Few individuals worry about credit risk, but the reality is that all households are exposed. Think of the situation in which a family loses money because they made advance payments to a contractor who did not complete a home-renovation project. This is credit risk!

Individuals also bear credit risk in their investment activities, just as insurers and corporates do. The individual manages credit risk in his or her selection of the mutual fund to invest in. The investor may choose to invest in a high-yield fund versus an investment-grade bond fund to extract more yield by taking more credit risk.

Finally, money deposited at banks generates credit risk. Regulators frequently shut down banks, which can lead to losses for their clients. In most countries, some protections are in place. In the United States, the Federal Deposit Insurance Company (FDIC) guarantees all deposits up to $250,000 per account.

WHY MANAGE CREDIT RISK?

An important aspect of credit risk is that it is controllable. Credit exposure does not befall a company and its credit risk managers out of nowhere. If credit risk is understood in terms of its fundamental sources and can be anticipated, it would be inexcusable to not manage it.

Credit risk is also the product of human behavior, that is, of people making decisions. Precarious financial circumstances that obligors may find themselves in result from the decisions that the company's managers have made. The decisions that they make are consequences of their incentives and the incentives of the shareholders whom they represent. Understanding what motivates the shareholders and managers is an important aspect of a counterparty's credit risk profile. We explore more of this thinking in Chapter 6, "Fundamental Credit Analysis."

In summary, weak management of a credit portfolio can be costly and can even lead to bankruptcy. As we review in Chapter 13, exposure to credit risk is capital intensive. A large equity base must be built to survive large and unexpected losses. With a credit portfolio, a large number of small losses are expected and manageable. However, there is also a small chance of large losses, which can be lethal.

All firms should devote significant attention and resources to credit risk management for their own survival, profitability, and return on equity:

- *Survival.* It's a concern primarily for financial institutions for which large losses can lead to bankruptcy, but even a nonfinancial corporation can have credit losses that can cause bankruptcy.
- *Profitability.* It sounds trivial to state that the less money one loses the more money one makes, but the statement pretty much summarizes the key to profitability, especially of low-margin businesses.
- *Return on equity.* Companies cannot run their business at a sufficient return on equity if they hold too much equity capital. Holding large amounts of debt capital is not the solution, either, because debt does not absorb losses and can introduce more risk into the equation. The key to long-term survival is a sufficiently high amount of equity capital complemented by prudent risk management.

During the 2007 crisis, certain global players performed much better than their peers, thanks to very powerful credit risk management principles that kept them afloat. In any economic environment and for any type of company, actively managing a credit portfolio can help increase the company's return on equity. In Chapter 13 we review the basic principles of portfolio management. In short, the objective is to maximize revenues for a given amount of capital allocated to credit activities.

CHAPTER 2

Governance

One individual or a group of individuals can make a bad judgment about a specific transaction. As a result, a firm can lose money—even a lot of money, if the transaction is sizeable—but it is unusual that a single transaction leads to the bankruptcy of a company. Serious problems that lead to bankruptcy occur when portfolios of toxic transactions are built. In the absence of fraud, what allows this to occur is a poor risk management framework and corporate governance failure. All professionals follow the rules, but either the rules don't function as intended, staff are not adequately skilled, origination lacks oversight, incentive systems reward the wrong goals, or the approval processes are flawed. When massive losses occur, investigations often reveal that all procedures were respected. It was a collective failure and there is nobody to blame.

Therefore, the question is: What is the best way to organize credit risk management in a large organization? The focus of attention must be on the processes that lead to risk taking—primarily origination, credit risk assessment, and approval processes. We are not saying that operations of Portfolio Management (Part Three of this book) and Mitigation and Transfer (Part Four) are not important as well, but the best way to avoid losses is to not enter into bad transactions to start with. There are no efficient portfolio management or mitigation strategies that can compensate for deficient risk-taking activities. When a bad portfolio of transactions is originated, it is too late, and there is a high probability that it will translate into heavy financial losses. Similarly, a good price, even far above market, can never compensate for a bad transaction and is not an excuse to justify a wrong decision.

If origination drives performance, then what drives origination? Most corporations' incentive systems reward top-line growth (in part because actual versus expected bottom-line growth is not immediately observable) and sometimes return on risk-adjusted capital. Originators will push for volume, expected margins, and expected returns, all of which are enhanced by showcasing their transactions in the most favorable light possible. In this environment, the risk manager must control quality.

To find a right balance between all stakeholders and clearly define risk management responsibilities, most organizations now rely on a framework presented in 2013 by the Institute of Internal Auditors in a position paper entitled "The Three Lines of Defense in Effective Risk Management and Control." At a high level:

- First line: business owners, who primarily own and manage risk.
- Second line: monitors and oversees risk performed by enterprise risk management, compliance, and legal. They establish policies and procedures and serve as management oversight for the first line.
- Third line: provides independent assurance of the risk management and risk monitoring provided by first and second lines of defense: internal audit, external auditors, and special audit committees.

Moreover, best practice for the governance system revolves around four key principles, which are critical to the quality of what gets originated:

1. *Guidelines:* Clear guidelines governing the approval of transactions generating credit risk.
2. *Skills:* Delegation of authority to committees and people with appropriate skills.
3. *Limits:* Setting up of limits.
4. *Oversight:* Qualified staff with adequate independence and resources.

GUIDELINES

Guidelines are a set of documents that explain the rules that must be complied with before a transaction is concluded. These guidelines are sometimes called "credit policies," "risk management standards," or some variation of these, all of which refer to the same thing.

To be efficient, guidelines must have the following characteristics:

- *Understandable:* Language must be clear and simple. Guidelines should be easy to understand and written in plain language. This is especially true for global organizations in which not every line manager is a native speaker. The guidelines are not a set of legal documents that establish a foundation to take action against an individual who breached them but rather an internal document whose purpose is to enable compliance. It may be a good idea to exclude lawyers from the initial drafting of guidelines!

- *Concise:* The size of the guidelines must be reasonable. If they are too long, no one reads them. A well-written document respects the reader's time and gets to the point quickly.
- *Precise:* The necessity to be short and understandable must not come at the cost of being overly general, which can render the guidelines ineffective. Guidelines that lack specificity can allow for bad transactions to fall through the cracks. Rather, the guidelines must address real-life situations in some detail so that the origination and line staff know what they have to do prior to closing a transaction.
- *Accessible:* All professionals who need the guidelines must first know where to find them. It seems obvious, but in too many cases, guidelines are buried in an organization's ever-changing document retrieval system. As a result, many professionals cannot even locate the most up-to-date set of guidelines. A simple and efficient way to make guidelines accessible is to prepare a one- or two-page summary that can be conspicuously posted on the company's intranet with reference to the name and location of the complete set. This will serve to remind staff of the risk management principles guiding transactions and of the whereabouts of the full set.

Creation and Approval Process

Guidelines are what ultimately protect the shareholders' capital of a firm and sometimes the firm's very existence. Bad human judgment is a common characteristic of poor transactions, but the executive management of a firm is ultimately accountable if the guidelines, either by direct authorization or omissions, permit certain transactions to occur.

This is why guidelines must be sponsored by a senior executive such as the chief risk officer or the chief financial officer and the approval of guidelines must be done by the Board of Directors. Companies listed on a stock exchange like the New York Stock Exchange must have the audit committee of the Board of Directors review risk management policies, so for these firms, the audit committee would have the ultimate oversight on the guidelines. In addition, most financial institutions have a separate risk committee within the Board of Directors, which would also be responsible for the oversight, review, and ultimate approval of these guidelines.

A process must be in place to maintain guidelines, keeping them up to date and in-step with the evolution of the business. They must, therefore, be reviewed and modified from time to time. It is also the responsibility of the most senior risk committee to request regular updates about the quality and the relevance of the existing guidelines. It is also good practice to review the guidelines after even a minor financial loss, because unclear or outdated guidelines could have played a part in it. The same holds for an event that happened and was never contemplated, and which may not have had consequences on the company itself, but could have. Some readers will remember that in April 2020, the price of oil was negative for a few days for technical reasons. Sellers of oil—via futures contracts—not only were not paid when they delivered oil but had to give $37 a barrel to buyers! How many institutions had guidelines protecting their capital in the case of a negative price? Most risk managers were more preoccupied by a spike in oil price and never considered it could become negative one day.

Promulgating and Maintaining Guidelines

The chief risk officer's office will own the guidelines, and it is this department's responsibility to draft, seek approval for, promulgate, and maintain the guidelines. In large organizations, this is a full-time job for one professional. It is crucial that this person has more than a basic knowledge of the underlying business as well as enough seniority for the following reasons:

- *Knowledge:* Guidelines must realistically reflect the way products and markets operate and evolve. Junior persons do not have a sufficient understanding of the business environment to either write good guidelines or to educate staff members on the guidelines' intent.
- *Politics/Diplomacy:* Authoring guidelines does not make anyone popular. Creating or modifying guidelines can be a power game between line managers/originators and risk managers, which will be contentious and involve significant negotiation. Senior people can better handle delicate situations and can better resist pressure.
- *Approval process:* As explained later, guidelines are approved at a very senior level of an organization. As such, they have to be sponsored and presented by staff who are credible with sufficient experience and knowledge.

The need to create new or significantly modify existing guidelines arises when a company enters a new business area, when markets experience change or innovation, or if operations change significantly, including mergers-and-acquisitions (M&A) activity. Even in the absence of these changes, existing guidelines need to be updated periodically since operations are never static.

After the 2007 crisis, all financial institutions strengthened their risk management functions and regulators paid more attention to the risk-taking activities. No doubt that permanent surveillance by regulators is a good incentive to maintain efficient guidelines.

Content of Guidelines

Guidelines should include, but need not be limited to, the following topics:

- Purpose of the guidelines
- Methodology for defining a transaction's key parameters
- Transaction approval and delegation of authority
- Process to deal with new products and new markets
- Process to review and update the guidelines
- Consequences of failure to follow guidelines

Breach of Guidelines

If the company is well managed, the breach of guidelines should be infrequent. A breach is a serious act, and in most financial firms, it leads to immediate termination of employment. No one is supposed to take more risk than what the Board of Directors has accepted. That is why it is so important that guidelines are known and understood.

Guidelines can have carve-outs for such variables as foreign-exchange volatility. For example, an originator may conclude a transaction that uses up the company's available credit limit for a particular counterparty but then finds the exposure over the limit due to exchange rate movements. The guidelines would have addressed this type of outcome and expressed limits on, for example, a local currency basis, since foreign-exchange management is usually handled by the treasury function.

A centralized database that captures information on transaction exposure and other key credit parameters as they relate to guidelines is a tool that enables their enforcement and also facilitates deal flow. Originators can do a quick look-up to see if their proposed transaction is permissible. Having such a system obviates the need to second-guess whether an originator knew the rules since the feedback is instantaneous. If an originator tries to enter a nonauthorized transaction, the system will reject it; and if the transaction is done anyway, the system provides documentation that it was unauthorized.

SKILLS

In a perfect world, all transactions would be approved by committees composed of the firm's most senior people. This is naturally not feasible, so the authority granted by the Board of Directors to the executive management of a firm has to be delegated further.

The rules to delegate authority constitute a central piece of the guidelines and a source of friction between risk management and the origination units. An old cliché in risk management circles is that risk management priorities are (1) not to lose money, and (2) to make money, in that order, and that business priorities are (1) to make money, and (2) not to lose money, in that order. To simplify, originators typically want maximum freedom that risk managers do not want to grant them. Originators have the responsibility to sell products and to grow the business. They have profitability objectives and they require freedom to execute their business plans. They want the ability to close transactions without having to garner approval from too many people. The role of risk managers is to see beyond the expected profitability of a transaction and to think of the consequences of a nonfavorable development.

Importantly, the risk management unit has no approval authority. It is not a profit center and, as such, risk managers play an advisory role in helping individuals or committees decide whether they want to enter into a transaction. This does not diminish the value of risk management but just reflects the fact that business managers are accountable for the top and bottom lines of their units.

Note that, for transactions meeting certain criteria, input or a recommendation from risk management may be required, and these criteria will be clearly stated in the guidelines. It is rare that risk managers have a veto right. If they strongly disagree, they must have a platform to express their opinion. A written memo must be attached to the documentation package for the credit committees. They must sit in the committees and have the opportunity to present their opinion in person.

The delegation of authority follows a two-step process:

Step 1: The assignment of fundamental parameters that characterize, from a risk management point of view, each and every transaction.

Step 2: The delegation of the approval authority based on these parameters.

An approval process must also be defined for transactions for which guidelines do not enable, due to complexity or uniqueness, the assignment of parameters. The guidelines may require that these types of transactions are automatically elevated to a high-level authority, such as a transaction committee, which may recommend further upward delegation.

Defining Risk Parameters

The most common parameters of a credit-sensitive transaction are:

- *Amount of exposure:* This represents an estimation of the maximum amount of money that a company can lose. The way to calculate this number depends on the nature of the transaction.[1]
- *Credit quality:* Each company must develop a scale to summarize the creditworthiness of each counterparty.[2]
- *Tenor:* This is the period of time during which there is credit exposure, at the end of which there is remaining financial obligation due by the counterparty. In the example of a loan, the tenor is the period between the closing of the loan agreement and when the last principal repayment is due.

Delegation of Authority

The simple rule is that the riskier the transaction, the higher the approval level must be. Transactions with a high exposure or a low credit quality or a long tenor necessitate senior-management attention and must be approved by committees staffed with people with the relevant level of knowledge, experience, and hierarchical level. On the contrary, small and short-tenor transactions with a high-quality counterparty can be approved at a lower level. Simple and straightforward transactions can even be approved by a single individual.

When a transaction enters the pipeline of a firm, the first step in the delegation of authority is to assign fundamental parameters to that transaction. It is then compared to the thresholds of the guidelines to decide who or which committee has authority to approve it. Figure 2.1 summarizes the escalation of delegation of authority and an example of approval authority can be found in Figure 2.2, in which the counterparty's credit quality is on the vertical axis, the delegation of authority is on the horizontal axis, and transaction exposures are represented by the values inside the figure.

---

[1]We present these details in Chapters 4 and 5.
[2]We present these details in Chapters 6, 7, and 11.

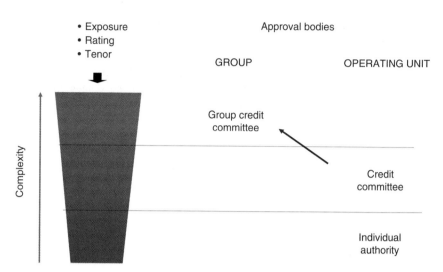

FIGURE 2.1   Approval Process

Exposure in U.S. dollars

Internal rating of the counterparty			
R1	150	200	250
R2	125	150	175
R3	100	125	150
R4	75	100	125
R5	50	75	100
R6	25	50	75
	Head of trading	Head of trading	Transaction committee	Executive risk committee

Recommendation of credit risk assessment unit

FIGURE 2.2   Single Transaction with a Tenor up to Five Years

Let's take the example of a three-year transaction with a counterparty rated R3 that generates an exposure of $130 million. The tenor is less than five years, so the chart in Figure 2.2 applies. The transaction must be approved by the transaction committee that has authority for an R3 counterparty up to $150 million, and, in addition, requires the recommendation of credit risk management, which is required for all transactions in excess of $100 million in this rating category.

The hierarchy for the authority delegation may begin with the individual originator, then progress to the business unit head, which may then be followed by a transaction committee that is made up of unit heads and relevant advisors, such as compliance, legal, and tax. Beyond a certain size, credit quality, and tenor thresholds, transactions will be delegated to an executive board or a credit committee, which is comprised of the firm's most senior management and would include, among others, the CFO, the chief counsel, and the CEO. Importantly, this authority delegation is cumulative, meaning each delegation level must approve the transaction. A transaction cannot go directly from the originator directly to the credit committee without first being endorsed by the intervening levels. The process we just described was for approval of single transactions. The approval of overall limits on counterparties follows a similar process.

Credit Committees

The highest level of approval is often called the credit committee and is staffed with the firm's most senior executives. The transactions that arrive here have a lot at stake and, as such, they follow a few basic principles:

- The quality of the decision is highly dependent on the quality and the diversity of people sitting on the committee. All disciplines must be represented to make sure that no aspect of a transaction is forgotten. The departments that must be represented include but are not limited to the business unit (i.e., profit center), risk management, legal, tax, compliance, and accounting.
- The charter of the credit committee must be part of the credit guidelines or other document detailing the approval process.
- Membership must be personal with limited ability to delegate.
- Originators must prepare an approval package. It must cover all aspects of the transaction and be distributed well in advance so that committee members have time to read it and request additional information or advice if necessary.
- There must be a respected chairperson who allows all parties to present their opinions and facilitates the discussion in a dispassionate manner.
- Originators bringing a transaction must understand that a committee can say no. A committee that never says no is not efficiently managed.
- If there is no consensus, a vote can be held.
- The discussions must be recorded with detail and accuracy via meeting minutes, distributed quickly after the meeting. If a transaction goes sour, one of the first documents that management and auditors ask for are the credit committee minutes.

SETTING LIMITS

Limits represent the absolute dollar (or other currency) amount of risk that a company wants to take, or, in other words, the maximum loss that a company is prepared to withstand. They are frequently called credit lines. Limits can be attached to counterparties, industries, countries and the concept is more complicated than it appears, because, for some transactions, the maximum loss in case of bankruptcy cannot be estimated in advance and depends on the market at the time of bankruptcy. This is the case for long-term supply/purchase agreements of physical commodities or derivative transactions. We explore the concept of dynamic credit exposure in Chapter 5.

To work around the uncertainty of certain exposures, combinations of limits are frequently used. For instance, a company may state that it is comfortable taking $200 million of risk on Company A but that exposure stemming from derivative transactions must not represent more than 50 percent of the total.

How to decide what the limits should be is more art than science. One can utilize value at risk models (Chapter 14) to make a link between the parameters of the exposure and the capital the company wants to risk with credit activities. Quite often, though, experience and gut feelings prevail. The executive management believes that a loss of, say, $150 million would be accepted by external parties such as shareholders, rating agencies, or regulators. So they set the absolute limit at $150 million for all counterparties but accept much smaller exposures on weaker names, based on their individual credit characteristics.

Ideally, all originators know the aggregate size of the credit lines for each of their counterparties. If several business units are competing for the same credit line for a particular counterparty, the credit line can be allocated to business in advance. The existence and size of the credit lines are actually a frequent source of tension between front offices and risk management teams. Originators' preference is to have preapproved limits so that they can start marketing prospective clients and not be in the undesirable position of generating business that is subsequently not supported by their firm.

OVERSIGHT

Risk management is instrumental to protect an organization's balance sheet. Efforts to originate and structure transactions are useful but, ultimately, choosing the right transactions is what distinguishes the good organization from the weaker ones. It is, therefore, essential that risk managers are qualified and work in an environment that enables them to perform their tasks efficiently.

Independence

The issue of independence is today much better understood than a few years ago. There must not be any compromise affecting the independence of the risk management unit. Two simple rules are:

1. It should never be located within a business unit with a profit center.
2. A risk manager's compensation should never be based on the profitability of the business.

All staff involved in risk management must have a chain of command that ultimately reports to the chief risk officer (CRO) and not a business unit head, to maintain independence and avoid conflicts of interest.

Many large companies have a CRO who reports directly to the chief executive officer. As such, they occupy the same seniority as the most senior business heads. Beyond the formal hierarchy and approval process, the reporting structure allows the CRO to informally influence the CEO. This is important not so much for any actual objections that the CRO may voice concerning a particular transaction or product, but more because the business unit heads know that this access is there, which should steer them toward complying with the guidelines.

Lastly, the CRO is likely to have privileged access to the risk committee and or the audit committee of the Board of Directors. To the extent that the directors are truly independent, which under Sarbanes-Oxley is increasingly the case in the United States, this feature may be the most critical element to ensure independence of the CRO.

Qualifications

Getting the respect of the business partner is a goal of risk managers. Conflicts are part of the job but they don't prevent mutual respect; to achieve it, it is essential that everyone speaks the same language. Business people do not have time to educate the risk managers, who would lose credibility and political capital if they would need to have fundamental elements of transactions explained to them.

As much as originators are confident in their skills, they do not mind hearing constructive criticism from time to time. Having quality risk managers as sparring partners helps them innovate and formulate a better proposition.

When the risk manager is weak, originators wait to involve him or her until later in the process and just for the purpose of obtaining the required recommendation.

Proximity to the Business Unit

As much as we advocate for a strict independence from the business unit, risk managers must be located organizationally and physically near operations since they need to have a full understanding of the underlying business. They must fully comprehend what motivates their peers, the customers, the vendors, and all parties involved in a transaction. Physical proximity allows risk managers access to this.

Although it is unusual for risk managers to be invited to business discussions with clients, a good credit risk manager who has gained the trust of the originator can bring value to a client discussion. In particular, when originators do not make progress with a client because of a term, condition, price, or limit, bringing in a risk manager who can diplomatically articulate the rationale for the firm's position can be persuasive or at least act as damage control on the relationship. Two caveats for accepting these invitations:

First, risk managers are not necessarily seasoned negotiators. Good negotiators always enter a negotiation with a very firm walk-away position. They know that they can be sensitive to a client's arguments during a live discussion and refrain from making decisions under pressure that they may regret later. Good risk managers must do the same. They must know in advance the absolute limits they do not want to breach and use the forum as a platform for conveying these limits.

Second, being too close to front office activities can backfire. The risk manager's raison d'être is to provide a different point of view and to protect the firm's balance sheet.

Open Mind

Let's finish with a soft factor. . . . One old cliché of risk management is that "a good risk manager does not say no but how." In other words, the art of risk management is not to refuse transactions, but to make suggestions that enable their acceptance. The good thing about this concept is that both the business and the risk management sides agree with it. Business people want to close deals and the risk manager who says no is a source of frustration. An effective risk manager understands their point of view and helps them succeed. Jobs in risk management are more interesting if they involve the ability to sit down with originators, discuss the details of a deal, and support its structuring.

FINAL WORDS

One sentence frequently heard in the financial industry is that the real head of risk management is the chief executive officer (CEO). This goes beyond the idea that the CEO is ultimately responsible for the profitability of the firm and that they will lose their job (and ultimately will give up their own future cash) for bad decisions. However, a company does not have to go through a quasi-death experience to realize how central risk management is to the day-to-day operations. What the statement really means is that the CEO has the absolute responsibility to make the whole organization respect risk management principles.

As each and every employee must be aware of the risks involved in doing business and must be committed to adhere to strict principles, it cannot happen that the senior management does not set the example.

What is expected is that the CEO and his direct reports support the established risk management principles and behave just as if they were directly in charge of risk management. When making strategic decisions, not only day to day transactions but also, for instance, mergers and acquisitions, the CEO has to involve his risk management department at the right time.

Although certain concepts are explained later in the book, we present here a map of the various steps to take when originating a new transaction (Figure 2.3).

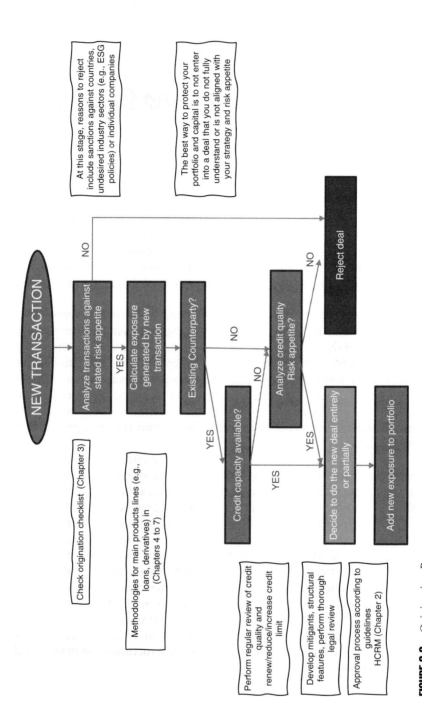

At this stage, reasons to reject include sanctions against countries, undesired industry sectors (e.g., ESG policies) or individual companies

The best way to protect your portfolio and capital is to not enter into a deal that you do not fully understand or is not aligned with your strategy and risk appetite

NEW TRANSACTION

Check origination checklist (Chapter 3)

Analyze transactions against stated risk appetite

Calculate exposure generated by new transaction

Methodologies for main products lines (e.g., loans, derivatives) in (Chapters 4 to 7)

Existing Counterparty?

Credit capacity available?

Analyze credit quality Risk appetite?

Reject deal

Perform regular review of credit quality and renew/reduce/increase credit limit

Develop mitigants, structural features, perform thorough legal review

Approval process according to guidelines HCRM (Chapter 2)

Decide to do the new deal entirely or partially

Add new exposure to portfolio

FIGURE 2.3 Origination Process

CHAPTER 3

Checklist for Origination

In the previous chapter, some key governance issues as they relate to activities generating credit risk were described. A good organization is not enough, though. The profitability of a credit portfolio is heavily impacted by the way all professionals involved in the process behave. It all starts with the handling of new transactions. In the context of this book, this is what we call origination.

Origination also matters for business deals that are not credit deals per se. In the ordinary course of business, companies assume credit risk in order to sell products and services, such as extending credit to a customer. For these types of transactions, the same principles about origination apply. Business heads will seek to generate volume and will want to make credit terms easy for clients. That extension of credit must follow the exact process described in Chapter 2, for example, establishing guidelines, setting limits, assigning parameters, and putting together an approval process that is clearly defined.

Since the best way to avoid credit losses is to carefully select transactions to enter, good credit risk management starts with origination. Even under pressure to generate revenues, smart organizations differentiate themselves by their ability to avoid bad deals and to select strong transactions. This is true for all businesses; entering into business arrangements with robust vendors and good customers is the difference between profits and losses.

There is no shortage of salespeople, internally and externally, to suggest deals and to put pressure on unit managers to accept them and on risk managers to opine favorably on them. Good managers will take a sober view of all transactions and move forward only with those that meet or exceed specific criteria. They will stay away from transactions for which the organization lacks expertise, including the ability to adequately structure or monitor a transaction. That said, no amount of structuring can make a bad transaction good.

What we will cover in this chapter are essential questions to answer when considering a new transaction—in short, a checklist. They can provide credit committees with a list of compulsory themes to discuss or, at a minimum, to be informed about. They can also serve as a basis of analysis to credit risk managers, even before they start the detailed credit assessment.

DOES THE TRANSACTION FIT INTO MY STRATEGY?

All business units must have a clear mandate known by stakeholders. For what we are interested in, transactions generating credit risk must be clearly identified in advance so that a proper organization—processes and people—is put in place.

We do not mean that one-off transactions should never be considered. There are sometimes market opportunities or commercial reasons that cannot be ignored. It is also legitimate from time to time to "test the water" as part of a business development exercise and to enter into a reasonably sized transaction in order to acquire knowledge and to develop some contacts in the marketplace.

The danger of accepting one-off transactions is that the existing skills may not be sufficient. As another old saying goes, "You do not know what you do not know." Well-tested structuring skills and back office infrastructure may turn out to be irrelevant when entering a new field. If a one-off transaction defaults, it raises eyebrows within an organization but, above all, outside parties may take a hard stance against doing business with the organization. The credibility of the firm's risk management framework is at stake.

Multiple examples were observed after the 2007 crisis. Traditionally conservative investors such as school districts, charity organizations, and retirement plans invested in structured credit products or invested in hedge funds. When the market turned, large amounts of money were lost and observers wondered what the institutions were thinking when they made their investment decisions. Lawsuits against intermediaries, in many cases investment banks, were filed but judges often considered that the investors were experienced enough and did not grant damages.

If compelling reasons exist to enter into a new kind of transaction generating credit risk, some basic principles must be followed:

- Elevate the decision-making process to a senior committee, not as a way to cover a unit from accountability, but in order to get additional points of view.
- Invest in external advice: well-chosen lawyers, accountants, consultants can provide valuable help.

- Document the thought and approval processes thoroughly.
- Make sure that all relevant departments in the organization are involved, for instance, transaction lawyers, tax specialists, accountants, and monitoring professionals.
- Last, but not least, *do not rush*. You should drive the timetable; do not let the counterparty do it. If you are not ready when the transaction must close, take a pass.

DOES THE RISK FIT INTO MY EXISTING PORTFOLIO?

For companies with existing credit exposures, it is necessary to assess a new transaction not only on its own merits but also within the context of the rest of its portfolio, or "the book." Among the considerations are:

- *Limits:* We explain in the previous chapter that limits must be set on counterparties, industries, products, and countries. The first thing to verify when confronted with a new transaction is whether the firm has authorized remaining capacity to assume more exposure and is, thus, in a position to transact.

  If the capacity is already exhausted, an increase of the limit can be requested, according to the processes in place. There may also be the possibility to hedge the credit exposure. As we will see in Part Four, there are some techniques available to mitigate credit exposures, such as the purchase of a credit insurance policy or a credit-default swap, which would enable completing a transaction in which the credit exposure is incidental but the transaction brings other value to the firm, such as meeting a client request or taking on a transaction generating a nice profit from its noncredit features.
- *Concentration:* Even if a transaction generates a credit exposure within the approved limit, it may not be compelling to do it. When a portfolio is already loaded with transactions of similar characteristics, doing a new one may impact concentration. In the Chapter 14 discussion of credit models, we see that, everything else being equal, imbalanced portfolios require more capital than well-diversified ones. That is why it is important that portfolio managers be represented in credit committees. They can provide an overview of the portfolio that complements the stand-alone analysis.
- *Critical mass:* A common misstep is to create an "orphan." From a portfolio management perspective, adding a new and uncorrelated transaction is beneficial. It brings some diversification that helps reduce capital

requirement and, therefore, increases the profitability. However, it creates more work for internal tax, accounting, and surveillance departments, among others, and the overhead cost and distraction created may overshadow the diversification benefits.

■ *Dry powder:* Credit and portfolio managers may opt to keep some reserve capacity to deploy when they expect to see more profitable opportunities coming in the future. Because credit capacity is a scarce resource, they may prefer to wait instead of originating new transactions that use up capacity. Since ordinary business operations create risk exposure, and the exposure uses capacity, a line manager may prefer to wait until pricing and margins improve so as to not run out of credit capacity at a critical moment.

DO I UNDERSTAND THE CREDIT RISK?

Having a thorough understanding of all aspects of credit risk present in a transaction sounds basic, but it is essential. When confronted with a new transaction, risk managers must take one step back and make sure that they truly understand the nature of the credit risk and its drivers.

For plain vanilla transactions that are well known and closed on a very regular basis, it may not be necessary to spend too much time. If a risk manager is assigned to a trading desk that closes a few similar transactions a day with the same pool of counterparties and well-tested documentation, the focus of their job is primarily the risk assessment of the counterparty.

Sometimes, however, what may seem to be plain vanilla is not, and there are two caveats:

1. Although financial markets evolve quickly, most changes are more a succession of small steps rather than quantum leaps. One participant creates a small variation of a well-known product, then another one builds on those changes, and so on. After a while, products can have undergone significant changes that modify their risk profile. The lesson is that, however, small, even a minor change must receive proper attention as, combined with other minor changes, they create a new breed of products that can have a very different risk profile.
2. One has to be careful with transactions that look close to something familiar. There could be some similarities with a well-known field but the devil lies in the details. Subtle differences can make a big difference. A risk manager must not assume that he knows a new product because it is similar to another. This can be very dangerous.

Consider, for example, a company looking to grow abroad. Although doing business abroad is similar in many ways to doing business at home, being able to properly document a sale and getting paid in a foreign company is a very different exercise than in one's own country.

Transactions of a new nature must be dissected thoroughly. Even if the general structure of the deal seems to be understood quickly, risk managers must not take shortcuts. The best piece of advice they can give is that there is no shame in asking questions. When originators invite risk managers to a meeting and explain quickly what the transaction is all about, all too often risk managers do not dare to speak up and to ask the good questions. Doing so is, however, a useful exercise that can reveal that originators and structurers themselves have missed or underestimated major risk factors.

DOES THE SELLER KEEP AN INTEREST IN THE DEAL?

There are three main cases where risk managers can request that the counterparty keeps an interest in a transaction, or "skin in the game," as it is usually referred to.

The first case is when a counterparty is selling a pure credit exposure it has originated. It's especially true if the counterparty acquired the exposure recently and tries to get rid of it immediately. Another red flag is when only certain types of exposures are selected out of a homogenous portfolio. In that case, "why are you selling?" is an indispensable question to ask. The seller may have good and legitimate reasons to sell, like reshaping of a portfolio or unwillingness to take on any (additional) credit risk. It could also be part of an efficient arbitrage strategy, when a counterparty finds a way to originate deals at a low cost and sell them at a higher price and realize a profit. However, there can also be an asymmetry of information, meaning that the seller has more information or simply more experience than the buyer, which can lead to adverse selection, in which the seller disposes of the risks that they know will not perform well and keeps the risks that they believe will perform well. Thus, buyers have to be particularly vigilant when sellers are getting rid of their exposures in a selective way.

The second case is when the seller can influence the performance of the exposure. For instance, a bank could be one of the largest clients of a computer software company, and should they decide to adopt a different technology and change providers, the software company would lose a large source of revenue and its creditworthiness would decline. It's therefore necessary to check potential business relationships between the institution willing to sell some exposures and the entity involved.

Note that some legal concepts are designed to protect buyers from sellers who may abuse their privileged information. A typical way to mitigate the risk of adverse selection is to require the seller to retain some exposure over a defined time period. For instance, the buyer may require the seller to keep 20 percent of the exposure unhedged throughout the lifetime of the transaction. The goal is to create an alignment of interest between the seller and the buyer. Also, buyers can obtain representations and warranties, which is essentially a legal affirmation by the seller that the data they provide are both correct and comprehensive and that they have fully disclosed any negative information.

The third case is when the counterparty that will assume the credit risk relies on the seller to perform certain credit-related functions. The most relevant example is trade credit insurance, a type of contract we explain in Chapter 19 and which enables a company to buy protection against the risk of default of payment of a customer (trade receivables). It would be too cumbersome for an insurer to approve each and every customers' buyers from a credit risk point of view and customers do not want to have their insurer decide to whom they are selling their products. Therefore, insurers typically grant discretionary limits, i.e., no preapproval is required but insurance coverage is available. However, this relative freedom is reserved only for counterparties that can prove that they have a solid credit risk management process in place and a good track record of low credit losses. In addition, policy wording includes an alignment of interest between the insurer and its customers in two ways. First, a deductible is imposed, meaning that only losses above an agreed threshold are covered. Second, above the deductible amount, losses are not fully covered but are shared proportionally; for instance, 90% is paid by the insurer and 10% is retained by the customer. Leaving the first losses to the insured customer and sharing them proportionally above the deductible amount is a good way to ensure that the insured customer will carefully select their buyers.

ARE THE PROPER MITIGANTS IN PLACE?

Mitigants are structural elements that help avoid or reduce a loss when a transaction deteriorates. Given the uncertainty around the counterparty's future creditworthiness, most transactions include some protection for the creditors. The idea is that transactions stay the way they are as long as the obligor performs close to its level at deal inception. If its situation deteriorates, some mechanism must kick in to protect creditors.

A simple example is a lease agreement. If the lessee defaults on its monthly payments, the lessor has the legal right to take back the asset. Mortgages are also classic examples of situations in which lenders can repossess a home when the borrower misses too many payments.

Because strong mitigants can avoid or reduce credit losses, when structuring a transaction, credit professionals must imagine what could go wrong and what can be implemented when it happens. Borrowers anxious to raise money are accustomed to mitigants and expect requests from lenders. The strength of the mitigant package depends very much on the competitiveness of the industry. When money is abundant, transactions are poorly structured and unfavorable to the lenders. When credit is scarce, borrowers are in a less favorable position and forced to accept stringent conditions.

Mitigating the risk of losses is a well-tested methodology that we will review in the case of derivatives transactions in Chapter 17 and for loans in Chapter 18.

Mitigants present a good opportunity for risk managers to demonstrate how creative they are. Remember the not-no-but-how attitude expected from risk managers. When they do not like a transaction, originators expect risk managers to propose solutions that enable them to say yes.

IS THE LEGAL DOCUMENTATION SATISFACTORY?

A decision to enter into a transaction involving credit risk is never complete before the legal documentation has been finalized. It is crucial for credit risk managers to make sure that lawyers do reflect in the binding agreements the conditions that have been presented by the business people and signed off by the relevant credit committee.

Credit risk professionals are rarely involved in post-committee discussions, but they should inquire on a regular basis about the status of the legal negotiations. At a minimum, they should be briefed prior to the finalization of the documentation to make sure that there have been no deviations from their recommendations during the negotiations.

It may sound trivial, but there are so many examples of transactions whose documentation is so sloppy that the basic rights of the creditors cannot be enforced.

IS THE DEAL PRICED ADEQUATELY?

In Chapter 13, which is dedicated to portfolio management, we mention the need, on a portfolio basis, to be compensated for the expected losses and for the amount of capital at risk, and this touches on credit risk pricing. However, we do not delve into the intricacies of pricing in this book because it is covered in great detail elsewhere.

Naturally, it is essential for entities taking credit risk to be able to calculate what this costs in order to make a profit on a risk-adjusted basis. Large financial institutions benefit from the work of quantitative teams whose role is to calculate the correct pricing for transactions, both prior to inception and during their lifetimes. They provide a neutral opinion to the credit committees.

Discussions about pricing in a credit risk management context can be very heated. Front-office people tend to think that the profitability of their transactions and the impact on their profits and losses (P&Ls) are off-limits to risk managers. A typical mindset can be summed up as "Tell me if you can recommend the transaction from a default perspective and I'll take care of the rest." In some cases, as we cover in Chapter 13, firms may establish transfer pricing schemes. Transfer pricing allows for business units to measure profits based on assigned costs; any one unit's costs may be above or below its true costs, but the scheme allows some transactions to subsidize others while motivating each unit to maximize its own P&L. A typical example is commercial loans. Loans have been priced very aggressively for a long time and they are priced below cost to the customer. All banks are nevertheless aggressively pursuing basic loans because they are gate openers, or loss leaders, for the bank's other, more profitable transactions. A basic banking relationship starts with participation in a commercial loan syndication that permits an introduction to the corporation's management and a chance to introduce value-added products.

As a result, credit assessment professionals should not be directly involved in pricing discussions. Portfolio managers are, however, indirectly involved by providing essential information to the pricing decision, such as expected credit losses and an estimation of the capital need.

A notable exception to adequate pricing is trade receivables, which, paradoxically, often represents the biggest source of credit risk for a nonfinancial company. Costs associated with trade receivables are rarely considered when a manufacturer sells its product to a wholesaler or a retailer. The focus is on the cost of manufacturing, marketing, distribution and all administrative expenses. However, when a major client defaults, some manufacturers have to write off large amounts of receivables, which directly impacts their net income. This credit risk exposure is usually not priced into the transactions, which implies that margins are smaller than they appear on a risk-adjusted basis.

DO I HAVE THE SKILLS TO MONITOR THE EXPOSURE?

Monitoring the evolution of a credit exposure is a key part of the credit risk management process. It is sometimes known as surveillance. Large financial institutions employ dozens of professionals dedicated to the surveillance of their portfolio.

In short, the main purpose of the surveillance activities is to detect, at an early stage, transactions whose performance is deviating from expectations. It can be a daunting task, and clear processes performed by skilled staff must be in place. Credit losses can be avoided or limited by taking actions at the appropriate time.

When a new transaction is presented to credit officers, the unit manager must verify that the firm has the ability to monitor the transaction's performance. First, what about the skills? If the new deal is similar to many others in the portfolio, it is likely that knowledge will not be an issue. On the contrary, if the transaction is of a new type, reviewing its performance over time may be challenging. The absence of skills is, in most cases, not a legitimate reason to reject a good transaction, but putting in place an efficient monitoring process prior to inception is appropriate. Training may be necessary.

Issues about the quantity and quality of data can also arise. Think of a transaction in a foreign country for which reports are produced only in a language that no one in the surveillance department understands. Also, what about transactions providing reams of data on a monthly basis? Are there IT resources dedicated to handling them? Does the company have the skills to sort out and interpret these data? A classic example is securitizations involving consumer assets like a mortgage-backed security. Updated numbers about key performance indicators, like 30-day delinquencies, are available on a monthly basis. A firm with only a few securities in its portfolio can analyze the data with a spreadsheet, but an asset manager with hundreds of securities could rapidly be overwhelmed and unable to detect downward patterns on a timely basis. As a result, it may not act quickly enough and may face unexpected losses.

Monitoring is a not a trivial function within a firm and should be allocated appropriate resources.

IS THERE AN EXIT STRATEGY?

Having an exit strategy means being able to hedge or sell a credit exposure at any time. In all organizations, priorities or risk appetite can change. A transaction that looks very attractive today can become a burden as time goes by. Just think of an investment firm heavily exposed to high-yield bonds that decides to exit the sector to concentrate on other asset classes.

The need to reduce credit exposure can also stem from the build-up over time of an imbalanced portfolio. A firm may be very eager to take a large exposure on a company, a country, or a sector at one point in time. As the business matures, they may end up with too much concentration and take too much risk or miss opportunities to enter into more profitable transactions. Another scenario is credit deterioration, in which it becomes necessary to reduce a company's exposure.

When building a portfolio, one should think of the challenges and costs to get rid of positions if needed. In fact, presenting options to unwind a credit exposure should be part of all investment decisions and credit approvals. Efficient credit committees should spend time grilling originators about their ability to eliminate credit risk should this become necessary.

Thinking about exit strategy is particularly appropriate for active investments like buying a bond or entering into a speculative derivative transaction. It is less relevant for an organization obliged to take credit risk to support other activities.

FINAL WORDS

Selecting good transactions is not a chance process, and there are many pressures within an organization to close deals. For most people, saying no can be harder than saying yes. There can be psychological reward for closing transactions, since this is a tangible accomplishment. Closed transactions are even symbolized by "salesperson of the month" awards and with deal "tombstones," which are essentially trophies awarded by senior management to deal teams for a closing. Thus, against these pressures, origination must be a highly disciplined and respected process within a risk-bearing organization.

Because it is harder to contain losses once they start than it is to avoid them in the first place, the risk-bearing organization must evaluate everything that can go wrong. What is the motivation of the seller? Does the organization have the institutional knowledge to understand and manage this risk? How is the risk correlated to others in the portfolio and does it fit the organization's strategy? Is the risk adequately priced and is the legal documentation adequate? Does managing this risk create opportunity costs for the organization and are there adequate resources to monitor it? If the deal goes bad, what are the options available? The firm must have complete and satisfactory answers to each of these questions to proceed with a transaction.

Credit Assessment

CHAPTER 4

Measurement of Credit Risk

The quantification of credit risk is an essential task, which is performed at the individual transaction level and at the portfolio level. In this chapter, we focus on individual transactions.

One number cannot sufficiently summarize individual transactions. No magic figure indicates whether a transaction is good or bad. No one figure allows for an ordinal ranking of transactions by quality. Rather, transactions have to be analyzed by several dimensions, four of which, taken together, are good barometers of risk. They are:

1. *The exposure:* The amount of money at risk.
2. *The probability of default:* The likelihood that the counterparty will default.
3. *The recovery rate:* The amount of money relative to the exposure that can be recovered in case of default.
4. *The tenor:* The time period in which some or all of the money is at risk.

These parameters are used to analyze and compare credit exposures. They also constitute the basis to decide who has authority to approve a transaction, as discussed in Chapter 2.

EXPOSURE

Exposure is the single most important number attached to a transaction because it represents, in most cases (some derivatives transactions are a notable exception), the potential maximum amount of money that could be lost in case of default. As such, it is a useful, albeit imperfect, gauge of absolute credit risk and of relative credit risk across transactions.

When the senior management of a company or the risk committee of the Board of Directors wants to get a sense of the amount of risk it is taking, the list of the largest exposures is a key document. Similarly, when banks are asked by stakeholders to disclose their relationship with a counterparty, an industry, or a country, they provide their exposures, often without additional details. It is not that the banks would not like to be more precise, but the explanations would not be understandable for most people and could create confusion. A good example is the difficulties faced by the airline and hospitality industries in 2020 during the COVID-19 pandemic. Investors and regulators wanted to know individual banks' exposures on the riskiest borrowers as a way to gauge the potential consequences of default on the balance sheets of these banks.

The beauty of exposure is that it is easy to understand and is a risk measure that is the closest thing to a common denominator.

Here stops the simplicity about the exposure, however! It may sound surprising, but calculating the exposure stemming from a transaction is not always straightforward. Internal discussions about credit exposures can be frustrating because in many cases assumptions must be made and uncertainty about outcomes remains. As financial transactions are more and more complex, the exposure report, which summarizes the credit portfolio of an institution, contains increasing amounts of fine print. Risk managers must take the time to discuss with senior management the limitations of the numbers they produce. If the situation underlying the transaction evolves differently from expected, the actual exposure can be very different from what is anticipated.

Let us mention a few things to be aware of in terms of credit exposure:

- The methodology to calculate the exposure is specific to each product and, as such, has to be clearly documented. An annex to the guidelines, which can be updated from time to time, is an ideal place to document the methodology.
- As precise as guidelines can be, they cannot anticipate all aspects of transactions in real life, particularly for new product areas or for one-off transactions. In these cases, the credit risk assessment team then decides on the methodology used to allocate the credit exposure on an ad hoc basis.
- For certain transactions like long-term supply agreements or derivatives contracts, the exposure cannot be observed easily and necessitates the use of statistical models. We introduce a common methodology in Chapter 5.

Which Exposure Number to Use?

As we discuss in Chapter 3, all firms establish credit limits they do not want to exceed. The exposure generated by a single transaction eats up the aggregate capacity the company has for a counterparty. It is, therefore, essential to allocate a reasonable number to each transaction. The challenge for the risk management team is to arrive at values that are both economically meaningful and take practical considerations into account. There is not one but several related exposure numbers that can be used.

Being conservative and avoiding surprises by using a high exposure number has the advantage of rarely underestimating the exposure. However, overestimating credit exposures is not efficient. First, establishing credit limits is an expensive process that may involve buying third-party data, travel, desktop research, production of detailed reports, and presentations to senior management. If exposures are measured conservatively and do not correspond to actual business and revenue, deploying these large resources cannot be justified. Second, business opportunities can be lost. No one wants to reject deals due to the lack of available capacity, whereas a finer analysis would reveal that the approved limit was adequate.

Conversely, setting a low number, as is possible for some products given the way they are structured—we will review examples below—can underestimate the exposure. The positive aspect is that if a company has appetite for $100 million on Counterparty A and if there is an agreement that one particular transaction generates $40 million of exposure, there is room to deploy more capital and increase revenue. However, actual losses may turn out to be higher than what was expected in case of stress or bankruptcy, and management and investors may be surprised if losses exceed $100 million as the exposure generated by the transaction turned out to be more than $40 million when Counterparty A defaulted.

We now introduce three concepts that can be used to set exposure numbers. They are:

1. GE = Gross exposure
2. NE = Net exposure
3. AE = Adjusted exposure

GE, NE, and AE are calculated with a three-step process, as shown in Figure 4.1.

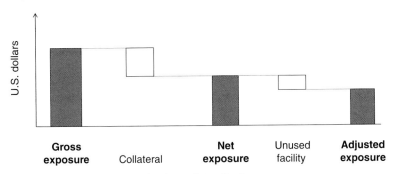

FIGURE 4.1 Gross, Net, and Adjusted Credit Exposure

In most cases, GE is the worst-case scenario, that is, the absolute amount at risk. Notable exceptions are long-term supply contracts of physical commodities and derivative contracts, in which the GE does not actually represent the worst case, a consequence of using the value at risk (VaR) methodology, which relies on historical data or simulations and confidence intervals rather than on absolute numbers. More details are provided in Chapter 5. GE represents the amount of money due by the counterparty and, therefore, the money at risk in case of bankruptcy.

For most transactions, the calculation is straightforward, because the GE is the notional amount of the transaction with the counterparty. When a company sells $100 worth of goods, the corresponding GE for the client is the value of the trade receivable, $100. When a bank lends $100 to a client, the GE is $100 + expected interest payments over the term of the loan.

Net exposure (NE) is defined as GE minus the amount of collateral pledged. The idea is that, if one entity has cash or cash equivalent collateral to support a transaction, GE should be adjusted to reflect the fact that the sale of the collateral assets would reduce a credit loss. If a creditor is comfortable with the value and the liquidity of the collateral posted, there is no reason not to adjust the exposure accordingly. Note that these adjustments are rare as it is unusual for a borrower or a customer to provide cash at the inception of a deal. One example is a prepayment by a customer when a contract is signed for delivery of a product or a service in the future. If the contract is $1 million and the customer pays 20% upon signing the contract, the GE is $1 million but the NE is only $800,000.

It is important to note that the collateral considered here is not of the same nature as assets used to secure a transaction like a lender receiving a lien on a piece of property which can be foreclosed if the borrower defaults. This is valuable and taken into account in the expected recovery rate of the instruments generating the credit risk, but does not reduce the exposure.

However, one has to be careful with the real value of collateral and pay attention to four fundamental checklist items:

1. Who owns the collateral in case of bankruptcy? This is a sensitive legal issue if more than one creditor claims ownership. Only collateral whose ownership is not disputed should be taken into account.
2. Can the collateral be valued? Unless the collateral is cash, valuation could present challenges. In case of uncertainty over the value, a discount or "haircut" to the notional amount of the collateral has to be applied. For instance, if the collateral is an asset worth $100 but whose value fluctuates, the creditor may apply a 20 percent haircut and would credit only $80 worth of collateral to the transaction's NE. Overestimating the collateral's value underestimates the amount of credit risk.

3. Can the collateral be sold? Collateral should consist of liquid instruments that can be sold easily.
4. Is the collateral correlated with the underlying exposure? If this is the case, collateral can be worthless. In one such transaction, a loan facility to a company was collateralized in part by shares of its parent company. The default of the subsidiary led to the default of the parent and the lender's collateral was worthless.

Adjusted exposure (AE) is the NE multiplied by the expected usage given default (UGD). Adjusted exposure is also called exposure at default (EAD).

What UGD captures is the expected rate of utilization of a facility in case of bankruptcy. Some transactions allow the counterparty to use a credit facility only partially. If the creditor has hard data showing that credit facility utilization is below the full amount most of the time, it can be reasonable to adjust the NE number downward by a certain ratio. Doing so reduces the need to review and approve large underutilized credit limits.

A good example of UGD in practice is a certain kind of commercial bank loan known as a revolver. It is structured around the ability of the borrower to draw and pay back money based on its needs. Borrowers pay a fee based on the notional amount, the GE, and an interest rate for the amount they draw. To maintain financial flexibility, large companies arrange multiyear facilities, regardless of whether they need the money. Banks that are competing for business are rather generous with this product and grant large capacity on relatively easy terms. As a result, the average usage rate in normal economic times is low, around 15 to 20 percent.

The challenge, for the lender, is to allocate a credit exposure. Should we consider the full notional amount (that is to say the GE), which is hardly used, or should we adjust the amount based on the borrowing history of the client or similar clients? In the real world, it is typically the latter. Banks consider that they will almost never be exposed to the notional amount and report exposure with a standard 20 percent usage assumption.

The decision is a difficult one to make for several reasons:

- Because borrowers can draw at any time at no cost (except the interest rate), their behavior is not predictable. If they need to finance an acquisition in a short period of time, they may draw 100 percent of their line. The bank would experience a sudden jump in the reported credit exposure.
- Revolvers can have long tenors, typically 5 years but up to 10 years. External circumstances can modify the behavior of otherwise predictable borrowers. For instance, in 2020, when it became clear that the COVID-19 crisis would have a long-term impact on the economy, many

companies drew on their revolvers to have rainy-day funds available. One example is Ford who drew down $15.4 billion out of two credit lines. Although they likely didn't need the cash immediately, they didn't want to experience the uncomfortable situation in which traditional lenders would turn their backs at a later point. In this recent situation, historical usage data was irrelevant.

■ As the name "usage given default" indicates, what is meaningful for risk managers is the usage factor at the time of the bankruptcy, not in normal circumstances. Even if loan facilities contain provisions to prevent distressed companies from borrowing (see Chapter 18 about risk mitigation), there can be situations in which borrowers are able to draw on their facilities shortly before they default. An historical average of 20 percent can become 100 percent when the company defaults.

The conclusion is that, although it is legitimate to reduce the NE amount by a reasonable amount for certain transactions like revolvers, setting the number requires circumspection and care.

We have introduced three ways to estimate the credit exposure stemming from a transaction. The relevance of these numbers is to allocate the approval authority and to provide the necessary input for quantitative analysis (more in Chapter 13). It is up to each firm to decide whether it wants to use GE, NE, or AE. The choice is dictated by both the underlying business and the risk management philosophy. There is not a good one or a bad one, just options with pros and cons. As we have seen so far, and we will continue to see, risk management is not an exact science; it draws on human judgment even more than quantitative analytics.

PROBABILITY OF DEFAULT

The *probability of default* (PD) is a statistical indicator that, as the name indicates, represents the likelihood that a counterparty will default during some future time period. Note that, in practice, the terms *probability of default* (PD), *default probability* (DP), and *default rate* (DR) express the same concept. There are a few fundamental notions to know about default probabilities:

■ It is never zero. Very strong entities have little chance to default, but one can never be sure. There is always a possibility that an otherwise reliable entity fails to generate enough revenues to honor its financial obligations due to management blunders, accidents, or changes in the competitive landscape. Not too long ago, the prevailing wisdom was that some companies, like General Motors, or countries, like the United States, were just too strong to default. These perceptions have clearly disappeared today. Similarly, the 2007 crisis has disabused us of the notion that some companies are simply too big to fail, meaning that their default would create so much damage to the economy that a solution will always be found to prevent it. General Motors did file for bankruptcy in 2009, but fortunately recovered very well since then. Large banks were supposed to be immune from bankruptcy due to the fear of a domino effect, that is, systemic risk that would bring down other institutions across the globe. One of the largest American financial institutions, Lehman Brothers, failed and was liquidated overnight, with its creditors losing tens of billions of dollars.

■ In 2020, governments all over the world borrowed heavily to support businesses and individuals impacted by the COVID-19 pandemic. For the fiscal year 2020 ending on September 30, 2020, the U.S. government deficit reached $3.13 trillion vs. $0.98 trillion the year before. The ability of highly rated governments to pay down their debt will certainly be in question. The common thesis is that governments with their own currencies cannot default because they have the power to print money. Yet there are more and more countries, even in the developed world, that rely too much on borrowed money. For instance, after the 2007 crisis, a few countries had to be bailed out by other countries or international institutions. Iceland, Ireland, and Greece are good examples. This is even the case for governments having their own currency, as we remember from the Russian default in the not-too-distant past. Who knows what will happen to Japan or the United States in the future?

■ It increases with time. Financial strength of borrowers tends to deteriorate over time, and companies have a higher chance of defaulting in the long term than in the short term. An implication of this observed pattern is that a PD has meaning only when it is defined for a given time period. It is not correct to state that an entity has a 0.3 percent chance of default. Rather, the same entity can have a 0.3 percent chance of default within two years and, say, a 2 percent chance within five years.

How does one calculate a default probability? There are several competing methodologies and all have one thing in common: reliance on a lot of assumptions. As such, they have to be calculated with caution. On a related point, credit analytic vendors sell data on default probabilities, and, for the same reason, these cannot be taken at face value. It is not that the data themselves are inaccurate, but how they are applied requires understanding the methodology used to compute the probabilities.

In this chapter, we focus on the most commonly used methodology to assign a default probability to a counterparty. In Chapter 7, we describe other ways that can be used in addition to, in conjunction with, or instead of this methodology.

Since default probabilities are not readily observable, they are typically determined by a two-step process:

Step 1: Analyze a counterparty's financial strength and assign a rating to it that represents its perceived financial strength.

Step 2: Using historical data, observe the default frequency of entities with similar ratings. The observed relative frequency is the estimate of the PD.

Step 1: Rating of a Counterparty

A credit rating is not an absolute measurement of financial strength but a relative one: an entity with a good grade is supposed to have a better chance to pay than one with a lower grade.

The idea is to analyze a company's operating environment, the strength of its management, its financial statements, and other drivers of its financial strength and then to assign a grade, either a letter or number, that summarizes its expected ability to face its financial obligations. For instance, a scale from 1 to 10 can be used. Strong companies are assigned an R-1 and weak companies an R-10 ("R" for rating).

Own or Internal Rating   The best way to assign a credit rating is with one's own internal credit assessment team. This is a resource-intensive activity that many large firms can afford to do but many small firms cannot. Large financial institutions have their own proprietary methodologies and their own rating scale. They employ specialized professionals whose main job is to perform credit assessments and assign ratings to their counterparties, based on publicly available as well as any private information they compile.

In Chapter 6, we review detailed criteria to take into account when assigning a grade to a corporate entity. In Chapter 11, we review criteria to take into account when assigning a grade to a noncorporate entity, such as a structured finance vehicle.

Rating Agencies   Most of the following discussion focuses on the role that ratings play for corporate borrowers, but note that rating agencies provide ratings for literally hundreds of thousands of entities, including sovereign countries, supranationals, municipalities, and public finance borrowers, most large companies around the world, and many structured finance vehicles. They provide an independent opinion of the credit quality of an entity, and they are used to support credit decisions such as lending money, loan pricing, or selling a product.

Rating agencies focus on companies that issue public debt because of the large demand from investors around the world for an independent opinion about the credit quality of the firms raising money. Importantly, rating agencies are paid by the entities seeking a rating because, without such a rating, issuing the debt would be, at a minimum, more difficult and, at worst, not possible. The agencies then publish their methodologies and ratings for all rated entities on their websites.

Although there are many rating agencies, some of which are highly specialized by industry or location, the significant global rating agencies are:

- Moody's Investors Services, owned by Moody's (U.S.)
- S&P Global Ratings (formerly known as Standard & Poor's or simply S&P), part of S&P Global (U.S.)
- Fitch Ratings, owned by Hearst (U.S.)

In addition, other rating agencies—including newly formed Kroll Bond Rating Agency and Morningstar Credit Ratings—also rate some entities. Figure 4.2 shows the typical process followed to allocate a corporate rating. It is in line with the best practice that we review in Chapter 6. Note that in the United States, A.M. Best, Fitch, Kroll Bond Rating Agency, DBRS, Egan-Jones, HR Ratings de Mexico, Japan Credit Rating Agency, Moody's, and S&P are nationally recognized statistical ratings organizations (NRSROs) and are regulated by the Securities and Exchange Commission (SEC) to: (1) protect users of credit ratings and the public interest; (2) promote ratings accuracy; and (3) ensure that ratings are not unduly influenced by conflicts of interest.[1] Canada, the European Union, the United Kingdom, and other countries also regulate approved or otherwise recognized rating agencies for the same purposes.

The main strength of the rating agencies is that they have dedicated analysts specialized in industry sectors who follow a relatively small number of entities. They have offices around the world to be close to the entities they are rating. Their desktop research is complemented by direct access to the executive officers of the firms. Ratings are so important that all CFOs of large companies issuing debt in the capital markets dedicate a good amount of time to support the rating agencies' due diligence processes.

In contrast, an analyst working for a financial institution or for an industrial company may not always have the luxury to speak with the company's management or to receive more information than what is made available publicly, in particular if the company is not a leading lender, vendor, or supplier.

---

[1] "The SEC's office of credit ratings and NRSRO regulation: past, present, and future," Jessica Kane, Director of Credit Research, Office of Credit Ratings, Las Vegas, NV, April 2020.

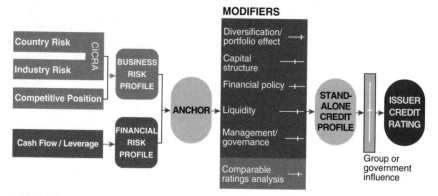

FIGURE 4.2   S&P Global Ratings Corporate Criteria Framework
Source: S&P Global Ratings, "Corporate Methodology," November 19, 2013.

Ratings are reviewed periodically—minimally each time financial statements are made available and more often if an event that may have a financial impact of an entity occurs. It is also customary for a company contemplating a major acquisition to inform the rating agencies prior to closing the transaction. The company will want to get an informal sense of what the reaction of the credit analyst will be. If a rating agency were skeptical about an acquisition and indicated a high likelihood of a downgrade, raising money to finance the transaction may become more costly, potentially jeopardizing the economics of the deal.

Rating agencies also pay attention to the competitive environment of the companies and can downgrade a company if they think that an external event may reduce profitability. For instance, a number of companies were downgraded in 2020 during the COVID-19 pandemic.

Over time, the agencies have developed different types of ratings to recognize differences between various types of financial obligations. The most important rating is the long-term "issuer" rating that corresponds to the assessment of an entity to meet its obligations maturing in more than one year. It is the most frequently used rating because it describes the general creditworthiness of the entity independent of a particular obligation, although it is understood to mean the senior unsecured credit rating because these obligations get first priority and because most creditors are exposed to this kind of obligation.

The major rating agencies' assessments are summarized by a letter system. Table 4.1 and Table 4.2 show S&P's and Moody's general ratings categories with their summary descriptions and how they generally correspond to each other. Note that S&P may further modify its letter grades with a [+] or [–] and Moody's with a number [1, 2, 3] to further distinguish the credit quality of obligors within a particular letter grade. Subcategories are known as notches. If a company is downgraded from A to A– or from Aa3 to A1, it is downgraded by one notch.

TABLE 4.1   S&P Ratings Scale

Standard & Poor's Ratings Scale
AAA   Investment Grade: Extremely strong capacity to meet financial commitments.
AA   Investment Grade: Very strong capacity to meet financial commitments.
A   Investment Grade: Strong capacity to meet financial commitments, but somewhat susceptible to adverse economic conditions and changes in circumstances.
BBB   Investment Grade: Adequate capacity to meet financial commitments, but more subject to adverse economic conditions.
BB   Speculative Grade: Less vulnerable in the near term but faces major ongoing uncertainties in adverse business, financial, and economic conditions.
B   Speculative Grade: More vulnerable to adverse business, financial, and economic conditions but currently has the capacity to meet financial commitments.
CCC   Speculative Grade: Currently vulnerable and dependent on favorable business, financial, and economic conditions to meet financial commitments.
CC   Speculative Grade: Highly vulnerable; default has not yet occurred, but is expected to be a virtual certainty
C   Speculative Grade: Currently highly vulnerable to nonpayment, and ultimate recovery is expected to be lower than that of higher obligations
D   Speculative Grade: Payment default on financial commitment or breach of an imputed promise; also used where a bankruptcy petition has been filed

Source: S&P website: www.spglobal.com, Intro to Credit Ratings.

TABLE 4.2   Moody's Global Long-Term Rating Scale

Moody's Long-Term Rating Scale Ratings
Aaa   Obligations rated Aaa are judged to be of the highest quality, subject to the lowest level of credit risk.
Aa   Obligations rated Aa are judged to be of high quality and are subject to very low credit risk.
A   Obligations rated A are judged upper-medium grade and are subject to low credit risk.
Baa   Obligations rated Baa are judged to be medium-grade and subject to moderate credit risk and as such may possess certain speculative characteristics.
Ba   Obligations rated Ba are judged to be speculative and are subject to substantial credit risk.
B   Obligations rated B are considered speculative and are subject to high credit risk.
Caa   Obligations rated Caa are judged to be of speculative or poor standing and are subject to very high credit risk.
Ca   Obligations rated Ca are highly speculative and are likely in, or very near, default with some prospect of recovery of principal and interest.
C   Obligations rated C are the lowest rated class and are typically in default, with little prospect of recovery of principal or interest.

Source: Moody's Rating Symbols and Definitions, published September 30, 2020.

One of the frequent criticisms of the rating agencies' production is that they are actually too slow to react. It can take several months before a company is downgraded, whereas the capital markets are expressing their opinion much more quickly by requiring higher interest rates on corporate bonds or selling the equity. This is certainly true, but the agencies are quick to point out that their credibility is based on stability. Their decisions have so much impact on the issuers' debt that they prefer to take the time to fully analyze a trend rather than to react quickly to events that may turn out not to be that relevant.

Once a company has been downgraded, getting back to the same rating is unlikely in the short term. Many companies that lost large amounts of money during the 2007 crisis were downgraded not only because their capital base had been eroded, but also because the agencies were disappointed by the magnitude of the bad decisions they had made. Years after the crisis had started, few large downgraded companies had regained their precrisis ratings.

There has been a lot of negative publicity for rating agencies after the 2007 crisis and some have even suggested that their actions played a key role in the debacle we experienced. It is fair to comment, though, that the criticism has been directed toward the structured finance, rather than the corporate ratings.

The agencies themselves recognized that they indeed lost their way. At one point in time, S&P was rating only four industrial companies AAA, the highest rating, whereas roughly 50,000 structured finance vehicles enjoyed the same coveted rating! In other words, the agencies considered that household names like Procter & Gamble, rated AA−, or IBM, rated A+, companies that had been around for decades, were more likely to default than obscure "special purpose vehicles" of all kinds created to facilitate the distribution of mortgage debt. As we all know, P&G and IBM are still very healthy companies, whereas thousands of vehicles previously rated AAA defaulted and generated billions of losses to investors.

To make things worse, few among the general public were aware of a rating agency's business model and discovered it after the crisis. The agencies are for-profit organizations. Their revenues come primarily from the entities that want to be rated who must buy their own ratings. When the mortgage market was booming, investment banks were pressuring the agencies to get fast and favorable ratings for the vehicles they were structuring. For the rating agencies, which can only expect to rate a finite number of companies worldwide, this provided a huge opportunity to increase revenues and profits. When the housing bubble collapsed and the AAA-rated vehicles defaulted in large numbers, the actions of the rating agencies were heavily criticized, and observers and legislators called for more regulation, which was delivered via Dodd-Frank and stronger oversight of NRSROs by the SEC in the United States, as well as enhanced supervision in Canada, the EU, and other jurisdictions.

The fact is that rating agencies have implemented major changes, including management reorganization and greater transparency, in an effort to regain credibility among investors. Corporate and sovereign ratings processes have remained reliable and intact, and today these ratings remain a key and trustworthy element of credit decisions made by corporates, banks, and asset managers.

Scoring Systems for Smaller Companies   Companies dealing with smaller counterparties may have to find alternative ways of assessing the credit quality if they are not otherwise rated. Ratings agencies tend to focus on larger entities, but many cover smaller entities as well.

The first challenge is to access financial data. Since 2000, public companies, under Regulation Fair Disclosure (Reg FD), must disseminate their financial statements and any other material information, including nonfinancial information, in a simultaneous fashion to the investing public, usually involving a combination of press releases, open conference calls, and website postings. However, nonpublic companies, many of which are small to medium size, do not provide such disclosure, so finding information on them is more difficult. In many countries, annual disclosure is required even for private companies, and some nonpublic U.S. corporations do make their financials available. Data vendors collect this information, format it, and make various adjustments to promote consistency, and then make it available for sale. The main data providers are:

- Dun & Bradstreet (U.S. focus), www.dnb.com
- Bureau Van Dijk (European focus—part of Moody's Analytics), www.bvdinfo.com
- Teikoku Data Bank (Japan), www.tdb-en.jp

The second challenge is to exploit the data. Although companies can analyze the information and prepare credit reports similar to what rating agencies do, when dealing with thousands of counterparties, which is not unusual for financial and industrial institutions, this process is prohibitively time and resource consuming. The practical alternative is to populate one's automated scoring systems with the data. The idea is to compute key ratios and weight them by coefficients to arrive at a number that summarizes financial strength.

Although this methodology lacks finesse, it is an efficient way to provide a first opinion of a counterparty, and it is unlikely that a creditworthy company would receive a low score or that a troubled one would receive a high score. More sophisticated systems can complement the numerical assessment with subjective information input by the analyst, such as management strength or the economic environment.

These types of scoring systems are actually extremely popular. The first widely publicized score was developed in the late 1960s by Edward I. Altman, then an Assistant Professor of Finance at New York University. It is called the Z-score and the formula is still widely used.

Some vendors that sell raw data complement the data they sell with their own scoring system. In addition to the ratio-based calculation, they can take into account other information, such as payment history. The largest vendors are again Dun & Bradstreet, Bureau Van Dijk, and Teikoku Data Bank.

Some companies prefer to develop their own models, making use of their judgment and experience dealing with defaulted counterparties. In that case, they buy data from the vendors mentioned earlier and populate their own systems with the supplementary information to generate ratings. One can also buy existing software such as Moody's RiskAnalyst™ that provide the platforms for incorporating the supplementary information with the basic financial data.

Hierarchy and Mapping   The final step in assigning a rating to a counterparty is to define a methodology to deal with multiple ratings sources. For the same counterparty, a firm can have its own internal rating in addition to different ratings by the major rating agencies. The goal is to obtain only one exploitable rating that will be the input of Step 2. There are three things to consider:

1. Establish a hierarchy. If a firm produces an internal rating, this typically ranks higher than the external ratings. The analyst does take into account external vendors' opinions but has full authority to assign the final rating. If a counterparty is not rated internally, then a hierarchy between the sources must be established. It is not unusual to place the major agencies' ratings ahead of the other values when available. The rationale is that the ratings from the ratings agencies benefit from human judgment, whereas other methodologies rely on automated processes.
2. Deal with inconsistencies. What to do when external vendors have different views? In such a circumstance, called a split rating, firms normally adopt a conservative posture and select the lowest indicator. For example, if a company is rated AA– by S&P and A1 by Moody's, the lower of the two ratings, A1, is retained.
3. Map the internal ratings with external ratings since, in the final analysis, the rating agencies have the historical data on the relative frequency of default, which is the basis for estimating the default probabilities, as we

will see next. It is, therefore, necessary to map one's own internal rating with the agency rating whose historical data will be used. If we again take our example of an internal rating scale of R1 to R10, a firm may decide to have R1 correspond to AAA/Aaa, and R2 to AA/Aa, and so on.

Step 2: Use Historical Data

Once a counterparty has been assigned a rating, the next step is to deduce a probability of default or PD. For establishing the PD, the idea is to observe the historical default frequency, made available by the rating agencies, of companies with the same rating.

It is straightforward and works the following way: If a company is rated AA today and historically AA-rated entities experienced a 0.5 percent default rate after five years, one can logically state that the probability of default of a AA-rated entity is 0.5 percent in the next five years.

Moody's and S&P regularly publish updated data on defaults, enabling risk management teams to better understand the likelihood of a counterparty defaulting and to select the best estimator for the PD.

Importantly, default frequency is not stable across economic cycles as can be seen in Figure 4.3. As one expects, recessions generate more defaults. When the economic environment is more favorable, defaults are scarce. The challenge is, therefore, to pick a PD that is representative across economic cycles.

Equally important to note is that cumulative default frequencies increase with time. Although the frequency of defaults among A-rated corporate borrowers may be close to zero in the subsequent year, but in five years the frequency is not close to zero, and will be even higher after 10 years.

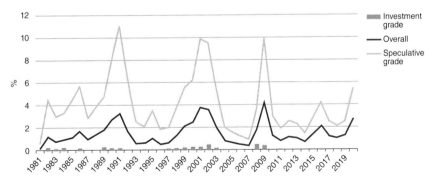

FIGURE 4.3 Global Default Rates: Investment Grade versus Speculative Grade
Source: S&P Global Ratings, "Default, Transition, and Recovery: 2020 Annual Global Corporate Default and Rating Transition Study," Chart 1, April 7, 2021.

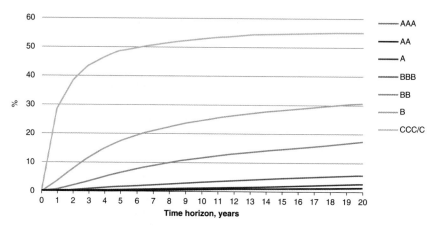

FIGURE 4.4 Global Corporate Average Cumulative Default Rates by Rating (1981–2020)
Source: S&P Global Ratings, "Default, Transition, and Recovery: 2020 Annual Global Corporate Default and Rating Transition Study," Chart 4, April 7, 2021.

The rating agencies publish both the one-year default frequencies by rating categories as well as the cumulative default frequencies over various elapsed time periods. Figure 4.4 shows default frequencies over time; note that default frequency rises for all rating categories over time. The single A borrowers have virtually no defaults over a short (one- to two-year) horizon, which grows to somewhat over 4 percent over a 20-year period. For BBB borrowers, the cumulative default frequency reaches about 10 percent over a 20-year period.

The two-step methodology we described is widely employed in the industry. In fact, since rating agencies refrain from stating that a particular rating corresponds to a probability of default, they publish all the necessary data to allow users to make this connection, thereby allowing each firm the flexibility to work with the numbers most relevant to its own analysis.

THE RECOVERY RATE

The recovery rate is the amount of money recovered upon default, expressed as a percent of the gross exposure. Rarely do credit losses result in the entire amount of the nominal exposure. Upon bankruptcy, creditors vie for residual assets and the legal structure of their claim influences the amount they ultimately recover. In Chapter 18, we discuss recovery dedicated to structural mitigants in more detail.

For the time being, let us mention the major elements that influence the amount of recovery:

- The total amount of assets available.
- The seniority of the position. Some financial instruments receive their share in priority. They are called senior creditors. Some rank second, and they are called the junior creditors. The more senior the creditor, the greater the recovery.
- The security package. Some loans or bonds benefit from a lien on some assets. In case of default, these instruments take possession of the pledged assets, and other creditors only benefit when the secured creditors are fully repaid. The recovery rate is usually estimated at transaction inception, and it affects the risk appetite of a firm toward a transaction that depends not only on the exposure level, but also on the amount that is expected to be lost on default. Because highly secured transactions have a high expected-recovery rate, firms can take on more exposure to these than to unsecured loans.

Recovery rates are estimated with historical data, also published by rating agencies. For example, many institutions exposed to credit risk having the equivalent to senior unsecured exposures consider that an acceptable recovery rate is between 40 percent and 50 percent. Additionally, S&P and Fitch are now selling recovery ratings for specific transactions, reflecting primarily their analysis of the collateral package obtained by the lenders.

Note that a widely used concept and term is *loss given default* (LGD), which is defined as one minus the recovery rate times the exposure. This reflects the net loss after recovery.

THE TENOR

Risk managers do not like long-dated transactions for two reasons: First, the long-term financial strength of a borrower is much harder to predict than its short-term financial strength, and second, as we now know, the default probability of a counterparty increases with time. In the discussion of guidelines in Chapter 2, the regular approval process is usually reserved for transactions with a tenor of up to three to five years, with longer dated transactions needing a higher approval level. In most cases, determining the tenor is straightforward because most financial arrangements have a clear end date. If a sale has a payment term of 60 days, the tenor is 60 days. If a loan must be repaid after 10 years, the tenor is 10 years.

There are naturally some exceptions that require adjustments. This is the case when transactions have a contractual tenor but experience shows that the repayment can be expected more quickly. If there is sufficient data available to support reducing the tenor, it is prudent to do so because otherwise sensible transactions might be rejected because they appear too risky. We will see later on that price and capital requirements for a transaction are highly influenced by the default probability. Being too conservative with the tenor translates into requiring a higher price than necessary and having to set aside too much capital, both of which could make the transaction uneconomical for either the lender or borrower. Setting a realistic tenor for a transaction is part of the common sense expected from a risk manager.

The most common example of the gap between contractual, or legal, tenor and expected tenor is residential mortgages. When individuals buy houses, they typically take out a long-dated, 30-year mortgage. Experience shows that few mortgages are paid according to the original schedule and that most of them are repaid within 10 years because of refinancing or a sale of the home. Estimating the prepayment rate of a pool of mortgages is absolutely necessary when analyzing transactions like mortgage securitization. Specialized software available on Bloomberg or INTEX enables analysts to estimate an expected tenor with a good amount of predictive accuracy.

DIRECT VERSUS CONTINGENT EXPOSURE

Financial institutions sometimes distinguish direct credit exposures and contingent credit exposures. The difference is whether money or goods have actually been exchanged or if there is just a commitment to do so. For example, funded loans are direct exposures because the cash is already out. Letters of credit (details can be found in Chapter 19) are contingent exposures because the bank makes only a commitment to disburse cash if certain well-defined events occur. Events are typically related to the performance of the obligor, such as finishing a contract on time and within budget.

If it is difficult to predict the probability of a commitment becoming a funded position, there is no reason to treat direct and contingent exposures differently. Both must be considered as exposures of the same nature and follow the same approval process. However, if reliable data on usage exist, an adjustment to gross exposure (GE) can be made, as described earlier.

What happens often is that, even if on the surface they look unrelated, the events that can transform a contingent exposure into a direct exposure and the financial distress of the counterparty are correlated. For a long time, a letter of credit (LoC) can remain undrawn as the counterparty is performing well. Then, when the counterparty starts facing financial stress and the quality of its operations declines, the LoC is drawn. Now, at the time of bankruptcy, the bank that issued the LoC is fully exposed. Thus, the notional exposure is the amount that matters when deciding whether to approve a credit line.

THE EXPECTED LOSS

Some of the concepts explained earlier are used to compute the expected loss of a transaction. Although we said in the introduction that the riskiness of a transaction cannot be summarized by a single number, the expected loss provides a number that takes into account the exposure, the default probability, and the recovery rate, and it is calculated in Figure 4.5.

Driver 1   **Driver 2**   **Driver 3**

Expected loss = Exposure × Default probability × (1 − Recovery rate)

FIGURE 4.5   Drivers of Expected Loss

Note that the expected loss is a statistical measure that, on a stand-alone basis, does not provide much information about a transaction. However, expected loss is critical for pricing transactions and has an important role in portfolio management. Although any one transaction is unlikely to produce the expected loss, on a portfolio basis, across many homogeneous transactions, the expected loss will be a fairly predictable number under certain restrictive conditions. We will defer our discussion of portfolio effects and statistical concepts as they relate to losses and the dispersion of losses around the expected value until later chapters (Chapters 5 and 13, primarily). However, we conclude this chapter with the statement that a single statistic cannot predict the loss behavior of any transaction.

CHAPTER **5**

Dynamic Credit Exposure

Unlike most loan facilities and other traditional transactions, certain financial arrangements generate a credit exposure whose amount is not a fixed number known at inception but, rather, one that changes over time. Two typical examples are derivative transactions of all kinds and long-term supply or purchase agreements of commodities. The credit exposure is not fixed because it will fluctuate with the value of an underlying product on which the financial arrangement is based. These exposures are known as dynamic credit exposures. A variety of transactions generate dynamic credit exposures and it is impossible to describe them all in detail. However, they typically share some key features:

- They involve transactions of financial instruments such as foreign exchange, interest rates, or equities or goods whose values fluctuate (e.g., commodities such as oil and sugar).
- They have a long tenor, typically several years.
- In some cases, there is no exchange of cash or goods up front.
- Both parties commit to make a payment or to sell/buy a product in the future, at terms determined in advance.

What creates the dynamic credit exposure is the difference between the predetermined conditions and the prevailing ones at the time of the expected payment or sale/purchase. The following two sections introduce the two most common families of transactions generating dynamic credit exposure: long-term supply or purchase agreements of physical commodities and derivatives transactions. We acknowledge that some of the concepts presented here are not immediately intuitive. Thus, we introduce them with examples rather than with theory.

The challenge for the credit analyst is to assign a credit exposure at the inception of the transaction because we want to know if the firm has credit capacity to enable the transaction. The common methodologies used for this are mark-to-market (MTM) and value at risk (VaR).

LONG-TERM SUPPLY AGREEMENTS

Long-term supply agreements involve one party committing to sell a product like oil or sugar for a long period of time and another one committing to accept deliveries and to make payments. The volume and price are set at the inception of the agreement and are valid until termination.

Let us illustrate long-term supply agreements with a concrete example. Utility companies, say, for example, Utility Corp., generate electricity from power plants they own and sell it to individual and industrial customers. They build power plants, which are expensive and require long-term financing, typically 10 years or longer. The financing faces the major challenge of forecasting expenses and revenues over a long period of time. Lenders need to be comfortable with the stability of the expenses, primarily the costs of operating the plant, and of the revenues generated by the sale of electricity to customers. A major portion of the operating expenses stems from the purchase of oil, a commodity. Prices of commodities fluctuate a lot, as shown in Figure 5.1, because they are influenced by rapid changes of macroeconomic conditions or by the occurrence of political events.

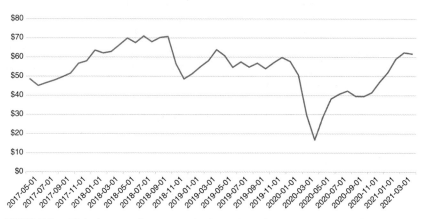

FIGURE 5.1   Global Price of WTI Crude ($ per barrel), May 2017–April 2021
Source: International Monetary Fund, Global Price of WTI Crude [POILWTIUSDM], retrieved from FRED, Federal Reserve Bank of St. Louis.

To avoid being exposed to the volatility of prices, which would make financing nearly impossible, utilities enter into long-term contracts with commodity producers and traders, like Traders & Co. In exchange for the commitment to be delivered a given quantity of oil, Utility Corp. agrees to buy a predetermined amount from Traders & Co. for a set price over a long period of time. In doing so, they eliminate their exposure to the fluctuations of the market price and their cash outflows are known in advance, which satisfies their financiers. The contract between Utility Corp. and Traders & Co. is known as a long-term supply agreement.

Let's examine the consequences of signing a supply contract for both companies if the basic features of the contract are:

- Traders & Co. will provide Utility Corp. with 100,000 gallons of oil per month.
- The agreed price is $3 per gallon.
- The contract is valid for five years.

From a cash-flow perspective, it is straightforward: Each month for the next five years, Utility Corp. will pay $300,000 to Traders & Co. and will receive the oil it needs to run its power plant.

Now let's imagine the following situation: Due to a strong economy, the worldwide consumption of oil increases, which drives its price up. One year after the inception of the contract, the price per gallon goes to $4. Utility Corp. made a good deal as it pays $3 for a gallon whose market price is now $4. Traders & Co. was caught off-guard by the large price increase and, due to a high volume of speculative bets, is going out of business and stops all deliveries immediately. Utility Corp. has no option but to find another supplier to replace Traders & Co. for the next four years. The new agreement reflects the prevailing market price of $4 per gallon instead of the $3 they used to pay to Traders & Co.

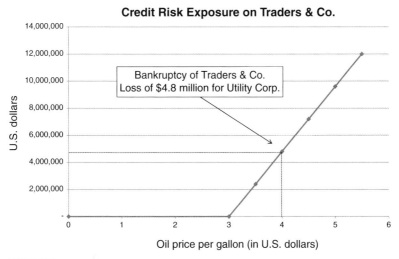

FIGURE 5.2 Loss for Utility Corp.

The financial loss for Utility Corp. generated by the bankruptcy of Traders & Co. is fairly easy to calculate. Each year, the extra cost is: 100,000 (gallons) × 12 (months) × ($4 – $3) = $1.2 million. Ignoring for the time being the time value of money, the loss for the four remaining years calculated at that particular moment in time totals $1.2 million × 4 = $4.8 million. The oil price, the exposure amount, and the dollar loss for Utility Corp. can be seen in Figure 5.2.

The supply contract, therefore, generated a credit risk for Utility Corp. because, when Traders & Co. defaulted, Utility Corp suffered a financial loss. Three main parameters influenced the magnitude of the loss:

1. The agreed price ($3).
2. The remaining lifetime of the contract (four years).
3. The market price at the time of Traders & Co.'s default ($4).

With the first two points alone, the situation would not be much different than from a bank loan. The notional amount of the loan and the amortization schedule is known at the time of the closing, so the credit exposure, which diminishes as time goes by, can be quantified at any time. What creates the dynamic exposure is the fact that the magnitude of the credit exposure depends on the market price at the time the calculation is made. Each time the price of the product underlying the agreement changes, the credit exposure changes. That's why it is dynamic. It cannot be calculated in advance, and its value will change frequently and can experience large swings in a short period of time.

This creates a serious challenge for a credit risk manager who is asked to sign off on the exposure to the counterparty. In addition to the long-term nature of the contract, which generates a high degree of uncertainty around the evolution of the credit quality of the supplier, the risk manager does not know with certainty the amount of credit risk his firm will be taking over the lifetime of the contract. We will present in the following sections the most common approach to deal with this situation.

DERIVATIVE PRODUCTS

Derivatives are financial instruments that companies use to hedge against risk or to speculate on price movements. The most common derivatives involve interest rates, foreign exchange, equities, credit, and commodities (e.g., oil). They are technically very similar. In most cases, there are no exchanges of cash at the inception (e.g., start date) of a derivative contract. However, the simple fact of entering into a contract generates a credit risk for the two parties involved.

We will use the example of an interest-rate swap to explain where the credit exposure comes from. In order to facilitate the presentation, we simplify some technical aspects of the transaction. Thus, what we describe will not perfectly represent the actual financial products sold by banks. Our goal is to make our readers understand the fundamental principles of dynamic exposures, and details have been omitted for this purpose.

Big Corp. needs to refinance an existing loan and borrows money from Large Bank. The main terms of the loan are the following:

- Loan amount: $100 million.
- Maturity: five years.
- Interest Rate: three-month LIBOR + 1.2 percent per annum.
- Frequency: five yearly payments at the end of each anniversary year.

The interest rate is not fixed but floats and varies according to the value of the London Interbank Offered Rate (LIBOR). Note that LIBOR is scheduled to disappear at the end of 2021. It will be replaced by various indexes, notably Secured Overnight Financing Rate (SOFR) for dollar denominated instruments and Sterling Overnight Index Average (SONIA) for pound denominated ones. LIBOR for a given term (e.g., 3 months) is an average rate at which large banks, like Large Bank, borrow money from each other to finance their operations. Its value changes daily. If, for example, LIBOR is 1 percent, Big Corp. will pay an interest rate of 2.2 percent. If LIBOR goes to 2 percent, the rate will become 3.2 percent. Figure 5.3 displays historical LIBOR rates for selected terms.

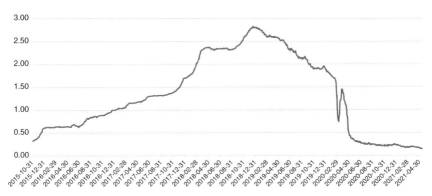

FIGURE 5.3   Three-Month LIBOR Based on U.S. Dollar, October 2015–May 2021, Quoted as Annual Percent
Source: ICE Benchmark Administration Limited (IBA), three-month LIBOR, based on U.S. Dollar [USD3MTD156N], retrieved from FRED, Federal Reserve Bank of St. Louis.

Big Corp. does not like the uncertainty around the interest rate it must pay on its loan, but it has no choice because all commercial banks lend money at floating rates and not fixed rates, so as to match the cost movement in their funding sources with the return movement from their loans. Fortunately, Big Corp. also has a relationship with an investment bank, Lemon Bank, whose trading desk is active in the interest-rate derivative market. Lemon Bank is willing to transform Big Corp.'s floating interest rate of LIBOR + 1.2 percent into a 5 percent fixed rate.

The two parties, therefore, enter into an interest-rate swap. This is a separate agreement from the loan between Big Corp. and Large Bank. Lemon bank is not involved in the contractual relationship between Big Corp. and Large Bank.

The main characteristics of the swap are:

- Notional (usually loan balance at the time the swap is entered into): $100 million.
- Maturity: five years.
- Payer: Big Corp. pays fixed rate of 5 percent per annum (swap rate).
- Receiver: Lemon Bank pays floating rate of LIBOR + 1.2 percent per annum.
- Frequency: five yearly payments.
- Original Cost: $0.

Entering into an interest rate swap removes the uncertainty about the fluctuations of LIBOR for Big Corp. They know that their expenses will be exactly $5 million per year until the maturity of the loan, regardless of the evolution of LIBOR. The payment they will receive from Lemon Bank will match exactly the interest payment they owe to Large Bank.

Each year, the exchange of cash will be:

- Big Corp. pays to Lemon Bank: $100 million × 5 percent = $5 million.
- Lemon Bank pays to Big Corp.: $100 million × (LIBOR + 1.2 percent). For instance, if, when payment is due, LIBOR is 4.8 percent, the payment is $100 million × 6 percent = $6 million. *(Note that in practice, Big Corp. and Lemon Bank will exchange on a net basis, so only one check is written at each settlement period. In this case, Lemon Bank will pay Big Corp. $1 million.)*
- Big Corp. pays Large Bank: $100 million × (LIBOR + 1.2 percent). In our example, the payment is $6 million.

Unfortunately, at the end of the first year and just before the first interest payment from Big Corp. to Large Bank is due, Lemon Bank faces some financial difficulties and is liquidated. As a result, the interest-rate swap with Big Corp. is canceled. To make things worse, the LIBOR has increased to 5.8 percent. The yearly interest payment on the loan from Large Bank is now $7 million, whereas Big Corp., thanks to the interest-rate swap, expected to pay $5 million. Big Corp., still interested in transforming its floating rate payments to Large Bank to fixed rate payments, in order to remove the uncertainty about the amount of its yearly payments until the maturity of the loan, replaces Lemon Bank with another bank, but now pays an interest rate of 7 percent instead of 5 percent.

Big Corp.'s financial loss due to the bankruptcy of Lemon Bank can be estimated, again ignoring the time value of money, at $2 million per year for five years = $10 million. By entering into an interest-rate swap, Big Corp. took a credit risk on Lemon Bank. As shown in the example, they lost money due to the inability of Lemon Bank to honor a financial obligation. Similar to the example of Utility Corp. in the previous section, the magnitude of the financial loss they incurred was not known in advance. It depended on:

- The agreed swap price (the fixed swap rate, 5 percent).
- The remaining lifetime of the contract (5 payments).
- The value of the LIBOR at the time of Lemon Bank's default (5.8 percent).

For a derivative transaction, the credit risk exposure cannot be estimated with certainty at the beginning of the contract. In addition to the agreed swap price and the time left on the swap, the prevailing LIBOR when the credit exposure is calculated has a major impact.

THE ECONOMIC VALUE OF A CONTRACT

The two examples just given illustrate the two main families of business agreements that generate a dynamic credit exposure. The fundamental thing to remember is that, once a contract has been signed, there is a possibility that one party loses money if the other party defaults, even if there is no exchange of cash or products at inception. As a consequence, the simple fact of entering into a transaction generates credit risk. The only case in which there would not be credit risk is if the market price of the underlying product were somehow constant, which naturally does not happen in real life.

As we saw in the previous examples, the amount of money that can be lost at any time is what it would cost to replace a defaulted counterparty. This is why the credit risk exposure is the replacement cost of the counterparty. It represents the economic value of the contract and corresponds to the mark-to-market (MTM) value of the contract.

MTM is a fundamental concept in finance. Within the context of this book, the most important meaning of MTM is that it corresponds to the valuation of the credit risk at any time, taking into account the prevailing market conditions. Note that there are other consequences of MTM that we review further on in this chapter. We will explain more about MTM in the following section.

Our two examples were, purposely, fairly intuitive because both companies had entered into long-term contracts to protect a business need, that is, to hedge the cost of oil and hedge the floating interest rate on a loan. There are situations in which the economic value of contracts is a little less easy to understand, especially when seeing a derivative transaction in which no money has been borrowed or no products yet sold. Let us illustrate this:

Going back to the example of Big Corp. and Lemon Bank, this time let's take the point of view of Lemon Bank and let's assume that Big Corp. defaults when LIBOR is at 3 percent. The floating interest rate is now 3 percent + 1.2 percent = 4.2 percent. Legally speaking, the bankruptcy of Big Corp. is a termination event of the swap and releases Lemon Bank from its obligation to honor the terms of the swap. It is, therefore, tempting to conclude the following: Because Lemon Bank did not lend money to Big Corp, the termination of the swap simply means that both parties are released from their obligations and there is no further settlement to consider. Lemon Bank will not receive $5 million per year from Big Corp. but will not have to pay $100 million × (LIBOR +1.2 percent) at prevailing LIBOR value over what would have been the remaining term. There is a loss of future revenues, but Lemon Bank cannot do anything about it.

This way of thinking is not correct. Big Corp. and Lemon Bank had entered into a derivative transaction and, at the time of the bankruptcy, Lemon Bank was expecting, at current LIBOR level, to have a net cash inflow of $800,000 ($5 million – $4.2 million) per year. Because there were five payments remaining, the MTM value of the contract or the economic value of the contract was, assuming expected future values of LIBOR to remain constant, $4.0 million.

Even if Lemon Bank did not lend money to Big Corp., they were expecting to make money on the contract, thanks to the favorable evolution of the LIBOR value. They had a credit exposure on Big Corp. that materialized at the time of their default. From an economic point of view, concluding a supply agreement or a derivative contract is strictly equivalent to lending money. Losing money that was lent and did not come back is exactly the same as not receiving an amount of money that is expected.

To make it clearer, let's present the situation of Lemon Bank in a different way. Let's assume that Lemon Bank did not have appetite for the interest-rate swap but just wanted to develop a commercial relationship with Big Corp. To cancel out their risk, at the same time they concluded the swap with Big Corp. they entered into the same swap but in the opposite direction with Better Bank. They committed to pay to Better Bank the fixed rate of 5 percent and Better Bank committed to pay them the floating rate of LIBOR + 1.2 percent. At the time of Big Corp.'s default, Lemon Bank owed $5 million to Better Bank, and Better Bank owed $4.2 million to Lemon Bank. Without the payment from Big Corp., Lemon Bank incurs a net cash loss of $800,000 and faces the potential to continue losing money until the maturity of the swap. However, whether Lemon Bank hedged their swap position did not matter. At the time of default, they incur an economic loss of $4.0 million, generated by the bankruptcy of Big Corp.

MARK-TO-MARKET VALUATION

We took a few shortcuts when calculating the financial losses of Utility Corp. and Big Corp. due to the bankruptcy of their counterparties. The purpose of the previous examples was only to explain at a high level the concept of dynamic credit exposure and MTM. For most credit risk managers, what is really important is to identify when transactions generate a credit exposure and to have a general understanding about its nature. The actual valuation of dynamic exposures is very complex. It is another science that typically involves sophisticated quantitative models. Thankfully, there is really no need to be able to calculate an MTM exposure to be a good credit risk manager. Naturally, the more one knows, the better, though.

In this section, we will endeavor to provide additional context around MTM so that our readers develop a good feel for the concept. To repeat ourselves, marking to market a contract means calculating its replacement cost, taking into account the prevailing value of the underlying product. In other words, how much money a company would lose if they would have to replace their counterparty by another one that would apply the prevailing market conditions.

There are three major parameters that influence the mark-to-market value of a contract and thus the credit risk it generates:

1. The predetermined conditions of the contract (e.g., $3 per gallon).
2. The time left in the contract. All things being equal, the longer, the larger the value.
3. The prevailing conditions at the time the computation is performed.

Let's review some key aspects of MTM calculations.

Time value of money is captured in the MTM calculation because the expected exchange of money or product takes place over time. Thus, we need to use the present value of future cash flows, and not the notional amount, which is a nominal figure that does not account for time value of money.

The MTM calculation can be done at any time, not just when a counterparty defaults. When one computes an MTM, the fact that the counterparty could default in the future has to be taken into account. There is some probability that the counterparty could default over the time period in question, and this possibility affects the economic value of the contract. So, in addition to the fact that prices vary since contract inception, the chance of default over the contract period is also a variable that influences economic value. This is what introduces complexity in MTM calculations. Reviewing and comparing the mathematical models used for these calculations would not bring much value to this book, so we will refrain from covering them.

MTM is a zero sum game for the two entities involved. If, at one point of time, the contract is worth $10 million for one entity, it is actually worth –$10 million for the other party.

If a transaction is entered at prevailing market conditions, the MTM value of the deal is zero at inception.

The MTM value of a transaction declines over time, all else being equal, since fewer and fewer payments will occur. This is known as the amortization effect. In our previous example, we made a rough calculation of MTM as a loss in a single year multiplied by the number of remaining years until the end of the contract. Again, this methodology was crude but enables us to understand that the shorter the remaining life of the transaction is, the smaller the MTM value. Ultimately, at the end of the contract's term, the MTM is zero, regardless of the prevailing market conditions, because there are no more payments expected.

MTM can be positive or negative. From a credit risk management perspective, only positive credit exposures are relevant. If a counterparty defaults when the MTM is negative, there is no financial loss, so negative numbers can be ignored. When exposure reports are prepared, only positive numbers are retained; otherwise the value is reported as zero.

MTM is more than a credit risk management concept; it is also an accounting one. The accounting standards (like the U.S. Generally Accepted Accounting Principles [GAAP]) require that some contracts have to be marked to market and distinguish those that do not have to be. The important thing to remember is that MTM valuations have an impact on the P&L statements of a company. Mark-to-market on contracts has to be reported as positive or negative revenue at the same level as the other operations of a firm. It may sound bizarre or irrelevant, but it just reflects the fact that some transactions involving products with fluctuating variables have an economic value similar to other value-creating or value-destroying activities of a company.

In a trading environment, MTM is computed daily, and, thus, the profitability of trading desk operations can be assessed on a real-time basis. The rationale is that a bankruptcy is not necessary to terminate a supply agreement or a derivative contract. It can be done on a voluntary basis if the contract is not needed any longer or for many other reasons. When a party decides to unwind an MTM-sensitive transaction, the other party may or may not accept, but if they do, they ask to be compensated at the market value level. It is logical since the counterparty may want to replace its partners and, to repeat ourselves, if they do so the new arrangement is done at the prevailing market conditions. They want to be paid for what it would cost them to replace their counterparty if they need and/or want to do so.

In case of bankruptcy of a counterparty, the positive MTM value of a contract is added to the list of liabilities at the same level as other senior unsecured financial obligations. The party that had a contract with a positive value with an entity that defaults is entitled to receive its share of the amount that will be made available to all creditors. Derivatives counterparties are considered senior unsecured creditors. This shows, again, the economic value of a contract.

Note that in many publications, the MTM value of a contract is defined as the present value of the future expected cash flows. The problem with this definition is that it makes sense only for transactions in which there is an exchange of cash flows, such as interest-rate swaps. The example of the supply contracts illustrates the shortcoming in this definition. The MTM value is present and is calculable even though there is no exchange of cash flows; rather, one party provides a commodity and the other one pays for it!

No doubt that the MTM value of a contract is an important number. It represents a good estimation of the amount of money that a company would lose at a particular point in time in case of default of the counterparty. That's why all banks, trading firms, or utilities like Utility Corp. have developed automated systems to compute MTM at least every day. When the financial markets close, the proprietary mathematical models are fed with the new data, and within a few hours, all MTM positions are available. The firms have access to the profitability of their business and, as far as we are concerned, to the credit exposures on all their counterparties.

For credit risk managers, the list of MTM values provides an overview of the exposures they have to manage. Those values have to be compared with the approved limits to make sure that the risks taken are in line with the firm's appetite. Furthermore, when a default occurs, many people inside a firm, such as senior management and compliance officers, and outside the organization, such as regulators, rating agencies, and equity analysts, want to know immediately what the financial consequences are. In an era when everybody is accustomed to receiving information on a real-time basis, risk managers need to have the MTM numbers handy all the time, for all contracts and on all counterparties.

VALUE AT RISK (VaR)

Alas, the computation of MTM values in quasi-real time is far from being enough for a credit risk manager. Mark-to-market is a snapshot of a credit risk exposure at the time it is computed. However, because the exposure is dynamic, the MTM methodology does not provide any information about what the range of exposure could be in the future. For risk managers, this range is what counts when deciding whether to enter into transactions, because they have to sign off on the credit exposures until they expire.

Imagine that there is a surge in commodity prices one day. When the credit risk manager arrives in their office the following day, they discover that some exposures have jumped by 10 percent compared to the day before. What do they do then? Try to figure out if it is still reasonable to face such high exposures on the weakest counterparties? Isn't it too late?

The price surge that triggered higher exposures may be impressive for one day but commodities are volatile, and it is neither the first nor the last time it will happen. Would it not be better if, at the time a new contract is considered, risk managers could have a methodology to assess, within a level of certainty, how high the credit exposure may reach during its life-time? Couldn't we extrapolate historical data to simulate how the new contract may behave as the price of the underlying product fluctuates? It would be imperfect, because future prices may differ from past behavior, but within a quantifiable level of certainty, we would have a reasonable estimation.

As you may have figured out, estimating the amount of future credit exposures that can arise from current contracts, that is, the range of MTM values, is a focal point of the credit risk management function. The range can be estimated statistically, and the outcome is a probability-weighted distribution of exposures from which the value at risk or VaR can be extracted. The VaR is the gross exposure (GE), as described in Chapter 4, attached to a transaction generating a dynamic credit exposure.

With MTM, we calculate the economic value of a contract based on the prevailing price, and we arrive at a point estimate. The idea behind VaR is to add a probability distribution dimension to the MTM concept. What is the likelihood that the price reaches a certain level and, if so, what is the corresponding MTM value of the contract?

For a particular product like oil or interest rates, historical price data are widely available for a long period of time, which gives us the relative frequencies of these prices. With enough data points on prices, the relative frequencies represent true probabilities, and, if plotted where the y-axis represents the relative frequency of occurrence and the x-axis represents the corresponding MTM value, we are able to generate a probability distribution as in Figure 5.4. For many physical and financial products, MTM values (prices) are normally distributed, consistent with the graphic in Figure 5.4.

FIGURE 5.4 Probability Distribution of MTM Values

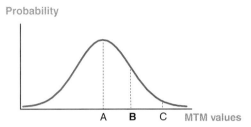

The area below the curve represents the probability associated with all possible outcome scenarios, which is 100 percent by construction. At a given MTM value, the area below the curve, up to that point, represents the probability of the product's MTM value being at or below that amount. For example, point A represents a 50 percent probability that the product's MTM will be at or below $65 and point B represents a 75 percent probability that the product's MTM will be at or below $90.

What risk managers are most interested in is the tail of the distribution, since values in the tail correspond to unfavorable outcomes. Risk managers are interested in knowing what the MTM values might be in the more extreme and rare cases, say 1 percent of the time or less frequently. Suppose the contract in question creates more credit exposure as prices rise. In Figure 5.4, risk managers are most interested in point C, which corresponds to the 99 percent probability of MTM values being at or below $100 million. Risk managers can, therefore, conclude, using the commonly used vocabulary, that the VaR of this contract, with a 99 percent confidence interval is $100 million. What it means is that we can have confidence that there is likely only a 1 percent chance that the credit risk exposure on the counterparty generated by this contract will be more than $100 million.

In the real world, entities will establish a confidence interval that fits their entity's risk appetite as set by the Board of Directors or the most senior risk committee. If a high value is chosen, there is a good chance that the entity will never be surprised by bad news. However, this strategy has opportunity costs because the transaction is assigned a high GE and consumes a lot of the scarce credit capacity that a firm allocates to a counterparty. Other profitable transactions would be rejected due to lack of available capacity on the same counterparty, whereas the likelihood of reaching the high credit exposure with the derivative transaction is small. In actual practice, many financial institutions set the confidence interval at 99 percent (corresponding to a 1 percent chance of experiencing losses beyond this point).

You may remember the concept of GE explained in the previous chapter. We mentioned that for transactions generating a dynamic credit exposure, the GE had to be computed using statistical methodologies. We also said that GE, for dynamic credit exposures, does not represent the worst case scenario. Most markets have, in theory, unlimited price limits. Recall the negative price of $37.63 per barrel of oil in April 2020, as traders who had committed to buy oil prior to the crisis did not want to take delivery due the economic slowdown at the time and were forced to resell it at no value and to compensate buyers for storage costs! Not only did they pay the agreed price to honor their purchase but they also remunerated someone else to get rid of their acquisition. Contrast this to the all-time high of $147.02 in July 2008. However, oil prices are, in principle, without limit, and the probability of reaching extremely high MTM values is close to zero but not zero. There is always a small chance that oil prices reach, say $500 per gallon, which would lead to a an extremely large MTM.

Let's not forget that, for most products, the big price moves will occur over time rather than suddenly. This gives risk managers the chance to take actions such as asking for collateral, buying credit protection, or unwinding the contract.

In most institutions, MTM and VaR calculations are performed outside the credit risk management team. Estimating and managing VaR exposures is the realm of what is known as market risk management. A market risk manager's job is, among other things, to define and implement methodologies to forecast future MTM values. The result of that work is then forwarded to the credit risk management team, which, before the conclusion of a contract, signs off on the methodology and judges if the associated GE is compatible with the firm's appetite. Once the contract is in the book, market risk management provides daily credit exposures for all dynamic transactions.

CHAPTER 6

Fundamental Credit Analysis

A basic requirement for any career in credit risk management is being able to perform a fundamental credit analysis. Within the credit risk management function, counterparty risk assessment employs the most professionals. The responsibilities of the credit analysts are to review the financial strength of entities that, in turn, is used to establish credit limits and approve transactions.

Senior executives who sit on credit committees also must have a thorough working knowledge of credit analysis because they are the ultimate decision makers in those credit committees. They must be able to quickly understand the credit reports produced by risk managers, to ask relevant questions, and then to make informed decisions using their judgment and experience.

The credit analysis of an entity revolves around the knowledge of:

- Its political, economic, regulatory, and competitive environment.
- Its management, products, and operations.
- Its financial status, such as liquidity, leverage, profitability, and cash flow, much of which is knowable through analysis of its financial statements.

In this chapter, we focus on fundamental concepts of credit analysis.

The deliverable of the work of a credit analyst is a credit report that summarizes the financial situation of an entity and that outlines its strengths and weaknesses. To be able to produce a credit report, analysts must have several essential skills:

- A strong understanding of the relevant accounting rules, such as U.S. Generally Accepted Accounting Principles (GAAP) or International Financial Reporting Standards (IFRS), used to prepare the numbers.

- Ideally, the credit analyst will have an accounting background strong enough to be able to perform some investigative analysis on the financial statements, not dissimilar to what a forensic accountant engages in.[1]
- A strong understanding of the macroeconomic, industry, and regulatory environment in which the entity operates.
- A strong willingness to be curious, skeptical, perseverant, and to ask questions when meeting senior managers of a company.

Imagine that a company is deriving most of its revenues from a product that is gradually becoming obsolete or for which its market share is slipping to stronger competitors. Or, suppose a pharmaceutical company is about to lose its patent protection on a key product. A company's financial statements are backward looking and may not reflect or predict these events; the credit analyst must look forward to understand the company's future profitability. In particular, large organizations not only employ a team of credit analysts, but also organize the team to allow the analysts to specialize by industry.

The relationship between a chief financial officer (CFO) of a counterparty and a credit analyst can be like a cat and mouse game. Some CFOs are very clear, but others can be purposefully enigmatic so as not to disclose much for a variety of reasons. CFOs of public companies are prohibited from disclosing material information unless it is done simultaneously to the general investing public; most CFOs choose to limit disclosure for competitive reasons and to err on the side of saying less rather than more. This facet of the credit analysis—the ability to glean additional information from a one-on-one with the CFO, is an integral component of the credit analysis, permitting a deeper investigation into the company's financial statements.

In practice, credit analysts often refrain from asking the tough questions. In an effort to maintain an ongoing relationship with the CFO, they are accommodating; yet, at the end of the day, if the analyst is unable to describe what a company's main risks are, they have failed at the key goal of the job. We present more detail of the accounting aspects of credit analysis in Chapter 16 and review key principles of the financial analysis next.

---

[1]For readers who would like to learn more about basics of accounting, we recommend *Essentials of Accounting* by Leslie K. Breitner and Robert N. Anthony (Pearson, 2012, 11th edition).

ACCOUNTING BASICS

There are three essential financial documents needed to analyze the financial situation of a company:

1. The income statement or statement of income also called profit and loss statement (P&L).
2. The balance sheet.
3. The statement of cash flows.

The P&L summarizes the profitability of the activities during a certain period of time like a quarter, half a year, or a full year. On a stand-alone basis, it does not say anything about the financial balances of the company, for instance, the amount of debt it raised to finance the assets that are necessary to operate or the amount of cash used or saved during the period, as the P&L is heavily influenced by accounting principles not generating or saving cash.

The balance sheet is a snapshot of an entity's financial situation (what it owns, what it owes, and how it was financed) at a particular past point in time. It does not say anything about its current or future profitability.

The statement of cash flows reflects sources and uses of cash to the company and thus captures the cash elements of the P&L and any changes to the balance sheet that impact cash balances.

At a very high level, the income statement, or P&L, reflects profitability, the balance sheet reflects financial robustness, and the statement of cash flows reflects a company's liquidity management. The credit analyst needs to work with all three documents as they form three pieces of a puzzle. They mean only so much on a stand-alone basis, and their simultaneous analysis enables the credit analyst to get a sense of the way the company performs.

Even more important than the three documents are the notes that accompany the financial statements. For large companies, the balance sheet, P&L, and cash-flow statement represent only a few pages of the financial reporting package, whereas, in contrast, the notes, often numbering over a hundred pages, constitute the bulk of the financial report, providing detail and critical information needed to understand the three documents.

Any company that secures external financing will be audited by an external firm. The external auditor's job is to verify that the financial documents are reported according to the accounting rules in place and that the financial numbers are representative of the company's situation. No investor would agree to lend or invest in a company for whom it did not secure an independent opinion of the accuracy of the financials. Thus, any company for which a credit analysis is being performed is likely to be audited. The biggest auditors are private firms known as the Big 4:

Deloitte, EY (Ernst & Young), KPMG, and PwC. Auditors must sign off on a company's financial statements, that is, they must sign a letter confirming their opinion that the financial statements give a true and fair view of the company's financial circumstances based on the information presented to them. If auditors have doubts about the data quality underlying the financial numbers, about the adherence to accounting rules, or about the ongoing viability of a company, they will qualify their opinion when signing off on the audit.

Financial statements are prepared for each legal entity. If an entity owns other entities, consolidated statements are presented in which the numbers of all entities are aggregated to present a comprehensive picture of the parent company. One important element in consolidated financial statements is that all intragroup transactions are eliminated in order to present the true economic picture of the business done with outside clients.

The Income Statement or Profit & Loss Statement (P&L)

The P&L shows two main categories: revenues and expenses. The outcome is either profit, if revenues exceed expenses, or losses, if expenses exceed revenues.

The income side shows primarily all sales recorded during the reporting period. The main expenses categories are selling, general, and administrative (SG&A); interest on debt; amortization/depreciation; and taxes.

Two key accounting notions about the P&L:

1. The accounting recognition of revenues and expenses is not related to an exchange of cash. For instance, the definition of a sale is a product or service that changes ownership (e.g., leaves the warehouse of a manufacturer). The sale of a product appears as revenue even if the customer has not yet paid or even if the product has not been delivered. The same holds true for supplies. They are recognized as an expense at the time the product is delivered and not when the supplier is paid. The rationale is that the P&L reflects the economic activity of a firm and not the timing of the payment or the way it manages its cash.
2. Some activities are not recorded in the P&L and trigger only balance-sheet entries. The main examples are the issuance or repayment of debt principal and the investment in plant and equipment. The reason, again, is that the P&L is meant to show the profitability of a firm's operations and not the investment needed to produce profits. Notably, what is found in the P&L is the interest paid on the debt because it is deemed to be an operating expense. Depreciation and amortization of long-term assets are also expenses, which we will explain below.

The Balance Sheet

The balance sheet presents, on a particular date, the assets that an entity owns, and how those assets are financed, either by liabilities (provided by lenders) or equity (provided by shareholders).

In principle, the balance sheet changes each day, due to activities such as sales of products, sales or purchases of assets, or changes in financing. In the real world, though, the balance sheet is prepared at the end of each quarter, primarily for companies having a legal obligation to do so, for example, for those listed on a stock exchange. For nonpublic companies, the balance sheet is usually prepared less frequently, say once to twice a year, since it is a time-consuming process. In addition, there is a long lag between the evaluation date and the day of publication—usually several months—which presents the analyst's first question: "What has happened between the date of the balance sheet and today?" Some balance sheet events may be publicly known but some may not, so this is always a good first question to ask.

Assets The assets are broken down into two main categories:

1. Current, or short-term, assets, which are assets the entity does not intend to own more than a few months or that can be transformed into cash quickly. Examples are trade receivables, i.e., invoices sent but not yet collected, raw materials, inventories, and liquid financial instruments like cash or marketable securities.
2. Long-term assets, which the entity intends to own for a long period of time. Examples are physical assets like an office building, a plant, or equity participation in another company.

The reason to separate current and long-term assets is to distinguish between what is owned temporarily as a result of the day-to-day operations and what is purchased with a long-term view. Because short-term assets and long-term assets are not financed the same way, this distinction is important to the credit analyst.

The credit analyst will attempt to adjust or revalue the assets to reflect what they would sell for if needed, that is, to value them on a fair-market value basis. There are several challenges with this.

First is goodwill. Goodwill, sometimes called "cost in excess," represents the premium paid during an acquisition for assets in excess of their book value. There may be legitimate reasons to pay more than book value for the acquired company's assets, such as cost savings that may result from the business combination. However, if the company had to sell some of these assets, it may receive fair value only. For transparency reasons, companies must separately report the fair value of the hard assets they acquired, and must revalue goodwill every year, writing down the value of this if necessary. There are many examples of large write-offs when a company was acquired at a high price in expectations of synergies or future profits that do not materialize. For instance, in December 2018, the tobacco company Altria took a 35 percent interest in e-cigarette maker Juul and valued the company at $38 million. Juul then experienced a series of lawsuits, and less than one year later Juul was valued at $12 billion and Altria recorded billions of dollars of write-offs.

Second, other intangible assets must be adjusted to reflect fair market value to the extent possible, such as patents.

Third, property, plant, and equipment are carried at amortized cost, which may be unrepresentative of fair market value. Finally, the valuation of invested and other financial assets must be scrutinized. In the United States, the Financial Accounting Standards Board (FASB) requires the reporting of certain assets and liabilities on a fair-value basis, and gives guidance on how to identify and account for assets and liabilities whose "fair-value" may not be easily observable with prices, therefore requiring estimation. FASB requires an identification of assets into three hierarchical categories, Level 1, Level 2, and Level 3, which reflect the degree of price observability, or in the case of estimation, the observability of inputs into the estimation process. Notably, the valuation of assets is to be presented as an estimate of what the assets would sell for in an orderly transaction. When a company's liquidity falls short, has large losses, or otherwise becomes financially challenged, its assets may not necessarily be sold in an orderly transaction.

Liabilities   The liabilities are monies owed to third parties that expect to be paid back, often with direct interest or indirectly through the issue price relative to face value, as is the case with commercial paper. Here again, one distinguishes two familiar subcategories:

1. Current liabilities that are supposed to be paid back within a few months.
   Examples are payables, that is, invoices received from suppliers or short-term debt, such as commercial paper.
2. The long-term liabilities, primarily long-term debt such as bank loans or bonds.
   Long-term liabilities include not just long-term debt and loans but all expenses associated with contracts through the current reporting period that can be reasonably expected in the future, such as pension liabilities, net of pension assets, which must be a particular focus of the analysis.

Shareholders' Equity   Shareholders' equity represents the residual interest in the company, meaning what would be left after all liabilities are extinguished. As owners, shareholders have a claim on the profits made, and they absorb losses in the event that the company has negative profits. The source of the equity is both paid-in capital, which represents the cost of the equity issued by the company in an equity offering—that is, what shareholders put into the company directly—and retained earnings, profits that were not paid out as dividends. Equity is the primary loss absorption mechanism for the company and of particular importance to the creditor. The larger the equity base, the more loss absorption capacity the company has and, thus, all else being equal, the more financially strong the company is from a credit perspective.

The Statement of Cash Flows

The statement of cash flows is meant to represent all the movement of cash during the same reporting period as the P&L. There are two formats for this schedule: the indirect method and the direct method, Companies can choose either or both methods for reporting. In the indirect method, the schedule begins with net income that is taken directly from the P&L. The statement of cash flows adjusts the P&L for all noncash entries to reconcile net income to net cash flow produced from operations because the P&L contains many noncash items. Noncash elements recognized in revenue are subtracted from net income and noncash elements recognized in expenses are added back to net income to arrive at cash flow from operations. In the direct method, cash flow from operations is arrived at directly, that is, from the sources and uses of cash rather than from making adjustments to the income statement. In both methods, cash flow from operations is one piece of the cash equation, supplemented by cash flow from investing and cash flow from financing. Net cash flow is then added to cash balances at the beginning of the reporting period to arrive at the net cash balance at the end of the reporting period. This end of period cash value will then match the cash balance as reported on the balance sheet.

- Cash flow from operations is the amount of money generated by the day-to-day operations of the business, such as collecting the proceeds of sales and paying for supplies, salaries, and other expenses. Sales recorded in the P&L represent products that were sold and services performed. As long as clients are paying on time, sales amounts correspond to cash inflows with a 30- or 60-day delay corresponding to the payment terms. Typical in a competitive environment is that a company extends its payment terms to maintain market share. Now, a wedge between revenue and cash inflow from sales has occurred, and net income overstates cash flow on a more pronounced basis, all else being equal. Working in the other direction are noncash expense items such as the amortization of goodwill and depreciation, which reduce reported profitability but not the cash balance of a firm.

- Cash flow from investing activities is the amount of cash generated by investment activities. For example, cash used to purchase a capital good is an outflow, and cash generated from the sale of plant or equipment is an inflow.

- Cash flow from financing activities is the third category on the cash flow statement and reports cash generated by financing activities, such as repaying debt (cash outflow), borrowing money from the bank or issuing shares (cash inflow). The dividends paid to shareholders and the buy-back of shares also appear in this category, whereas, somewhat counterintuitively, interest income paid on a bank loan is reported in cash from operations.

What's notable about the cash-flow statement is that, although generally speaking, more cash is better than less, a company's increase in cash over a period is not necessarily a good thing, and a decrease in cash is not necessarily a bad thing. For example, a company can underinvest, which would manifest itself in lower cash outflow, and cash balances would increase, all else being equal. A company could take on too much borrowing, and cash inflow would rise, and this increase is not necessarily a good thing. As for cash from operations, companies that are growing rapidly have large appetites for working capital (the need to pay suppliers before collecting sales revenues) and are likely to have negative cash flow from operations, but this is a good problem. Companies that are in a state of decline could be selling goods from inventory, and not growing, in which case the cash flow increase reflects the decline.

Smell Test

Even before knowing the details of a company's financial statements, an experienced analyst is able to quickly form an opinion about a company. To do this, he would rely on a few key indicators that provide a high level gauge of credit quality. These are:

- *Size:* The bigger the sales the better. Although not all large companies are financially strong, large companies tend to be healthier than small ones. Medium-sized companies, even profitable ones, are usually niche players that can be vulnerable in an economic downturn, are more susceptible to losing their competitive advantage, and may not have the market power to secure adequate pricing.

In addition, corporate governance is normally more robust in large firms. Compare this to small- and medium-sized companies that may still have family roots or governance tightly woven in the local community and, in both situations, are slow to reorganize when the profitability decreases.

Finally, large companies normally have multiple bank relationships and, thus, greater access to financing, which is especially helpful in times of stress.

That size is helpful for creditworthiness is a general principle and there are naturally some exceptions. For instance, the gradual growth of e-commerce has led to new companies fighting for more market share in order to build a dominant position, regardless of profitability. It can be worrying for a credit analyst as the growth is typically financed by banks and a change of heart from lenders can jeopardize the very existence of these unprofitable companies. The same can be true for companies relying on a new technology. Building an infrastructure and building scale can be expensive and not profitable. A good example is the electric car manufacturer Tesla, whose sales grew from $4 billion in 2015 to $31.5 billion in 2020 but made a profit only in fiscal year 2020.

■ *Profitability:* The primary indicator of profitability is net income. Making money on a regular basis is a good sign of financial health. However, most companies are not immune from the broader economy and, from time to time, hit bumps in the road. A one-off drop in income or even negative income is not necessarily a bad sign; the key is to understand why. A one-off disposition of a loss-making unit, a reversal of a tax asset, and reorganization charges are usually not indicative of a sustained reduction in profits.

A company like Caterpillar, a manufacturer of heavy equipment for the construction and mining industry, is very dependent on investments in public and private infrastructure and its sales and profitability tend to be cyclical. In 2015, they generated close to $47 billion of revenue and $2.5 billion of net income but in 2016 generated only $38.5 billion of revenue and incurred a small loss before rebounding and reaching $54 billion in revenue and $6 billion in net income in 2019. Then, like many companies, their 2020 results were heavily impacted by COVID 19 and sales and profitability declined significantly to $41 billion and $3 billion respectively. This is typical of a well-managed firm: Although susceptible to events it cannot control, the management team is able to respond.

What is more problematic and yet hard to spot are those companies that have been profitable and then record a bad year due to bad decisions, which should be of concern to analysts, because this calls into question such companies' long-term abilities to generate enough profits to meet their financial obligations.

- *Rating:* The firm's rating(s), either external (such as Moody's or Fitch's) or internal (company proprietary), should reflect the counterparty's strengths, and such ratings are good predictors of a company's credit-worthiness.

- *Debt/equity ratio:* Assets of an entity are financed using borrowed money and/or by funds provided by shareholders. Corporate finance *practice* encourages leverage, that is, the use of debt (borrowed money) versus equity to fund assets, since it provides a tax shield and, in addition, is thought to lower a company's weighted cost of capital given that debt is nominally cheaper than equity. Note that financial practice conflicts with theory regarding the use of debt to lower the cost of capital. Modern corporate finance *theory* posits that a company's cost of capital is invariant to leverage (in the absence of taxes). On this issue, we are on the side of the theory, since, from a credit perspective, high leverage translates into more credit risk and, thus, a higher cost of credit. There is no free lunch.

  Although there is no fixed rule for the threshold that separates too much leverage from an acceptable amount, and because each company's situation is unique, for a rule of thumb, a one-to-one ratio is not a bad starting place. This means that the shareholder's equity should be at least equivalent to the amount of long-term debt provided by banks and bond holders. This proportion is usually indicative of a conservative financial structure.

- *EBITDA:* EBITDA stands for earnings before interest, taxes, depreciation, and amortization. It is a relatively easy value to calculate from the P&L, and it represents a proxy for the cash generated from operations (since depreciation and amortization are noncash expenses) before payments are made for interest and taxes. EBITDA provides a good indication of the amount of money available for finance, investment, and other charges, and it is usually compared to items like the amount of interest payment. This concept is explained more fully later.

  The main difference between EBITDA and cash flow from operations is that the former does not take into account uncollected sales revenues and unpaid expenses during the reporting period. For a company operating with stable growth, these uncollected and unpaid items do not introduce much distortion between the two measures.

- *Market capitalization:* For public companies, this is a relevant credit indicator on two fronts. First, a company's access to equity markets makes it more creditworthy since equity is an important form of financing, and from a creditor's perspective, the best form of financing since equity has only a residual claim on a company's assets. Thus, if two companies in the same industry have similar earnings, the company with the higher market capitalization is likely to be financially stronger, both because the equity markets have signaled that they believe that profit growth is there, and also because companies with high market capitalizations relative to their earnings can raise equity more cheaply (i.e., with less dilution to existing shareholders), both of which benefit the creditors. Here again, exceptions include fast-growing companies disrupting established business models like Tesla, whose market cap in May 2021 was more or less 8 times that of General Motors and 16 times that of Ford.

Second, equity financing necessitates equity analysis, which is useful for the credit analyst, much as the work of a credit analyst is helpful to the equity analyst. Equity analysts try to forecast the future profits of the company, and in assessing this earnings power, they take into account the same risk factors that are relevant in a credit analysis. The caveat with equity analysis is the potential for exuberance on the part of the analyst. In strong equity markets, the future of companies looks bright and ultimately may fall short of the analyst's expectations. The equity markets have proved to be exuberant and badly wrong on a regular basis. Think of the bad calls made on dot-coms and telecommunications. On the contrary, credit analysts are not predisposed to making optimistic forecasts since the creditor has limited upside.

A TYPICAL CREDIT REPORT

Many firms with a credit-analysis function develop their own format for presenting credit reports to ensure consistency across analysts and uniformity in reporting to make decision making easier for senior management. We sometimes hear discord about standardization, and that credit analysts should emulate equity analysts who produce more idiosyncratic reports to catch their reader's attention. On the contrary, we do not recommend allowing analysts to present reports the way they want because rigor and discipline are fundamental to the credit-analysis process. Professionals involved in the credit assessment should agree on a format and stick to it, and such a format will permit opportunities for the analyst's qualitative assessment.

Although credit analysis relies heavily on interpretation of the numbers presented in the financial statement, the qualitative assessment of a company is not less important. Good analysis relies equally on qualitative and quantitative reviews. Numbers tell only one part of the story. Moreover, the numbers reflect the past, not the future, and a credit decision, such as whether to lend money, is often made with a five-year horizon, sometimes more. The analyst must be convinced that the company will be able to meet its obligations in the future.

We have presented a template here for the structure of a credit report. A typical credit report will contain the following sections: General information, including an executive summary on the background on the company; the transaction; the industry and competitive landscape; a qualitative assessment including the company's strategy, ownership, management, and environmental risks; and a quantitative assessment that includes a detailed analysis of the company's financial statements and estimations of future income.

General Information

Background of the Company   This first section presents an executive summary of the company including:

- A summary of the company's history, activities, and key financial and operational numbers.
- Recent significant news such as management changes, new products, mergers and acquisitions.
- The internal rating or scoring, if any; otherwise, external ratings.

The Transaction   This section presents a summary of the transaction contemplated with the counterparty, if it is what motivates the production of a credit report. If the submission is a regular review and renewal of a credit limit, this is what must be indicated.

The description of the transaction must be relatively short but detailed enough so that readers understand the main parameters. At a minimum, the following must be presented: overview and purpose of the deal, other participants (if any), pricing, and covenants.

Relationship and Approval Process   In this section, the history and profitability of the relationship is presented together with an explanation of the approval process, based on the guidelines. For instance, if capacity is sought for company ABC with an R2 rating, a requested limit of $160 million, and a tenor of four years, then approval is delegated to the credit committee of the investment banking department with a compulsory recommendation from the credit risk assessment unit.

Rating and Recommendation The final part of this section is the internal rating, the rationale for its assignment, and a recommendation about the transaction and/or the credit line.

Qualitative Assessment

Performing a qualitative assessment is like playing with Google Maps. You start at the global level and zoom in until you reach the CEO's office in the headquarters of the firm. The analysis must contain at least the following four sections.

Political, Economic, and Regulatory Environment More and more companies have global operations, so analyzing the country risk today is not as straightforward as it used to be. The review should at least cover the largest and most strategic markets, as well the potentially problematic areas. If a company relies for growth on emerging markets, a thorough review of the risk landscape is a must. For all markets, the main topics are the following:

1. *The political situation*

    Is the political environment stable in which strikes, riots, confiscation of assets, bans on currency transfer, and other such events are unlikely?

2. *The macroeconomic environment*

    Is the fundamental demand for the product growing or not? If it is, how fast? Are the credit markets able to supply attractively priced credit on attractive terms?

3. *The regulatory risk*

    Can the company be affected by new compulsory rules that would impact its profitability? This is a growing area of concern for many companies because, in many industries, regulators are more and more active. In the United States alone, constraints like the Volcker Rule (interdiction for banks to use internal resources to speculate in the capital markets) modifies the earning power of financial institutions.

4. *Other operational factors*

    Can the company be affected by events such as catastrophes, natural disasters, and product or environmental liability? For example, the COVID 19 pandemic exposed the operations of many companies to material weaknesses in their supply chains, causing business interruption, lost revenue, and higher costs of production.

5. *Industry/competition*

This section gives an overview of the structure of each industry in which the company operates. If a company is present in several markets, each market should be studied separately. Examples of what is covered include the size of the market, market growth, product and customer segmentation, the number of key players, the pricing trends, barriers to entry and exit, and the drivers of revenues. A critical component of this overview is through a review of the competitive landscape.

Then, for each market, one must describe the positioning of the company and its strengths and weaknesses. This type of analysis has been employed commonly since the 1970s using the famous SWOT paradigm, which stands for the assessment of Strengths, Weaknesses, Opportunities, and Threats. Other techniques beyond a SWOT analysis work as well, as long as they capture the same facets of the company's relative positioning in its industry.

Strategy and Key Risk Factors This section presents a thorough review of the company's strategy, both at a high level and specific strategic initiatives. Annual reports and investor conference presentations, made available on the investor relations pages of a company's website, provide a lot of information as well. For smaller companies, a meeting with the senior management is a must to understand better what the priorities are and how the company is preparing its future.

It is a good idea to perform a thorough review of the risk factors and to check how they are addressed by the company's strategy. If an analyst meeting a company executive really wants to ask the most famous question in risk management, "What keeps you awake at night?" this is the time!

Ownership Structure The ownership structure is critical to credit risk management since the shareholders of the company are agents of the creditors, as outlined at the end of this chapter. Debt holders and lenders having no governance rights cannot force the hand of shareholders if a company needs a capital injection to stay afloat. The interests of the lenders and shareholders are not aligned, and the value of the debt is directly affected by the amount of equity the company has issued. Thus, understanding the ownership structure permits the credit analyst to understand nuances of the trade-offs between the values of debt and equity, who has the incentive to take risks, and who bears the downside of a risky strategy. Although many aspects of credit quality are a function of the industry, the quality of the management team, the competitive positioning, and so forth, credit quality is also a choice variable for the shareholders. Therefore, understanding their point of view is a key aspect of a credit analysis. A stable group of long-term investors with a clear strategy is, from a credit point of view, preferable. Their tenure signals that they are fairly risk adverse, a risk preference more closely aligned with that of the debt holders.

An equally important aspect of the ownership is the overall quality of the directors, who directly represent the interests of the shareholders. Given the complexity of the operations of today's corporations, the directors must be up to the task of providing well-informed and well-executed oversight with teeth, in addition to strategic direction, none of which is an easy task.

Management Just as shareholders are agents of the debt holders, management is an agent of shareholders. Just as there is a misalignment of interests between debt and equity holders, a similar misalignment exists between shareholders and management. First and foremost, the compensation plans of the senior and upper management must be well understood to know what is motivating them. For example, a compensation plan heavily weighted toward out-of-the-money warrants will tend to give management incentive to take excessive risk, since only "home runs" trigger a payday. This risk-taking behavior is beyond what the shareholders desire, which is itself beyond what the debt holders desire. A plan weighted toward a comfortable but predictable salary feels a lot more like what the debt holders' pay-off looks like, and these managers might be more inclined to not take big risks. Typically though, directors set compensation of the senior management team to resemble the pay-off of shareholders—warrants are large parts of the compensation scheme, and together with deferred bonuses, in addition to typically large salaries, the management team's pay-off will look similar to a shareholder's.

Recently, pressure from shareholders led to more transparency and disclosures on management's compensation principles worldwide. In the United States, detailed information and numbers are typically not included in the annual report or in the 10-K form but in the Proxy Statement, which is the document distributed to shareholders prior to the General Assembly of shareholders. It contains the agenda of the meeting and the list of topics that will be submitted to a vote. Note that the shareholders' vote on executive compensation is only advisory and the ultimate numbers are decided by the Board of Directors and its compensation committee.

An equally important aspect of management is the overall quality of the team. Experience, turnover, succession plans, and track records are knowable, which provide information regarding the quality of management. A management misstep can easily squander a company's fortunes, even if that company has a history of making money and a strong competitive position in a growing industry.

It is well within the credit analyst's job to offer an opinion on the quality of management even without much to go on. The credit report is the venue in which the analyst can and should be encouraged to speak up.

Quantitative Assessment

The last part of the report is dedicated to the analysis of financial statements. In this area, there is no shortcut. The analyst must have access to the most recent documents in an understandable language. It can be a challenge for companies located in foreign countries, and the assistance of a professional knowledgeable with the local accounting principles and language may be required.

A common challenge is dealing with private companies that do not publish results. It is hard to imagine a credit analyst providing a recommendation without having the ability to perform a basic review of the financial statements.

In the real world, there are a number of large but private companies that do not share documents with their business counterparties. It is often a power game between the company and its counterparties; the company makes exceptions for banks since they supply much needed liquidity lines but deny access to other creditors like suppliers or insurance companies. Some companies give access to a data room in their headquarters. There, analysts can consult documents but are not able to make copies. In extreme cases, computers are not allowed and only handwritten notes are tolerated. It is up to each creditor to decide if such a high level of privacy, even with business partners, is acceptable or not.

Financial Statement Summary   A summary of the financial statements must be prepared either as an introduction to this section or in an appendix. It is also helpful to have the latest audited (annual) report as an addendum to the report for easy reference. Again, standardization across the assessment function helps here, allowing the most commonly used numbers and ratios to be easily found. Key balance sheet, P&L, and cash-flow statement numbers will comprise the bulk of the financial-statement summary.

Figures for at least four fiscal years are recommended to enable a review of the company's performance over a meaningful period of time. A creditworthy company will have fairly consistent performance over time. Less solid companies may experience ups and downs or a negative trend, detectable by comparing the performance over a number of years.

Summary statistics may include those that we already described (size, profitability, rating[s], debt/equity ratio, EBITDA, and market capitalization) and those we will expand on later, together with some other metrics that we find to be appropriate across most industries and countries.

Capital Structure   In addition to the debt/equity ratio that we mentioned earlier as part of our smell test, there are other indicators to pay attention to:

- Goodwill plus intangible assets as a percentage of total assets. Intangible assets represent patents, trademarks, and other sources of franchise value, such as brand recognition. Should the company have to monetize these assets, it would be unlikely to monetize them anywhere near the carrying values, and shareholders' equity would be reduced accordingly. This is why this number is important, because equity represents the company's loss absorption capacity. If the loss absorption capacity is actually smaller than the nominal value of equity, this fact needs to be highlighted, and this ratio helps to do just that. For instance, U.S. telecom giant AT&T carried $135 billion of goodwill at the end of 2020, representing 26 percent of total assets as a consequence of numerous acquisitions.
- Off-balance-sheet obligations. Accounting governance bodies (such as the FASB) have made significant progress recently regarding disclosure of off-balance-sheet obligations from such items as derivatives and future lease obligations. Yet, some future obligations, particularly contingent obligations, are still not reflected in the financial statements of a company. A good example of this is derivative transactions. Some of these may lead to cash outflows in the future if the underlying products evolve in a nonfavorable direction. Thankfully, in most accounting jurisdictions, companies now report these types of contingencies in the notes accompanying the financial statements. It is the job of the credit analyst to have reviewed and understood the financial consequences of these transactions.

Liquidity and Cash Flow   A company's liquidity position has become a centerpiece of most credit reports. In the recent past, the analyst would just look to see that the maturity of the various debt facilities was spread over time and that the cash flow from operations was sufficient in the event of refinancing difficulty.

The start of the 2007 crisis was a real turning point. Many companies took refinancing for granted, almost an administrative task. As we all know now, this was a severe miscalculation. Investors simply refused to lend to certain entities and industries. The financial sector, which was dependent on short-term funding due to its low cost, was hit particularly hard.

The inability to refinance short-term instruments like commercial paper (generally described as debt maturing within 270 days) led directly to the bankruptcy of Lehman Brothers. The bank, like many others, was overly dependent on the willingness of investors, including other banks, to buy its debt each day.

A similar phenomenon was observed in the fall of 2011 when several European countries were on the brink of defaulting. Investors, concerned by the exposure of banks to the countries primarily affected by the crisis, lost appetite for their short-term debt instruments. This was especially true in the United States, where money-market funds stopped buying debt issued by major European banks, which, as a result, were forced to announce to their clients that they would reduce loans denominated in dollars because they had difficulty supplying dollars. Worse, in October 2011, the French and Belgian governments agreed to dismantle the bank Dexia, which also faced a liquidity crisis. At the time of the decision, the short-term financing needs were close to $100 billion. If, on average, the maturity of the debt were six months in length, the daily refinancing needs were close to $500 million! This was not sustainable, all the more so because funding was primarily used to finance a bond portfolio whose yield was much lower than Dexia was paying on its debt, a position known as negative carry in finance.

These examples show the vulnerability of banks that rely on wholesale funding, which is funding from lending institutions and institutional investors, as opposed to retail deposits. The lesson for credit analysts is to scrutinize their counterparty's liquidity sources, and secure confirmation that, at any point in time, (1) the company's cash balance is sufficient to cover most expenses, (2) that they can draw on large bank facilities committed on their behalf, and, (3) more important, they have extended the maturity of the debt to prevent a refinancing wall in any single year. For large banks, which are heavily reliant on short-term debt, one must assess if the amount of debt being refinanced every day is in line with the appetite of the capital markets.

The internal and most important source of liquidity for most companies is cash from operations. We can observe cash flow from operations from the cash-flow statement, using historical cash flow as a gauge and making necessary adjustments based on any changes to payment terms and so forth. A stricter gauge of liquidity is free cash flow, which is simply cash from operations less the cash required for capital expenditure to sustain the business. Both amounts should be compared with what the company needs to meet its contractual financing obligations.

Debt Service In principle, the debt-to-EBITDA ratio computes how many years it would take a company to pay off its debt. The numerator is the debt and the denominator is the repayment capacity, that is, the cash income available for debt service and taxes. Notably, various types of debt can be included or excluded from the numerator. A conservative approach would include senior, subordinated, and other liabilities to capture total debt. Or, the debt value can be the net of the company's cash position to arrive at net debt.

In many financial institutions, this ratio is used to size the maximum amount of debt that a company can support. A limit can be set at, say, 2.5 times for investment-grade companies, and banks, typically, do not lend money to companies with ratios in excess of 2.5.

The EBITDA-to-interest expense ratio is known as a coverage ratio. It shows how many times the amount of interest due is covered by the profit from operations. As interest expenses are not the only source of cash outflow from EBITDA (note taxes), the ratio is expected to be large for investment grade companies.

Other leverage ratios of interest are the funds from operations (FFO) to total debt and the debt to total capital ratio. Table 6.1 shows indicative ratios used by S&P to assess a company's financial risk profile for purposes of assigning an issuer rating.

Profitability No surprise that the net income is the most relevant indicator of profitability. What is interesting, though, is to break down the profitability into several categories to assess the cost structure of a company. To this effect, the most useful ratios are:

- COGS / Sales: COGS stands for cost of goods sold so this ratio indicates the amount of raw materials, labor, and manufacturing expenses (aside from depreciation) going into the products sold. Companies in mature markets and price-sensitive industries are expected to have a high ratio,

TABLE 6.1 Cash Flow/Leverage Analysis Ratios—Standard Volatility (partial)

	FFO/Debt (%)	Debt/EBITDA (x)
Minimal	Greater than 60	Less than 1.5
Modest	45–60	1.5–2
Intermediate	30–45	2–3
Significant	20–30	3–4
Aggressive	12–20	4–5
Highly leveraged	Less than 12	Greater than 5

Source: S&P Global Ratings, "Corporate Methodology," November 19, 2013, Table 17.

which translates into thin profit margins. Companies in high-tech industries typically have a low ratio and, as a consequence, high margins. *Gross margin* is a term that conveys the same information and is defined as 1 – (COGS / Sales).

■ SG&A/Sales: SG&A stands for selling, general, and administrative (expenses). This ratio reflects general overhead such as salaries, rent, and advertising. The objective of this ratio is to indicate how efficient the operations of a company are. A high ratio shows expensive operations and is not favorable. A low ratio demonstrates that the company is efficient and cost conscious, saving funds on behalf of investors.

■ Operating income is defined as Revenues – COGS – SG&A – Depreciation. It is also called EBIT, which stands for earnings before interest and tax. This metric recognizes that, although depreciation is a noncash expense, it serves as a proxy for the capital expenditure that the company must make, on average over time, in order to remain competitive and, thus, must be considered in the claims on the company's cash flow.

Pro-Forma Financials   Whenever possible, we recommend making projections of the financial statements and ratios for future years. The projections would be made using best estimates of the key drivers of the key variables, such as sales and cost of goods sold, together with a financial model that allows business variables and metrics to interact with each other. The great value of the projections is that they permit sensitivity analyses, so that the credit analytics can be made more valuable by considering a base case, a down-side case, and a worst-case analysis.

Competitor Ratios   In addition to gathering numbers and computing ratios for the company being analyzed, preparing a summary of key ratios for its major competitors is a valuable output. For instance, if the company being analyzed has an SG&A/sales ratio of 22 percent, this number becomes much more meaningful if the ratio typically seen across its competitors is 18 percent. One might conclude that the company has a potential cost issue, which increases its credit risk because less money is available for debt service.

AGENCY CONFLICT, INCENTIVES, AND MERTON'S VIEW OF DEFAULT RISK

Thus far, we have discussed credit risk as a feature of an obligor's financial wherewithal, such as profitability, leverage, growth prospects, and other indicators of creditworthiness. However, the corporation's managers, working on behalf of shareholders, are making decisions behind the scenes. Their decisions directly impact the corporation's credit risk profile. Incentives play a large role in the decisions managers make, and this human element may be as important as the inanimate features of the company in terms of its credit risk profile.

We end this chapter by characterizing creditors as having what's known as an "agency" conflict with shareholders. The conflict stems from creditors having virtually no control over the strategic, financial, or day-to-day decisions of managers, or over the shareholders who are represented by the managers. Coupled with this, the conflict arises from creditors and shareholders having different incentives. Their incentives are different because their risk/return profiles are distinctive, and this distinction arises from the capital structure of the firm. We all know that the capital structure of the firm is a key piece of a firm's risk profile. However, the question is really "risky for whom?"

We outline the incentives of the creditors and shareholders that give rise to the fundamental agency conflict between the two groups. Understanding their different incentives is a critical element of a fundamental credit analysis, as we have explored thus far in this chapter. Another critical element of a fundamental credit analysis is an understanding of how a corporation's capital structure affects the risk/return profile of shareholders and creditors and, thus, impacts the creditworthiness of the company.

Understanding the agency conflict sets up an alternative way of thinking about credit risk as first postulated by Robert Merton, a Nobel laureate, in 1974. Later, we introduce what's known as the Merton Model, which provides the foundation for alternative estimations of credit risk that we cover in Chapter 7.

The Agency Relationship

In normal circumstances, creditors are neither directors nor officers of a corporation, and, thus, they have no governance rights over the corporation that they lend to. Creditors' rights are sometimes nonexistent (e.g., receivables, derivative transactions) or only narrowly stipulated in the covenants of the lending agreements.

The company's directors and officers, who represent, first and foremost, the interests of the shareholders who appointed them, make decisions that affect creditors. Thus, shareholders (themselves represented by the Board of Directors and management) can be considered an agent of the creditors. Although creditors have not technically hired shareholders to act as an agent, they understand that, by virtue of extending credit, shareholders will make decisions that impact them. The decisions that shareholders make range from new product development, R&D investment, key hiring decisions, and the corporation's capital structure. Since these decisions affect the corporation's profitability and risk profile, they affect the value of the debt and, thus, they impact creditors directly. If shareholders make a decision that impacts creditors negatively, creditors cannot force their hand; they have to take a back seat.

Acknowledging the agency relationship is a good starting point when evaluating whether to assume credit risk on a counterparty. At the end of the day, shareholders will make decisions in their own interest. If their interests are aligned with the creditors', then there is no problem. However, this alignment of incentives is the exception, not the rule, to this relationship.

Alignment of Incentives

What separates the incentives of the shareholders from those of the creditors is a disparate risk/return profile. They share neither losses nor gains in a proportionate way. When losses occur, shareholders pay first, with the losses eating into retained earnings or paid-in capital. Creditors, in contrast, would not experience losses until shareholder's equity is exhausted. When gains are made, shareholders get all the upside, with creditors receiving a prenegotiated capped amount, that is, the par value of what is owed and interest. Thus, the shareholder's pay-off profile is highly asymmetric; while they can lose their total investment, they have tremendous upside. The pay-off profile for lenders is also asymmetric, but less so, and less disperse with effectively no upside and a smaller chance to lose their total investment.

Thus, shareholders' incentives are influenced by two main forces.

1. Shareholders are highly incentivized to take risks since this has the potential for large gains.
2. Shareholders are in a first-loss position, so any new capital they inject into a company with precarious finances is prone to being lost.

Thus, shareholders have less incentive to make investments when their companies are in need of capital, since the investment may end up going directly to paying off the creditors.

To illustrate the first point, suppose that a manufacturing company can move its operations overseas where costs are significantly lower, which would double margins. However, in so doing, they run the risk of disrupting their supply chain, since doing business overseas is an untested strategy. Management, acting on behalf of shareholders, may elect to undertake the risky strategy since this has an attractive upside but runs the risk of not panning out, whereas the status quo would safely cover the obligations to creditors. Note that creditors have far less to gain from this risk taking and are more prone to losses.

To illustrate the second point, suppose that a company needs a capital injection of $50 million to repay debt and stay afloat. Without new equity, shareholders will realize their equity losses and creditors will face losses of $50 million. Shareholders can elect to inject $50 million, and in so doing, ensure that creditors get paid. However, there may be no assurances that the company will make future profits to recover their invested equity; thus, in the minds of shareholders, the new capital injection may be tantamount to throwing good money after bad. Creditors want the equity capital injection; shareholders may be unsure of the value of this strategy.

The creditor is most interested in being repaid. There is no upside and only downside, thus the preference for the status quo—that is, for no volatility. The creditor extended credit on some basis, and thus wishes this basis to persist. New strategies, M&A activity, alterations to the capital structure (new borrowing) are all causes for alarm, and many lending covenants prohibit such activities, since these activities present opportunities for losses to occur.

Part of the risk manager's job is not just to evaluate credit risk, but also to assist the line manager with not-no-but-how approaches to enabling transactions that create value. Knowing up front what the company's management is likely to want and how this will impact the company's probability of default is a key input to the negotiation and structuring of a credit transaction.

Capital Structure

As introduced earlier in this chapter, capital structure refers to the amount of debt and equity that the corporation has to fund its assets. To summarize from above, the corporation's capital structure is a key determinant of its risk and therefore credit profile and directly impacts the value of its debt. Simply, the greater the amount of equity relative to debt, the higher the value (price) of the debt, because the debt has less risk. Similarly, less equity means a lower value (price) of debt, because the debt has more risk. A large equity base means that there is a large layer of funds to absorb losses before the losses attach to the debt, since equity is in the first-loss position. Thus, more equity means that the debt is more likely to be repaid, which reduces its risk and thereby enhances its value.

Thus, understanding the ownership structure permits the credit analyst to understand nuances of (1) the trade-offs of risk and return in terms of the values of debt and equity, (2) who has the incentive to take risks, and (3) who bears the upside and downside of a risky strategy, particularly as it relates to the creditors being able to exert very little control.

This understanding also sets the stage for thinking about credit risk in a novel way, known as the Merton model.

Merton Model

Robert Merton, together with Stanley Black and Myron Scholes, pioneered options pricing back in the 1970s. A significant contribution to finance theory as it relates to their work on options pricing was Merton's model for pricing a bond's default risk.[2] In his paper Merton expresses owning equity stock in a company as equivalent to simultaneously owning a European call option and selling a put option on the company's assets, with the strike price being the value of the company's debt. Note that the option portfolio (own a call and sell a put on the firm's assets) has the identical pay-off as owning the equity outright. Thus, for an investor, buying equity is effectively buying an option on the underlying assets of the company.

At maturity, the value of the assets will be either greater than, less than, or equal to the debt. Since the call option's strike price is the value of the debt, if assets are worth more than the debt, the debt can be paid off (i.e., the option is struck) and the equity holder claims the assets. Yet, if the value of the company's assets is below the value of the debt at maturity, the call option is worthless and expires without being exercised. That is, shareholders simply walk away, leaving bondholders with debt that cannot be extinguished with the company's assets, i.e., defaulting on the company's obligations.

This framework puts shareholders' incentives in perspective. Unless their option is in the money, they will not exercise it and, thus, will walk away from their obligations to creditors. Because shareholders enjoy limited liability, they can effectively stick their losses on creditors. Therefore, default amounts to what is effectively an economic decision by the shareholder based on cold facts. Note that "sticking" losses to the creditors is sometimes referred to colloquially as "putting" losses to the creditors.

Merton sees default simply as arising from the value of the company's assets falling short of the value of debt at maturity. As a consequence, credit risk is a function of the likelihood that debt will exceed assets at maturity. This likelihood of default is determined by three variables, plus a discount factor: the time to maturity (lessens the likelihood), the volatility of the company's operations (increases the likelihood), and the existing distance between assets and debt (lessens the likelihood). The greater this positive distance, or "in the money" distance, the lower the chance that at maturity the assets value will fall beneath the debt value. This is where capital structure comes into play. If the company has significant equity funding relative to debt, the larger is the distance to default and, thus, the lower is the chance of default.

---

[2]Robert Merton, "On the Pricing of Corporate Debt: The Risk Structure of Interest Rates," *Journal of Finance* 29, no. 2 (May 1974).

If we could model which companies are likely to have the value of their assets fall below the value of the debt between now and the time that the debt matures, we would know which companies are likely to default. Other researchers have filled in some missing pieces, such as estimating some unobservable variables such as the volatility of a company's operations and the market value of the firm's total assets, which has given the credit risk manager new tools to estimate default risk.

FINAL WORDS

The relationship between creditors and shareholders, the lack of alignment of incentives, and risk/return profiles as impacted by the capital structure are each central to the credit risk manager's evaluation of an obligor's risk profile. In addition, they are also central components to Merton's characterization that default is a rational and deliberate decision made by shareholders if their equity stake is worthless. In addition, Merton's corporate bond pricing model expands the ways in which default risk is estimated. Pioneering the new ways were Kealhofer, McQuown, and Vasicek, who developed the "KMV" model for estimating default risk. They picked up where Merton left off, doing the empirical research that allows the default drivers in Merton's model to be mapped to usable probabilities of default. In Chapter 7, we explore further how the KMV approach, now part of Moody's Analytics, and others like it have introduced alternative estimations of credit risk.

Alternative Estimations of Credit Quality

Predicting default is a high-stakes exercise for any entity taking credit risk. An underestimate means the difference between profit and significant losses. An overestimate means a foregone profitable opportunity. Fundamentally, the assessment of default risk drives the yes/no decision about entering a transaction. If the risk is deemed acceptable, the strength of the counterparty dictates the type of transaction, the exposure, the tenor, and, last but not least, the price.

We see in Chapter 2 that the most common methodology for summarizing credit quality is the use of a rating based on an internal review, a rating agency, or a credit-scoring specialist. Then, a probability of default can be mapped to the rating using the historical default data compiled by rating agencies like S&P, Fitch, or Moody's. This way of estimating a probability of default is the oldest and the most widespread on a global basis. What has changed over time, though, is that methodologies used have become more sophisticated, and data are more plentiful (e.g., historical, peers).

In parallel, the development of quantitative research in the past few decades and the advent of analytics have opened new possibilities. Since the early 1990s, considerable resources have been devoted by researchers and companies of all kinds, from start-ups to large banks, to develop alternatives to human-judgment-driven ratings.

In this chapter, we describe alternatives to the traditional methodologies that have been embraced by the financial sector and, to a much lesser extent, by industrial corporations engaged in credit generating activities. What these alternatives share is a reliance on capital markets information. Many people used to think that there was little to learn from the markets about fundamental credit issues. We know now that this was a mistake. Credit and capital markets are too often like neighbors who do not talk to each other although they have a lot in common. We can now extract data from traded instruments, such as stocks or bonds, to estimate a probability of default. Given the global growth in the credit default swap (CDS) market, we can extract valuable and fairly precise information, on a real-time basis, about the perceived credit quality of companies.

In the following sections, we review the most compelling alternative techniques.

THE EVOLUTION OF AN INDICATOR: MOODY'S ANALYTICS EDF™

Moody's Analytics Expected Default Frequency or EDF™ is one of the most popular alternative indicators used in the financial industry to estimate the probability of default of counterparties. Most banks and insurance companies in the world subscribe to a Moody's service called CreditEdge™ that provides EDFs™ on more than 38,000 publicly traded companies in the world. The penetration of CreditEdge™ among industrial corporations is low, primarily due to the high cost and less coverage of their counterparties.

In order to rely on EDFs™, it is indispensable to have at least a basic understanding of the methodology behind its estimation process and to be aware of its limitations. The methodology has its foundation in Merton's seminal 1974 paper introduced in Chapter 6, which we review in detail in the following section.

The Merton Model Foundation to Moody's Analytics EDF™

A significant contribution to options pricing and finance theory was Merton's work in describing how a shareholder's equity stock can be expressed as a call option on the firm's total assets. Referring to our comments in Chapter 6, we describe shareholders as agents of creditors and default as essentially a choice variable for shareholders. In the Merton Model, if the market value of the firm's assets is below the market value of the outstanding debt at maturity, the call option is worthless, since the strike price is the value of the debt. Owing to the limited liability that shareholders of corporations enjoy, meaning they cannot be sued as the result of actions taken by the corporations' officers and directors, the shareholders effectively have a put option for the outstanding value of the debt in excess of the market value of assets, meaning they can stick debt holders with losses without ramification.

There is a significant amount of financial mathematics underlying the theory, but there are two basic theoretical pillars from Merton's paper underlying the EDF™ approach. The first is to express equity as a call on the firm's assets. As discussed in Chapter 6, we know that if the market value of the firm's assets falls below the outstanding value of the debt, the equity owners will walk away, that is, default on their debt obligation. Thus, if we could model which firms are likely to have the value of their assets fall below the value of the debt between now and the time that the debt matures, we would know which firms are likely to default. The trick is knowing the market value of the firm's total assets since these are not directly observable; only the book value of total assets are (and the market value of equity and the book value of debt, which get us only partially there).

The second pillar uses Black-Scholes options pricing theory to find the market value of a firm's assets. In Black-Scholes, under a set of assumptions, an option's value can be determined by five key variables: (1) the value of the underlying asset (the market value of the firm's total assets), (2) the volatility of the market value of total assets, (3) the option's strike price (the outstanding value of the debt), (4) time to expiration on the option (the debt maturity), and (5) the risk-free interest rate. We know (3), (4), and (5) and we know the value of the option, so we could solve for the market value of the assets if we only knew the volatility of the market value of assets. This, too, is estimable (albeit mathematically intensive), and thus we can solve for the market value of assets. What's of ultimate importance is that the market value of assets is modeled as a random variable that changes over time, and there are numerous values that it can take.

The credit analyst worries about those cases in which the value of the firm's assets could fall below its debt value. Thus, the analyst is interested in a tool that estimates the possible values and their likelihoods that assets can take at maturity, that is, a distance measure that tracks the gap between asset and debt values. This need gave rise to the pioneering work of what's now known as Moody's Analytics EDF™.

Expected Default Frequencies (EDFs™)

In the late 1980s, a good 10 years after Merton had published his research paper, there was no commercial application of the Merton Model. Analysts may have used it, but it required additional research, data collection, and an IT application developed from scratch. At the same time, financial institutions around the globe were managing growing credit portfolios due to the concentration of the banking industry and the development of the asset management business. Three individuals with academic and asset management backgrounds, Stephen Kealhofer, John (Mac) McQuown, and Oldrich Vacisek, anticipated the market demand for alternatives to rating agency ratings and created KMV Corporation.

Their best idea was to recognize that financial institutions did not need one more consulting firm hired to develop internal systems. They realized that the smartest strategy was to provide clients with a tool that simply directly delivered probabilities of default. The KMV founders thus performed fundamental research, collected data, and calculated the EDFs™.

KMV developed its own version of the Merton Model and spent a lot of time studying defaulted companies in order to transform the distance to default into a default probability. They did so using econometric methods that estimate and parameterize how actual defaults correlate to technically modeled defaults.

They then sold their clients a subscription to the EDFs™ that were updated monthly. The last piece of their vision was unparalleled customer service. A hotline was to be staffed 24 hours a day, and customers were invited to visit the company's chaotic offices located in a former warehouse of the Dole food company, where the three founders made themselves personally available.

The main advantage of the product is that it provides a default probability directly. Unlike other methodologies, there is no need to develop additional formulae or to manipulate data. One just has to enter the name of a company into Moody's CreditEdge™ platform and up pops the current EDF™ as well as its recent trend (Figure 7.1). The drivers behind the EDF™, namely market leverage and asset volatility, are also plotted as can be seen from the example of Caterpillar in Figure 7.2.

Despite the high price of the product, the company met immediate success. From the mid-1990s, no sizeable bank could avoid being a KMV customer. The interface delivering EDFs™ was installed on the computers of thousands of credit professionals all over the world. Additionally, KMV developed a portfolio management application that was equally successful.

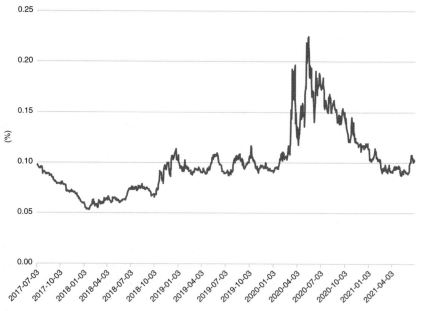

FIGURE 7.1 Moody's One-Year EDFs™ for Caterpillar until June 30, 2021
Source: Moody's Analytics, CreditEdge™.

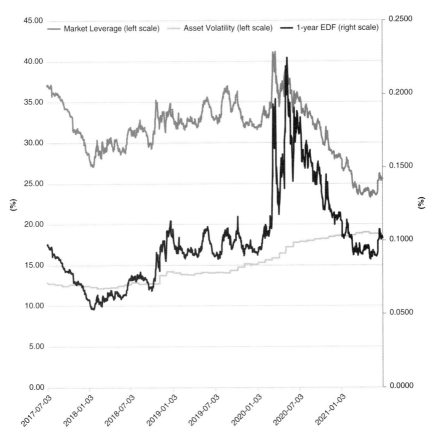

FIGURE 7.2 Drivers of EDFs™ for Caterpillar until June 30, 2021
Source: Moody's Analytics, CreditEdge™.

Thinking that the company had reached its growth objectives and could face competition, the three founders, who were the majority shareholders together with senior executives, sold their company in 2002 to Moody's for $202 million. Today, EDFs™ and other related products are sold by Moody's Analytics and delivered online.

Pros and Cons of EDFs™

More than 20 years after their introduction, Moody's Analytics EDFs™ remain widely used and highly relevant to estimate the default probability of a company. The main advantages of EDFs™ are the following:

■ Expected default frequencies are a neutral numerical estimation with a forward-looking view. The main driver of the EDFs™ is the market value of equity, which aggregates the entire market's view on the company's balance sheet and future prospects.

- Expected default frequencies are a bridge between the credit and equity markets. Expected Default Frequencies metrics, therefore, benefit from the collective judgment of innumerable market participants about companies' abilities to generate cash flow in the future. A negative perception of equity investors generally translates into a higher EDF™. This makes sense since poor equity performance typically reflects less earning potential and low flexibility to raise money if needed.
- Expected default frequencies are updated every day and, therefore, reflect all information available in the markets, including up-to-the-minute information. By comparison, it is extremely rare for a rating agency to downgrade a company immediately even after a noteworthy event. They first place the ratings under review, which can take several weeks before leading to a downgrade. Expected default frequencies are recalculated and disseminated every day. Moody's Analytics regularly publishes case studies showing that the EDFs™ are much quicker than the rating agencies to forecast the difficulties of a company that eventually defaults.

There are also well-known shortcomings to the EDF™ approach, and users need to know them. They are:

- Some of the fundamental principles behind the calculations are proprietary and not transparent to users. The expression "black box" is often heard regarding EDFs™. First, some mathematical concepts used to calculate the market value of assets are not revealed. Second, the ultimate EDF™ is the result of mapping the distance to default, essentially an index value to a probability. The mapping makes use of empirically generated estimates of probabilities given distance measures, meaning, actual default rates are observed and mapped to modeled distance measures. The mapping, as with any statistical procedure, has sampling variability, and users are not given much the insight into the sampling variability and statistical estimation techniques employed. One can understand that Moody's Analytics competitive advantage stems in part from the development of proprietary techniques, and they have an excellent predictive track record, which they highlight. However, some professionals are not comfortable with the idea of basing credit decisions on unknown parameters.
- The EDF™ population contains many companies with high default frequencies, yet they can survive for months or even years. To a large extent, this reflects the nature of default forecasting, where the future can never be known with certainty.

- The EDF™ methodology relies on the book value of debt. At best, companies publish new numbers on a quarterly basis. The first consequence is that Moody's Analytics can misestimate a company's financial situation if the level of debt changes considerably between reporting periods.
- The equity market is volatile, so EDFs™ will be volatile as well as can be seen in Figure 7.1. It can be argued that some events that move the stock price of a firm may not be relevant from a credit perspective. Credit decisions, like lending money or buying a bond, are generally made with a long-term perspective so this volatility is not a desirable characteristic. This is one of the judgments that experienced credit professionals must make when using metrics like EDFs™.
- By its nature, the EDF™ public firm model only works for publicly traded companies that comprise a small segment of the entire universe of companies. To address this issue, Moody's Analytics has developed a private firm model as well called RiskCalc™.

EDFs™ represented a breakthrough in credit analytics. Their appeal is in being forward-looking, reflective of mostly current market information, accessible, and easy to use. They are limited in use to analyzing companies that are publicly traded and, as with most market-based metrics, are susceptible to perhaps more volatility than the fundamentals of the credit exposure merit.

From EDFs™ to Ratings

Expected default frequencies are expressed as a default probability within a certain time horizon, typically one year. As can be seen in Table 7.1, Caterpillar had a 0.1016 percent EDF™ within a one-year time horizon on June 30, 2021. Many analysts prefer to summarize creditworthiness with a rating versus a default probability and, thus, the default probabilities can be expressed with ratings equivalents. Using historical data, Moody's Analytics translates EDFs™ into ratings. Table 7.1 presents the example of Caterpillar. In essence, if this company's one-year EDF is 0.1016 percent and the average population of companies with a 0.1016 percent one-year EDF has a rating of Ba1, then this particular company has an Ba1 equivalent rating. Note that the Moody's Analytics ratings-equivalent EDF™ does not necessarily match the company's rating by S&P or Moody's. The Moody's Analytics rating equivalent is a forward-looking measure for a company that could be different from its current, actual rating. The Moody's Analytics rating equivalent is based on an EDF™ whose inputs were described earlier. In contrast, the rating agency's rating is based on a detailed analysis of the firm's financials, its operations, the quality of management, and a qualitative approach overall in which human judgment plays a key role.

TABLE 7.1   Moody's One-Year EDF™ Implied Rating for Caterpillar

Date	One-year EDF™	Implied Moody's Rating
June 10, 2021	0.097%	Baa3
June 30, 2021	0.1016%	Ba1

Source: Moody's Analytics, CreditEdge™.

Other Vendors

Moody's Analytics EDFs™ is the most popular product in the market due to its long and successful history. Other vendors have similar products. One such vendor is the Kamakura Corporation (www.kamakuraco.com), which has a default probability estimator called the Kamakura Default Probability (KDP).

CREDIT DEFAULT SWAP PRICES

At a high level, a credit default swap (CDS)[1] can be thought of as insurance against credit risk, although the CDS is executed as a derivative transaction and not with an insurance policy. Purchasers of CDSs buy protection against the risk of default of an entity. If the entity defaults, the CDS buyer receives a certain amount of money from the CDS seller.

CDS prices, therefore, reflect the buyers' and sellers' views on the creditworthiness of an entity. The higher the perceived credit risk, the more expensive the price. In addition, CDS prices reflect the other market conditions, such as the overall supply and demand for protection in the marketplace. Other factors influence CDS prices as well, such as the credit risk of the seller, the liquidity risk of the CDS instrument itself, and the mark-to-market (MTM) risk of the CDS. Notably, unlike a bond, the movement of interest rates has no effect on the CDS prices since there is no cash-flow or funding component to the transaction.

The liquidity risk is the inability to exit the position if needed. Large broker-dealers typically provide a market to buy and sell CDSs and there is an unwritten understanding in a CDS contract that both counterparties can, in normal economic circumstances, unwind (i.e., cancel) the transaction at any time.

The MTM risk is described in Chapter 20. In short, CDSs, like other derivative instruments, have to be valued every day, and this daily valuation can generate unrealized gains or losses. Since the seller must hold capital to support that risk, the CDS price includes a (small) provision for market risk.

---

[1]Chapter 20 is dedicated to credit default swaps. For readers not familiar with CDSs we recommend reading Chapter 20 before going through the following section.

TABLE 7.2   Three Corporate CDS as of May 28, 2021

Reference Entity	Conventional Spread (bps p.a.)
Boeing Co. (Ticker: BA)	129.98
Amazon.com, Inc. (Ticker: AMZN)	35.37
Nike, Inc. (Ticker: NKE)	29.12

Source: Bloomberg, May 28, 2021.

Where to Find CDS Prices

Credit default swaps are not traded on exchanges but are traded over the counter, meaning they are bilateral contracts between two parties. The nature of the transaction implies minimum price transparency but, in order to develop the market, major dealers provide price indications with data vendors. In addition, some contracts are processed through independent clearinghouses that record the prices of the transactions they clear.

There are three main sources of prices:

1. Investment banks and dealers: If a firm already has a relationship with a bank or a broker active in CDS trading, it can ask for a quote or at least a price indication. This constitutes the most reliable source since they would likely indicate a level at which they would be ready to trade.
2. IHS Markit (www.markit.com) purchased Fitch Solutions pricing service in 2016 and provides daily CDS prices on close to 4,000 entities. Some prices are observed, others are evaluated, and less than 500 entities are frequently traded. Note that S&P Global and IHS Markit agreed to merge in November 2020 and the transaction was expected to close in the second half of 2021.
3. Bloomberg L.P.: Bloomberg is a subscription service that provides global information and data of many varieties plus selected trade support services for many traded instruments. It publishes CDS bid-and-ask quotes for companies, sovereign debt and structured securities, as well as other information relevant to the CDS market, namely tenor, terms, and volume.

Table 7.2 shows selected corporate CDS as of May 28, 2021.

What to Do with CDS Prices?

Credit default swap prices are helpful tools and serve several functions. They take the pulse of credit markets by reacting to overall macroeconomic conditions, sending most prices up when the economy slows and down when conditions improve. In Figure 7.3, pricing on a basket of five-year CDS for more than 100 U.S.-based investment grade corporates is shown from January 2020 to May 2021. This index is called CDX.NA.IG and is reset every six months; its composition changes slightly, so prices between series are not exactly comparable. Figure 7.3 includes Series 33 from January 1, 2020, until March 19, 2020; Series 34 from March 20, 2020, to September 18, 2020; Series 35 from September 21, 2020, to March 19, 2021; and Series 36 afterwards. The March 22, 2021, reset led to a five bps upward price.

What is interesting to notice is that early 2020, the U.S. economy was doing well and the index was at a low level. When the COVID-19 pandemic impacted the world economy, the market reacted with a sharp increase of spreads due to a fear of decline of creditworthiness and a lack of risk takers, before gradually going back to a lower level when traders started to expect a return to normality.

For individual credits, CDS prices also are essential tools for credit analysis, as described next.

Provide Early Warnings   Credit-default-swap prices react quickly to market news and reflect the instant view of capital markets participants on a specific company. Because these transactions do not involve funding, namely any large advances of cash, sellers can sell contracts quickly and buyers can buy them quickly. As a consequence, CDS prices are highly sensitive to the perceptions of the actual and prospective buyers and sellers, and the prices

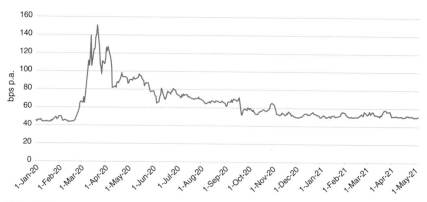

FIGURE 7.3   Index CDX.NA.IG, Five-Year CDS, January 1, 2020, to May 5, 2021, Series 33, 34, 35, and 36
Source: IHS Markit.

move quickly. CDSs can be used as part of the surveillance efforts to raise immediate attention on entities that may face problems. In most cases, CDS prices will react much more quickly than rating agencies' ratings changes and, thus, they constitute early warning signals of problems that may be coming. In large financial institutions, surveillance departments set up automatic downloads of CDS prices on a daily basis and receive alerts for price movements exceeding a threshold, for example, +/– 5 percent in a single day.

Take, for example, the crisis in the hospitality industry triggered by the COVID 19 pandemic. Credit-default swaps for Marriott reflected the market's growing uncertainty about the creditworthiness of the company. Figure 7.4 is the five-year CDS price for Marriott debt; one can see that the perceived decline in credit quality is reflected in the evolution of the CDS price. Whereas the spread was 35 bps p.a at the beginning of 2020, it was 405 bps p.a. by mid-March 2020.

In addition, when contemplating a new credit transaction, researching the past and current values of CDS prices can be helpful. Imagine that two potential counterparties have the same internal rating, the same external rating, yet very different CDS prices and or price histories. Although there may be supply and demand drivers of the pricing discrepancy, as we will see later, there may be some fundamental reasons already known by capital market participants not yet recognized by the handful of (ratings) analysts who follow the company.

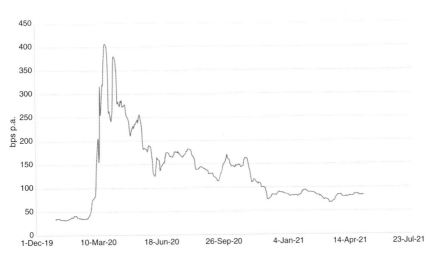

FIGURE 7.4   Price of Five-Year CDS for Marriott
Source: IHS Markit.

Pricing   The best thing about a CDS is that it provides an actual price. Pricing credit is a complex task and having access to what major financial institutions are comfortable charging for the credit risk of a company on a stand-alone basis is extremely useful. As a matter of fact, many firms use the CDS price as a benchmark and would not consider entering into a credit transaction at a price below the CDS market.

However, comparing a CDS price to a credit transaction of a very different nature has caveats:

- The tenor can be different. The most liquid CDS contract has a tenor of five years. For some names, it is possible to find a price for one, three, or seven years. Transforming a 5-year CDS price into a 2.5-year CDS necessitates developing a methodology and employing assumptions, both of which introduce uncertainty.
- The recovery rate can be different. A key parameter of a credit transaction is the expected recovery rate, as seen in Chapter 2, which is the proportion of the notional amount of the transaction not expected to be lost in case of bankruptcy. CDS contracts work off a senior unsecured reference security, which will experience some level of recovery, and the expected recovery is built into the CDS price. If a credit transaction has a different estimate of recovery, the CDS benchmark would need to be adjusted to reflect the differential in the recovery rates.
- CDS transactions are small, typically $5 million or $10 million. A much larger credit transaction would deserve a higher price if it uses more of the risk-taker's credit capacity for that name.

Caveats When Using CDS Prices

In the late 1990s, when the CDS market started growing in earnest, companies that had specialized in the sale of credit opinions, such as the rating agencies or KMV Corporation, were concerned that CDS prices would become the undisputed market benchmark making their products and services obsolete. The same way that stock prices are freely available, there was a sense that CDS prices would replace all other information sources.

Even though the CDS market became a cornerstone of the financial markets as anticipated, CDS prices have not replaced other sources of information. They are viewed as complementary to ratings, but no serious institution would ignore ratings and replace them with real or implied CDS prices, for the following reasons:

- Very few entities have actively traded CDSs. The universe of active companies is less than 500. The market is dominated by a handful of large dealers like J.P. Morgan, Deutsche Bank, and Morgan Stanley, who concentrate on the same names. There is not enough demand for credit protection on smaller companies for these large institutions to develop a significant market.

■ Given the narrowness of the market, some vendors extrapolate information from the CDS market to present implied prices for entities for which a CDS market does not exist. However, this process requires so many assumptions and approximations that we can only recommend a good level of caution in using implied prices. Entities may present a very similar profile in the implied pricing methodology yet have very different creditworthiness.

■ CDS prices can be greatly influenced by noncredit events and be distorted to a point that they do not reflect default risk. They may be influenced by technical factors as well, that is, the economic environment of buyers and sellers. Let's illustrate this by two examples:

1. When an issuer hits the market with a large bond issue, some investors may want to buy the bonds but not keep the credit risk attached to them. To protect themselves, they buy a CDS contract. All of a sudden, there is a surge in demand for CDS contracts that drives the price up, to a point that it does not reflect the true credit risk. The price increase is the result of a momentary imbalance between buyers and sellers of protection and it has nothing to do with the fundamental strength of the issuer.

2. Before the COVID-19 pandemic, analysts were confident in the strength of the U.S. economy and spreads were generally low. Then, when the economy started slowing down, the perceived riskiness increased and more institutions were willing to buy protection than to sell protection, which translated into a sharp increase of CDS prices as can be seen on the price of the CDX.NA.IG index in Figure 7.3.

This volatility in CDS prices is also illustrated in Figure 7.5. Here we show the CDS of Walmart, the large U.S. retailer. which held at the time a stable credit rating credit rating of AA (S&P), Aa2 (Moody's), and AA (Fitch). Note the spike in its CDS from February 2020 to April 2020, during the most uncertain days of the crisis; the CDS gradually retreated to more or less the same level as before the crisis. Walmart enjoyed a stable rating over the same period, and although the macroeconomy around the company was in jeopardy, its fundamental credit characteristics arguably did not change much.

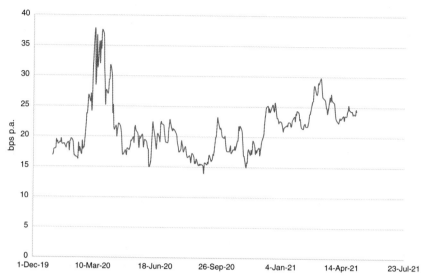

FIGURE 7.5 Price of Five-Year CDS for Walmart
Source: IHS Markit.

BOND PRICES

Investors in corporate bonds take a direct credit risk on the issuers. When a company has financial difficulties, it defaults at the same time on all financial obligations including bank loans and bonds. It is, therefore, legitimate to try to extract credit risk information from the prices at which bonds are sold in the market. There are, however, a few major obstacles that we summarize here:

- The biggest problem is that bond investors take more than credit risk, first and foremost, interest rate risk as bonds are typically issued with fixed interest rates. When interest rates go up, bond prices fall. They also take liquidity risk, that is to say the ability to sell the instrument quickly and without much discount to a quoted price. Finally, bonds may have embedded options, such as early redemption, that can heavily influence their values.

    Bond prices, therefore, include risks of a very different nature from credit risk. Even if the credit risk of an issuer does not change, its bond price may change. The price of a bond alone is not a reliable indicator of credit risk. To obtain the credit-risk premium contained in a bond price, one has to develop a methodology to isolate the credit risk component from the observable price. Credit spreads represent the difference between what a noncallable bond with credit risk—such as a corporate bond—yields, and what a bond with no risk—a U.S. Treasury, for example—of the same tenor yields. The credit spreads are indicative of the issuers' credit risk and represent what bond buyers demand as extra compensation for taking this credit risk. Credit spreads are available from various market data publications or can be roughly estimated by subtracting a U.S. Treasury yield from a bond yield of the same maturity.

However, credit spreads are not perfect indicators of credit risk because market technical factors are at play in any bond's price, and therefore in their yield. For example, the market may be saturated with a certain issuer, even of excellent credit, and bond buyers' willingness to buy more of a given name may be limited. This would drive down the price, drive up the yield, and drive up the credit spread, and this upward movement would not reflect any change in creditworthiness. The same holds true for liquidity factors. Some bonds are highly liquid, and their yields would be lower than those bonds that are illiquid, all else equal. If one were to observe or calculate credit spreads of the liquid and illiquid bonds that are otherwise identical, some of the spread would reflect illiquidity, not credit risk.

Characteristic of the bond market is that any given bond may be illiquid, meaning not traded frequently. Bond investors tend to be institutions such as pension funds, endowments, and insurance companies with a longer-term view and with lower turnover. There are so few transactions that it is unusual to have pricing data that adjust on a daily basis.

■ Bond prices are not transparent. Hand-in-hand with the infrequency of trading, price discovery is an issue for bonds; at any one time it's unclear what the current market value of a bond is. Most bond trades still occur bilaterally through brokers although both the NYSE and the Nasdaq exchanges now have platforms for bond trading.

■ In summary, extracting credit information from the bond market presents challenges. Yet with the rapid development of the CDS market, the need to exploit bond market prices declined considerably since the CDS market offered a substitute. However, extracting pure credit prices from the bond market data is always possible, and those prices can be used and interpreted in the same way as CDS prices.

FINAL WORDS

Although consensus may exist for many companies regarding their credit quality, which is often the case for the strongest and weakest firms, ratings agencies and EDF™ methodologies can deliver very different opinions about the relative quality of companies. This is no surprise given that the two methodologies are completely different. To repeat ourselves, rating agencies are, by choice, slower to react than the capital markets because they need time to fully analyze and incorporate news and structural trends, and ratings are designed to be invariant to the economic cycle. They also have a downward bias, meaning that downgrades are more frequent, and once downgraded, it is hard for a company to be upgraded. The capital markets react quickly and can reverse their point of view quickly and symmetrically. How many times has a company's stock fallen after an announcement only for the share price to recover after a few days when investors realize that the news is not as bad as they thought? The discrepancies resulting from the different approaches offer an opportunity for the credit analytics team to pay closer attention to them.

As seen in Chapter 2, firms must establish a hierarchy of available indicators of creditworthiness so that credit decisions are made on a rules basis as opposed to a discretionary basis. Whatever the chosen hierarchy, the information in a credit report must include all available indicators.

CHAPTER **8**

Consumer Finance

Part Two of this book is dedicated to the assessment of individual credit transactions, as opposed to the management of a portfolio of individual transactions, which is covered in Part Three, and mitigation techniques that will be described in Part Four. However, as the vast majority of this book deals primarily with corporate debt rather than with consumer debt, we will discuss all major aspects of consumer finance in this chapter. This includes financial instruments generating credit exposures on individuals, portfolio management principles, some mitigation techniques, and a brief overview of the regulatory environment in the United States.

As we describe in Chapter 1, many companies, primarily financial institutions, take credit risk on individuals, as we may need to finance our durable goods and our fundamental household investments such as buying a house. In the largest economies of the world, debt owed by individuals can be as large as corporate debt! However, when we present household debt we exclude mortgages (see Chapter 1), since the vast majority of these are secured by the GSEs and therefore present little to no credit risk to the investor who has funded the mortgage. Including this debt would make the United States household debt about the same size as corporate debt.

For small transaction amounts and regular shopping, credit cards are gradually replacing cash and personal checks, so credit card companies are generating very large and growing portfolios of consumer debt. Larger purchases like houses or cars are usually financed by medium-term and long-term loans provided by banks and specialty finance companies that are exposed to household debt as well.

Analyzing the credit quality of an individual bears some similarities with the assessment of the creditworthiness of a corporate but also major differences. Whereas corporates are required all over the world to prepare financial statements at least once a year, the same requirement does not exist for an individual: no income statement, no balance sheet, and no statement of cash flows are available. The annual tax return filed by individuals has one main purpose, which is to assess the taxable revenue of an individual or family in order to calculate the amount of income tax due to the State or Federal Treasury. But the tax return says nothing about expenses and existing debt. Revenues are only one indicator of creditworthiness for an individual. One can make a lot of money, which may or may not be reflected in the tax return, given the intricacies of the tax codes, but spend much more than what was made, and no document will show it. Similarly, a tax return will not reveal the amount of debt a household already carries. Prior to the Tax Cuts and Jobs Act of 2017, a federal tax return might shed light on a filer's mortgage by looking at the interest deduction and grossing this amount up using an estimated interest rate. But not everyone itemized, and as of 2017, there is no longer a deduction. More data is needed to make sound lending decisions and we will see in this chapter techniques developed by financial institutions with the support of data provided by independent credit reporting agencies like Experian, Equifax, and TransUnion.

Whereas the creditworthiness of a corporate typically does not change overnight, except if fraud is involved or during times of extreme volatility in the financial markets, the financial situation of a family can change quickly due to major life events like a loss of employment, a divorce, disease, or a death. The potential volatility of the ability of an individual to repay their debt is a major driver of a lender's decision in extending credit.

A recent example is the unprecedented economic crisis triggered by the COVID-19 pandemic in 2020. Public health officials were taken by surprise by the rapid spreading of the virus and had to take drastic measures to protect the health of their citizenry. Among other things, travel restrictions and the closing of restaurants, schools, and sports arenas were imposed overnight. To compensate for the loss of economic activity, governments worldwide reacted by launching stimulus packages including increased unemployment insurance benefits, forgiving or providing forbearance on loans, and extending subsidies to businesses. But it was not enough to prevent a massive increase in unemployment all over the world. In the United States alone, more than 20 million jobs were lost in the first half of 2020 and the unemployment rate grew from 3.5 percent at the end of 2019 to a peak of 14.7 percent at the end of April 2020, before retracting to 6.1 percent at of the end of April 2021, as can be seen in Figure 8.1. The actual impact on the economy may be more pronounced than the unemployment statistics show because there was a corresponding decline of the number of people in the labor force, largely due to the need for those previously employed to stay home and care for children and the elderly. The labor force participation rate (Figure 8.2) dropped from 63.4 percent to 60.2 percent between January 2020 and April 2020 before rebounding somewhat to 61.7 percent by April 2021 (U.S. Department of Labor, Bureau of Labor Statistics; data are seasonally adjusted).

Credit losses for lenders are volatile and depend on the strength of the job market as most households have limited liquid assets available and rely

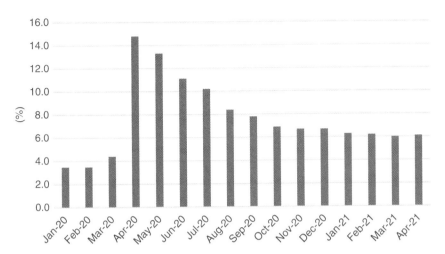

FIGURE 8.1   U.S. 2020 Monthly Unemployment Rate
Source: U.S. Bureau of Labor Statistics.

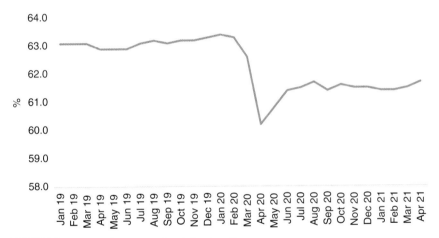

FIGURE 8.2   U.S. Labor Force Participation Rate
Source: U.S. Bureau of Labor Statistics.

on their monthly income to honor interest and principal payments on their debt. The low level of savings is one of the reasons why consumers borrow in the first place. This is particularly true for non–real estate debt like auto loans, student debt, credit card, and other forms of personal loans. When the economy flourishes and unemployment is low, losses tend to be predictable and low enough for lenders to make a profit. When the economy slows down, borrowers lose their jobs and stop paying back their debt, which translates into higher losses for lenders. Besides the tragic situation for

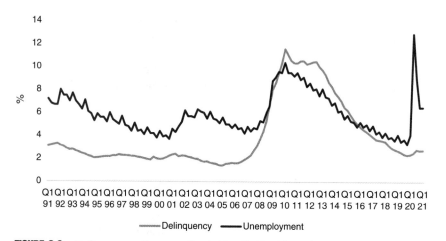

FIGURE 8.3   Delinquency Rate on Single-Family Residential Mortgages and Unemployment Rate, Seasonally Adjusted
Source: Board of Governors of the Federal Reserve System (retrieved from FRED, Federal Reserve Bank of St. Louis), and U.S. Department of Labor, Bureau of Labor Statistics.

families who may struggle to buy groceries or make mortgage payments, the sudden change of the economic environment can have a devastating effect on lenders. Thanks to the various stimulus packages in the United States in 2020, the high level of unemployment did not translate into more delinquencies on consumer debt at the time this book went into press. Delinquencies may not have risen notably because the spike in unemployment was a shock that dissipated quickly, as unemployment levels have receded. As one can see in Figure 8.3, delinquency on mortgages increased sharply with the 2007 crisis, and generally closely tracks the unemployment rate.

WHAT IS CONSUMER FINANCE?

Consumer finance, or household finance, refers to financing activities by individuals. For centuries, individuals have entered into financial transactions with each other, with the government, or with financial institutions in order to finance the purchase of essential products and assets to improve their daily lives. The most obvious example is real estate. Buying a house is a major goal for families but few have enough savings to pay cash. The only way to finance the acquisition is to borrow money—from a family member, a friend, or more commonly from a bank or a specialized financial institution. It's always a long-term engagement as most individuals borrow for a very long period of time, given the high purchase price of the house, increased by all transaction costs and renovation expenses, as compared to their annual income.

Once limited to real estate and other durable, physical assets like cars, individuals can borrow on an intra-monthly basis in going about their daily lives, such as paying for groceries, clothes, school, or even a vacation. Replacing cash payment at the grocery store with tapping a credit card or using a cell phone equipped with Apple Pay is also a type of household finance as the individual is enjoying a product before paying for it a few weeks later when the balance on their credit card linked to Apple Pay is due. This is, in essence, borrowing!

SEGMENTATION OF CONSUMER FINANCE PRODUCTS

Before describing the major families of consumer finance products, let's segment them based on their fundamental characteristics: first, whether the borrowing is a fixed amount or a revolving line of credit and, second, whether the borrowing is secured or unsecured.

Fixed Amount and Revolving Facilities

Fixed amount means that the amount of the loan is fixed at the beginning of the transaction between the individual and the lender. The borrower has no ability to increase the amount of the loan after the closing of the transaction. The principal amount reduces over time (amortizes) as the borrower makes their monthly principal and interest payments. They can also make extra payments and even pay off the loan at any time with or without a prepayment penalty, after a preagreed period. Prepayment penalties are sometimes imposed by lenders when borrowers pay-off part of all their loan too early. The main reason is that lenders want to be guaranteed a minimum of interest income to cover expenses to originate and underwrite it and to make a minimum profit.

Revolving means that borrowers are entitled to draw and pay back any amount of money from their accounts as long as they do not exceed the credit limit fixed at the outset. A typical example are credit cards where individuals rarely spend the same amount of money each and every month and have the flexibility to spend the amount they want up to the limit set by the issuer. Home equity lines of credit, or HELOC, described further on in this chapter, are also revolving instruments.

Secured and Unsecured Products

Similar to corporate debt (see Chapter 17), consumer debt can be secured or unsecured. Secured means that the lending agreement includes a lien on the asset being financed. The borrower owns the asset as long as they are current on their scheduled debt repayment. If the borrower misses payments on principal or interests, the lender has the right to seize or repossess the asset. After the legal process of repossession is completed in a legal process called foreclosure, the lender will sell the asset and use the proceeds to repay all unpaid amounts, principal, interest, fees, and expenses. If the proceeds are greater than the amount due, the net proceeds will be given back to the borrower. In most cases though, the amount recovered by the sale of the asset is smaller than the amount due from the borrower and the lender will record a financial loss.

With the notable exception of student debt, secured lending is the norm for high borrowing amounts and long-term financing, regardless of the credit quality of the borrower, because there is too much uncertainty about the credit quality of individuals for lenders to not protect themselves in case of borrower default. It's basic risk management and applies to all segments of the population. Even multimillion dollar properties purchased by wealthy families are secured. The good thing is that there are limited constraints for the borrower. If borrowers pay what they committed to when they borrowed, they will not feel the effect of the lien. However, the property cannot be used to secure additional debt with the same level of priority of payments. It can only be used to secure a second lien with subordinated loan like a HELOC (see further on). Only in case of default will borrowers run the risk of losing their assets (the collateral).

In some cases, loans can also be secured by financial assets like checking accounts, saving accounts, or certificates of deposits (CDs). In case of missed payments, the lender can access funds available in the checking and saving accounts, if any, and seize CDs. The legal term is "right of offset" and can be used for mortgages or personal loans but is typically limited to accounts held in the same financial institutions as the lender.

Unsecured means that, in case of default, the lender does not have direct access to any assets owned by the borrower. If negotiations fail to trigger repayment of the amount due, the lender will have to force the borrower into personal bankruptcy and become a general creditor, sharing the proceeds of what can be recovered with other creditors, if any.

Table 8.1 segments the various consumer debt products along the two dimensions secured/unsecured and fixed amount/revolving.

TABLE 8.1   Segmentation of Consumer Finance Transactions

	Secured	Unsecured
Fixed amount/amortizing	Mortgage Auto loan Personal loan (infrequent)	Student loan Consumer/personal loan
Revolving	Home equity line of credit (HELOC)	Credit card

MAJOR FAMILIES OF CONSUMER FINANCE PRODUCTS

For many individuals, buying a house is a lifetime dream, and also imposes financial discipline, which can be challenging for a borrower and can curtail lifestyle choices for most of their lives. A big part of individuals' disposable income is dedicated to servicing the debt they incurred when they purchased their home. As a result, in all major economies, the vast majority of consumer debt is housing debt. As Table 8.2 shows, at the end of 2020, total consumer debt in the United States reached a record $14.88 trillion, representing 71 percent of nominal GDP (source for GDP: U.S. Department of Commerce, BEA). Of this consumer debt, mortgage debt was the largest component at $10.31 trillion.

Mortgages

Mortgage is the generic term used to describe monies borrowed by families to buy a house or a condominium. The root of the words "mortgage" and "amortize," *mort* is French for "die" since the mortgage debt is designed to diminish and eventually go away over the term of the borrowing. Most mortgages carry fixed monthly payments: a portion is used to pay interest due on the balance (balance multiplied by interest rate) and the rest to repay principal (fixed payment minus interest). Hence and as illustrated in Table 8.3, principal repayment grows over time and interest payments decline over time until the borrowed amount is fully repaid.

In this example, we show a 30-year (360 month) $100,000 mortgage with a 3 percent interest rate. The calculation of the monthly payment can be made with Microsoft Excel function PMT.

TABLE 8.2 Segmentation of Consumer Finance Balances as of Q42020

Product	U.S. Consumer Debt, $ billion
Mortgage loans	10,310
Auto loans	1,370
Student loans	1,570
Credit card debt	756.3
HELOC	374.2
Personal loans	323.6
Retail credit card debt	79.9
Other	115.2
Total	14,880

Source: https://www.experian.com/blogs/ask-experian/research/consumer-debt-study/

TABLE 8.3 Example of Fixed Payments Mortgage

	Month	Beginning Balance	Monthly Payment	To Interest	To Principal	Ending Balance
	1	$100,000	−$421.6	−$250.0	−$171.6	$99,828
	2	$99,828	−$421.6	−$249.6	−$172.0	$99,656
	3	$99,656	−$421.6	−$249.1	−$172.5	$99,484
	4	$99,484	−$421.6	−$248.7	−$172.9	$99,311
	5	$99,311	−$421.6	−$248.3	−$173.3	$99,138
	6	$99,138	−$421.6	−$247.8	−$173.8	$98,964
	7	$98,964	−$421.6	−$247.4	−$174.2	$98,790
	8	$98,790	−$421.6	−$247.0	−$174.6	$98,615
	9	$98,615	−$421.6	−$246.5	−$175.1	$98,440
	10	$98,440	−$421.6	−$246.1	−$175.5	$98,265
End of	11	$98,265	−$421.6	−$245.7	−$175.9	$98,089
Year 1	12	$98,089	−$421.6	−$245.2	−$176.4	$97,912
Year 10	120	$76,251	−$421.6	−$190.6	−$231.0	$76,020
Year 20	240	$43,974	−$421.6	−$109.9	−$311.7	$43,662
Year 30	360	$421	−$421.6	−$1.1	−$420.6	$0

Buying a house using a mortgage is also a form of personal savings. Borrowers are required to make monthly payments, usually fixed, which over time become equity in the house as the interest/principal paydown ratio falls, as can be seen in Table 8.3. Mortgages create mandatory savings that are realized as real estate equity over time. This is true even if the buyer overpays or real estate values fall. In our example above, if the property was valued at $125,000 when the mortgage was taken and the down payment was $25,000, then the equity of the borrower was $25,000 at the time of acquisition. After 10 years, if the house is still valued at $125,000, the borrower's assets will have grown to $48,980, which is the original $25,000 equity down payment plus the paydown of the mortgage of ($100,000 − $76,020).

The property can be a single detached house, a multifamily house (i.e., a building with several independent units), or a condominium. Mortgage loans can be used to finance a primary residence, a second residence (e.g., a weekend or a vacation home), or even an investment property.

There are many other kinds of mortgages in the market, notably:

- Adjustable-rate mortgages or ARMs are common in the United States. Their interest rate is fixed for a period of time, for example for three years, then varies after the fixed period based on the interest rates prevalent in the financial markets. These mortgages expose borrowers to volatility in payments. If rates go down, mortgage payments go down, but if rates go up, payments go up as well. When rates rise, borrowers can be in for a sudden brutal surprise. It's one of the triggers of the 2007 crisis that we review in Chapter 21.

- Negative amortization mortgages do not amortize but, on the contrary, the principal balance grows over time as the borrowers' fixed payments are not enough to cover the interest due. In the example shown in Table 8.3, if monthly payments are less than $250, the borrower cannot cover the interest due and this shortfall becomes part of the balance owed that grows over time.

- Interest-only (IO) mortgages are nonamortizing loans as well. Borrowers do not repay any principal but make fixed monthly payments equal to the amount of interest due. In our example of Table 8.3., if the monthly payment is $250 the mortgage balance neither grows nor amortizes, but remains the same during the lifetime of the mortgage.

Both negative amortization and interest-only loans are enticing products for someone who cannot afford to pay high regular payments and intends to sell their house and pay back their mortgage in a short to medium time frame. However, these loans have often been offered to borrowers with low income or low net assets with the expectation that their house would gain in value and thereby enable a refinancing with more equity. When this appreciation did not materialize, it led to higher default rates than traditional mortgages experienced.

The origination of a single mortgage for a borrower involves many distinct roles, typically involving multiple entities:

Mortgage brokers: They are typically independent consultants whose job is to help borrowers understand their financing potential, to present the various products available, and to introduce them to potential lenders with the best (cheapest) conditions. If the borrower's credit history is poor, their mission is to find a lender who will accept the borrower's credit risk. They are remunerated by a commission, typically 1 to 2 percent of the loan amount, paid by the borrower or the lender. For a long time, mortgage brokers were small companies or even individuals introduced to clients by realtors and working in a traditional way. Today, these kinds of services are gradually performed by FinTech companies whose mission is to connect borrowers and lenders online, in a fully automated way. One of the leaders of tech-enabled mortgage brokerage in the United States is LendingTree.

Lenders: The lender is the financial institution that provides funds to borrowers to purchase their property. They are primarily well-known "brick and mortar" commercial banks like Wells Fargo, JPMorgan Chase, or Bank of America in the United States.

However, non–bank lenders actually originate far more mortgages than traditional banks. More than half of mortgages are originated by nondepository institutions and, of these, the vast majority are not affiliated with a traditional bank.[1] In the United States, companies such as Quicken Loans, a subsidiary of Rocket, or Provident Funding are among the largest lenders. Lenders are responsible for making underwriting decisions. This means they decide to approve a loan and provide funding, or to reject it if they do not like the creditworthiness of the borrower or other attributes of the transaction, such as the purchase price of the house, location, or insurance coverage. They define their own risk appetite—borrower's credit profile, attributes of the security (the house), whether they are overexposed to a particular geographic area, whether the mortgage conforms to the underwriting rules of the Government-Sponsored Enterprises (Fannie Mae, Freddy Mac, Ginnie Mae, and the NCUA), who in turn will either directly buy mortgages from the mortgage lenders or insure those same mortgages that are sold to the broader investment community. The lenders set the interest rate that reflects their assessment of the risk. They are also responsible for the loan documentation, which sets out all the terms and conditions of the financial transaction.

Risk takers: Lenders are not necessarily the ultimate risk takers. Their roles vary from country to country but in the United States, the lender facing the borrower is rarely the ultimate risk taker on the mortgage, because in most instances, the lenders originate the mortgages and then sell them to investors. This frees up their resources for funding new loans and generating new revenue from origination. There are a variety of ways for a lender to sell the loans they originate. We show in Chapter 11 that residential mortgages are often repackaged and sold as part of a structured transaction called "securitization." The structured transactions create securities, known as residential mortgage-backed securities (RMBS). These securities are sold directly to institutional investors or to government-sponsored enterprises (GSEs) like Fannie Mae or Freddy Mac. The securitization process usually involves a repayment guaranty of each and every loan provided by the GSEs. The role of the GSEs is crucial. It removes the risk to investors of nonpayment by borrowers. With the removal of this risk, investors are incented to invest in RMBS.

---

[1]*Source:* Federal Reserve Bulletin, November 2017, Table 10, "Lending Activity by Type of Institution."

The RMBS securitization provides an outlet for lenders to sell the mortgages that they originate, which in turn makes lenders willing to originate and provide funding to individuals to buy houses. Thus, without a guaranty from a GSE, investors would not purchase financial instruments backed by mortgages, lenders in turn would not have the appetite and funds to finance mortgages, and families would not be able to borrow.

Servicers: The role of the servicers is not very well known as they operate in the background. They perform all administrative tasks after a mortgage has been concluded. Their main role is to make sure that payments are made by borrowers, that the documentation of the loans remains accurate, and that the ultimate risk takers are properly paid on time. As long as a borrower pays their mortgage regularly, they will not interface with the servicer. However, if a borrower becomes delinquent, it's the servicer's job to try to collect the money. Efficiently servicing a loan requires simple things like having accurate information about the borrowers, such as their email address, phone numbers, and hours at which they can be reached in the event of a late or missed payment. The servicer's operations must be adequately staffed so that borrowers are called regularly and that their individual situation is discussed. That's why the quality of the servicer is very important during a financial crisis. In 2007–2008, large banks that were well organized and had the financial means to properly staff their servicing activities experienced fewer defaults than smaller or less financially strong companies. The worst performances were recorded by lenders who had contracted with third-party servicers without the wherewithal to stay on top of the delinquent loans. Simply put, if borrowers are not contacted quickly and regularly after they become delinquent, there is little chance that they will try to work out a solution with the lender and stay current. This can significantly increase the amount of credit losses.

Auto Loans

Auto loans are a simple product related to the financing of a new or used vehicle. It's offered in the United States by financial institutions like Capital One Financial Corporation or JPMorgan Chase or by companies affiliated with car manufacturers. Examples are Ally Financial—former GMAC and related to General Motors—Ford Motor Credit Company, or Toyota Financial Services. Loans are funded either directly by the lender or via securitization products, which is explained in Chapter 11.

It's estimated that 85 percent of the vehicles sold in the United States are financed. There are two main financing products available: a financed sale and lease. In a sale, the borrower owns the car with money provided by the auto loan. The loan is repaid by monthly installments for a period typically between three and five years. In a lease, the car is owned by the finance company and the individual pays a down payment and then monthly a fixed amount during the agreed period, typically three years. At the end of the lease, the individual has the option of giving the car back or to purchase the vehicle. Both products are secured lending. If the borrower missed payments, the finance company will repossess the car.

The most challenging aspect of lease financing for the lender is the residual value of the vehicle at the end of the lease. Financial models supporting the loans and the securitization schemes are based on the expectation that vehicles will be sold at a certain price at the end of the lease. Failure to collect the expected amount can generate credit losses and put stress on the ability of the lender to repay their investors. Some insurers have tried to create a "residual value insurance" product, but without much success.

Student Loans

Student loans are taken by students to finance their college education. It is an old product developed to help students and their families pay for their tuition. There is typically a grace period until graduation during which no repayment is due. It is an unsecured product that relies only on the commitment of the student to repay their loan when they begin earning income. Student loans are sometimes guaranteed by family members.

In the United States, the Department of Education manages roughly 90 percent of all student loans through various programs. The rest are offered by private finance companies, including Sallie Mae, a former government-sponsored enterprise privatized in the 1990s. Funding sources are primarily asset-backed securities (see Chapter 11).

Credit Cards

Credit cards are often viewed by individuals as a means of payment but, for a finance company, issuing a credit card is equivalent to granting a loan. Merchants are typically paid by credit card companies two or three days after the purchase, whereas customers pay their balance a few weeks later at the earliest. The credit card issuer therefore needs to fund, on a temporary basis, purchases made by their customers, taking a credit risk.

In the United States, credit card debt is like a consumer loan as holders are not required to pay back the balance of their account regularly.

They receive a monthly statement, but they have the option of paying it in full with no interest and no cost or to delay repayment, which incurs hefty interest costs. It is estimated that half of the credit card holders do not pay their monthly bill in full but carry a large and costly balance. These customers can be very profitable for credit card issuers but they also carry a lot of risk because a high balance on an expensive and unsecured instrument like a credit card loan means that the borrowers have no liquidity, and sometimes no ability to pay back, with limited income, and in some cases living from paycheck to paycheck. In most countries outside of the United States, credit cards are not loans as the individual does not have the ability to carry a balance for more than 30 days. They have to pay back the full amount monthly and if not, are delinquent. Outside of the United States, the consumer loan industry has developed in other ways, as reviewed below.

Similar to other consumer finance products reviewed previously, credit card issuers use a mix of funding sources to advance payments to their network of merchants. A company like American Express relies on sources like deposits from their banking business, bonds, loans, and securitization.

Home Equity Lines of Credit (HELOC)

Home equity lines of credit (HELOC) are consumer loans secured by a real estate asset. The concept is to use the equity embedded in the ownership of a house, without selling the house, to provide funding for other needs. For instance, if an individual owns a home valued at $100,000 with a mortgage carrying a balance of $50,000, there is $50,000 in equity. The individual can borrow up to $30,000, bringing the total amount of debt secured by the house to $80,000, in line with most conventional mortgages where loan-to-value (LTV) of 80 percent is the norm. The $30,000 is the size of the credit limit but the HELOC allows the borrower flexibility to draw on the limit and pay it back partially or fully anytime during the lifetime of the facility, which is generally 10 years. The interest rate is much lower than that on a credit card, as the loan is secured, but typically slightly higher than that on a mortgage, as it is a second-lien product, and due only on the outstanding HELOC balance. Similar to mortgages, the product is provided by financial institutions, large banks, and specialty finance companies, and funded by institutional investors via deposits from customers or securitization.

HELOCs are a second-lien product. This means that the primary mortgage lender is first to be repaid in the case of default, and the HELOC lender is second to be repaid, and only after the primary mortgage lender is repaid in full. In the example above, if after a default of the borrower, and subsequent foreclosure on the house, the proceeds of the foreclosure after expenses is $75,000, the primary mortgage lender will receive its full $50,000 and the

HELOC lender receives only $25,000, realizing a $5,000 loss. This explains why HELOCs are riskier than mortgages for a lender and warrant a higher interest rate.

Consumer Loans

Consumer loans are unsecured facilities individuals can take on to finance whatever purchases they would like. They are mostly popular outside the United States in countries where credit card balances must be repaid monthly and do not allow individuals to delay payment of their purchases.

The industry is being disrupted by FinTech companies that market to, originate, and provide loan servicing directly to individuals via the Internet. The ability to offer personal loans online without having a network of retail branches has provided an opportunity to new entrants. Interesting enough, not only start-ups funded by private equity firms are entering this market, but large institutions historically not involved in consumer finance have also entered the market. A notable example is Marcus (named after Marcus Goldman), created from scratch in 2016 by Goldman Sachs.

ASSESSMENT OF CREDIT QUALITY

The key challenge for personal finance lenders is to assess quickly the likelihood of being repaid by a large number of customers whose financial situations can change quickly. Life events like job loss, divorce, or a disease can brutally change the creditworthiness of an individual, complicating the risk management of consumer finance lenders. Increasingly, these lenders rely on predictive analytical models, and make use of a wider array of information on the borrowers, such as social media, to complement their traditional sources of information produced by credit bureaus.

Basic Information

The first step for lenders is income verification, which is obtained by gathering basic information from the borrower and their families. Individuals who are employed can easily demonstrate their revenues by providing pay stubs. Lenders typically require documentation on the most recent months, and sometimes most recent years, which enables them to verify the stability of the income and to avoid fraud. Self-employed people without regular income create more challenges for lenders who have to rely on other data points described below.

For all, the second basic document required by lenders is the individual's federal tax return, which in the United States is the Internal Revenue Service's (IRS) form 1040 and accompanying forms. In addition, all employees are required to provide a summary of wages and all sorts of compensation they receive annually. The IRS's forms W-2 (for salaried employees) and 1099 (for independent contractors) are typically required by lenders, especially for large borrowings like mortgages.

In most countries, tax documents and pay stubs are the only reliable sources of information available. They provide relevant information but do not indicate anything about existing debt or payment history. Lenders have to rely on declarations made by borrowers, which may not always be accurate.

Consumer Credit Reporting Agencies

Fortunately for lenders, the need to assess the creditworthiness of a borrower and to predict their ability and willingness to pay back the debt owed has led to the creation of dedicated independent private companies known as consumer credit reporting agencies or simply, credit bureaus. In the United States, market leaders are Experian, Equifax, and TransUnion. Outside of the United States, these credit bureaus are also active, providing various services but are sometimes limited by local privacy and bank secrecy regulations or by the quality and availability of data.

Their business model is based on collecting information on individuals from all companies that have extended credit to the individuals, including utility companies like electricity or mobile communications providers. When establishing electricity service to a residence, the utility company is providing credit to a borrower. A service, in this case, electricity, is being provided before the utility collects payment. Because there is a chance that the individual will not pay for the service, this is credit risk for the utility. Utility companies routinely require the social security number of the new customer for the precise purpose of checking the credit history with a credit bureau. The social security number is the primary identifier used to track an individual's credit history. A low credit score may require the customer to prepay for the estimated usage of the serviced. Whenever a company requests an individual's social security number, it is almost certainly making the request to run a credit check on the individual from the credit bureau. In turn, many of these companies then provide the credit bureau with a payment report on the individual on a going-forward basis. This pattern builds an individual's credit history

The individual's credit history is summarized by a score reflecting the individual's history of repayment and ability to pay current debt. Financial institutions like banks and credit card companies and other businesses, such as utilities, are therefore both supporting the credit bureaus by providing information about their clients (e.g., opening of a new account,

1. **Payment history (35% of your scores)**
   Whether you've paid past credit accounts on time
2. **Amounts owed (30% of your scores)**
   The amounts of credit and loans you are using
3. **Length of credit history (15% of your scores)**
   How long you've had credit
4. **New credit (10% of your scores)**
   Frequency of credit inquires and new account openings
5. **Credit mix (10% of your scores)**
   The mix of your credit, retail accounts, installment loans, finance company accounts and mortgage loans

FIGURE 8.4 FICO® Methodology
Source: Fair Isaac Corp., www.ficoscore.com, "FICO® Score Education."

outstanding balance, payment incidents, late-payment frequency) and are also the main clients of the credit bureaus as they need the scores to help their underwriting process. The impact of the credit bureaus on the ability for a family to finance their needs is enormous as a history of late payments or a personal bankruptcy translate into a low score that can close access to borrowing. Individuals have the right to be informed of their credit score.

Fair Isaac Corporation is the main provider of analytical models to compute a credit score. Their methodology is summarized in Figure 8.4. They sell their models to credit bureaus that, thanks to credit data collected from financial institutions and other enterprises, compute the FICO® Score. As companies are not necessarily reporting their history to all of the three agencies, an individual's score can vary from one agency to another. Fair Isaac is also selling industry-specific FICO® Score models that take into account the type of credit (e.g., credit card, auto loan) that the borrower is considering.

Credit scores are updated regularly and can be obtained from one of the credit bureaus. Many credit card companies and banks provide real time data on their websites as well. Figure 8.5 summarizes the interpretation of a credit score. During the 2007 crisis, the expression "subprime" became popular. There is no standard definition of a subprime borrower but as the name indicates, it refers to individuals with a low credit score, typically with a FICO® Score below the 620–670 range. The dominant reason behind the 2007 crisis was the high volume of mortgages granted to subprime borrowers (and to borrowers who did not provide income or asset documentation) who defaulted on their loans.

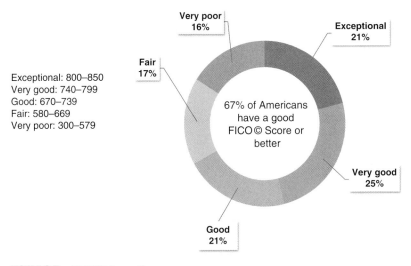

Exceptional: 800–850
Very good: 740–799
Good: 670–739
Fair: 580–669
Very poor: 300–579

67% of Americans
have a good
FICO © Score or
better

FIGURE 8.5   FICO® Score Ranges
Source: Experian www.experian.com, "What Is a Good Credit Score?"

Equipped with basic tax information summarizing the income of a borrower and a FICO® Score reflecting their liabilities and credit history, lenders still have to decide to whom they want to extend credit. It's not a straightforward decision as the information they have reflects past performance, which as the old saying goes, is no guaranty of future results. Another objective is to avoid "false negatives," such as rejecting an application as the result of the outcome of an algorithm that would otherwise fit the lender's risk appetite.

DECISIONS BY LENDERS

Income, asset, tax records, FICO® scores, and other data points define the creditworthiness of a borrower. Lenders must then decide to whom they want to lend money, based primarily on the type of credit being requested and their own strategy and risk appetite, both at the individual and portfolio levels. As always in financial services, lenders must first design the ideal profile of customers they want, and then make case-by-case decisions to produce the portfolio they want.

Experienced lenders with a long history and large-scale portfolios supplement public information with their own research to be able to maximize the number of borrowers and at the same time to reduce the amount of credit losses. With the advance of artificial intelligence and predictive analytics tools, it is a rapidly evolving topic. Data science is becoming critical for companies to be able to exploit their own data and to incorporate outside information for building a sustainable competitive advantage. Lenders are now supplementing traditional financial information with data scraped from borrower's social media footprints, where data mining and advanced analytics may indicate that an individual's repayment likelihood is highly correlated by certain types of activities on social media. A large amount of new data is becoming available and has the potential to sharpen the profile of a potential borrower and predict with more accuracy their future behavior.

Risk management is very different for fixed and revolving facilities. For fixed facilities such as mortgages and auto loans, key decisions are made prior to the execution of the legal documents and lenders have no opportunities to reduce their risk once the funding has occurred. Lenders of revolving facilities, on the contrary, like credit cards or HELOCs, can adopt more dynamic strategies and modify the terms of the loans at any time. They can react to a deterioration of the credit quality of a specific borrower, such as reducing limits or charging higher interest rates, or modify the terms of an entire segment of their portfolio, affecting thousands of individuals at the same time.

Mortgage Lenders

Prior to funding, but after credit approval, mortgage lenders have ways to strengthen their position and to reduce the risk of losing money. They can adapt the mortgage they are willing to underwrite based on the profile of the property and require other structural mitigants. Here are the main mitigating techniques to reduce risk:

- Loan-to-value ratio (LTV): this is the amount of money lent compared to the appraised value of the property. If a house is appraised at $100,000, a lender will typically limit the LTV to 80 percent and lend no more than $80,000. The remaining $20,000 is financed by equity (savings) from the borrower. The objective for the lender is to build a cushion to reduce or eliminate losses in case of default. Upon default and subsequent foreclosure, the lender's recovery on the property would have to be less than $80,000 before losses are incurred. As the mortgage is paid down over time, the LTV declines, which naturally mitigates the lender's risk, as the borrower's equity rises providing more cushion. If they repossess the asset when for example $75,000 is still due on the mortgage, they have a good chance to recover more than $75,000, which would eliminate their losses even after paying for all expenses related to the foreclosure process and even if the value of the property declined below the original price of $100,000.

- Interest rate: Lenders can set the interest rate on the mortgage based on the perceived riskiness of the borrower. They will require a higher rate for lower credit quality, taking the risk that higher monthly payment increases the default risk!
- Mortgage insurance: For mortgages with LTVs in excess of 80 percent, lenders can require the borrower to purchase a mortgage insurance policy covering the credit risk between the LTV accepted by the lender (i.e., 80 percent) and the actual LTV. Taking the example above, if a lender is comfortable with an LTV of 80 percent but the borrower cannot contribute $20,000 but only $10,000 of equity, the lender will agree to provide $90,000 in financing if a mortgage insurer guarantees to accept the first $10,000 of losses in the event of default. In the United States, government-sponsored enterprises (GSE) like Fannie Mae and Freddy Mac purchase loans from lenders if they conform to certain guidelines, including an LTV no higher than 80 percent, and require mortgage insurance to cover up to an additional 10 percent points of LTV, that is up to 90 percent.
- Escrow account: Lenders can demand that a certain amount of money is deposited in an escrow account when the transaction closes or at regular intervals such as bundled with the regular mortgage payment. These extra funds are then available to repay the debt or the property tax if the borrower faces temporary financial difficulties. This can be an efficient way to mitigate credit risk for borrowers with seasonal income.
- Property insurance: Lenders require borrowers to secure a homeowner's insurance policy to cover all perils that the property may be exposed to. The lender must approve the policy to insure that there is adequate protection, such as from fire, wind, and flood. In some instances, insurance policy payments are collected up front and put into an escrow account. In other cases, insurance is "forced-placed" where the lender secures the policy directly on the property and bundles the policy payments into the monthly mortgage payment. Lenders require that borrowers maintain an adequate property insurance policy for the whole duration of the mortgage.
- Title insurance: Because mortgages are secured loans, the lender must be the sole owner of the property in case of foreclosure. Without the right of ownership, the lender could not recover its investment in a foreclosure. The risk that is covered by title insurance is that another entity claims ownership of the property. The title insurer would indemnify the lender in case it turns out it is not the sole beneficiary of the sale of the property.
- Life insurance: In certain countries, a life insurance policy covering the death or the disability of the borrower is required by the lender.

Interestingly enough, mortgage lenders have to make all risk management decisions prior to the execution of the legal documents but borrowers have flexibility and choices during the lifetime of the transaction. They can prepay their loans whenever they want and without penalties after a short period of typically one year. This happens naturally when people move and sell their house but also frequently in a declining rate environment. Borrowers can shop around and refinance their house with another less expensive mortgage from the same or another financial institution. It's close to a nightmare for a mortgage lender as refinancing deprives them of quality revenue and often translates into a decline of portfolio quality as only borrowers who are not attractive enough for other lenders keep their original loan whereas creditworthy households have been observed to flee *en masse*.

Revolving Facilities

Decisions to be made by credit card companies when they receive an application are straightforward: First, to issue or not to issue a card and, second, if the application is approved, the size of the credit line. Given the competition in the marketplace and the sizeable marketing costs associated with the acquisition of a customer, they have to make quick decisions when they receive an application.

Credit card issuers typically do not even require tax information but only basic data about employment and income. What they collect from prospective customers is supplemented by FICO® scores. But this traditional hard data does not tell the whole story of a customer. Their willingness and ability to pay their credit card debt can change overtime and be dependent on other factors. Credit cards issuers are becoming more and more sophisticated to predict the behavior of potential customers thanks to the quasi-infinite possibility that data science offers now. They can obtain and integrate more data in their decision-making process. They can compare applicants with similar profiles, such as living in the same zip code, changing addresses or jobs at similar frequencies. Then, with the help of proprietary algorithms exploiting the trove of the data they have accumulated, they can be more accurate in predicting future delinquencies or nonpayment.

For existing clients, credit card issuers must actively monitor the behavior of their customers and design early indicators of potential of default (what credit card professionals call "run-ups"). Here again, predictive models based on artificial intelligence technology and exploiting previously unused data like spending patterns or reaction to promotional offers can help. A customer spending less and less each month could be an early indicator of upcoming financial stress and require close monitoring. Someone reacting regularly to a promotional offer like earn double miles when buying groceries may indicate financial stress and signal to the issuer they have to monitor closely the activities on the account. Once they decide to act, issuers have many tools at their disposal such as reducing or, in extreme cases, cutting the amount of the credit line available (which also reduces their customer's credit scores), increasing fees and interest rates to dissuade clients from using their card, or closing inactive accounts (before they start tapping into new lines of credit).

Beside the creditworthiness of the borrower, lenders of HELOCs focus on the property serving as a collateral to the loans. They use a very similar process as the one described above for mortgages, with particular attention to the primary mortgage as their second-lien position means that in case of default they will recover the funds that are left only after the primary mortgage has been fully repaid.

REGULATORY ENVIRONMENT

Consumer finance products are a necessity to help people fund the purchases of durable assets, manage unevenness between income and expenditure, and encourage savings habits through real estate investment. But these same products can lead to an excessive debt load and destroy people's lives, and in the case of 2007, even imperil the world economy. Governments all over the world are fully aware of the need to regulate the consumer finance industry to protect individuals and the financial system as a whole. Regulations have tightened after 2007 to avoid a repeat of the 2007 crisis. There is a delicate balance between enabling the distribution of a variety of financial products that can improve the lives of families and curtailing abusive practices (e.g., lack of disclosure excessive fees) by some market participants.

In the United States, as a result of the 2007 crisis, the business is regulated by the Consumer Financial Protection Bureau (CFPB) created in 2010 and governed by the Federal Reserve Bank. It was part of the impactful Dodd-Frank Wall Street Reform and Consumer Protection Act, named after Senator Chris Dodd and Congressman Barney Frank who introduced it. The CFPB is responsible for regulatory supervision of most personal finance products and the debt collection industry.

One of the regulator's objectives is to make sure that consumers understand what they are committing to when borrowing. In the United States, the Truth in Lending Act (TILA) sets mandatory disclosures by financial institutions. The two other main objectives are to protect consumers against unfair, deceptive, or abusive activities and prohibit discrimination in credit transactions based upon borrower characteristics such as sex, race, religion, and age. Federal fair lending laws on this topic include the Equal Credit Opportunity Act (ECOA), the Fair Housing Act (FHA), and the Home Mortgage Disclosure Act (HMDA).

CHAPTER 9

State and Local Government Credit

STATE AND LOCAL GOVERNMENTS

Our discussion of public finance herein will be limited to the credit risk of state and local governments in the United States. To understand state and local government credit risk, one first has to understand who the obligor is and what collateralizes or secures their obligations. That sounds straightforward, but the public finance category includes many very different types of entities, not all of which are state and local governments. Generally in the United States, cities, towns, and boroughs that are incorporated places that have elected officials and the right to tax their residents are municipalities, which are local governments. Counties are local governments that are not incorporated and are subdivisions of their states. State governments are of course governments. Local agencies that are governed by state and local governments that provide services for the public good are "municipal agencies." Agencies can be state-level, city-level, or multi-jurisdictional level. These entities are all public entities. The "public entity" category extends beyond what is a municipality, and includes state and local governments, as well as their agencies.

Note that the term *municipality* is sometimes used to refer to the whole public finance sector, including all state and local governments, municipal agencies, and government-related enterprises, largely because the asset class "municipal bonds" is the convenient catch-all category used in the bond market that includes state bonds, city bonds, county bonds, agency bonds, and bonds issued by nonprofit institutions, such as universities, charter schools, and health care providers. But state governments, counties, and nonprofits are not technically "municipalities." Yet state governments, state and local government agencies, counties, and nonprofit and certain public benefit corporations share the characteristic that, under many circumstances, they pay neither sales, property, or income taxes, and the bonds that they issue often have the characteristic that their interest income may be tax-exempt at either the local, state, or federal level, or some combination of the three, for the bond investor.

The U.S. Constitution grants rights to states to make decisions that affect their citizenry. States grant rights to local governments and agencies. The local governing body cannot exercise its authority over its citizenry unless particular rights are explicitly granted to a local governing body by state statute. As with municipalities, a county's authority is limited to the charter granted by its state. The organization and separation of powers across state and local governments is complex and varies by state. The state and local government finance that accompanies the organization and separation of powers is as well. Decisions that a state or local government or agency makes can impact the value of municipal bonds as well as other obligations. Therefore, jurisdictional governance plays a role in the overall credit profile of these entities.

In particular, the role of agencies and public benefit corporations, such as a housing authority, further complicates the landscape. While we are looking at the credit risk associated with the obligations of state and local governments, we acknowledge that the obligations of government-related entities, such as housing authorities, may be explicitly or implicitly enhanced by state or local government resources. Therefore, a full understanding of the credit risk of state and local governments would include, for each state and local government, what government-related enterprises they are supporting, and some expectation of what expected and contingent support they may provide.

EXPOSURE TYPES

There are several categories of assets that have risk to the creditworthiness of state and local governments: short- and long-term debt securities (bonds), loans, trade payables, and public pension fund benefits. Figure 9.1 shows the breakdown of the obligations.

Note that retirement benefits are actually larger than bonds in terms of total indebtedness and have the potential for becoming larger over time as benefits' values are linked to longevity and in some cases to inflation. These pension benefits are net of the assets that are in the pension plans, meaning that these are the unfunded liabilities. The total pension obligations, gross of assets held in the plans' trusts, are in excess of $9 trillion. Loans typically represent only a small portion of total obligations of state and local governments, and total approximately $22 billion.

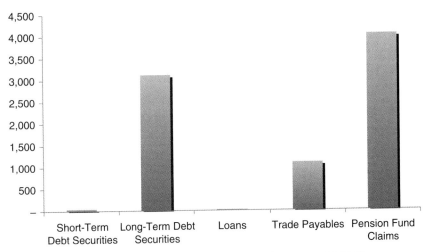

FIGURE 9.1   State and Local Government Liabilities by Type, USD Trillions
Source: Federal Reserve Bank Flow of Funds, Z.1, Table L.107, Q4 2020.

Bonds

There are several types of bonds issued by state and local governments:

- General obligation bonds (GOs) are backed by ad valorum tax revenues and appropriations of states and localities. GOs are issued to fund day-to-day government operations.
- Revenue bonds are backed by sources other than taxes, such as revenues generated by the project or assets that are financed by the bond proceeds such as a stadium. Revenue bonds may be issued either by a government or by a municipal agency. They are issued to fund specific public purposes, with the exception of industrial development bonds, which may be issued to fund select private purposes as well. Industrial development bonds are issued via an Industrial Development Authority, which is a conduit to provide funding for private companies for the purposes of economic development, and depending on the use of the funds, may be eligible for tax exempt status as determined by the use of the bond proceeds.
- Certificates of Participation ("COPs") are similar to revenue bonds in that the investor is repaid with revenues generated by a project, and the COPs are not issued directly by a government but by a municipal agency.
- Double barrel bonds are backed by revenues generated by the public project being financed as well as the full faith and credit of the sponsoring state or local government.

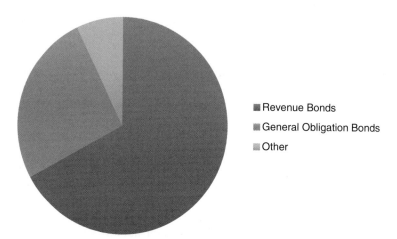

FIGURE 9.2   Revenue, GOs, and Other Municipal Bonds, by USD Volume of Trades
Source: Municipal Securities Rulemaking Board, EMMA, 2020.

The vast majority of bonds issued are revenue bonds, constituting two-thirds of all municipal bonds outstanding as can be seen in Figure 9.2.

Trade Payables/Trade Credit

In Figure 9.1, trade payables (or alternatively, trade credit) is approximately USD 1.1 trillion. These are shorter term liabilities and payables and may include items such as tax refunds owed to taxpayers. Such payables include traditional trade credit, such as payments due for services to school bus companies, waste management services, and payments to other service providers who bill the city, state, or county directly.

Pension Obligations

Pension plan obligations of states and local governments are benefits owed to their employees, former employees, and retirees. The plans themselves are separate legal entities over which the state or local government has a fiduciary responsibility. Note that within a government, there will be multiple plans. Teachers may have a plan, and firefighters, judges, municipal employees, and other groups are likely to have their own dedicated plans. Funds cannot be comingled across plans.

Defined benefit (DB) obligations are a source of credit risk to employees, former employees, and retirees in the plans ("plan members") when plans are underfunded, which is the case for the vast majority of governments. For the defined benefit plans, the credit risk exists because the government or agency could simply become unable to make payments into the funds over time, and thus default on its contractual obligations. Benefits received by current and future retirees could fall short of what was expected based on the contract or terms of employment.

The government or agency has made promises to make specific payments to retirees and in many cases, their survivors. Benefits may have guaranteed COLAs (cost of living adjustments), making the annuity stream a growing annuity. These obligations can also grow with improvements in longevity, i.e., people living longer. Once the government has contributed funds to the plans, these assets cannot be accessed by the state or local government for other purposes. Even in cases where a government has fully funded the obligations, asset values can fall and liabilities can increase so a fully-funded position is not locked in.

The funds set aside to collateralize the obligations are generally insufficient. As shown in Figure 9.1, unfunded pension liabilities are approximately $4 trillion, and total pension liabilities are over $9 trillion, indicating less than a 50 percent funded ratio when averaged across all state and local governments. Each entity will have a different funded ratio; some governments have fully funded their pensions and some have barely funded their pensions. On an entity-level basis, half of the states are at least 70 percent funded, as seen in Figure 9.3.

The pension obligations themselves are very difficult to modify. State and local governments may not have understood the financial implications of their retirement benefit promises as many governments are struggling to keep up with funding their obligations on past service. They may look to find ways to reduce their obligations, but generally they cannot. Rules vary

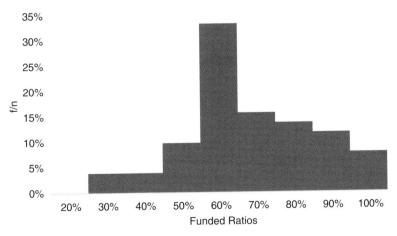

FIGURE 9.3 State-Funded Ratios as of FY 2019
Source: Municipal Solvency Research LLC.

by state, but in many states, past contractual obligations cannot be modified without changing the law or state constitution. New hires are subject to new contracts or new employment terms, whose benefits may differ from existing employees' benefits. And the size of the pension benefit associated with future service for existing employees can sometimes be modified as well.

For example, a city may have a contract where retirement benefits are based on final average salary times number of years of service times a 2 percent crediting rate. When that contract expires and a new contract is agreed to, the retirement benefit may be based on a 1 percent crediting rate. Future years of service would be based on the 1 percent and past years on the 2 percent. The benefit is immutable for earned service, but not for future service beyond the contract period.

Defined contribution (DC) plans have little credit risk. The employer agrees to make specific contributions into the pension fund during each employment year, and makes no promises about the size of the fund upon retirement. It is possible, however, that deferred payments into the plan are never made by the employer. So, there is some short-term credit risk even for defined contribution plans.

The typical size of the unfunded liability of a defined benefit plan of a state or local government is about $50,000 per member, in present value. Across states the per-member value is $56,000; across the United States' larger 200 cities the value is $63,600; and across the counties where these cities are located, the value is $44,000.[1]

Other Post-Employment Benefits (OPEB)

Other post-employment benefits (OPEB) are largely comprised of health benefits during retirement, but may also include life insurance and disability insurance. Employees who retire may do so before reaching Medicare eligibility at 65, and then after becoming eligible, they may still have benefits from the government or agency for health care benefits not otherwise covered by Medicare. In addition, the spouse of a retiree may also be covered under the plan, and the spouse may be younger than the employee, and thus garner more benefits long-term than the employee. The plans may or may not provide survivor benefits.

Benefits vary greatly from government to government, and there is usually a participation of the retirees for premiums, for health-savings account contributions for high-deductible plans, and for co-pays. The plans are usually managed on a pay-as-you go basis, so their funded levels—that is, assets set aside for benefit payments in the future based on past service—is typically low. Hence, this is a credit risk for the plan members on their current or

---

[1]Pality. Data as of the latter of FY2018 or FY2019.

former employer. Governments and agencies routinely change the structure of the plans and participations as labor contracts are renewed.

Protections for OPEB benefits vary considerably by state, and, generally, the protections are not as clear as those for pension benefits. Some states protect retiree health benefits either through the state's constitution, through statute, or through common law. Nearly half of U.S. states do not have explicit protections on retiree health care benefits. In 2015, there was a U.S. Supreme Court ruling (*M&G Polymers v. Tackett*) that found that when language is missing in a contract regarding the duration of benefits, then a court should not infer that the benefits were meant to last for life.[2]

If there is no explicit guarantee that health care benefits will be paid for life under the current terms, then employees and retirees should not be viewing these as guaranteed entitlements. However, unions do try to protect benefits, and contractual negotiations often end up preserving benefits, and certainly may lead employees and retirees to expect to receive these benefits in retirement.

Holders of State and Local Bonds

The household sector is the largest direct holder of municipal bonds. Households own roughly 44 percent of the bonds outstanding. In addition, mutual funds own municipal bonds, and the biggest holder of mutual funds is again the household sector. The household and mutual fund sectors combined hold up to 72 percent of the bonds outstanding, therefore, the vast majority of these holdings is the household sector, either directly or indirectly (see Figure 9.4).

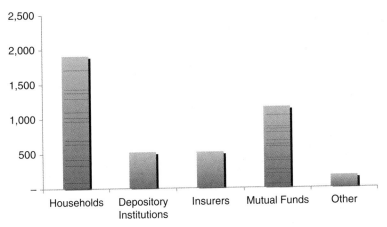

FIGURE 9.4   Holders of Municipal Securities, USD Trillions
Source: Federal Reserve Bank Flow of Funds, Z.1., Table L.212, Q4 2020.

---

[2]Pew, "Legal Protections for State Pension and Retiree Health Benefits," May 30, 2019.

ASSESSING CREDIT RISK

Historical Credit Experience

State governments have no history of default. Puerto Rico, which is not a state but a U.S. territory, filed for bankruptcy in 2017.

State governments have had very few ratings actions by independent rating agencies as well. Since the 1960s, when many states were first issued ratings, S&P has made very few ratings upgrades and downgrades for the 50 states. Alabama has had only two ratings changes since 1960, and Iowa only one since 1963. California, an outlier, has had 20 ratings upgrades and downgrades since 1968.[3]

At the local government level, S&P reported a low annual default frequency rate of 0.01 percent from 1986 to 2019 of tax secured bonds. Most local governments are highly rated and are issuing bonds that are secured by tax revenue or appropriations.

During the Great Depression, the number of local governments that defaulted numbered in the thousands. State and local finance is highly dependent on taxes, and taxes are dependent on the economy. Sales and income taxes are directly dependent, and property tax revenue is indirectly dependent. With the onset of the Great Depression, property owners simply had no resources to pay their property taxes.

With the economic impact of the 2007 crisis, we witnessed again an uptick in defaults and bankruptcies, with 13 local governments that sought protection from creditors.

More recently, after the recovery from the 2007 crisis, Moody's reported only seven impairments or defaults of local government GO bonds since April 2010. In 2019, a strong economic year, S&P reported 11 defaults in 2019 of local public finance bonds. However, these defaults were comprised of seven housing bonds, three health care bonds, and one higher education bond. There were no defaults by local governments.[4]

The COVID pandemic may unearth financially weak state and local governments, in particular those governments that were already facing stressed situations. The federal government did step in with CARES act and ARPA act aid which totaled, as of May 31, 2021, over $4 trillion. These funds were certainly welcome but may not be enough to help a struggling city, town, or county, either from direct payments or as indirect support via taxpaying individuals and businesses that received funds. Many of the cities

---

[3]S&P Global Ratings State Ratings History.
[4]USPF Default Rates by Sector, S&P, May 15, 2021.

that were already struggling are experiencing population flight as a consequence of COVID and the lockdowns, which will add to financial stresses. It is possible that impairments or defaults of local governments may emerge as a consequence.

Rating Agency Methodologies

Ratings provide a good indication of credit quality. The ratings agencies will rate GOs separately from revenue bonds, and will rate all affiliated taxing authorities separately, for example, a school district or a government-related issuer, such as a public benefit corporation. They consider the explicit or implicit assistance that a government will provide (such as a state to a city) along with that entity's creditworthiness, and also the recovery aspect of the issue, should a government default.

Among the most important factors that Moody's uses in evaluating the creditworthiness of a GO issue is the size of the tax base, the quality of the local government management, debt levels, unfunded pension levels, the government's operating history, the size of the General Fund, and income demographics. They evaluate the stability of the revenue base, the ability of a local government to reduce spending, and the degree of organized labor.[5]

Laws about Budgeting and Borrowing

General obligation bonds are subject to balanced budget requirements and total debt limits on the amount of borrowing that states and localities can undertake. Each state has its own laws on limits.

Revenue bonds and COPs are not subject to constitutional limits on borrowing by state and local governments. Revenue bonds are not subject to these restrictions due to a legal provision known as the Special Fund Doctrine (which incidentally allows for state and local governments to establish authorities to issue revenue bonds). This doctrine "provides the foundational exception to the restraint on GOs in that non-GOs may be validly issued if paid from revenue other than taxes—water rents, sewer rents, electric utility rates, highway tolls, and the like—which are derived from a public enterprise that provides a public service from a discrete source of revenue."[6]

---

[5]Moody's Investor Service, "U.S. Local Government General Obligation Debt," January 26, 2021.

[6]K. Bond, "Conduit Financing: A Primer and Look around the Corner," NYSBA *Government, Law and Policy Journal* 11, no. 2 (2009).

The limits on the amount of debt that can be issued are high, and generally may not constrain a government borrower. Generally speaking, other obligations, such as pensions and OPEB, do not factor into the limit setting. These obligations are forms of debt just as bonds are. However, with pensions and OPEB, these debts have variable interest rates (governments often vary their contributions year by year, and can diverge from the actuarially determined crediting rates) and allow for negative amortization, meaning, the unfunded balances generally can grow. State and local governments are increasing their awareness of retirement debts that are growing versus amortizing over time, and are setting targets on funding levels.

Solvency Metrics

The General Fund is the main working capital account of a government. The General Fund takes in the tax revenue and general government fees and pays the expenses of the general government operations. Other funds, such as Fiduciary Funds for the pensions or Proprietary Funds established for special purposes, such as the sewer service, will collect revenue and pay expenses out of those funds. If there is an appropriation or a requirement for the general government to make contributions to other funds, such as pension contributions, cash in the General Fund may be used to make the payments. As a consequence of managing the cash flows in and out of the General Fund, it is this fund that gets looked at to provide a snapshot of the government's financial condition. The General Fund presents a good picture of current liquidity, and sometimes governments may also have established a distinct Rainy Day Fund, which can get added to the General Fund balance to provide a more complete indication of liquidity.

However, for overall solvency, the General Fund balance does not provide a picture of solvency because the General Fund does not take into account long-term liabilities.

The Government Wide balance sheet provides a complete picture of financial condition, taking into account all assets and all liabilities. Many state and local governments report a negative Net Position, which indicates technical insolvency. This means that obligations accrued as of the reporting date cannot be satisfied with the government's assets. Many governments have a positive Net Position but a negative Unrestricted Net Position. This indicates that obligations as of the reporting date cannot be satisfied with the government's liquid assets, which suggests that obligations can be met but to do so would require liquidation of some of the government's capital assets. These two positions—negative Net Position or a negative Unrestricted Net Position—do not seem to be a hot-button issue, perhaps because governments have the ability to raise taxes to correct imbalances. However, as we saw with Detroit, Puerto Rico, Long Beach New York, New York City, and many other mainly metropolitan areas, if taxes are raised or essential services cut back, residential and commercial tax payers will move out and this will erode the tax base, which will worsen the overall financial condition and prospects. So there is a practical limit to a government's statutory right to raise taxes and this taxing ability should not be seen as a panacea for fiscal imbalances.

Recovery: Bankruptcies and Other Credit Events

Local government bankruptcy filings are relatively infrequent events. Bankruptcies are filed under the Chapter 9 statute of federal law known as "Municipal Bankruptcy." Note that the term "municipality" under federal law also pertains to counties and government agencies that collect fees for services.

During the Great Depression of the early twentieth century, there were 4,700 defaults of local governments due to nonpayment of property taxes. However, federal bankruptcy law—protection—did not at that time extend to municipalities. Congress reacted, and passed legislation to extend bankruptcy protection to municipalities. The Supreme Court subsequently ruled that extension as an unconstitutional infringement on the sovereign powers of states. In 1937, a revised bankruptcy act was passed that respected the governance of states.[7] Since then, there have been fewer than 500 municipal bankruptcy petitions filed. The intent of municipal bankruptcy is for municipalities to reach agreement with creditors, for parties to agree to a plan of adjustment, such as extended maturities, adjustments to principal and interest payments, and a plan for taxes and pensions. Municipal bankruptcy is not designed to be a mechanism to liquidate government assets and to distribute proceeds to creditors.[8]

The next colossal economic crisis, this time in 2007, precipitated several insolvencies and bankruptcies of local governments, including Stockton (California), Boise County (Idaho), Detroit (Michigan), Mammoth Lakes (California), Harrisburg (Pennsylvania), Washington Park (Illinois), Gould (Arkansas), San Bernardino (California), Central Falls (Rhode Island), Jefferson County (Alabama), Prichard (Alabama; second filing, the first being in 1999), Vallejo (California), and Westfall Township (Pennsylvania). With

---

[7]James E. Spiotto, Primer on Municipal Debt Adjustment, 2012.
[8]U.S. Federal Judiciary, Office of U.S. Courts.

the help of the state, New York City narrowly avoided bankruptcy in 1975, and in 1994, Orange County (California) filed due to a liquidity crisis brought about by risky investments. The Detroit bankruptcy was the largest in U.S. history, with $18 billion in total obligations, nearly $10 billion of which were pension and other post-employment benefit obligations. The plan of adjustment was multifaceted and involved significant debt forgiveness. Recovery on the various classes of debt obligations ranged from 10 percent to 74 percent, with 100 percent of the pension obligations fully funded.[9] Note that revenue bonds may perform better under bankruptcy. Whereas payments on general obligations, including GO bonds, are halted during bankruptcy, payments on revenue bonds, considered "special revenue," may continue.

Not all states allow municipalities or incorporated counties or public agencies to file. States retain sovereignty over their jurisdictions and some states opt to not allow for filings or allow it on a limited basis or only to cities and not counties. Georgia and Iowa explicitly prohibit municipal bankruptcy. Some states do not authorize municipal bankruptcy but have other workout arrangements for financially distressed local governments. Fifteen states allow bankruptcy subject to conditions, and twelve states authorize municipal bankruptcy filings under Chapter 9. This Handbook cannot do justice to the legal treatment across all 50 states of local governments that become financially stressed and either default or are about to default on their obligations, but the key takeaway is that each state is idiosyncratic and retains sovereignty as to how to handle a local government that cannot meet its obligations. In short, measures that a distressed local government will take either in bankruptcy or other reorganization is uncertain, and thus, how the various obligations will perform as it relates to recovery is difficult to predict.

MANAGING CREDIT RISK

Credit Enhancement

Municipal bonds are insurable via a financial guarantee product. In the United States, regulation of insurance products is on a state-by-state basis, and the insurers authorized by states to underwrite the risk of nonpayment of municipal bond interest and principal are known as financial guarantors. They take large risks on the bonds in terms of limits—typically they

---

[9]U.S. Bankruptcy Court, Eastern District of Michigan, July 18, 2013.

underwrite the entirety of an issue, and because the risk of loss is very small, few reserves are posted. Any loss that does occur would be therefore covered by the insurer's capital base. Because all of the capital needs to be available for the very infrequent but very large loss, these insurers do not insure other perils, only bond defaults. Therefore, they are known as "monolines." Assured Guarantee and Build America Mutual (BAM) are two active major players in the industry. In the 2000s, some monolines underwrote defaults on structured securities, in particular, nonagency mortgage-backed securities. Needless to say, they suffered huge losses and insolvencies and reorganized. Their municipal bond business has performed to date, but the municipal bond industry was impacted, and many, such as the Financial Guarantee Insurance Company (FGIC) and Ambac, stopped underwriting new business. New companies were formed, including BAM, an industry mutual, and Berkshire Hathaway, which established a monoline to both insure and reinsure public finance obligations, which has since become inactive.

If a bond is insured, meaning it benefits from a financial guarantee, then in the event that the municipal issuer does not make an interest or principal payment, the financial guarantor steps in and pays investors their principal and interest and then seeks recovery from the issuer. Issuers pay for the insurance. By virtue of the bond being less risky, the insured bond can be issued at a lower yield thereby giving the municipality more cash for its issue. The guarantee is an important facet for the issuer, in particular smaller issuers that investors may have never heard of, or issuers whose credit rating is not triple-A. The presence of the guarantee removes risk and makes the market function more smoothly. The guarantor, by its ability to hold a well-diversified portfolio of bonds that it insures across many jurisdictions and across many types of bonds and maturity structures, achieves diversification in a way that is not possible for one of the largest players in the municipal bond investor pool—the high net worth individual. The muni bond that is "wrapped" with a financial guarantee (aka bond insurance) will enjoy an enhanced credit rating and will sell more quickly and for a better price.

Most bonds are not insured though. In 2020, for the approximate $4 trillion in the municipal bond asset class outstanding, two large active insurers, Assured Guaranty and BAM, insured approximately $172 billion and $75 billion, net and gross of reinsurance, respectively.[10]

---

[10]Assured Guaranty Ltd. 2020 10-K, BAM Quarterly Operating Supplement, March 2021.

Diversification

Apart from credit enhancement, diversification is a readily available way to mitigate the credit risk of state and local governments. In the United States, 38 states issue GO bonds, and thousands of cities, towns, and counties issue both GOs and revenue bonds. While GO bonds are exposing the bond holder to the creditworthiness of the local government, revenue bonds are exposing the holder to the financials of a public project, which may or may not expose the investor with the contingent credit risk of the local government, depending on whether a backstop is provided by the local government. Bond buyers can select a variety of geographies, size of obligors, type of obligation, maturity, and coupon type (fixed or variable), thereby eliminating idiosyncratic risk and interest rate risk almost entirely. The credit risk remaining is of course systematic risk, that being the overall economy and its impact on tax revenue and expenditures (state unemployment insurance programs, other social services), as well as project revenue and fees. Economic downturns can be localized, a risk that can be mitigated via geographic diversification, but nationwide-events, such as the 2007 Crisis or COVID, cannot be diversified away entirely. Some losses will not be diversifiable, but local (and state) government defaults and impairments are still very infrequent events, even under extreme economic conditions.

Other Credit Events

Municipalities will find themselves in financial distress usually long before they file for bankruptcy. Financial distress is not uncommon, and the COVID epidemic created financial stress for many local governments. A recent example of this is Long Beach, New York. It experienced fiscal deficits even before COVID, had to raise taxes significantly over several years, saw its credit rating slashed, and was faced with the potential of not being able to fund its daily operations. In 2020 and again in 2021, the city issued Deficiency Notes—short-term borrowing to cover budgetary shortfalls, buying the city time to address its fiscal issues.

This is a type of a credit event—the need to issue a Deficiency Note to cover a funding gap—which gives a clear signal that operating cash flows are insufficient, and therefore the ability to make debt service is called into question. Bond insurance on the town's prior bond issues covers shortfalls on those issues, but the deficiency bonds and tax anticipation notes are not insured.

In addition, there are many facets of state and local government and their affiliated state and local agencies that are manifestations of credit events beyond what happens to municipal bonds.

First, if the issuer's revenue falls short or if expenditures are larger than projections, and its ability to meet its debt service is jeopardized, the issuer has the ability to raise taxes. Municipalities, agencies, and other local governments have the right to tax residents or business activities to meet their GO bond obligations. Cities, towns, and counties tax their residents with property taxes, fees, and may have sales and other taxes that would apply to nonresidents as well. This ability to tax is a form of credit enhancement for certain bonds. In addition to bonds being issued to repay debt with specific streams of revenue, such as income or sales taxes, GOs are issued with this specific provision that bond investors will be paid back even if this requires increasing taxes to do so. Municipal agencies may also have the right to tax people based on their residency, such as a school district or a fire district. The immediate or first response to financial stress or distress is to raise taxes, and the taxpayers are essentially in a first-loss position.

Second, local governments have monopoly privileges for essential services, such as water and sewer services, either via direct ownership or governance or regulation over the essential service providers. They can set fees, make investments, and approve bond issuance, all of which impact both the residents dependent on the services, taxpayers, and the finances of the agency or regulated entity. If the essential service provider becomes financially stressed, the governing jurisdiction can approve fee increases or can delay capital improvements. The immediate response impacts not the bond holder but the fee payer or taxpayer.

Third, the governing jurisdiction makes decisions that can put various stakeholders at odds, across bond investors, fee payers, and tax payers. As an example, suppose that a local government decides to enact a curfew for public health purposes, as it did with COVID. Local businesses, such as restaurants and bars, will be open fewer hours, and the demand for parking at the municipal parking lot declines. The parking lot was constructed with the proceeds from the issuance of a revenue bond, but now the revenues are below projections, and the parking garage may subsequently default on the revenue bonds that it issued. So, in this example, while the parking authority itself was a good credit and did not stray from its business plan, the decisions made by the local government impacted the business environment that had a consequence on the liability issued by the authority, and thereby the assets that its investors hold. In this example, the citizenry enjoys a public safety benefit but municipal bond investors are worse off.

FINAL WORDS

Because state and local finances are complex, and laws pertaining to state and local government are complex, state and local finance is not well understood. There are many bond issuances, and relationships across state and local governments and their agencies are also not well understood, hence the importance of financial guarantee companies, who play an active role in credit enhancement and step in when there is a default, and the ratings agencies that seek to untangle and understand the myriad of relationships across entities and evaluate how these relationships affect creditworthiness.

However, not all bonds are insured, implicit support of related governing entities is not a guarantee, explicit support may not be reliable, and recovery in the event of default is more complex than credit risk associated with corporate issuers because the application of bankruptcy laws vary significantly by state. Each situation of financial stress, impairment, default, or bankruptcy has been and may likely continue to be a unique experience.

CHAPTER **10**

Sovereign Credit Risk

SOVEREIGN BORROWERS

Sovereign credit risk refers to the risk taken by investors when lending money to countries. There have been a multitude of credit events involving sovereign borrowers in the past 50 years, and as with most other credit events, the events have arisen from borrowing too much, combined with a macroeconomic event or recession, or, in the case of emerging markets, growth not materializing as rapidly as originally anticipated.

Sovereign borrowers are governments of both developing and fully developed economies, including the Group of 12, which have the most developed capital markets, well established laws, and, all things being equal, stable political climates. These borrowers—the countries themselves—will have the political will and means to make good on their debts. Sovereign borrowers can also be the governments of emerging markets as well as those that are nearly as developed as the Group of 12 countries.

There is a range of markets that sovereign borrowers can tap. These are the private capital markets, meaning, the global bond market made up of pension funds, mutual funds, other institutional funds, ETFs, and insurance companies who are buyers. These markets can be both domestic and foreign. There is also the supra-sovereign market that lends: The World Bank, which makes longer-dated loans to developing country governments often for infrastructure, and the IMF, which provides short term liquidity facilities to governments and others such as the International Investment Bank. The sponsor investor-governments behind the World Bank and the IMF consist of the most developed economies. These and other supranational organizations issue debt on the capital markets and use the proceeds to make investments in sovereign nations. As with most areas in the capital markets, these market participants, and sovereigns such as the World Bank and the U.S. government, can be both borrowers and lenders.

TYPES OF SOVEREIGN BONDS

The types of instruments are numerous. Many structures and instruments are developed for a particular need that arises at the moment. However, the important characteristics of the debt instruments are threefold: (1) Is the borrowing denominated in the home currency or in an external currency? (2) Is the borrowing done in the home country or is the borrowing accessing markets outside of the country? And (3) are there any guarantors of the bonds, for example, from a multinational institution or other sovereign?

If the sovereign borrower is borrowing in its own country using its own currency, borrowing from local lenders, then there is no exchange rate risk and there is little jurisdictional risk. The risk of not being repaid is somewhat reduced because sovereigns who have their own currency may have the ability to print money to repay debts denominated in their own currency. Therefore in exchange for what would be higher credit risk the lender has more exposure to inflation risk. If more currency is created simply to repay debts, this increases the money supply and, all else being equal, this will create inflation. Inflation causes losses to the lender. If a lender is promised a yield of 8 percent, and if inflation is 6 percent, then the real return is 2 percent. The lender is recouping their investment but it's worth 6 percent less than what was promised. This is a form of loss to the instrument, but it is caused by inflation directly. There have been numerous inflationary events caused by governments printing money not only to pay debts but to buy goods and services. High inflation ensues, and real returns, that is nominal yields less inflation, can easily become negative.

The inflation-linked sovereign bond asset class is large and active for the most developed economies. The U.S. Treasury issues inflation-linked bonds, such as Treasury Inflation Protected Securities (TIPS), whose yield rises and falls with inflation. The U.K. similarly issues inflation linked gilts, and this is an active market. Investors have a large appetite for these securities. In exchange for a lower real return upside, the investors eliminate the downside risk of experiencing negative real yields in excess of expectations. Note that as of July 2021, many sovereign nations have nominal bond yields that are negative, and barring a deflationary environment, investors expect their real returns to be negative as well.

Many sovereign bonds are issued in currencies other than one's own, such as in U.S. dollars, in Japanese yen, or in euros. With these bonds, investors do not have to worry about inflation nearly as much, and as a consequence, the yields do not need to include a premium for inflation risk. However, the issuer must worry about exchange rate risk. If investors need to be repaid in an external currency, the central bank of the sovereign needs to either have foreign exchange reserves or be able to buy foreign exchange in order to make debt payments. This presents significant exchange rate risk for the sovereign issuer. Sometimes a sovereign will restrict private enterprises' access to foreign exchange, making it difficult for them to purchase raw materials or needed goods and services, which hurts their business and is detrimental for the local economy.

As for the second characteristic, whether the issuer is selling bonds into the domestic or foreign markets, many sovereigns seek to borrow outside of their home countries. This strategy is a sensible one since it is always good for a borrower to have a diversified source of funding. A sovereign may use its own borrowing to develop its capital markets, and issuing bonds in external markets helps to get global investors more comfortable with them as a borrower. If the borrowing is done in local currency on top of this, this is a way to gain trust and confidence in their currencies. Default rates for local currency issues are lower than for foreign currency issues. For example, the five-year cumulative default for a BBB issuer in local currency is 1.05 percent versus the same statistic of 1.79 percent for a BBB issuer overall (which includes both local currency and foreign currency issues).

SOVEREIGN DEBT MARKET

The active market for traded sovereign debt has 54 nation borrowers. These borrowers tend to be the industrialized countries. Most are rated investment grade, but not all, and several defaulted in 2020—such as Argentina and Lebanon. The market is sizeable, dominated by U.S. Treasuries (USD 22 trillion), but also large issuances of the U.K. (GBP 2 trillion), France (EUR 2.35 trillion), Germany (EUR 1.65 trillion), Canada (CAD 1.46 trillion), Australia (AUD 825 million), and China (CNY 26.4 trillion).

CREDIT ANALYSIS

The steps in a fundamental credit analysis for a sovereign borrower are not dissimilar from those of a corporate, state, or local government borrower. First is a review of the leadership ("management"), the economy, the political landscape ("industry"), the uses of funds, the country's financial strength and ability to repay, and finally remedies, should a default occur.

Is the leadership transparent or corrupt? Is the leadership committed to pursuing prudent fiscal policies, including keeping spending growth limited,

TABLE 10.1   Fitch Sovereign Average Cumulative Default Rates: 1995–2020

(%)	Year 1	Year 2	Year 3	Year 4	Year 5	Year 6	Year 7	Year 8	Year 9	Year 10
AAA	–	–	–	–	–	–	–	–	–	–
AA	–	–	–	–	–	–	–	–	–	–
A	–	–	–	0.37	0.79	1.26	1.79	2.37	3.05	3.83
BBB	–	0.50	1.05	1.39	1.79	2.26	2.46	2.75	3.06	3.43
BB	0.24	0.50	0.80	1.12	1.47	1.55	1.99	2.83	3.04	4.08
B	1.64	4.53	7.08	9.52	10.71	12.06	13.41	13.69	14.35	13.37
CCC to C	30.77	32.35	36.36	37.50	37.93	42.31	37.50	36.36	35.00	31.58
Investment Grade	–	0.15	0.32	0.50	0.71	0.94	1.10	1.28	1.49	1.73
Speculative Grade	2.27	3.74	5.28	6.61	7.24	7.94	8.52	8.97	9.29	9.23
All Sovereigns	0.88	1.53	2.21	2.81	3.15	3.53	3.84	4.11	4.34	4.46

Source: Fitch Ratings 2020 Transition and Default Studies.

debt leverage low, markets open, money supply stable, and taxes appropriate so as to not choke off growth? Will the leadership be able to withstand competition from other political forces? And if not, is the political landscape stable enough to allow for peaceful government transition with voting integrity and would another elected leadership honor debts of a previous administration? What are the economic prospects of the country? Is its economy growing or shrinking? Is it exposed to the fortunes of a single commodity such as oil? Is the need for borrowing well understood? Is there growth in national income, is the debt modest, can the governments make its debt service, and is there a plan for repayment?

Fitch's Sovereign Cumulative Default table is presented in Table 10.1 for the past 25 years through 2020. For investment grade credits, the historical experience shows no defaults on a one-year basis, and no defaults for AAA and AA borrowers on a 10-year basis.

Transitions of sovereign credits are relatively stable, other than the outlier year of 2020 owing to the pandemic. The credit transitions on a five-year basis, for example, show more stability than those for corporates (see Table 10.2).

TABLE 10.2   Fitch Sovereign Transition Matrices: 1995–2020, Five-year

No.	(%)	AAA	AA	A	BBB	BB	B	CCC to C	D	WD
285	AAA	87.72	9.82	–	2.46	–	–	–	–	–
258	AA	14.73	66.67	8.14	5.04	2.71	1.16	–	–	1.55
254	A	–	15.35	70.87	11.02	1.18	–	0.39	0.79	0.39
336	BBB	–	–	19.35	61.61	16.07	0.60	–	1.79	0.60
340	BB	–	–	2.35	27.65	46.47	21.18	0.29	1.47	0.59
308	B	–	–	0.32	3.90	18.83	53.57	3.25	10.71	9.42
29	CCC to C	–	–	–	3.45	6.90	17.24	3.45	37.93	31.03

Source: Fitch Ratings 2020 Transition and Default Studies.

In a typical year, for sovereign issuers rated by Fitch Ratings, there is about a 1 to 1 downgrade to upgrade ratio. During 2020, as a result of the pandemic, the ratio jumped to 16:1. Even during 2009 in the aftermath of the 2007 crisis, the ratio jumped to only 7:1. Downgrades in 2020 occurred not only due to the direct impacts of the pandemic on government revenue, slowdowns in GDP, and direct health and containment costs, but also because governments reacted aggressively with stimulus spending, and the ensuing fiscal imbalance and stress this is expected to cause. Fitch Ratings' downgrades of issuers, combined with its upgrade of issuers, caused the average rating of this category to fall overall in 2020 from BBB to BBB–. The wave of COVID related sovereign defaults in 2020 included the following nations: Argentina, Ecuador, Lebanon, Suriname, Zambia.

Yields on sovereign bonds are also indicative of the credit quality of the obligor. Yields are conduits of information on credit quality that reflect the global market's views, which is an information set larger than a single team of credit analysts at an investment fund or rating agency. However the yields also reflect other risks such as currency and inflation. The yields also reflect the supply and demand technicals of the market. Buyers may simply want more of a name, and will buy, driving yields down, and issuers may need to issue more, driving prices down and yields up. Many yields on sovereign debt have been negative in nominal terms. Unless there is deflation, a negative nominal yield means a negative real yield. Why then would these yields be negative? Of the developed markets, sovereign bonds are alternatives to holding cash and to holding highly rated corporates and other low credit-risk asset classes. Since the 2007 crisis, governments worldwide have loosened monetary policy, putting more cash into the financial system, and this cash needs to be parked somewhere. Highly rated sovereign debt, such

TABLE 10.3   Sovereign Yields, Selected Issues

Yields on Sovereign Debt, Five-year Tenor	
U.S. inflation linked	−1.808%
United States	0.796%
Germany	−0.622%
Greece	−0.121%
Peru	−3.748%
Philippines	0.854%

Source: Data from Bloomberg, July 14, 2021

as U.S. Treasuries, is one such place. But by all means, many sovereign issuers are currently selling debt at far lower yields than the United States, and many issuing at negative nominal yields. And note the differential between the yields on a five-year Greek bond and the spread on the Greek CDS. The bond yield is negative and the CDS is paying the default risk taker a considerable premium to the bond yield, which suggests that investors have motives beyond pure credit risk taking when buying the bonds.

Table 10.3 outlines recent yields on some sovereign debt.

MITIGATION

As with all credit exposure management, preventing bad exposure in the first place is the best technique for mitigating risk. Portfolio construction is an effective mitigant, where credits would be selected that are as uncorrelated as possible to underlying drivers such as the same export commodity, or highly dependent financial markets, e.g., the United States and the U.K. Diversification would also consider political risk, so that geopolitical concentrations might be minimized. Geographic concentrations could also present natural catastrophe risks, so portfolio construction would be mindful of concentration in such areas as the Caribbean. Inflation and other macro concentrations present a risk, and closely related to inflation risk is currency risk, as the more in-country inflation there is relative to trading partners, the more pressure there is on one's currency value.

There are capital markets products to address three main types of risk to sovereign debt: credit, including political risk, inflation, and currency. There are markets for credit default swaps (CDS) for sovereign countries, currency swaps, and inflation swaps. Table 10.4 shows the CDS spreads on selected sovereign credits (see Chapter 20 for details about CDS prices).

TABLE 10.4   Five-Year CDS Price on Selected Sovereign Credits, in Basis Points

France	21.41
Greece	71.00
Portugal	28.08
United States	9.33

Source: Data from Bloomberg, July 14, 2021.

DEFAULT AND RECOVERY

When a sovereign borrower becomes overextended, a variety of things may happen. The sovereign may selectively default, meaning choose to not pay certain creditors. The sovereign may seek extensions on maturities, exchanges of outstanding bonds for new bonds with extended maturities, lower interest payments, lower par value, or some combination. Often, the remedies sought are with the help from the IMF and other sovereign nations. It is in the interest of the sovereign borrower to work with its creditors so as to have access to the capital markets in the future. It is in the interest of creditors to find a workable solution, because without a solution, their bonds may be worthless.

However, the solution, whether lower interest payments, principal, or longer maturities, results in the diminution of the value of the bonds, which no creditor wants. Some creditors do not participate in the restructuring, and can take their claims to a court and try to enforce the contract that is the bond, with the hope of a full recovery. These creditors are known as "holdouts." This stymies the restructuring process, and can leave fewer funds available for the creditors participating in the restructuring. The holdout creditor must still rely on the goodwill of the sovereign because the holdout, almost always, cannot seize the assets of a sovereign nation. When a sovereign nation defaults, there is a negotiated restructuring, the difficulty of which may be influenced by the actions of the holdout creditors.[1]

The IMF has rules regarding negotiated settlements known as the "Paris Club." Because the IMF's permanent members, which are the larger industrialized nations, have extended credit to other sovereigns, the IMF has a rules-based packaged solution for borrowers when they start to lose their

---

[1] Buchheit, Lee. 2013. "Sovereign Debt Restructurings: The Legal Context." In *Sovereign Risk: a World without Risk-free Assets? Proceedings of a Seminar on Sovereign Risk Including Contributions by Central Bank Governors and Other Policy-makers, Market Practitioners and Academics, Basel, 8–9 January 2013.* Bank for International Settlements, BIS Papers No. 72, 107–111, July.

ability to pay. The package requires political buy-in of the borrower as well as fiscal reforms, formerly known as austerity measures. Other multilateral organized negotiated settlements have included Brady bonds, which were pioneered by Nicholas Brady during the Mexican debt crisis, when Mexico's sovereign bonds were exchanged by bond holders, primarily commercial banks, for Brady Bonds that were collateralized by U.S. Treasury bonds. Brady bonds continue to be a mechanism for sovereign nations to issue debt.

FINAL WORDS

Restructurings can work well for creditors and obligors. Mexico repaid its Brady Bonds, and Greece, which defaulted in 2012, had its debt restructured (exchanged), and now Greek bonds with maturities up through five years are trading at negative yields. Even defaulting multiple times, as Argentina has done over the years, does not seem to have an impact on a sovereign's ability to tap the capital markets.

CHAPTER 11

Securitization

We begin with a definition: Structured credit is a type of product in which the risk of loss for investors or lenders has been stratified into nonproportional amounts. As an example, if a bank makes a loan and holds the loan on its balance sheet, and the borrower defaults, the bank assumes the loss net of any recovery. This credit product is straightforward and not structured. Other financial products, like the asset securitizations covered in this chapter, involve techniques like the pooling of assets and the creation of credit-sensitive instruments in which investors do not share the losses proportionally. This is what is called structured credit.

Structuring credit risk allows for a more precise and efficient matching of lenders' risk appetites with counterparties' needs for risk transfer, and allows for pricing that can be better discriminated. Most securitizations, with the notable exception of some securities issues by government-sponsored enterprises (GSEs), involve the structuring of the credit risk, and, hence, these two terms are used interchangeably.

Securitization gained its foothold in the mortgage market in the 1970s as commercial and investment banks realized that it was possible to originate loans, keep the relationship with the borrowers, but transfer the credit risk to institutional investors. By doing so, banks could maintain full service to their customers without having to raise capital and keep long-dated mortgages on their balance sheets. To this day, the mortgage-backed securities market is the largest single fixed-income asset class in the United States after U.S. Treasuries. Basically, when a bank wants to lend money to a borrower to buy a house, it sells the note on the borrower into a large pool of similar mortgages that are combined, standardized, and divided into units (the securities) that are then sold to institutional investors, who, in turn, pay cash that the bank uses to make the loan. There are a few remaining banks who provide mortgages on a "buy and hold" basis, meaning, they fund the mortgages via traditional banking sources (deposits) and retain the mortgage loan on their own balance sheet. Most mortgages are financed almost exclusively by securitization. Other consumer assets like credit-card receivables or auto loans are also securitized and sold to institutional investors.

In the aftermath of the 2007 crisis, securitization activity of mortgage loans by nongovernmental entities, which had reached close to $1.3 trillion in 2006, came to a halt and securitization of other types of assets also reduced significantly. With many securities defaulting, investors had become reluctant to put money into new transactions. Banks were not able anymore to fund their mortgage loans and were prepared to stop offering loans to their customers. As the U.S. government wanted to help families acquire a home, government-sponsored enterprises (GSE) like Fannie Mae or Freddy Mac were asked to intervene. They essentially replaced institutional investors and became the main buyer of mortgages, absorbing the bulk of new loans originated by banks.

More than 10 years later, investors' appetite for nonagency mortgage-backed securities (MBS) remain low, as can be seen in Figure 11.1. As institutional investors slowly came back to the market and more and more deals were executed, the COVID-19 pandemic led to a record level of unemployment, which reminded investors of the risk associated with consumer finance and reduced the level of new issuance.

About the same time, changes to accounting guidelines on consolidation of special purpose vehicles (SPVs) and similar entities impacted the securitization market as well. We discuss both derecognition and consolidation guidelines in Chapter 16. In summary, the accounting benefit of securitization has

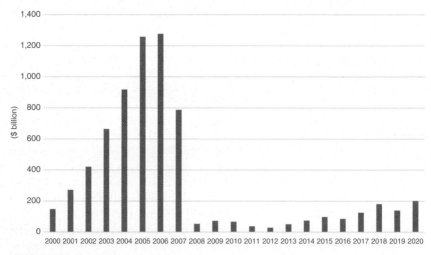

FIGURE 11.1 Nonagency MBS Issuance
Source: Data from SIFMA (Securities Industry and Financial Markets Association).

largely gone away. Given that regulatory capital generally rises in tandem with the amount of assets on a bank's balance sheet, the regulatory capital benefit that accompanies the accounting treatment has also diminished.

Regardless of the volume of new issuance, credit risk managers should understand the basics of asset securitization, since they are likely to be exposed to these transactions.

Market participants do not always use the same names and acronyms for securitized products, which can be confusing, but here are the most common definitions, and more explanations will be provided in the rest of this chapter:

- ABS: Asset-backed securities is the most generic term used to designate securities sold to investors as the result of a securitization scheme.
- MBS: ABS supported by a pool of mortgages are called mortgage-backed securities. RMBS is for residential properties and CMBS is for commercial real estate.
- CMO: Collateralized mortgage obligations are MBS but several classes of securities called "tranches" are created and bear different risk/return profiles.
- Nonagency RMBS or simply RMBS: MBS supported by residential mortgages issued by a non-governmental financial institution. Individual mortgage loans are not guaranteed by a GSE and investors can only rely on the repayment of the loans by individual borrowers to get their money back.
- Agency MBS refers to securities issued by a GSE when there is only one class of bondholders. They are also called pass-through securities. This is the major exception where all investors take the same risk and are remunerated the same way in a securitization scheme.

ASSET SECURITIZATION OVERVIEW

Asset securitization refers to the creation of securities that are used to fund asset purchases and borrowing, such as residential and commercial mortgages, auto loans, and student loans. In a typical asset securitization scheme, the following sequence of events takes place:

1. Investors buy securities called asset-backed securities (ABSs).
2. The proceeds of the sale of the securities are used to lend money to a pool of borrowers to purchase a specific asset (e.g., cars).
3. The borrowers make regular interest and principal payments according to a schedule.
4. The interest payments made by the borrowers are used to pay interest to the investors in the ABS.

5. The principal repayments are used to either gradually amortize the securities or to fund new loans to borrowers to replace the ones that have been fully repaid.

Asset securitization is a technique that enables both the funding of loans and the transfer of the associated credit risk to capital market investors. The initial attraction of securitization for banks was that they could originate and make profits on loans without actually holding these capital-intensive assets on their balance sheets—they simply sold them to investors, whose proceeds were used to fund the loans. Because certain investors in turn have minimal or no regulatory capital requirements (e.g., hedge funds, individuals, pension funds, mutual funds), this arrangement is more capital efficient. In addition, banks are able to maintain client-lending relationships but without the drag of the capital cost. In many securitizations, the bank also retains the servicing rights to the loans and thus maintains an additional touch point with clients, who may be unaware that their loans have been sold.

The mechanics of the securitization involve a special purpose vehicle (SPV) that issues the securities. Although the loans are on the SPV's balance sheet, because of accounting rules, the SPVs must be consolidated somewhere—they cannot be orphans.[1]

Apart from accounting benefits, securitization is truly unique because it isolates different functions traditionally performed by banks—origination, funding, underwriting/structuring, assuming credit risk, and servicing, typically thought to be undissociable, and allows different entities to specialize on what they do best, as described next.

Functions within the Securitization Process

There are several functions within the securitization process that are important to understand, including the following:

- *Origination:* Originating amounts to finding customers who need financing. Retail banks like Citibank or Wells Fargo specialize in origination and in maintaining their client relationships by offering clients a suite of products for which the banks do not have a risk appetite, such as building on the checking-account relationship to arrange a mortgage or finance a car purchase. Securitization enables nonbank entities to originate assets as well since there is no need to be able to self-fund

---

[1]See Chapter 15.

these assets to sell a product to a consumer. The bulk of mortgages are originated by nonbank companies like Quicken Loans offering their products online and without a network of brick and mortar depository branches.

- *Funding:* Funding transactions means finding the cash needed to advance to the borrowers. Traditionally, the monies came from client banking deposits or from loans, bonds, or commercial paper issued by banks. Now, investors specialize in providing funding through investments in ABSs that, in normal economic circumstances, provide them earning stability and liquidity (i.e., they can be easily sold).

- *Structuring/underwriting:* Investment banks structure transactions and receive fees without taking much risk. Structuring and/or underwriting transactions means designing the terms, conditions, and caring for all associated logistical details in a way that aligns incentives among borrowers and all other stakeholders to minimize credit risk and other costs.

  Since ultimately the credit risk is being borne by many securities holders, as opposed to one entity that underwrites the transaction for its own book of business, the underwriting function has transitioned into a structuring function with many stakeholders' interests considered.

- *Assuming credit risk:* Assuming credit risk means bearing the risk of loss of not being fully repaid by borrowers. Traditionally, banks made profits on this function, by charging interest that more than offset the expected losses and cost of capital. Investors now specialize in taking (a portfolio of) credit risks, which earns them a relatively consistent return in excess of noncredit risk bearing investments, such as U.S. Treasuries. As explained above, institutional investors' appetite for consumers' credit risk has been limited since the 2007 crisis and today the U.S. government via GSEs is once again taking the bulk of mortgage loan credit risk.

- *Servicing:* Servicing the transaction means collecting interest and principal payments; managing escrow accounts for any taxes and insurance; complying with various laws and regulations, such as the Truth in Lending Act (TILA); and managing delinquencies, workouts, and recoveries when borrowers do not repay or pay late.

The Building Blocks

Credit risk managers are primarily involved in the analysis of ABSs when their firms are considering investing in these securities. The credit analysis of ABSs requires a review of all aspects of the transaction, which is vastly more complicated than analyzing the financial statements of a corporate borrower.

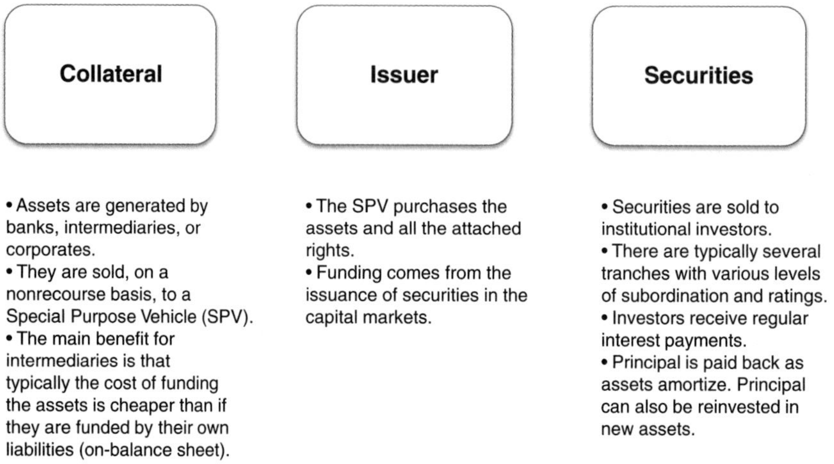

Collateral	Issuer	Securities
• Assets are generated by banks, intermediaries, or corporates. • They are sold, on a nonrecourse basis, to a Special Purpose Vehicle (SPV). • The main benefit for intermediaries is that typically the cost of funding the assets is cheaper than if they are funded by their own liabilities (on-balance sheet).	• The SPV purchases the assets and all the attached rights. • Funding comes from the issuance of securities in the capital markets.	• Securities are sold to institutional investors. • There are typically several tranches with various levels of subordination and ratings. • Investors receive regular interest payments. • Principal is paid back as assets amortize. Principal can also be reinvested in new assets.

FIGURE 11.2   Building Blocks of a Securitization

Securitized transactions are complex in nature because they involve many participants, lengthy and rather complicated documentation, and various cash flows among several parties. The legal documentation provides detailed explanations about the rights and obligations of each party, and each transaction may have its own deal-specific issues, which adds to the complexity. For instance, commercial mortgage-backed securities rely only on the cash flow generated by specific properties to service the debt and not on the general ability of a borrower, individual or corporate, to repay its debt.

The ABSs are issued for the exclusive purpose of funding assets, and the payments made by the borrowers whose loans are part of the transaction are used to make payments on the securities. Investors in ABSs rely on the performance of the pool of loans to be repaid, hence the term *asset-backed*. Regardless of the complexities of an individual deal, three building blocks apply to all securitizations, as represented in Figure 11.2.

THE COLLATERAL

The primary purpose of a securitization is to finance individuals or companies seeking to purchase a home, a car, or a piece of commercial real estate. A securitization does not usually involve only one financial asset; that is, one mortgage or one auto loan, but, rather, many assets. A transaction to finance mortgages is built around, for instance, 1,000 mortgages. Assets are normally of the same nature; credit card receivables are not mixed with student loans. The expression *collateral* refers to the pool of assets that are funded.

Thus, the first step of a credit risk assessment is to thoroughly understand the collateral since there are so many drivers that make collateral nonperform and cause default. As we describe in Chapter 8, there are many types of consumer debt assets and the credit risk manager needs to understand in detail what kind of underlying finance transactions is involved. As a reminder, in addition to the technical characteristics of the financial instruments, the behavior of the borrowers has to be taken into account. During the 2007 crisis in the case of nonagency mortgage-backed securities, mortgage borrowers first stopped paying because of insufficient funds. This was one driver of nonperformance. Later, borrowers strategically defaulted on their loans because they owed more than the value of the home. This was a second driver of nonperformance. Third, since the homes provided collateral, and the recovery on these homes was far less than 100 percent of the outstanding balance, this was another source of nonperformance. In addition, the documentation in many cases was so poorly prepared and the legal entanglements of the mortgages so complex that servicers had trouble realizing recoveries for securities investors, which translated into a high inventory of homes hung up in the courts and which ultimately went into foreclosure.

Before investing in ABSs, one must be fully convinced that the collateral is strong enough to generate enough cash flow to service the interest and the principal of the securities. In the following sections, we present a nonexhaustive list of fundamental topics to review and fully comprehend.

Collateral Assessment

The originator is the entity finding the borrowers and structuring the debt product. Historical data show that the performance of ABSs varies greatly by originators. In a same-asset class (e.g., mortgages), originators can experience very different levels of delinquency. Well-established originators such as large banks typically have better results than smaller, less experienced entities, which have a strong need to close business to stay alive and tend to be less diligent when assessing the creditworthiness of a borrower and less thorough when structuring a loan. Since originators of ABSs do not keep the credit risk associated with the loans they structure, it can be tempting to take shortcuts to generate the necessary volume to issue an ABS transaction. Credit analysts must, therefore, review the history and situation of the originator. The risk assessment of an originator includes a review of its:

- Financial strength.
- Background and reputation of its management.

- Loan-underwriting guidelines: How detailed are they? Are they known to employees? Are they systematically respected? Are exceptions granted and properly justified and documented?
- Experience and training of the staff.
- Track record: Quality originators must be able to demonstrate the performance of the assets they structured in the past.
- Access to information: Do underwriters have access to relevant data about borrowers? Do they understand how to interpret the data?
- IT system: How well is the company equipped to handle clients' data?

The product is the type of financial obligation being securitized. There are dominant families of securitized products, such as mortgages, auto loans, or credit-card receivables, but also unusual and less frequent ones. Even among the most frequent types, some subtleties can be introduced, so attention is required. Like any credit transaction, the product that populates the ABS must be thoroughly understood. Ideally, risk managers should interview the originator and review the legal agreements with the borrowers to make sure they fully understand the type of products they invest in.

The 2007 crisis showed that originators created new mortgage products, called "affordability products," to attract a new population of borrowers. Not only did investors not fully understand how they worked but, more importantly, they were so different from the traditional mortgages that historical performance used to analyze the transactions was largely irrelevant. This was a large driver of the wave of default and also a lesson for all actors of the industry and the regulators. Today, mortgage loans are more conventional and better understood by borrowers.

Marketing information about ABS transactions should include detailed profiles of the borrowers, because their ability to pay the debt in the ABS and any security the collateral possesses influences the performance of the ABS.

The risk analysis, therefore, focuses on the borrowers' credit quality, whether they are individuals or corporates. For corporate borrowers, the methods outlined in Chapters 6 and 7 are applicable for the credit quality analysis. For individual borrowers, refer to Chapter 8.

Leverage, the amount of debt used relative to the equity in a borrower's funding of an asset, must be taken into account. In the case of an auto ABS, the size of the loan relative to the money put down on the car purchase is an important marker for the credit quality. Similarly, for a home mortgage, leverage is measured by the loan-to-value (LTV) ratio, which measures the size of the loan relative to the size of the asset purchased, with a higher ratio signifying more debt and less equity, which strongly influences a borrower's propensity to repay.

The quality of the security package underlying the debt obligation is also important. Later in this chapter, we will provide some detail on features of the securities themselves that drive credit performance as they relate to ABSs.

The diversification of the borrower pool is also crucial. Diversification avoids a single event jeopardizing the entire transaction. For securitizations involving corporate assets, there are typically limits per borrower (e.g., a single borrower cannot constitute more than 3 percent of the total pool), per industry sector, and per country. Deals involving individuals are naturally diversified because the borrowed amount per household is small compared to the total size. Typical in mortgage securitizations is geographic diversification so as to reduce exposure to regional economic factors. The experience in Texas in the 1980s and Michigan and Nevada in the late 2000s illustrates the benefit of this tactic. Limits on any one state may be imposed, including those with historically higher default rates, such as California. Diversification reduces unsystematic risk, but the borrower pool, no matter how diversified, still faces systematic risks of a macroeconomic nature. Pools involving primary residences tend to perform better than portfolios with a large proportion of second homes and investment properties so limits can be imposed as well.

Finally, there are two types of collateral, each of which requires a different approach:

1. *Static collateral:* They amortize over time and are not replaced when they pay off, that is, the proceeds pay back principal on the securities. Mortgages and auto loans fall into this category. Credit analysts must focus on each individual asset present at the inception of the transaction, as they remain in the deal until maturity.
2. *Revolving collateral:* When the underlying assets are short-term (such as credit-card receivables), the originator has the option during the revolving period to use the proceeds of the repayments to invest in new assets rather than paying back the securities. This complicates the credit risk analysis, because the original pool that is reviewed at the time of the investment may not reflect the characteristics of the pool at any later time. The performance of the securities primarily depends on the quality of the assets that are purchased over time.

The investment process of the originator must, therefore, be reviewed more thoroughly because the people and processes in place will select future assets. Additionally, some protection clauses are added to stop the reinvestment process on the occurrence of events, which can modify the credit profile of the collateral. When it happens, the transaction enters into early amortization and the proceeds of the repaid assets are used to amortize the securities. The transaction is, therefore, shorter and the securities have a higher chance to be repaid, since assets of lesser quality will not be purchased. Examples of events that can trigger early amortization are a change of ownership of the originator or if key people leave the firm. We review this in more detail in Chapter 18.

THE ISSUER

The issuer is the entity issuing the asset-backed securities. It is not a traditional company but a special-purpose vehicle or SPV, or sometimes called a special purpose company (SPC) or special purpose entity (SPE). It is created for the transaction and is dissolved when the transaction terminates. It has a very narrow scope of activities because investors seek to severely limit what it can do in order to protect the value of their investment.

There are multiple forms of SPVs depending on the type of transactions they are created for. Most SPVs formed in relation to a conventional consumer asset securitization in the United States are incorporated in Delaware, whereas SPVs related to collateralized debt obligations are incorporated in the Cayman Islands. Some have directors, and some do not. It has no real management (operations are usually outsourced) and does not own anything other than the financial assets funded with the proceeds of the sale of the securities.

Technically, investors in ABSs face the credit risk of the SPV since it is the entity that issues the securities. However, because the SPV is a shell company that owns only the collateral, apart from the risk of the collateral, there is little credit risk associated with the SPV as a counterparty.

There are, however, important details to review concerning the structuring of the SPV when performing the credit risk assessment of ABSs, itemized here.

- The SPV must fully own the collateral. This is a legal concept, and lawyers perform the verification for true sale and perfected security interest, which, at a high level, ensure that the SPV has secured all the rights of ownership of the assets and their corresponding cash flows.
- The SPV must be fully isolated so that no one other than the securities holders can claim the ownership of the assets. The legal concept is called "bankruptcy remote." As the name suggests, it means that the bankruptcy of any entity related to the SPV, even remotely, and the SPV's business must have no consequences on the SPV itself. The SPV must be strictly independent from any other party, especially the ones that contribute the

assets. The main situation that has to be avoided is that the creditors of a business partner to the SPV that defaulted claim that they own it or its assets. If the transaction is not properly structured, they may try to access the SPV and its assets to maximize their recovery. This issue is crucial but routinely performed by the team in charge of the legal analysis of the ABS.

■ The SPV does not employ any staff, and all operations are outsourced to service providers. The servicer is an entity hired by the SPV to handle its day-to-day operations related to collateral management. The credit analyst must be comfortable with the ability of the service providers to perform their tasks. The main task is to ensure that borrowers pay what they owe to the SPV and to handle all negotiation and collections when dealing with delinquent borrowers.

■ The credit analysis of an ABS includes a review of the servicer's financial strength, the quality of its operations, and its track record. The two key aspects of the review are staffing and systems: Do they have enough qualified professionals to handle thousands of assets? Have they invested in an IT infrastructure enabling the constant monitoring of the borrowers' performance? The legal documentation typically includes a back-up servicer who steps in when the servicer fails to perform as expected or disappears. When the financial situation or the performance of a servicer declines, a "hot back-up servicer" is typically activated, meaning that they start receiving the same information as the main servicer and are prepared to step in at any time. This helps to mitigate the loss of experience when the transfer occurs. Change of servicers happens relatively often, especially when servicers are smaller entities.

■ The trustee is an entity hired by the SPV to perform tasks like verifying that the legal obligations contained in the documentation are met, that the various stakeholders (e.g., investors, rating agencies) are properly informed or that payments to investors are made. Trustees are generally affiliated with large banks and, historically, few credit related issues have emerged.

THE SECURITIES

An entity that invests in an ABS is purchasing securities issued by the SPV. Most securitization transactions involve the issuance of several series of securities, each with a different risk profile, in order to reach more investors who have varied risk and return appetites. These series are called tranches, which are at the heart of structured credit transactions.

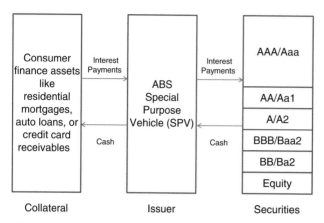

Consumer finance assets like residential mortgages, auto loans, or credit card receivables	Interest Payments → ← Cash	ABS Special Purpose Vehicle (SPV)	Interest Payments → ← Cash	AAA/Aaa
				AA/Aa1
				A/A2
				BBB/Baa2
				BB/Ba2
				Equity
Collateral		Issuer		Securities

FIGURE 11.3 Basic ABS Structure

Figure 11.3 expands the schematic from Figure 11.2 to show (1) the key entities involved: the borrowers associated with the collateral, the SPV that issues the securities, and the investors who purchase the securities; (2) the key instruments, namely the collateral and the securities; and (3) the cash flows associated with the transaction such as the initial funding of the SPV through the investors' purchase of securities and the periodic interest payments from the borrowers to the SPV and then from the SPV to the investors.

Investors choose the tranche they want to invest in according to their investment objectives. What primarily differentiates the various tranches is their position in the subordination hierarchy, also known as the "waterfall," which prioritizes the payments. When funds generated by the collateral are available, they are distributed in priority to the tranche that occupies the highest position in the waterfall. When all the money due to that tranche is paid, the remaining funds are used to pay the next tranche, until there are no more funds available. Since the investor expects payments over a certain period, funds collected may not be entirely distributed but may be set aside in a reserve to meet future payments in the event that the assets do not generate enough cash flow to make required payments.

The tranche on top of the waterfall has the lowest probability of default because it receives or has rights to the available funds first. It has, therefore, the highest ratings and, as the least risky tranche, pays investors the lowest spread over Treasury yields relative to all other tranches.

It is not unusual for an ABS to offer five or more tranches. Table 11.1 shows one example of a $500 million CMBS securitization offering six tranches, which corresponds to six distinct bond issues.

TABLE 11.1 Illustrative Commercial Mortgage Back Securitization

Security	Rating	Original Principal	Term	Spread (in basis points per annum)
Class A	AAA	$330 million	3.00 years	70
Class B	AA	$50 million	4.00 years	90
Class C	A	$50 million	4.75 years	115
Class D	BBB	$30 million	5.25 years	140
Class E	BB	$20 million	6.00 years	200
Residual/Equity		$20 million		

The aggregate amount of bond offering (tranches) below any given tranche is known as the subordination amount; this is why the structure is sometimes called senior/subordinated. Subordination is a form of credit enhancement, because it represents the volume of accumulated defaults a transaction must experience before the tranche in question defaults. In the example shown in the table, the Class A tranche benefits from $170 million of subordination. The total original collateral amount is $500 million. When the principal repayment starts, the Class A tranche is paid first. As long as there is $330 million of principal repayments received in the transaction—that is, less than $170 million of defaults—Class A is fully repaid. For amortizing transactions without reinvestments in new collateral assets, funds are typically used to pay interest to all tranches before it starts repaying principal to any tranche. Because principal on the highest tranches is repaid first, the average life of the high tranches is generally shorter than the lower tranches.

Transactions in which principal repayments are made in the order already described are known as sequential payers. Sometimes the transaction can be structured with some portion of the repayments being pro rata, at least until a certain point, for instance 50 percent of the principal, but these are rare. In these transactions, lower tranches with higher coupon rates are reduced in size more quickly than the sequential payers. Although this is obviously not favorable to senior investors, the pro-rata structures reduce the cost of funding.

Tranche sizes are a function of supply and demand. Investment banks that structure the transactions have a feel for investors' relative risk appetites. They also have the ratings agencies evaluate the riskiness of and assign a rating to each tranche. They then fine-tune the amount of subordination needed to achieve both the targeted ratings and size of the estimated investor demand for each tranche.

Assessment of Securities

The credit risk analysis of an ABS transaction requires a thorough review of the waterfall. The goal is to understand how all the cash received from interest, principal, and credit enhancement is allocated, both in amount and timing, to tranches and to third parties. Each tranche's position in the waterfall is the main driver of the creditworthiness of the securities of an ABS transaction, but there are other structural elements that also influence the credit quality for each security class and those elements kick in if the performance of the collateral is not as expected. We expand upon this as we discuss mitigation techniques in Chapter 18.

Commonly, waterfalls include much more nuance than what is shown in Figure 11.3. Payments for taxes, audit fees, management, and other fees also factor into the waterfall. A securitization will be comprised of many security types, each with varying principal and or interest timing and amounts designed to meet an investor's appetite or aversion to prepayment exposure. Cash for the securities is received in a highly prescribed order based on the performance of the collateral. Note that a tranche more junior in the waterfall might be paid off sooner than tranches above. So, in addition to a security's place in the waterfall, credit quality will also depend on the actual security type and how that security is allocated cash.

We cannot stress enough that each securitization or structured credit deal is nonhomogeneous, with the devil lying in the details. We underscore that the securities' prospectus, which captures all these details, is required reading for the credit risk manager.

MAIN FAMILIES OF ABSs

Many types of assets have been securitized in the last few decades, a few with regularity. The securitization market is also primarily a U.S. issuer market. We next discuss those asset classes that credit analysts are most likely to encounter. Table 11.2 presents an overview of issuance in 2020.

TABLE 11.2   2020 Issuance of Consumer Assets Securitization

Product	Outstanding ABS (as of December 31, 2020)	2020 ABS Issuance
Residential Mortgages (excluding proportional Agency MBS)	2,179	651
Auto Loans	206	108
Student Loans	144	19
Credit Card Debt	68	3

Source: Data from SIFMA (Securities Industry and Financial Markets Association), USD Billions.

Residential Mortgage-Backed Securities

Residential mortgage-backed securities (MBS) is the largest asset class after U.S. Treasuries and, thus, merits our attention. Before the crisis, this asset class was appreciated by investors for its stability, liquidity, and sheer market size. Until the early 2000s, the vast majority of MBS were guaranteed by the federal housing agencies, Fannie Mae, Freddie Mac, Ginnie Mae, the Federal Housing Administration, the Federal Home Loan Bank, and the National Credit Union Association and, thus, there was virtually no credit risk in these securities. Although only Ginnie Mae, the Federal Housing Administration, and the smaller National Credit Union Administration were guaranteed by the full faith and credit of the U.S. government, the market treated the other agencies as if they were effectively guaranteed by the government as well. As it turned out, the market's estimation was correct and the 2007 crisis saw the bailout of Fannie Mae and Freddie Mac and the temporary guarantee and conservatorship of these entities by the U.S. government.

Most of the securities issued by government-sponsored enterprises are structured as "pass-throughs" in which there is no tranching, and each security created from the pool of mortgages is treated *pari passu*—meaning on equal footing with all others—to receive interest and principal, and no waterfall of preferential repayments exists. As a reminder, they are called Agency MBS. When they are tranched and different series of securities are supported by the same pool of mortgages, they are called collateralized mortgage obligations (CMOs) although some market participants refer to them as Agency MBS as well, so be careful!

The early part of the 2000s saw the explosive growth in MBS not guaranteed by the federal housing agencies, and the bulk of these non-agency guaranteed securities that were created were designed with structured tranches as described earlier. Refer to Figure 11.1. For both the federal housing agencies, which have for decades assumed credit risk on residential mortgages, as well as the investors in this asset class, important underwriting criteria and information critical for credit analysis include the following:

- The type of product: Conventional first lien mortgage versus second lien or home equity line of credit (HELOC).
- If the interest rate is fixed rate or adjustable.
- The credit quality of the borrowers: High FICO scores (prime borrowers) versus low FICO scores (subprime borrowers).
- The leverage of each mortgage measured by the loan to value (LTV) at origination: If a house has a value of $100,000 at the time of loan origination and the loan is $70,000, the LTV is 70 percent. If the borrower defaults, the bondholder would lose money only if the house, after foreclosure, is sold for less than the outstanding mortgage balance. The average LTV of an MBS transaction is, therefore, a good indicator of its

quality for two reasons: First, a lower LTV means that the house has less of a pricing threshold to meet on liquidation, given default. So, if the housing sector declines, there is more cushion. Second, a lower LTV means a higher down payment by the borrower, who puts more skin in the game.

- Who originated the mortgages, a bank or a specialty finance company.
- The amount of documentation supplied by the borrower: Historically, a special carve-out of borrowers was accommodated by mortgage originators for those borrowers who had cash (i.e., undocumented) income— for example, for well-to-do, otherwise-creditworthy families operating cash businesses. The loans were still considered prime (or A quality) but their documentation failed to meet the Freddie, Fannie, or Ginnie underwriting standards. Thus, they were dubbed alternative-A mortgages and had a market acceptance. In the early 2000s, the category was corrupted, and uncreditworthy borrowers were enticed to take out mortgages on houses they could not afford without the onus of supplying information on job income, a pay stub, or a bank statement showing cash reserves.
- Geographic location of the collateral: Although a low LTV provides a cushion against low recovery on losses, given default, if the particular housing submarket is poised for a correction, the cushion, although looking large at origination, may be inadequate. It is important to track a mortgage bond's current market LTV, not just the LTV at origination or only on an amortized basis. The publication of the Case Shiller index (housing prices for major Metropolitan Statistical Areas) as well as FHFA's (Federal Housing Finance Administration, formerly OFHEO) house price index enable the tracking of current LTVs.
- The prepayment option: Well beyond the scope of this book is the prepayment variable embedded in most mortgages, which complicates the analysis of MBS securities, including the credit analysis. Since most mortgages allow borrowers to prepay without a penalty, borrowers can exercise this option, meaning selling or refinancing, if it's in their interest. Since homeowners often will sell their homes if they are unable to pay the mortgage, the prepayment option will get exercised if a homeowner's finances deteriorate sufficiently. However, if the current LTV exceeds 100 percent, then this option cannot be exercised, and the borrower might, instead, exercise his put option on the mortgage (if there is one, which depends on the jurisdiction) by simply putting the losses on the house (equal to the house value less its debt) back to the bondholder. Second, when rates fall, the prepayment option becomes in the money, but only so for borrowers whose creditworthiness is still strong. Thus, over time, with prepayment, the credit mix of borrowers in the pool is likely to change for the worse. Loan seasoning, or the average loan age, is an important pool characteristic for this reason. Seasoning also affects

prepayment; after about 30 months, the rate at which mortgages prepay levels off and becomes more stable. Various investor and investment-manager service providers, such as Bloomberg L.P. and Intex Solutions, sell tools to enable analysis of prepayment and scenario testing.

Commercial Real Estate

Commercial mortgage-backed securities, CMBSs, are packages of commercial real estate loans. The structure and the analysis of a CMBS is similar to that of a nonagency MBS because, in both cases, loans are related to real estate collateral values, and the commercial real estate borrowers have their creditworthiness analyzed, albeit with more intensity, along the lines of how a corporate borrower would. A key difference is that most CMBSs are not structured to fully amortize but, instead, are designed to be refinanced. Given that little amortization is built in, the LTVs at origination for these bonds tends to be low—for example, 50 or 60 percent, as compared to a residential mortgaged-backed bond that conforms to most federal housing agency standards of 80 percent. The lower LTV helps to mitigate the refinancing risk such that, in the event of forced liquidation, full recovery is more certain. Another distinguishing feature is that far fewer loans, but larger loans, are in the collateral pool, and if a loan becomes delinquent or looks as if it may, the servicers are much more proactive in working with the borrowers to closely monitor and manage the repayments.

Other Consumer Assets

Many other assets are packaged into securities. The predominant assets in this category are auto loans, credit cards, and student loans. Securitizations are issued by banks and nonbank financial institutions.

Auto loan securitizations are used to finance car purchases for buyers. Often, car manufacturers use finance subsidiaries to finance auto purchases. The securities in the ABS are typically medium term because the car loans backing them are medium term.

Asset-based securities are one of the major sources of financing of credit card companies. For instance, roughly 20 percent of American Express's debt is composed of securitization of its credit card receivables. As credit card receivables are short term in nature (most people pay their debt on a monthly basis), this is the main category of revolving collateral. Debt repaid by consumers is used to invest in new collateral.

Student loans are long-term in nature because students borrow during their college years to finance their education and repay when they work.

Other Transactions

Securitization has also been used occasionally for more specialized financing transactions when investors have an appetite for a particular asset class.

Future flow transactions cover assets that will be created in the future, in contrast to mortgages or auto loans that are existing financial assets. A typical example is the financing of the infrastructure construction in commodity production, such as mining, which requires a lot of money up front. The company that sponsors such a scheme grants the revenues generated by the output of the mine to the investors in the securities. For example, a mining company receives a loan from an SPV and uses that money to develop a site. When it enters into production, the receivables from the sale of the coal or iron ore are owned by the SPV, and the proceeds are used to service the securities. It is called future flow because the receivables are generated over time but not at the time of origination. This technique is reserved for projects in which the existence of commodities is certain and there is little business risk involved. Because investors need certainty about the sale of the product, the mining company enters into long-term purchase contracts with several clients in order to lock in amounts sold and pricing, and to diversify the sources of revenues.

Whole-business securitization has been used to finance acquisitions, similar to leverage buy-outs, primarily of restaurant chains. The idea is to exploit the regular royalties paid by the franchisees to their company. The expected cash flows are captured by the SPV to service the securities. Well-known examples include Dunkin' Donuts or pub chains like Punch Taverns in the United Kingdom.

Diversified payment rights (DPRs) is a technique that has been used by banks in developing countries to borrow money in hard currencies such as U.S. dollars. There is a regular and relatively predictable flow of money sent by people living in the United States to their relatives living in emerging economies. An SPV is established to provide U.S. dollars up front to a bank domiciled, for example, in Turkey. In exchange for the up-front dollars, the Turkish bank gives the SPV the right to collect the dollars sent during a certain period of time by the people living in the United States. Investors in the SPV would have to become comfortable with the ability of the Turkish bank to have enough of its customers receiving money from abroad.

SECURITIZATION FOR RISK TRANSFER

Thus far, we have described securitization as a technique to fund financial assets, which applies to the vast majority of transactions in the marketplace. However, there are notable exceptions in which securitization is used exclusively to transfer risk to the capital market. In these cases, the proceeds of the sale of securities are not used to fund assets.

These transactions work essentially like insurance policies, but the entity purchasing risk protection—that is, seeking risk transfer—does not want to find itself having bought the protection from an entity that itself is unable to pay. Unlike most insurance policies, the securitizations involving risk transfer fully fund the promise to pay, were the prespecified loss event to occur. When the securities are sold to investors, the proceeds are kept in an escrow account (and invested in low-risk securities, such as U.S. Treasuries). The protection buyer pays a premium, and this payment, together with the income on the investments in the escrow account, is used to make coupon payments to the investors. If a loss event occurs, the funds in the escrow account are transferred to the protection buyer, and the investors forego some or all their principal. Absent an event, the money is used to make principal payments to pay back the securities holders.

Here again, securitization technology is used to match the sponsors' objective with investors' risk appetite. Several tranches with different risk/return profiles are created so that investors of various natures can purchase the security they prefer based on their investment objectives. Conservative investors interested more in principal protection than in high yields will buy tranches high up in the capital structure which can only be eroded in case of extreme losses. More aggressive investors like hedge funds may focus on the lowest tranches which generate good returns but whose principal is at a greater risk of partial or full loss. An example of an insurance-linked security is described below.

Essentially, these transactions remove the counterparty credit risk associated with the transfer of another form of risk. The motivated reader will quickly note that not all counterparty risk is eliminated from these transactions. Note that an SPV that receives the proceeds normally turns around and invests them, so the SPV faces its own counterparty credit (or investment) risk, which is shouldered directly by the protection buyers. If the investments fall in value, the SPV has no other sources of funds to make the investor whole. Often, the SPV elects to enter into a total return swap in which a counterparty agrees to pay a certain return to the escrow account in exchange for cash up front, thereby assuming the investment risk. Even in this instance, risk is not removed because, although the investment risk is removed, there remains counterparty credit risk. In one instance, an SVP had a total return swap agreement with Lehman Brothers in which Lehman received the proceeds and promised to pay a certain total return on the monies. When Lehman collapsed in 2008, not only did the SPV not receive its promised return, it did not fully recover its principal.

The advantage of this technique is that it allows protection buyers access to alternative markets populated by investors like hedge funds who are comfortable in taking unusual risks in exchange for a high expected return. Let's mention two examples:

1. Credit-Linked Notes (CLNs): Notes (i.e., securities) are issued by an SPV, the proceeds of which fund an escrow account established to make payments to a protection buyer should a predetermined credit event occur. Typically, the credit event risk is higher than with most assets in asset securitizations. If the credit event occurs, the note investors are not fully repaid their principal. Investors in these notes typically have a higher risk tolerance and are seeking higher expected returns than in traditional ABS securitizations. Mortgage insurers like Arch Mortgage Insurance Co. are regular issuers of CLN, backed by pools of residential mortgages. One recent example in 2020: Arch purchased $1.5 billion protection via three "Mortgage Insurance-Linked Notes—MILN" transactions called Bellemeade Re.

2. Insurance-Linked Securities (ILS), also known as catastrophe ("Cat") bonds, are used by insurance and reinsurance companies to protect against catastrophic events like earthquakes or hurricanes. It is a form of collateralized reinsurance allowing insurance companies to protect their balance sheets and their earnings against extreme catastrophic events. The idea of tapping the capital markets to reduce their exposures goes back to the late 1990s but remained marginal until not too long ago. With an outstanding volume of $30 billion and an annual issuance around $10 billion worldwide, the ILS market today represents 5 percent of the total capital invested in the reinsurance sector. The motivation for investors is to buy securities not correlated with other types of fixed income instruments, which is always of interest for a portfolio manager. They can buy an instrument that cannot be replicated by any other investment product.

The mechanism is as follows, as can be seen in Figure 11.4: The insurance company enters into a reinsurance contract with an SPV, which sells securities to investors, the proceeds of which fund an escrow account. The insurance company pays a premium to the SPV and these premiums, together with the investment proceeds of the escrow account, are used to pay the coupons on the securities. The reinsurance contract references a specific natural catastrophic event like a hurricane making landfall in Florida or an earthquake occurring in Japan in a defined period of time. Then the contract stipulates the criteria that would trigger a payment from the SPV: either a dollar amount of losses incurred by the insurance company, in case of an "indemnity" transaction, or a set of criteria like the epicenter of the earthquake and its magnitude

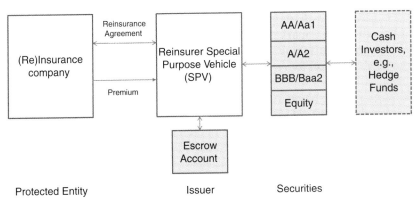

FIGURE 11.4   Insurance-Linked Securitization Structure

in case of a "parametric" deal. The amount paid by the SPV is commensurate to the severity of the event, which explains why the various securities sold by SPV do not have the same risk profile and are rated differently by the rating agencies. If the catastrophe occurs and the conditions for payments are met, the monies invested in the escrow account are used to pay claims to the insurance company, and, consequently, investors suffer a partial or total loss of principal.

For the investors, the credit risk analysis is limited to the way the proceeds of the sale of the securities placed in an escrow account are invested, as we learned from the Lehman collapse mentioned earlier. The biggest part of the analysis is the insurance risk. Experts must verify if they agree with the scientific and actuarial analysis of the sponsor and of the rating agencies, and investors decide if they have appetite to take, for instance, a 1-in-100-year risk that a major earthquake hits the Tokyo area during the lifetime of the transaction.

CREDIT RISK ASSESSMENT OF ABS

Unless an institution is involved in the collateral warehousing business, which we describe in the following section, most credit risk managers' involvement in the securitization world is to review the strength of an ABS. We have already described essential reviews to perform on the collateral, the issuer, and the securities.

These tasks are mainly qualitative in nature, which is essential to form an informed opinion about the overall quality of the investment, and to detect weaknesses or flaws. In most cases, securitizations are a seller's market, in which originators and investment banks structure transactions to meet their own objectives, subject to what they perceive the market will bear. From time to time, the buyer can influence the transaction and demand a change to the terms, conditions, or pricing, which can have a profound impact on the soundness or profitability of a deal. Good transactions usually are differentiated from weak ones in the details, and the credit risk manager's job is to understand the details. In summary, no detail can be overlooked, and experience and specialization are paramount.

Virtually all ABS transactions are rated by at least two major global rating agencies. The methodologies they use to allocate ratings are described in technical material available on their websites. After the large amount of defaults experienced in the late 2000s, the agencies have strengthened their processes and issued new sets of criteria. A particular scope of interest has been the verification of the quality of the collateral and of the originators' processes.

Ratings are based on the qualitative assessments described previously but also on analytical models. Most sophisticated investors do not rely exclusively on the ratings but have their own models. They can be developed from scratch or purchased from vendors. The most popular one is INTEX (www.intex.com), which is the de facto industry standard. INTEX has a very large library of current and past deals. The models permit users to make changes to key assumptions to see how the transactions perform under different scenarios.

The rating agencies' models work with a two-step process that, although simplified, is essentially as follows:

Step 1: Estimate the probability of default of the collateral. Using historical data and a set of assumptions, models are built to generate a loss distribution (i.e., a series of all possible outcomes) with corresponding expected relative frequencies of the collateral performance over time.

Step 2: Input the loss distribution into a model of the ABS's cash flows to identify the scenarios and their likelihoods for a cash flow shortfall to occur, on a tranche-by-tranche basis. The probability of a tranche facing an interest or principal shortfall determines the rating assigned to the tranche.

In this chapter, we identify many reasons that financial institutions participate in the securitizations. A final reason is that, since most ABSs are used to fund high-quality assets, the ABS often secures a high rating, often higher than the sponsoring institution. It is sometimes said that securitization is reserved for the "crown jewels" of a firm. By giving up future revenues generated by quality assets, sponsors are able to structure strong transactions that secure strong ratings. Strong ratings translate into low funding rates, so securitization proves to be an efficient tool to raise well-priced, even economical, cash for these institutions.

WAREHOUSING RISK

We mentioned earlier that the sale of securities to investors is the first step of a securitization program and that the proceeds are used to fund asset purchases. Although technically the case, the mechanics are such that prior to being funded by the money coming from the sale of securities, the collateral assets are purchased by an intermediary and then sold to the SPV the day the securitization deal closes.

An intermediary, typically related to the originator or the investment bank structuring the securitization, purchases the assets (i.e., funds the loans or mortgages) at the point of sale. When enough loans have been accumulated, and the aggregate volume matches the expected size of a prestructured and preagreed on securitization transaction, the SPV purchases the loans from the intermediary.

The intermediary is warehousing the assets, and the period during which the intermediary accumulates assets is called the ramp-up period. From a credit perspective, the intermediary takes a significant amount of risk because the planned securitization could fall through and the intermediary could be left holding long-dated assets, which have credit risk since defaults could occur or the intermediary may realize losses when selling the loans.

This risk is known as a warehousing risk, and it is a risk faced, not by the ABS investor, but by investment banks and originators. In order to receive the mandate to structure securitizations, investment banks often have to offer warehousing financing facilities, that is, liquidity lines to fund the assets. The sharing of the ultimate warehousing risk between the originator and the structurer (investment bank) depends on prevailing market forces. When investment banks are competing for mandates, they may agree to bear 100 percent of the risk. When the market is harder, banks request that originators share some risk. If a transaction fails and the collateral is sold at a loss, the originators and the structuring bank share in losses, based on the risk-sharing terms agreed on up front.

At the peak of the mortgage securitization market in 2006–2007, some global banks were exposed to more than $10 billion of warehousing risk and some lost significant amounts of this money due to their inability to complete and permanently fund the transactions as originally envisaged.

Warehousing risk presents such a significant exposure that much of the conventional mortgage market has innovated a way around this by operating through the TBA (to-be-announced) market. Prior to actually funding mortgages, investment banks presell pools of MBS based on defined characteristics such as LTVs, average FICO, geographic concentration, and coupon rates. In this way, mortgage originators can make commitments and arrange for funding at closing, without having to hold funds indefinitely or originate loans that then cannot be placed in a securitization.

FINAL WORDS

It is impossible to present securitizations today without mentioning their central position in the 2007 crisis. The biggest sources of investor losses stemmed from investments in structured mortgage products and related securities, such as collateralized-debt obligations (CDOs, discussed in Chapter 12), which were primarily invested in mortgages. Most losses were, therefore, due to credit exposures that had been analyzed with the methodologies we just described.

Many observers believe that, without innovations in the securitization markets, the origination of mortgages would not have been possible. Many borrowers, who subsequently defaulted, would not have been able to find lenders to finance their houses without these structured products. Some people view these mortgage products as being "weapons of mass destruction" that created the real estate bubble that collapsed and led to one of the worst financial crises ever.

However, the securitization technology is now 50 years old, well understood and appreciated by institutional investors, and a powerful component of the financing strategy of originators of consumer debt and corporate equipment. Outside MBS, issuance of other types of ABS experienced a dip after the 2007 crisis but came back to early 2000s levels after 2014. The growth in the market may be limited due to the accounting and regulatory constraints of securitization technology, but certain industries like (re)insurance have been able to develop real interest from investors for securitized products and to find an additional source of capital to support their business.

Considering the key role played by securitization in the capital markets, it's essential that any credit risk manager understand the basic concepts described in this chapter and even consider specializing in ABS, as knowledgeable professionals are always in demand in the job market.

CHAPTER 12

Collateral Loan Obligations (CLOs)

Collateral loan obligations (CLOs) are a special type of asset securitization, where the collateral is composed of loans to noninvestment-grade corporates. CLOs play a fundamental role in the distribution of such loans, as banks are active in originating and structuring them but are not interested in keeping them on their balance sheet as their probability of default is relatively high and, therefore, they require a high amount of capital. Notes issued by CLOs are purchased by institutional investors motivated by the ability to acquire a diversified portfolio and to receive an attractive return on investment.

Prior to the 2007 crisis, market participants used the more general term *collateralized debt obligation* (CDO) as collateral could be either loans to noninvestment-grade companies for CLOs or tranches of mortgage-backed securities for ABS CDOs. The peak of the market was reached in 2007 when more than $600 billion worth of CDOs were issued globally. As institutional investors completely lost appetite for residential mortgages not guaranteed by government-sponsored enterprises like Fannie Mae, ABS CDOs do not exist anymore. Today, the market is smaller, limited to CLOs but banks, hedge funds, pension funds, and insurance companies invest new money in CLOs that provide funding for roughly 50 percent of the noninvestment-grade loan market in the United States, much less in Europe. The other 50 percent of the loans stay on the banks' balance sheets or are purchased individually by institutional investors. In 2020, close to $120 billion of CLOs were issued in the United States and €30 billion in Europe.

CLOs first came to market in the late 1990s. The fundamentals of the product have not changed much since its introduction but step-by-step structural fixtures have evolved to improve the quality of the notes. We present here only a high level introduction so that readers understand the basics of CLOs and the market.

OVERVIEW OF THE CORPORATE LOAN MARKET

CLOs involve loans to corporates so let's review briefly the corporate loan market, which can be broken down into three categories:

1. Loans to (large) investment-grade companies are unsecured and the borrower can draw money if and when it needs to do so. They are called *revolvers*. They typically stay on the balance sheets of commercial banks primarily because the risk of default is low and the capital required by regulators to hold these loans is low. Also, they serve as anchors of a banking relationship, so large banks retain them for purposes of strengthening the relationship.
2. Loans to (large) noninvestment grade companies, also called leveraged loans or high-yield loans, are fully funded and secured by a first lien on the borrower's assets. In the United States, most banks always had a limited appetite for these loans, since they are both risky and require large amounts of economic and regulatory capital. As a consequence, they are primarily sold individually or into CLO pools. Buyers, third-party cash investors, are other banks, pension funds, insurance companies, or, more recently, private equity funds like KKR & Co. or Apollo Global Management.
3. Loans to small- and medium-sized enterprises (SMEs), involve entities with only tens or hundreds of millions of dollars of revenue. They are originated by specialized units of large commercial banks and by regional banks, where together with customers' deposits, they represent their main assets. CLOs are also a way to fund them.

WHAT ARE CLOs?

Collateral loan obligations (CLOs) refers to securitization transactions in which the collateral consists of loans to noninvestment grade companies. Any given CLO is commonly identified by the special purpose vehicle (SPV) that issues the securities sold to capital-markets investors and uses the proceeds to buy loans issued by corporate borrowers. Investing in a CLO means buying securities issued by the SPV which technically owns the loans.

On the liability side, the method of structuring different tranches of equity and debt, each with a different level of seniority, is the same as what we describe in Chapter 11. Several classes of debt, rated between AAA and BB, and equity are created and backed by the cash flow generated by the pool of noninvestment grade loans. Transactions are possible when the weighted average coupons paid on the securities is lower than the amount of interest paid by the loans to the CDO, thus enabling equity investors to be properly compensated for the risk they take. The expression ABS is not used to describe securities issued by a CLO. Instead, they are commonly referred to as notes.

There are several families of CLOs regrouping transactions of the same nature according to three main dimensions.

1. **Purpose of the deal:** *Arbitrage CLOs* designate transactions built to fund loans issued by noninvestment grade companies. The term *arbitrage CLO* is used for these transactions because they are based on the arbitrage between high interest rates on leveraged loans and lower weighted average interest rates on the CLO notes. *Balance sheet CLOs* are risk transfer transactions structured by banks to protect their balance sheet against the risk of default of loans.
2. **Risk transfer technique:** *Cash CLOs* means that the CLO SPV purchases the loans from the banks that originated them using the proceeds of the sale of the CLO notes. *Synthetic CLOs* means that the loans stay on the balance sheet of the bank that originated them, but the risk attached to the loans is transferred to the CLO SPV via a contract similar to a credit default swap, which we review in Chapter 20.
3. **Type of loans:** Most CLOs involve *broadly syndicated loans*, which means loans that are too big to be originated by a single bank so banks act together to make the loan collectively, a process known as *syndication*. Other CLOs involve senior secured loans to smaller companies. These transactions are called middle-market CLOs (MM CLOs). They represent roughly 15 percent of the outstanding U.S. CLOs by both count and volume.

A specific CLO is a combination of these three dimensions although arbitrage CLOs are typically cash CLOs, which is natural as their goal is primarily to fund the loans, and balance sheet CLOs are typically synthetic as sponsoring banks only want to transfer the credit risk attached to the loans, not sell the loans.

The attractiveness of CLOs for investors resides in the superior return they generate compared to similarly rated instruments. Table 12.1 shows the spread over LIBOR of CLOs as it compares to the spread over LIBOR of corporate bonds as of September 6, 2019. Note that, for noninvestment-grade tranches, the CLO spreads are significantly greater than the bond spreads.

TABLE 12.1   Guggenheim CLO 2019-1 Ltd./Guggenheim CLO 2019-1 LLC:
Example of CLO Structure and Pricing, September 2019

Tranche	Interest Rate Spread over Three-Month LIBOR (%)	Balance ($ million)	Preliminary Rating	Corporate Bonds Spread over U.S. Treasuries (%)
A-1A	1.43	250.00	AAA (sf)	1.51
A-1B	1.90	6.00	Not rated	n/a
A-2	2.10	42.00	AA (sf)	1.61
B (deferrable)	2.67	30.00	A (sf)	1.83
C (deferrable)	3.70	24.00	BBB-	2.37
D (deferrable)	6.98	16.00	BB-	n/a
Subordinated Note		37.10	Not rated	n/a
TOTAL		405.10		

Source: Data from S&P Global Ratings – Presale report dated September 6, 2019

New issuance of arbitrage CLOs grew significantly in mid 2000s then dipped after the 2007 crisis due different factors. First, investors had lost appetite for structured products in general, despite the fact that the performance of CLOs was strong and was not affected by the crisis. Second, even though interest rates on leveraged loans were relatively high, frequently in excess of 3.5 percentage points over LIBOR, the market expects high coupons on CLO notes, as can be seen from Table 12.1, which made the arbitrage described earlier difficult. If the weighted average coupon paid on the various classes of notes is too high, the loan portfolio does not generate enough interest payments to service the CLO debt.

As the economic activity gradually recovered, interest rates declined and investors looking for performing assets with good historical returns helped the CLO market recover quickly. As mentioned earlier, in 2020, close to $120 billion of CLOs were issued in the United States (Figure 12.1) and close to €30 billion in Europe (Figure 12.2).

ARBITRAGE CLOs

Arbitrage CLOs are a well-established product performing an essential role in the distribution of leverage loans and the provision of a high-yielding product to institutional investors. Next, we describe the structure, the collateral, and the collateral manager of these CLOs.

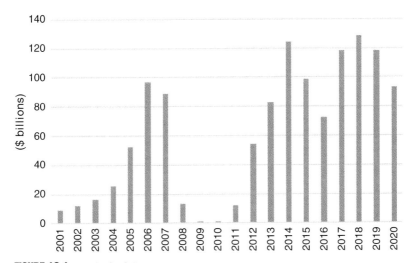

FIGURE 12.1   U.S. CLO Issuance.
Source: LCD, an offering of S&P Global Market Intelligence.

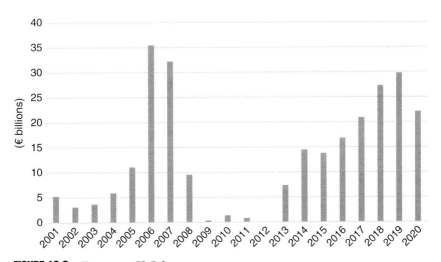

FIGURE 12.2   European CLO Issuance.
Source: LCD, an offering of S&P Global Market Intelligence

The Structure

Like all securitization schemes, an arbitrage CLO is centered around a special purpose vehicle that raises money by selling notes to investors and uses the proceeds to purchase loans. This is an example of a cash flow CLO, as there

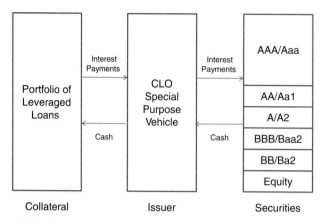

FIGURE 12.3   Arbitrage CLO Structure

is a real exchange of cash between the investors, the SPV and the borrowers. The SPV is created with an expected lifetime of several years exceeding the legal life of a typical leveraged loan. Although investors start receiving interest payment right away, principal repayments are typically deferred by a few years as proceeds from repaid loans are reinvested in new loans.

Several tranches of notes are created. They differentiate themselves by the priority of payment. The most subordinated ones absorb the first losses on the portfolio. The most senior ones benefit from the credit enhancement provided by the subordinated notes and are typically rated AAA/Aaa. CLOs are not very large. The typical size is a few hundred million dollars and rarely exceeds $500 million. Figure 12.3 shows the typical structure of an arbitrage CLO.

The Collateral

There are no limitations on the type of loans that can be included in an arbitrage CLO, but the market is centered on noninvestment grade companies, both relatively large and publicly rated (broadly syndicated leveraged loans), and on loans to small- and medium-sized enterprises (SMEs). They are attractive for CLO investors as, in case of default, they historically provide higher recovery rates than other asset classes. As we explain in Chapter 17, this is primarily due to the fact that these loans are always secured by some of the issuers' assets. In case of bankruptcy, the pool of creditors controls the fate of the defaulted company. They can resell whole or part of the company, or, if liquidation is deemed to be a better option, they repossess the assets and sell them, which provides a high recovery. Leading investment banks like Bank of America or J.P. Morgan originate and structure the loans to develop relationships with borrowers (and their owners for those controlled by large private equity companies like KKR or Blackstone), earn fees, and sell them other services like M&A advisory. Because they have no appetite to retain the risk, they sell pieces of the loan in a process known as syndication to traditional institutional investors, either directly or via CLOs. Note that CLOs are not the only funding source for leveraged loans. In 2019, the net supply in the United States was estimated at around $200 billion and slightly more than half were absorbed by CLOs—the rest were sold as individual loans to mutual funds, asset managers, insurance companies, and other investors. Examples of mutual fund investing in leveraged loans are the exchange-traded funds (ETF) Invesco Senior Loan (Ticker: BKLN) or SPDR® Blackstone Senior Loan (Ticker: SRLN).

The Collateral Manager

Managing the loan portfolio and making investment decisions is the role of a collateral manager, who makes the initial selection of loans that investors can see but, just as importantly, makes future investment decisions, as arbitrage CLOs are dynamically managed. This means that the portfolio of loans is not static. The collateral that the investors see when making their investment decisions will not be the same as when the transaction matures. The main reason is that, even if leveraged loans have a legal maturity of five to seven years, they are often repaid early. When a loan is repaid or sold prior to maturity, the proceeds are not used to repay the notes but to invest in new loans. Reinvestments are typically required for several years. However, when economic uncertainties arise, the reinvestment period shortens so that investors get their money back and can evaluate their options. Whereas reinvestment periods shorter than three years are contractually featured in only about 10 percent of the CLO deals, this proportion reached 90 percent in the first part of 2020 due to the uncertainty created by the COVID-19 pandemic.

The second major role of the manager is to monitor the performance of each individual loan. This includes reviewing financial statements when they become available but also speaking frequently with the borrower's management team. If signs of deterioration surface, the manager has to make a decision, either to keep it in the CLO, at the risk of experiencing a loss in case of default later on, or to sell it at a discount. When loans default, CLO managers owning large positions may become part of the creditors' committee and try to extract the most value for investors.

When considering an investment in the CLO, thoroughly reviewing the profile and track record of the manager is essential. We will come back to this topic later.

In the early 2000s, when the CLO market was growing at a fast pace, many management firms were created. As managers' fees are relatively high, a small management outfit could survive with mandates for only a few CLOs. When the market shrunk in the aftermath of the 2007 crisis, a good number of these firms disappeared and their mandates were transferred to larger companies. There was a wave of consolidation and larger firms managing more assets were created. New managers also emerged and in 2019, more than 100 different managers issued CLOs in the United States and close to 50 in Europe.

Market leaders are subsidiaries/divisions of large banks, insurance companies, and private equity firms such as Blackstone or The Carlyle Group. Table 12.2 lists the top 10 CLO managers ranked by principal liabilities.

BALANCE SHEET CLOs

Banks with large commercial loan portfolios need to hedge some of their positions from time to time. This is particularly true for the loans made to small- and medium-sized enterprises (SMEs), which are riskier and require a lot of regulatory capital.

To protect their balance sheet and reduce their regulatory capital requirements, the banks structure CLOs, that transfer the credit risk of a portfolio of loans to the capital markets. One of the main differences with arbitrage CLOs is that no collateral manager is involved. The bank selects the portfolio and places it into the CLO. When loans are repaid, the transaction either gradually amortizes (called a static transaction) or the portfolio is replenished with similar loans meeting predefined criteria so as to maintain the same average credit quality.

Cash Flow Balance Sheet CLOs

When banks are not prevented, from a commercial or legal perspective, from selling the loans, they do so. The structure of the CLO is then exactly the same as the one presented earlier in Figure 12.3. Notes are issued by an SPV and the proceeds are used to physically purchase loans from a bank. Such transactions are examples of cash flow CLOs.

This type of transaction has always been rare. Their sizes are much larger than those of arbitrage CLOs. One of the largest ever made was issued by Lloyds Bank (UK) in 2012, a $2.4 billion transaction called Sandown Gold 2012-1.

TABLE 12.2 CLO Manager Ranking by Principal Liabilities (Debt + Equity) as of March 31, 2021

Rank	Manager	U.S. CLOs Par ($bn)	No.	Middle Market CLOs Par ($bn)	No.	European CLOs Par (€bn)	No.	Total CLOs Par ($bn)	No.
1	Blackstone Credit	21.27	36	0.80	2	9.64	24	33.40	62
2	Credit Suisse Asset Management	26.65	38			5.08	11	32.61	49
3	Carlyle Group	21.32	39	0.78	2	7.91	18	31.39	59
4	PGIM	20.52	38			7.52	17	30.27	57
5	Ares Management	19.38	36	2.56	5	3.82	9	26.43	50
6	Apollo Global Management (Redding Ridge)	17.02	26	4.30	7	3.15	8	25.03	41
7	CIFC Asset Management	22.88	39			1.18	3	24.27	36
8	Golub Capital	6.14	13	16.54	25			22.68	38
9	KKR	12.73	25	0.51	1	6.43	14	20.80	40
10	Octagon Credit Investors	20.68	37			5.92	13	20.68	37

Source: Creditflux.

Synthetic Balance Sheet CLOs

Banks sometimes want to transfer the credit risk of a loan but either cannot or do not want to sell the loans to investors. As we review in Chapter 20, that is where credit default swaps (CDSs) come into play. It is actually the very reason they were created in the late 1980s. Contrary to cash flow CLOs, which purchase loans with cash, synthetic CLOs acquire the credit risk attached to the loan, and do not acquire the loan itself, via a CDS or a risk transfer transaction mirroring the CDS technique. The loan stays on the balance sheet of the originator. That is why the market refers to them also as synthetic CLOs by comparison with cash CLOs.

To avoid confusion, let us clarify that the expression *synthetic* refers to the fact that the transfer of credit risk is achieved with a CDS or a similar technique. The term *balance sheet* refers to the fact that the purpose of the transaction is to protect a loan portfolio that stays on the balance sheet of the issuing bank. In other words, *synthetic* and *balance sheet* refer to two different characteristics of these transactions and are compatible. The former is related to the technique used to acquire the assets, the latter to the motivation of the issuing bank.

Borrowers are not involved in nor are they aware of the transaction. Loans remain on the bank's balance sheet and, in case of financial difficulty, borrowers negotiate with the bank, not with capital market investors like hedge funds, as they might in a cash CLO.

To facilitate the execution of the transaction, the bank, anxious to protect its portfolio, does not transfer the credit risk of single entities but on a portfolio of entities, which becomes the reference portfolio of the CLO. The amount of protection on each entity does not have to be the same. The transaction can reference $10 million on certain names and $5 million on others.

Also the bank does not necessarily protect its entire exposure. In the CLO it can include $10 million on a borrower, whereas its full exposure is $15 million. What dictates its choice is (1) the amount of unhedged exposure it is comfortable retaining, and (2) the necessity to create a homogeneous portfolio without peak exposures.

One major characteristic of these transactions is that the bank, which does not need cash but only credit risk transfer, does not buy protection on the aggregate notional amount of the portfolio but on a small portion. For instance, a bank can protect a portfolio of loans with an aggregate amount totaling $2 billion but purchase only $300 million of protection. It is reasonable because, in normal economic conditions, only a small proportion of borrowers will default. In our example, if less than 15 percent ($300/$2,000) of the loans default, the bank is fully protected. What motivates its decision is the size of the regulatory or economic capital that is transferred, compared to the cost of doing so.

As no cash is needed to finance the acquisition of the loans, the CLO could, in theory, enter into credit default swap transactions with CDS writers. In case of default in the reference portfolio, the CLO would collect money from the CDS counterparties and compensate the bank for its losses. In reality, investors in subordinated tranches of CLOs are specialized funds with a low credit quality. The CLO, in order to be able to indemnify the bank in case of default in the reference portfolio, cannot take a credit risk on the CLO investors. Therefore, full cash collateralization is required. That is to say, an investor who is ready to take a credit risk of up to, for example, $25 million in a CLO tranche has to deposit in advance $25 million.

The collateralization is achieved through the issuance of credit-linked notes or CLNs, which we present in Chapter 11. Notes are sold but the proceeds are placed into an escrow account and invested in liquid and high-quality collateral. If the reference portfolio experiences a default and the CDO has to pay the bank under the term of the CDS, the CDO draws cash from the escrow account. Absent default, the money held in the escrow account is given back to the investors when the transaction matures. Figure 12.4 shows a schematic of a synthetic balance sheet CLO.

Frequent in the early 2000s, these deals are rare now. However, S&P Global Ratings issued in September 2020 a presale report for a synthetic balance sheet CLO transaction involving Goldman Sachs, called Goldman Sachs Banks USA Credit-Linked Notes Due 2025 (see Table 12.3).

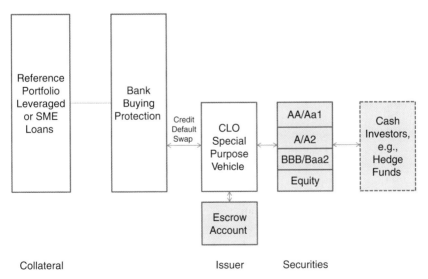

FIGURE 12.4   Synthetic Balance Sheet CLO

TABLE 12.3   Goldman Sachs Banks USA Credit-Linked Notes Due 2025

Tranche	S&P Preliminary Rating	Balance ($ million)	Subordination (%)	Interest Rate (%)
Super senior tranche	Not rated	2,695.00	12.50	n/a
Senior mezzanine tranche	A (sf)	98.56	9.30	2.95%
Junior mezzanine tranche	BBB– (sf)	86.24	6.50	5.20%
First loss tranche	Not rated	200.20	0.00	n/a
TOTAL		3,080.00		

Source: S&P Global Rating—Presale report dated September 24, 2020.

Even more interesting, Goldman Sachs's objective was to protect its investment-grade unsecured revolving loans, not high-yield ones. The portfolio was composed of 148 borrowers and the aggregate balance was $3.08 billion. As a good illustration of what was described earlier, Goldman Sachs purchased protection on only $184 million with the CLO/CLN structure.

Performance of CLOs

The overall performance of CLOs is excellent as loan underwriters strive to structure solid products and CLO managers select carefully the deals they want for their investors, monitor closely the performance of each loan in their portfolio, and actively manage them when one or several loans' quality is declining. Rating agencies have also imposed more subordination for a given rating versus their requirements in the past. S&P estimates that in 2020, AAA securities benefited in average from 35 percent of subordination against 28 percent pre-2007 crisis requirements. As a result, of the more than 12,000 CLO tranches S&P rated globally since they started covering the sector, less than 100 defaulted, and none of them was rated AAA. However, the COVID-19 pandemic has the potential to stress many CLOs, especially in Europe, as a result of lockdowns and other restrictions imposed by public health officials in many countries. The drop in economic activity is unprecedented and, as a result, many highly leveraged companies whose loans were purchased by CLOs may default, stressing CLOs as well. Rating agencies were quick to react and either downgraded notes or placed hundreds of tranches on review for possible downgrade.

ABS CDOs

ABS CDOs have completely disappeared today. Up until 2007, they were primarily used to finance nonagency mortgages to individuals and investors. With the 2007 crisis investors lost all appetite for the asset class.

ABS CDOs were considered to be one of the most complicated financial products ever invented and simply understanding them was a complex endeavor. The structures of the ABS were complex and the quality of the collateral hard to assess as the borrowers represented a previously untapped market (e.g., subprime) as well as new forms of instruments (low documentation and high loan-to-value loans). Even experienced, well-resourced, and sophisticated professionals had trouble analyzing them.

The main source of the complexity resided on the asset side: ABS CDOs invested in ABSs issued by SPVs that funded consumer assets. A typical ABS CDO owned more than one hundred securities, each being backed by a pool of consumer assets, sometimes as many as 1,000 mortgages. To really understand the assets that the ABS CDO owned, on had to go through the ABS, which was complex enough, because an ABS' prospectus is a long and dense document, and drill down to the individual loan level. In the previous example, a CDO would have an economic interest in $100 \times 1,000 = 100,000$ mortgages. This involved the handling of a high volume of data and an actual ability to exploit it.

ABS CDOs differentiated themselves by the credit quality of their assets. We saw that ABSs are issued at diverse levels of priority of payments that influence their default probability and, therefore, their ratings. A typical ABS transaction involves more than 10 tranches rated between BBB/Baa2 and AAA/Aaa. High-grade ABS CDOs invested in tranches rated AAA/Aaa, AA/Aa1, and occasionally A/A2. Mezzanine ABS CDOs purchased the lowest tranches, between BBB/Baa2 and A/A2, and were, therefore, riskier.

Anyone interested in credit risk management must understand the history of ABS CDOs because they played a central role in the 2007 crisis. As we saw, ABS CDOs offered an additional distribution channel for ABS. Traditionally, ABS were purchased by long-term investors such as pension funds or insurance companies. The investment process was rigorous. Each security was dissected to thoroughly understand the underlying collateral and the structure of the deal. If satisfied, the investor would place an order. ABS CDOs brought to the market a new breed of investors, competing with the traditional ones. The success of ABS CDOs was such that the vast majority of nonagency residential mortgage-backed securities were purchased by CDOs.

The most conservative investors were focusing on high grade ABS CDOs, thinking that they were safer investments than mezzanine CDOs. It was a reasonable assumption because the track record of AAA/Aaa rated securities was outstanding, so investing, via a CDO, in a portfolio of AAA/Aaa securities seemed like a safe bet. Alas, when borrowers started to default, the expected strong lines of defense embedded in the structure exploded quickly, and many tranches defaulted, regardless of their ratings. The wave of RMBS defaults triggered the default of the CDO notes as well, which led to tens of billions of losses for investors.

The exponential development of ABS CDOs was a result of two major factors. First, banks, notably European ones, were flush with cash to invest. As ABS CDOs were large, up to $2 billion each, they provided great opportunities to deploy cash quickly. The banks were, however, not interested in taking the credit risk associated with the ABS CDO notes. They much preferred the stable and high credit quality of other financial institutions, notably monoline insurance companies and other large and highly rated insurance companies. Insurers were attracted by the potential revenues and the low-risk profile of ABS CDOs, but they did not want to deploy cash to buy notes and wanted to leverage their AAA and AA ratings. Their focus was on the AAA/Aaa rated tranches that were large in size (sometimes up to $2 billion) and low in default probability—so low that they were called the super-senior tranches.

This is where CDSs were used and provided the key ingredient: Banks purchased the ABS CDO notes and, at the same time, the bank purchased protection on these notes from insurers via a CDS. These became known as the negative basis trade in which the CDS spread paid was less than the credit spread embedded in the CDO's coupon paid to them, seemingly providing a form of arbitrage, or risk-free profit, for the bank. The bank was essentially providing a funding mechanism (buying the CDO), not taking much risk, and making a profit. Figure 12.5 illustrates the structure of the negative basis trade.

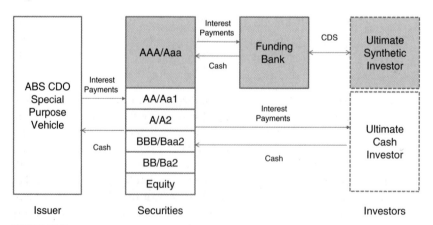

FIGURE 12.5 Negative Basis Trade for Super-Senior AAA/Aaa Tranche

The convergence of a high amount of liquidity available, the appetite of insurers, and the allure of making riskless profits were the major reasons behind the rapid expansion of the ABS CDO market. Once they had secured the commitment of a funding bank and of the insurer, which could represent 95 percent of the total amount of notes to sell, investment banks structuring ABS CDOs had to sell only the most subordinated notes. They were typically purchased by hedge funds and pension funds, or retained by the banks themselves. Thus, these transactions were relatively easy for the bank to execute.

All the CDOs created at the same time by the largest players like Merrill Lynch, now part of Bank of America, and UBS were actively looking for ABS to purchase, which created a strong incentive for mortgage originators to create assets. Thus, attractive mortgage products were created to entice individuals to take on mortgages to buy real estate.

We will not elaborate further on this topic but wanted to provide our readers with an overview of the techniques used in the mid-2000s to finance consumer assets and, notably, mortgages. As we saw, ABS CDOs and CDSs played crucial roles.

CREDIT ANALYSIS OF CLOs

In Chapter 11, we provid a framework for analyzing a securitization scheme that provides a basis for understanding CLOs. In the following, we give an overview of other relevant topics for CLOs.

Quality of Collateral

Each CLO comes with special parameters that constitute the guidelines that the collateral manager must respect when building the portfolio and reinvesting the cash available during the lifetime of the structure. These parameters provide a first opportunity for investors to judge if they are interested in the CLO or not.

The first criterion to check is the quality of each individual loan composing the CLO's asset. Not all leveraged loans have the same structure, and some of them are inherently prone to default. Collateral managers are commonly restricted from purchasing too many risky types, such as second liens or debtor-in-possession loans that are extended to defaulted companies. We review these loans in Chapter 21 in the context of bankruptcy. It is typical to have a minimum high threshold, e.g., 90 percent of first-lien senior secured obligations. Then, there is a low ceiling for loans rated CCC/Caa, typically less than 10 percent.

One of the key parameters is the weighted-average rating factor, or WARF. This is a number that's calculated with a formula developed by rating agencies. For instance, Moody's assigns a rating factor of 1 to a loan with a default probability rating of Aaa, a rating factor of 360 to a loan rated Baa2, and a rating factor of 1,350 to a loan rated Ba2. The first step to calculate the WARF is to compute the product of the par amount (e.g., $10 million) of each loan by its rating factor (e.g., 1,350). Then, we add the value obtained for all loans in the portfolio, and the WARF is the result divided by the par amount of the entire portfolio. A CLO with a minimum WARF of 2,000 has, on average, a better portfolio than a CLO with a target WARF of 2,300. The higher the number, the more aggressive the CLO is. The loans, and notes, may generate higher interest payments but the risk of default is also higher.

Another parameter is the weighted-average spread, or WAS. Arbitrage CLOs, not created to protect a balance sheet but to distribute leveraged loans, are based on the principle that, by creating tranches of different ratings, the aggregate interest payments on the notes are less than the amount of interest generated by the collateral assets. To verify that this is actually the case, CLOs are created with a minimum WAS, which guarantees that when assets are selected, the amount of interest they pay is taken into account. A weighted-average coupon (WAC) is also computed and the difference between WAS and WAC provides a good indicator of the strength of the CLO—the higher the better. Overall, WAS guarantees that there is enough cash generated by the assets to service the notes and provide a decent return to equity investors.

We mentioned earlier that leveraged loans are highly secured by some assets of the borrowers. In case of default, the lenders can access the assets in priority, thus increasing the recovery. A few years ago, rating agencies started forecasting the recovery in case of default (which we discuss in Chapter 17) and assigning a recovery rating. CLOs typically include a weighted average recovery rating or WARR aimed at selecting assets subject to a minimum amount of expected recovery, which improves the creditworthiness of the CLO.

Recently, rating agencies started paying attention to environmental, social, and governance (ESG) risks as well. For instance, a high proportion of loans extended to the energy or the chemicals sector would be considered a significant risk factor.

Finally, let us mention various parameters designed to avoid concentration and create diversification in the portfolio. The most common ones are the single obligor concentration (typically less than 3 percent), the maximum industry sector concentration, and the diversity score, also calculated with a formula proposed by rating agencies.

Structural Mitigants

Because the CLO's assets are risky by nature, structural mitigants are in place to accelerate the repayments to notes buyers if the portfolio deteriorates. The general principles are explained in an earlier chapter, but let us mention the two most important tests for a CLO.

The first one is the overcollateralization test or O/C test for a specific tranche. It is a ratio measuring the aggregate notional of assets over the notional of the tranche and the previous tranches. The exact calculation is a little complicated, but the idea is that there is always more collateral than the outstanding amount of notes to be repaid. Similarly, all CLOs include interest coverage, or I/C, ratio, aiming at ensuring that the collateral pool generates more interest payments than the amount of interest to be paid to investors in the notes. Breaching an O/C test or an I/C test commonly triggers the immediate amortization of the CLO. The notes become immediately due, no new investment is allowed, and interest payments to junior investors are suspended (or diverted) until senior investors are fully repaid.

Assessing the Manager

In today's market, collateral managers are strong companies, as the smallest entities did not survive the 2007 crisis. However, there are still notable differences between managers. The main areas to pay attention to are:

- Track record: Most managers have been involved in the management of CLOs for a number of years. The best indicator of their performance is the behavior of their CLOs over the years and particularly at times when defaults were high. Assessing the performance of their CLOs during the 2007 crisis period provides a real-life test. Investors can verify how many CLOs experienced O/C test breaches, if dividends payments to equity investors were suspended, and how long this lasted. Also, one of the key questions is how many loans in their portfolios experienced default. When asking this question, note that sometimes managers sell loans at deep discounts slightly before the loans default to improve their statistics.
- Financial strength: Not all managers have the same level of funding, which can be an issue because it is indispensable for managers to have the necessary resources to hire quality professionals and to invest in a robust infrastructure. Some managers are part of large organizations with access to resources. Some are much smaller firms or they are independent and only involved in the management of CLOs. Investors should not be afraid to require full disclosure of the financial statements.

■ Key personnel: The quality of the staff is obviously important. Good portfolio managers are professionals who have been involved in the business a long time and who have a deep knowledge of the way the market works. Some individuals are so necessary to the performance that it is usual to have a key-man provision that allows investors to change managers if these individuals leave the firm.

Quantitative Analysis

To assess the quality of the notes issued, rating agencies and investors run scenarios to simulate defaults of loans, based on the ratings of each loan, and level the correlations between loans. The outcome of the scenarios, together with the notional amount of each loan, their expected recovery rates, and the various structural elements of the CLO enable researchers to build a cash-flow model leading to a probability of default of each tranche of notes issued by the SPV.

Portfolio Management

Credit Portfolio Management

We have focused so far on the origination and analysis of individual transactions and provided methodologies to assess the credit risk generated by a new deal. Should we be satisfied and consider that this is enough to protect a firm's balance sheet?

The answer is a clear no. What we are missing is the portfolio dimension as each new transaction contributes to the complexion of all existing transactions combined, the total of which is not equal to the sum of its parts. Even if each single deal satisfies all the firm's risk criteria, concluding too many of them can lead to the creation of an unbalanced portfolio loaded with exposures of the same nature, which is dangerous.

The role of the credit portfolio management (CPM) unit is to take a big-picture view and manage the risk of the portfolio in its entirety. Credit risk assessment and CPM are two complementary disciplines, staffed with people having different background and skills. The former focuses on individual deals, and the latter concentrates on the entire portfolio. Credit portfolio management is more strategic in nature, and, based on the firm's risk appetite, it sets the vision for the portfolio it wants to create and the direction that the originators should follow. If originators cannot execute this, if external events lead to unwanted changes, or if the firm changes priorities, then CPM implements corrective action.

Credit portfolio management has evolved significantly over the last 20 years. Once reserved to large banks with large portfolios, it is now implemented by most institutions that actively generate credit exposures. Two main factors contributed to this phenomenon: analytical tools and liquidity.

In the late 1980s, analytical tools took a leap forward when computers became more efficient and widespread. Mathematical models were developed and provided the foundation of modern CPM activities. Nowadays, all large financial institutions and some corporates have models to perform data-intensive and complex analysis. In addition, data have become more plentiful, and now market data such as default correlations across obligors, industries, and so forth are inputs into models. Once hard to obtain, the necessary data are now widely available because many vendors collect, process, and sell the data in a user-friendly format.

By liquidity, we mean the ability to buy and sell exposures when needed. In the not so distant past, few methods existed to get rid of unwanted positions. A few pioneers were trying to develop the CPM concepts and knew what actions should be taken in an ideal world, but implementation was nearly impossible. Without the ability to execute rebalancing transactions, CPM remained an academic exercise. Things changed in earnest in the late 1980s when a few banks engineered the development of new products, notably credit default swaps and credit securitization, which provided financial institutions with a toolbox to work on optimizing their portfolios.

Credit portfolio management is a discipline that requires significant resources, human and financial. As a result, developing a fully fledged CPM function is not realistic for all firms. Although it is inconceivable for a large financial institution not to invest in CPM, smaller companies with stable, modest, or unsellable portfolios may not be able to justify the resource allocation. The risk management function must be pragmatic and must size its CPM capabilities to be appropriate to the credit exposures assumed. Building a state-of-the-art credit risk management framework is not done in a day. It typically starts with establishing discipline around the origination process. Credit portfolio management, being one of four components (as a reminder: origination, assessment, CPM, transfer) of the credit risk management process, competes for resources with the other components and should not come at the expense of other parts of the chain, such as fundamental credit analysis.

That being said, hedge funds need to have all tools in place when they start trading, because modern financial techniques enable them to grow a portfolio rapidly. Credit portfolio management will be identified as a fundamental function during the development of the business plan, and execution should start immediately. Another example is financial institutions that are heavily regulated. As we discuss in Chapters 14 and 15, methods developed by CPM teams are indispensable to calculate the amount of capital at risk. Some regulators may not grant the permission to start a business if the entity has not developed the infrastructure necessary to perform the analysis and report compulsory numbers.

Our suggestion is, therefore, to thoroughly consider one's own situation, to review what the objectives are, and to adopt a realistic strategy. If needs and resources are limited, a simple approach to portfolio management is sufficient.

In the sections that follow, we describe three different levels of CPM activities practiced by companies that have significant credit risk exposures. Companies will generally scale their CPM activities to their needs and resources. For example, a highly sophisticated process would be inappropriate for a small or midsized firm for which credit exposure is a by-product of its core business. Implementation can also be gradual and scalable. As progress is made or major changes occur in the portfolio, the next level can be considered, which might include a comprehensive cost/benefit analysis that measures the benefit against incremental staffing, software, and other IT expenses.

LEVEL 1

Basic CPM consists of the minimum activities that need to be performed by any company exposed to credit risk. It does not require sophisticated analytical capabilities but common sense, a well-managed organization, and skilled people. The focus is on prudent risk taking via strict limits, on the knowledge of the composition of the portfolio, and on the monitoring of its performance. Elementary defensive actions can be taken to protect unwanted or deteriorating exposures. This is an adequate level of CPM for companies taking credit risk as a by-product of their core activities (e.g., trade receivables) or involved in simple transactions.

The techniques described below are relatively simple to execute and appropriate under what we have labeled Level 1 CPM. They meet the objective of limiting concentration risk and thereby reducing credit risk in the aggregate. They do not require a large infrastructure and can be implemented by most companies.

Aggregation

Managing a portfolio of credit exposures starts with measuring the accumulation of risk for each counterparty, which is called aggregation. Chapter 4 describes the three ways to measure the exposure: GE, NE, and AE. The chapter focuses on individual transactions and proposed a methodology to measure the credit risk for each and every deal. There is nothing to add about this approach as this is the way to work with transactions viewed in isolation. As the first CPM step, we measure the accumulation of risk across multiple transactions on a counterparty-by-counterparty basis. One division of a firm may sell a product to Company ABC, generating a trade receivable, and another division may enter into a derivative transaction with the same Company ABC, generating a dynamic credit exposure. The two exposures must be aggregated because if Company ABC were to default, losses would be experienced on both exposures.

This first CPM step requires identifying all companies that are related and how they are related. The ultimate parent needs to be identified along with each subsidiary and affiliate on a global basis. The default of one company belonging to a group may trigger the default of some or all associated entities. Even if they do not all default, the default of a subsidiary may indicate the inability of a group to support an affiliate, which may signal financial weakness. The ultimate parent may also default and that may trigger the default of some or all affiliated companies. When a multinational company files for bankruptcy protection, it's not unusual that all group entities, including foreign subsidiaries, file for bankruptcy at the same time. It is, therefore, prudent to consolidate exposures based on the ultimate parent company and on all its subsidiaries. By quantifying and monitoring the exposure this way, the worst-case scenario is more likely to be captured. This is not as straightforward as it sounds as sometimes domestic or foreign subsidiaries do not bear the same name as their parents. Inputting properly the name of the parent and all its subsidiaries in the organization's database is essential to track global activities with the same entity.

For those entities that have only partial ownership or for joint ventures, there is no general rule but a judgement call is needed. The risk manager must understand the role of the partially owned company, and if there is a chance that the default of one entity triggers the default of the other one, then exposures should be aggregated.

In implementing this measurement system, a central database that groups all exposures must be developed. This task is so essential that some large institutions have a unit fully dedicated to it. The unit is staffed by professionals who know the organization well enough to surface all types of transactions generating credit risk. This function benefits from diplomacy since business managers are prone to deny that their products bear any credit risk to avoid having to abide by yet another set of guidelines or be subject to another level of approval, or have their turf stepped on by a risk manager.

Reporting

Risk management must provide frequent and regular updates on the content of the credit portfolio. The report must also be user friendly and allow its readers, primarily senior management, to quickly assess key exposure metrics. It is common for banks to prepare a daily summary report since exposures can change quickly, with new transactions coming on, old transactions running off, and changes in market prices that affect the exposure.

The credit reports must contain essential information to explain the quality of the portfolio and problematic exposures. At a minimum, it should present:

- Largest absolute exposures (compared to approved credit limit).
- Largest weak exposures.

- Biggest deterioration/improvement of creditworthiness with corresponding exposures.
- Large new transactions.
- Breakdown by products and business units.

Credit Limits

Chapter 2 presents the concept of credit limits. As a reminder, a credit limit is the absolute amount of exposure a firm wants to take. In creating and setting limits, there are a few basic principles to consider, and minimally they should be:

- Applicable to counterparties, industries, countries, product categories and or asset classes.
- Set in advance and changed infrequently. Although limits can be updated from time to time, ad hoc or frequent limit upsizing to accommodate transactions should be avoided.
- Enforced. In major banks, a transaction that breaches an approved credit limit is a cause for termination of employment. At a minimum, the operational risk management unit should investigate why it happened, because it may be the result of a flawed process, such as data capture. In addition, regulators may review limit breaches as an indicator of poor internal control.
- Subject to judgment and review. Establishing a credit limit is as much an art as a science. Analytical models can help but, in most institutions, they are ultimately based on the experience of senior risk management and consensus with other senior management and even directors, taking into consideration how a loss would affect earnings and the reputational costs that may ensue—how large a loss from one counterparty would shareholders, rating agencies, and clients tolerate?
- Set for multiple exposure metrics. Chapter 5 discusses the measurement of potential exposure for dynamic exposures: VaR (value at risk), which does not represent the worst-case scenario, or when relevant, the total notional amount, which does. So when setting limits, in addition to VaR-based GE, the notional amount of the transactions, when relevant, can be also taken into account.

Surveillance

Surveillance refers to the monitoring of the performance of the transaction and counterparty after the deal has been closed. In some companies, surveillance is considered as the ultimate back-office function because it is internally focused and most of the work performed is considered to be of secondary importance. Experience shows that this is wrong. Surveillance departments must be properly staffed and given appropriate resources because they are first to detect that a transaction is not performing as expected or that a counterparty shows signs of stress. By informing the relevant teams in the organization that will review the issues and take necessary actions, they can avoid large losses.

Here are a few recommendations for an efficient surveillance process:

- Include surveillance sign-offs on new major transactions. We do not say that they perform a key function in the structuring of a deal but involving them in new major transactions or initiatives can make structurers aware of potential issues that were problematic with other transactions. Surveillance specialists can also extract conditions from the counterparty up front, such as regular reporting under a certain format, which should be anticipated before the deal has closed.

- No one should assume that the surveillance department can quickly adapt itself to new types of transactions. Allow time for the department to get up to speed and allocate a budget for its resource needs. The learning curve can be steep and an efficient monitoring process can take months to put in place and require significant resources. For example, when a firm enters a new country, it will have trade receivables from that country. Although the firm may have the experience to monitor the creditworthiness of its domestic customers, it will have no experience with the receivables from its new international customers, and its regular processes of reviewing financial data and monitoring the evolution of the legal environment may be insufficient. One-off structured transactions are another place where the surveillance professional may miss important signals. Thus, when requested to approve a new transaction, a credit committee should know that the surveillance department may not be in a position to perform its usual task. Alternatives would be needed, because knowingly performing surveillance that is handicapped is not an option.

- Agree on a surveillance schedule for each transaction rather than using a one-size-fits-all approach. Not all transactions are uniformly difficult to monitor. Some are stable enough to require only infrequent reviews, whereas others deserve to be monitored more frequently. Each transaction and counterparty should have its own review period, such as monthly, quarterly, or yearly.

- Distribute portfolio-level surveillance reports on a monthly basis. They can include a status of the performance of the main lines of business, transactions, and a progress report on transactions that have deteriorated and for which corrective actions have been recommended and implemented.

■ Set up regular meetings to review the most problematic cases and take corrective action, which may include purchasing protection or handing over a transaction to a workout department. To be useful, the meetings must be more than recommendation forums. They must be staffed by people with the authority to make decisions and, more important, a budget for executing mitigation transactions. Allocating a yearly budget to the surveillance team avoids lengthy discussions about cost allocation, and, most important, the team can react more quickly as a credit deteriorates.

■ Regular meetings must ideally also take a forward-looking view and include people who can anticipate future problems. Economists can add value in that respect and provide useful input that can trigger preventive actions and lawyers as well if new regulations or recent verdicts may impact the firm's counterparties.

Mitigation

From time to time, firms originating credit exposures may want to transfer the credit risk they took on a counterparty to another firm. There are two main reasons for wanting to do so:

1. The counterparty's creditworthiness declines after conclusion of the transaction(s).
2. For commercial reasons, the firm accepts a transaction that bears credit exposure beyond its appetite for the counterparty. In this case, the difference between the assumed exposure and the available credit limit is hedged.

In Part Four, we cover the major techniques available for mitigating credit risk by transferring it to another party. There are ways to transfer the risk that are relatively simple to execute for the company that falls into this Level 1 category.

LEVEL 2

Intermediate CPM requires analytical skills and tools, because the focus here is on the amount of capital at risk and on profitability. Most commodities-trading companies, insurance companies, and other financial institutions practice CPM at this level.

Quantification of the Capital at Risk

Because large unexpected losses occur in any portfolio and current period profits are insufficient to absorb them, a cushion has to be built in, in order to protect the firm against the risk of insolvency. Until the late 1980s, it was difficult to quantify the amount of losses that could occur because of constraints on computational power and access to data. Thus, it was difficult to size the amount of capital to set aside to cover such losses.

Thanks to the development of quantitative methods and the advent of modern computing power that can manage joint probability distributions, it is now more feasible to perform this sizing. This concept is known as portfolio value at risk (VaR) or more specifically as it relates to credit exposures, portfolio credit value at risk (CVaR). We cover this in Chapter 14, and we, therefore, do not expand upon further here. Its quantification is a cornerstone of CPM activities for all major financial institutions.

Allocation of Capital and Profitability at Individual Transaction Level

After having developed a methodology to calculate the amount of capital at risk at the portfolio level, it is possible to allocate the aggregate amount to individual transactions. There are various techniques for coming up with an allocation scheme. One of the simpler methods is to calculate the overall capital needed for the total portfolio and then recalculate the need with all exposures included, except for one. The extra, or incremental, capital needed for the total portfolio relative to the but-for-one portfolio is the capital required for this one transaction. A similar process can be conducted for all transactions in the portfolio.[1] Also, the motivated reader will note that by virtue of portfolio effects, the incremental capital needed for a transaction is smaller than the average capital need for each transaction, since each transaction's capital need is calculated based on an existing portfolio that already benefits from diversification that all other transactions have brought to the table.

The capital allocation process is useful for pricing transactions. Since capital is expensive, its cost must be covered by transaction revenue thus must be built into the pricing. The next logical step is to calculate all costs associated with each transaction, including internal costs, which may not be easy to allocate or even visible, such as overhead and other surveillance costs.

The pricing equation must be fully loaded with all these costs: operating, overhead, and, most important, the cost of capital.

---

[1] In Chapter 14, we elaborate on how to calculate the capital for the whole portfolio.

The benefits of being able to compute the profitability of each transaction are multiple, including the fact that it helps to negotiate if one understands the transaction's total cost on a fully loaded basis. It also helps to prioritize transactions, which helps to allocate resources, allowing transactions with low profitability to be deemphasized in favor of transactions with high profitability.

Stress Testing

Stress testing refers to evaluating the economic consequences of unexpected but plausible events that may impact the performance of the counterparties, and, thus, of the entire portfolio. Stress testing is done to evaluate how the portfolio will behave in extreme circumstances. The extreme circumstances can reflect historical extremes, or values beyond these that have not yet been experienced. It is prudent to evaluate how a portfolio will perform under both types of scenarios—historically experienced extremes and yet-to-be-experienced extreme events. In both cases, each firm must identify the main factors that influence the financial performance of its portfolio, and there is no one-size-fits-all approach or scenarios; they are company specific. Calculations can be done parametrically, using historical probability distributions, if the joint probability calculations are manageable, or they can be numerically simulated, which usually requires computational capacity. The numerically simulated approach has the benefit that many extreme values, correlations as well as nonlinear relationships, can be specified, and the computer does the computation work. These methods suffer to some degree in that their results provide less transparency as to the ultimate causes of the portfolio value output under the extreme environments.

To illustrate, consider a bank heavily exposed to steel companies, which are highly dependent on energy to produce their material. An increase in oil prices typically decreases the profit margin of steel companies, because they cannot pass on much of the cost increase to their customers. Rising energy prices, therefore, translate into higher credit risk. A stress or what-if scenario could test what would happen in the case of a persistent period of high energy prices. The risk assessment team may assume that if oil price stays above $150 a barrel for more than six months, 50 percent of steel companies could be downgraded by three notches (e.g., from A/A2 to BBB/Baa2) and that 15 percent of the B/B rated companies may default. The CPM then runs its capital model with the modified default probabilities for the steel subportfolio and is able to conclude that, in such a case, $500 million additional capital would be necessary for the bank to maintain the same level of solvency.

Prior to the 2007 crisis, stress scenarios were performed but were not taken very seriously and were often based on optimistic outlooks. Postcrisis, a new world emerged as people realized that inconceivable scenarios like a prolonged and deep drop of house prices and double-digit defaults were plausible. Today, most financial institutions dedicate more resources to stress testing and are more open-minded about the plausibility of these events.

As a result of the crisis, regulators are also putting more weight on stress testing. The Federal Reserve Bank in the United States conducts stress testing on U.S. member banks on an annual or more frequent basis. The latest test results, from June 2021, show that U.S banks are well capitalized, able to withstand a severe global recession. The recession environment tested included the following circumstances: Substantial stress in commercial real estate and corporate debt markets; the U.S. unemployment rate rising by 4 percentage points to a peak of 10-3/4 percent; U.S. gross domestic product (GDP) falling 4 percent from the fourth quarter of 2020 through the third quarter of 2022; and a sharp decline in asset prices, including a 55 percent decline in equity prices.

All of the 23 banks tested passed that specific scenario. While their collective losses would be in excess of $470 billion, with nearly $160 billion losses from commercial real estate and corporate loans, their capital ratios would decline but would still be more than double their minimum requirements.[2]

The Fed had restricted some activities of banks during the COVID pandemic, and based on the results of the stress tests, these restrictions were lifted and banks now revert to the normal restrictions imposed by the Fed. When banks do not pass the stress tests, the Fed restricts share repurchases and dividend payments in order to rebuild capital in order to absorb the shocks and extreme events.

Hedging Strategy

Rather than dedicating resources to monitor risks that are not welcome, some positions can be hedged. A hedging strategy, although defensive in nature, is proactively performed. An efficient way to orchestrate the implementation of a hedging strategy is to hold regular hedging meetings involving representatives of various units:

- CPM, as part of the risk-management function, leads the exercise and makes recommendations on overall portfolio characteristics and return targets.
- Risk assessment, as part of the risk-management function, provides analysis about the performance of counterparties and industry sectors.

---

[2] Board of Governors of the Federal Reserve, Press Release, June 24, 2021.

- Surveillance as part of the risk-management function has ongoing involvement with each transaction and can opine on the performance of transactions and trends and will suggest hedging actions.
- Originators also offer their opinions about client sensitivities concerning hedging. For obvious reasons, some clients do not like to hear that their partners have sold or hedged their positions. It is therefore legitimate to forego the use of a hedge to avoid creating friction with a client. However, as we discuss at the end of this chapter, the members of the origination team may not be allowed to discuss the possible hedging techniques, since they have had access to clients' material nonpublic information and securities laws could be violated.
- Structurers are in charge of deal execution but, by the surveillance stage, they have handed off responsibility to the CPM team and may provide input to and assist CPM with implementation of the hedge, sale, or unwind of the transaction, should it be needed.

Rebalancing Transactions

Portfolio management activities aim to minimize the amount of capital deployed and generate the highest return on it. Firms that have appetite for credit risk demonstrate so by setting limits on risks they are prepared to retain and by allocating a certain amount of their capital to credit-related activities.

The CPM team, then, must make the best use of the resources (capital) it is given by senior management, that is, it must optimize the use of the capital available. This means shaping the portfolio in a way that meets certain business objectives but also provides the highest risk-adjusted return to shareholders. The goal is to generate the maximum amount of income with a given amount of capital and to do so in such a way that the capital amount reflects the portfolio's risk. Fine-tuning the portfolio by replacing transactions that provide little income relative to capital with those that produce more income relative to capital is a good way to achieve this goal. Optimization can be performed at the counterparty, industry, or country level. Another simple way to reduce the amount of capital consumed is to diversify the portfolio and avoid concentration. We discuss this topic again in Chapter 14.

At the single counterparty level, optimization of the portfolio is another reason it is crucial to be able to assess the profitability and the marginal impact on the overall capital of each transaction. A review of all sources of exposures can be performed and priority given to the most favorable deals. For instance, a bank may sell or hedge a mildly profitable loan to a counterparty to make room for a more profitable derivative transaction with the same counterparty. The two transactions may generate a similar exposure or use an equivalent amount of capital, but if the loan generates less income than the derivative deal, the firm is better off selling the loan and executing the derivative transaction. This concept is known as the velocity of capital, which means the speed at which capital is redeployed to new transactions. Velocity is desirable, since it means that the firm has the ability to free up and redeploy capital when needed, maximizing its usage and redeploying it to higher-yielding transactions.

This type of rebalancing activity requires an intelligent employee compensation scheme and effective governance to avoid political conflicts. In the example mentioned earlier, the business unit that owns the loan is likely unwilling to sell it because it contributes to a client relationship and to revenues. Its managers would have to be compensated in some shape or form by the business unit that will replace their exposure. We are about to describe the exception to the rule that risk management does not have a P&L interest.

LEVEL 3

An active CPM strategy integrates portfolio management concepts in the day-to-day operations of a company. As the concept is enticing but the implementation delicate, few banks are actually practicing it. Those that are have large portfolios and are assuming credit risk as a primary line of business.

In these instances, the CPM team may, in fact, have a profit and loss (P&L) responsibility. Thus far, we have characterized the risk-management function as decidedly not a profit center. However, after deal execution, transactions become the assets of CPM, and in some instances CPM's profitability is measured as any other business group.

Transfer Pricing

Transfer pricing traditionally refers to intracompany transactions like the allocation of expenses for shared services or charges associated with the purchase of a product or a service from an affiliate.

The concept is extended to financial institutions that may employ a "funds transfer pricing" scheme to create the proper incentives for divisions so that they may focus on their area of expertise. In the risk-management context, the key idea of transfer pricing is to dispossess business units of their exposure immediately after closing a transaction. The ownership is transferred to the CPM group by selling the exposure via a funds-transfer price such that the originator can recognize income, which then shifts the performance burden to the CPM group, which has the responsibility to manage the portfolio it owns.

The acquisition of the exposure by CPM is executed at market price, irrespective of the amount that the business units obtained from the client. Suppose that an investment bank participates in a loan facility in order to create a relationship with a large prospective client, even if it knows it is underpaid on the credit facility (as is often the case). The client is charged 3 percent on a $100 million loan. Credit portfolio management buys the exposure from the origination unit and demands to be paid market price, which is 3.5 percent. The shortfall of revenue is, therefore, 0.5 percent or $500,000 per year, which will be absorbed by the P&L of the origination unit. The CPM receives its needed 3.5 percent. In this way, if the institution needs to shed the exposure and sells the loan to the market, or hedges it, it has priced-in this cost. To the extent that market pricing does not move against the firm, CPM is made whole.

Note that pricing a deal based on the prevailing market conditions is not at odds with the costing that we discussed earlier in which all costs are considered, including the cost of capital. In fact, the internally calculated cost needs to be compared to the market price. If it's less, then the deal makes sense. If it's more, the deal should not be done since, from the firm's point of view, the market is underpricing the transaction. Using market price as a benchmark for actual deal pricing is becoming more widely utilized. However, there are still many transactions that either don't use market prices as a gauge or don't have access to market prices because the transactions are illiquid and there is not much price discovery.

Some banks have thoroughly implemented funds-transfer pricing, as they believe that it provides discipline, transparency, and accountability. It is, however, quite complex to put in place and can create acrimony across business units.

Acquisitions or Swaps of Exposures

As we discuss in the next chapter, the amount of capital dedicated to credit risk can be reduced by adding diversification to the portfolio. Active CPM can involve the acquisition of exposures that the business is not able to generate.

For instance, a bank may not have any presence in the food sector, whereas analytical studies reveal that it would provide diversification to the portfolio. The CPM group can be proactive and purposefully acquire exposures in the sector. A straight acquisition via credit-default swap or purchase of participations in commercial loans can be executed.

Another technique is for two institutions with unbalanced portfolios to engage in an arrangement that's profitable to both parties by swapping exposures. The concept is that one institution's peak exposure may be a low exposure for the other institution, and vice versa. Thus, the two exchange peak/low for low/peak, each institution benefiting from a newly rebalanced portfolio that is less capital intensive.

ORGANIZATIONAL SETUP AND STAFFING

Credit portfolio management is either a corporate function attached to the chief risk officer or part of a business unit like investment banking or capital markets and, thus, it either contributes to a P&L or has responsibility for one. The latter case is found in institutions that, in addition to the transfer pricing and incentive alignment requirements, are so diversified (e.g., active in commercial banking, investment banking, and asset management) that it makes more sense to have CPM specialists reporting to people who understand what they do. In all cases, they are independent from the origination units, the same way the credit risk assessment team is. Contrary to the risk-assessment team though, CPM interacts only infrequently with the business units because they are not involved in individual transactions.

A large part of what CPM does is analytical in nature, so a large number of staff will have strong quantitative backgrounds. Hedging transactions are executed via the internal trading desk, if there is one. Otherwise, CPM deals with external dealers.

The Private Side and the Public Side

In cases where an institution has access to nonpublic information, it has to be careful when it executes hedging transactions. It is illegal to execute certain financial transactions based on information that not all market participants have, because this may constitute insider trading. Prosecutors all over the world are harsher and harsher with traders gaining from privileged access to material nonpublic information.

A firm in regular contact with its clients and counterparties has routine access to information that is not shared with the public. It is legitimate for a borrower or client to disclose nonpublic financial statements and other relevant information in the deal origination process. It is also fine for a firm to make a credit decision based on what it knows. Problems occur when the CPM team has access to material nonpublic information and uses this private information to hedge an exposure.

Firms wanting the flexibility to hedge some of their positions need, therefore, to isolate the staff deciding on new transactions from the staff that may be buying protection or selling the risk back to the market—that is, a clear separation has to be built. Banks refer to the "private side" and the "public side" of the business. This can lead to the duplication of certain functions like credit assessment. Two separate teams are in charge of assessing the credit quality of counterparties. The one on the private side receives private information and recommends accepting or declining a credit exposure based on what they know. The CPM is on the public side and relies exclusively on public information as the basis for recommending hedging some exposures.

THE IACPM

Finally, let's mention that the development of CPM in major financial institutions around the world led to the creation of a dynamic professional organization, the International Association of Credit Portfolio Managers (IACPM), based in New York. Close to 100 financial institutions are members. Its website (www.iacpm.org) and newsletters offer valuable information, including a freely available white paper called "Sound Practices in Credit Portfolio Management" that presents a fundamental framework to develop a CPM function.

FINAL WORDS

Credit portfolio management's role is to aid the firm in establishing a well-diversified portfolio. Its input occurs at all stages of a transaction's life cycle—at the point of origination, in the deal pricing, as transactions accumulate within the portfolio, and in executing exit and mitigation strategies to keep the portfolio in balance. Well-managed CPM reduces overall capital requirements for the firm, regardless of whether the firm is a Level 1, 2, or 3 participant. For firms further along in their CPM functionality, CPM can also increase the velocity of the firm's capital, which is a value-enhancing strategy. Credit portfolio management, although typically a support unit, is increasingly becoming integrated with business units. When the firm's originators have access to nonpublic information, CPM must be separated from the other parts of the firm with that information, if they want to be in a position to hedge or sell exposures.

CHAPTER 14

Economic Capital and Credit Value at Risk (CVaR)

The question we address in this chapter is how to quantify the amount of capital necessary to support a credit portfolio. We begin by defining capital since capital itself has various meanings. We then describe credit value at risk, or CVaR, a technique widely used for quantification. We describe what it is, how to interpret it, how it's calculated, and how the risk manager can influence it. Lastly, we cover CVaR's role in the risk manager's toolbox and its limitations.

By supporting a credit portfolio, we mean to not only avoid bankrupting one's institution but keeping it in good standing with all constituents—customers, regulators, ratings agencies, and creditors. The way in which capital supports a credit portfolio is by absorbing unforeseen or unexpected losses.

A company can easily manage expected losses, and because it expects them, their occurrence can be reasonably quantified, and interest income or revenue can be collected to offset them. For these losses, capital is not required. The problem arises from unexpected losses. Losses can be bigger than expected because, for example, the number of defaults is larger than expected, high exposures are hit, recovery is less than anticipated, or a combination of all these factors. The capital absorbs these losses. Its presence is like a cushion in the unlikely event that credit losses are far greater than expected and current earnings are insufficient to cover them.

The expected performance of a credit portfolio is characterized by a high probability of experiencing small losses and a low probability of very large losses that can wipe out the organization. Small losses are generated by defaults of entities to which a company has either low exposure or high recovery. Frequent but small losses are not an area of concern. Even in a favorable economic environment, there are always a good number of companies that default as a result of issues that are specific to them and not to their environment. These frequent losses are expected from a statistical point of view, meaning we expect them to occur in the aggregate. However, among all entities composing a large portfolio, nobody knows which ones will default. The strategy is, therefore, to factor in the expected losses into a pricing decision.

Large losses are problematic because they can jeopardize the very existence of an entity. If the portfolio has been properly managed, with little concentration of exposures, it takes more than one default to generate a large loss. Most often, large losses result from an above-average frequency of defaults that are large in size due to a large exposure and/or low recovery value.

CAPITAL: ECONOMIC, REGULATORY, SHAREHOLDER

From a credit risk management point of view, equity constitutes capital because only equity, not debt, can absorb losses. To illustrate, if a firm has $100 million in debt and $200 million in equity and losses amount to $250 million, then the losses burn through all of the firm's equity and cause losses to the debt holders. The borrower will default on its debt obligations, and the firm will not continue on a business-as-usual basis. A series of actions will ensue, starting with a bankruptcy filing. If the firm had more equity, say $300 million, it would survive this event (though having lost $250 million of the $300 million) and continue business as usual, though perhaps to a lesser degree.

More capital is, therefore, better, except for the fact that more capital makes attaining shareholders' expected return targets more difficult. Thus, getting the capital number right is critical for an organization's survival. Too little capital means an insufficient cushion, and the company faces a quick death. Too much capital results in inadequate shareholder returns, which may cause shareholders to sell their shares, replace management, or seek strategic alternatives.

There are several meanings of capital within a risk-bearing organization: economic capital, regulatory capital, and shareholder's capital, which we outline next.

Economic or Risk Capital

Economic capital for the risk-bearing organization exists to serve as a buffer against unexpected losses, and it is not intended to be spent. It is different from working capital or investment capital. It is sometimes called risk capital. The amount of economic capital needs to be significant, and the greater the risk, the more capital is required; this is why credit transactions, which are inherently risky, are known as being capital intensive.

Firms dedicate considerable resources to figuring out the right amount of capital. Major financial institutions employ large teams of specialists to focus on this task. Smaller firms will find numerous vendors and consultants who supply models and perform the required analysis. Either way, economic capital is an internal amount set by management so that the firm can withstand even dire circumstances.

Once the size of the economic capital is determined for a whole portfolio, it is allocated to individual transactions for pricing purposes to ensure that returns compensate for the risks taken, to allocate risk-bearing capacity across the organization, and to measure and reward performance across business units. One common measure of performance is risk-adjusted return on capital known as RAROC. It is calculated as the return margin (net income) divided by economic capital.

After describing regulatory and shareholder capital, the balance of this chapter is devoted to the measurement of economic capital using the CVaR technique.

Regulatory Capital

Regulators impose minimum capital requirements on financial institutions, which we explore further in Chapter 15. The regulators' mission is to protect the public's deposits, other funds, and the financial system in general, and they set capital requirements based on their views of the risks inherent in the company's undertakings. They have a low tolerance for risk, so they generally set high capital requirements so that their regulated entities stay solvent, even in extreme circumstances. Although the regulator's view of risk may be loosely aligned with a firm's view, the regulator will not give full credit for the quality of a firm's risk underwriting or for the finesse in which it constructs a well-diversified portfolio. By necessity, regulators will rely more heavily on a formulaic approach that will miss many details on exposure, the chance for loss, mitigating factors, and portfolio effects, all of which affect the firm's risk profile.

Notably, banks have historically considered regulatory capital requirements to be onerous. Their own economic capital calculations are typically usually significantly less than regulatory capital but, clearly, both banks and regulators were optimistic in their capital calculations prior to the 2007 crisis as the largest financial institutions were forced to accept emergency capital injections, and other banks failed in record numbers.

Banks are still reluctant to measure the profitability of their business based on regulatory capital; they prefer economic capital, even if they obviously cannot ignore what the regulator imposes on them. What is important to remember is that, even in an environment in which regulators strive to impose higher capital requirements, banks are not prepared to abandon the efforts to measure, at least internally, their performance based on economic capital. In the foreseeable future, economic capital will remain the yardstick that will drive business decisions and reward performing units.

Shareholder Capital

Shareholder capital is the book value of equity. It is the value that is visible to the outside world, whereas economic capital is a management number. Regulatory capital may be knowable, but it may not be widely disseminated.

Shareholder capital is also used for signaling. Even if a firm measures performance and makes strategic resource decisions based on economic capital, it may wish to hold actual shareholder capital in excess of this amount. One important signaling constituent in the outside world is the rating agency, and a major driver of a firm's credit rating is actual equity held relative to its risk exposure. Even if a firm perfectly estimated its economic capital to equal $5 billion, it may choose to hold $7 billion in shareholder equity just to remove all doubt to the outside world, especially the rating agencies, about its own creditworthiness.

Shareholder capital can be larger than regulatory capital but not smaller, at least not for a long period of time. If it were lower, the company would be out of compliance, and regulators could force the company to take action, including handing over control. Thus, financial firms will hold capital in excess of the regulatory minimum. Shareholder capital can be larger or smaller than economic capital. If it is well in excess, managers will return some equity to shareholders. If it is smaller, managers are doing a poor job of running their business.

To recap, credit is a capital-intensive activity because large losses can hit any portfolio. To prevent insolvency and to keep the business in good standing, firms engaged in credit activities must hold a large amount of capital. Apart from making sure that the firm can survive high losses, the economic capital number is used to:

- Provide an ordinal ranking of the riskiness of products and business units.
- Measure risk-adjusted return on capital, since the capital reflects risk.
- Allocate capital to the areas with the highest risk-adjusted returns.
- Reward units that generate large returns relative to their capital allocation.

DEFINING LOSSES: DEFAULT VERSUS MARK-TO-MARKET (MTM)

Before we proceed, let us take one step back and explain something that we have voluntarily ignored so far in this book. We have defined credit risk as default risk. We focused on the possibility of losing money as a result of insolvency of a counterparty in order to introduce major concepts of credit risk management in an intuitive way.

There are actually two distinct views of credit losses: The default view, which we have adopted so far, and the mark-to-market (MTM) view. Both views of losses share the same objectives of assessing the performance of a credit exposure and of calculating the amount of capital at risk, but they take different paths to get there, based on how losses are defined.

Certainly, some firms consider losses only as those arising from default. Even when a counterparty gets downgraded, if the firm believes that the counterparty will repay, its view of the exposure doesn't change much—no losses are expected and, thus, it is "money good." Such firms take what is known as a default view to compute economic capital. The vast majority of industrial companies with a portfolio composed of trade receivables or loans or leases to clients (vendor financing) and many insurance companies for exposures stemming from traditional business activities such as trade credit (re)insurance (we are not referring to asset management or derivatives activities) use this approach. In part, this view arises from the lack of a liquid market for these exposures. If there's no real market for the exposures, if the firm intends to hold onto the exposures it creates, and if the obligors make good on their payments, then there are no losses unless there's a default.

The alternative view is what is known as an MTM approach, which we introduce in Chapter 5. Large financial institutions measure their performance not based exclusively on the number of defaults in their portfolio but, rather, by the economic value of the exposures they hold. They experience losses (gains) if the market price of their credit exposures falls (rises). The market price could fall based on a default, but it also could fall based on a myriad of other events, including subtle changes in the market's perception of the creditworthiness of a particular counterparty or of borrowers in the aggregate. The market price could change based on what's known as technical factors, meaning changes in the supply and demand for the credit exposure thought to be independent of changes in the credit fundamentals. The most obvious event that causes a change in market price is a downgrade by a rating agency, which would impact the MTM value of all exposures associated with this counterparty. Note that changes in ratings—both downgrades and upgrades—happen far more frequently than default.

To illustrate, assume a firm charged 50 basis points per annum to take a credit risk on Company ABC when it was rated AA/Aa2/AA (by S&P, Moody's, and Fitch, respectively). If ABC is downgraded to A+/A1/A+, the risk premium demanded by investors would increase from, for example, 50 bps to 80 bps p.a. The higher yield on the credit risk translates to a lower price of the asset, and thus the firm would lose money on an MTM basis.

Note that the paper (MTM) loss would become a realized loss if the firm decides to exit the position, and yet no default has occurred.

The advantage of an MTM approach is that, in concept, it is based on the market's view, which compiles all available information about an asset, including the creditworthiness of the obligor, and summarizes the information into a price. The disadvantages with using market prices (that is, spreads) to measure credit risk are twofold. First, we cannot readily observe market prices of credit obligations for most obligors, since those credit exposures are not publicly traded. Second, changes in spreads encompass technical factors; market vagaries; and the macroeconomy, including what is happening on the other side of the world. Arguably, if a sovereign nation were to default, this could cause a credit crunch worldwide, which might impact all borrowers and cause prices of credit assets to fall and hence spreads of industrial corporates in the United States. However, often when spreads increase, we may be uncertain whether this reflects an increased likelihood of default or a factor unrelated to creditworthiness.

For purposes of explaining the calculation of economic capital (with the CVaR method) in the simplest and most intuitive way, we will stick to the default view of credit risk while giving readers only a flavor for the MTM approach.

Accounting and the CVaR Calculation

We will now say a few words about accounting. Readers unfamiliar with the various accounting treatments of credit assets may wish to read Chapter 16 first, in which we review some relevant accounting aspects of credit risk, or they may skip ahead to the next section.

The language used in both U.S. Generally Accepted Accounting Principles (GAAP) and International Financial Reporting Standards (IFRS) as it relates to recognizing and valuing credit exposures is not dissimilar from the language used in determining economic capital, so it bears clarification up front.

Companies account for their credit assets in various ways, based on a variety of factors, including the type of credit exposure (loan, bond, credit card receivable), the companies' intentions about whether they will hold the exposure until maturity or sell it beforehand, and the extent to which a decline in the exposure's value is attributable to creditworthiness, and if this decline is expected to result in default.

The default risk approach to credit risk appears on the surface to be consistent with a buy-and-hold accounting treatment, and the MTM approach seems consistent with the available-for-sale accounting treatment for a bond. Thus, the two views of credit risk could easily be confused with the accounting treatments. What we'd like to underscore is that the choice of methods (default or MTM) to calculate CVaR is not necessarily dependent on the accounting treatment of the asset.

CREDIT VALUE AT RISK OR CVaR

Credit value at risk is the methodology firms use to size the amount of economic capital needed to support credit activities. It allows the firm to define the amount of losses it is prepared to withstand. Credit value at risk, a dollar loss number, is a special case of VaR whose concept is introduced in Chapter 5. Implementation of VaR can be fairly complex. In this chapter we restrict our discussion to a high-level presentation of CVaR.

If the question is asked, "How much can my organization lose from credit exposures?" the logical reply must be, "Everything!" However, this is neither helpful nor realistic. First, not every entity will default even in extreme loss situations. Second, if an organization had to set aside an amount of capital representing a large proportion of its potential exposure (GE) it could not survive since this business would be completely unprofitable. Instead, CVaR looks at the question in a three-step statistical framework:

1. Over what time horizon are we concerned about losses?
2. What is the probability of losses of a certain size occurring?
3. How confident do we want to be in our ability to withstand losses of some predetermined level?

The Time Horizon

To evaluate how bad losses can be, we need more time specificity for two reasons.

First, in most circumstances, the longer the time period, the larger the loss. For example, it is unlikely that losses in a given day will exceed losses in a year because volatility in credit quality increases over time. In Table 14.1 we present a one-year credit transition matrix from Fitch for corporate credits on a global basis from 1990 to 2020. What can be seen is that there is an overwhelming chance that the rating, within one year, remains the same, especially for highly rated entities. The table reads that an AA rated entity has a 85.88 percent chance of remaining rated AA and only a 0.05 percent chance of defaulting one year later, based on historically observed migration.

In Table 14.2, we show the same matrix capturing rating transitions over five years, that is, a cumulative five-year credit transition matrix.

TABLE 14.1   Fitch Global Corporate Finance Average One-Year Transition Rates: 1990–2020

Average Annual

No.	Rating	AAA	AA	A	BBB	BB	B	CCC to C	D	WD
853	AAA	88.51	5.16	0.23	–	–	–	–	0.12	5.98
6,014	AA	0.12	85.88	8.81	0.33	0.02	0.02	–	0.05	4.77
18,876	A	0.01	1.54	88.75	5.07	0.37	0.05	0.03	0.05	4.14
21,451	BBB	0.005	0.10	2.73	87.70	3.37	0.32	0.10	0.12	5.55
8,833	BB	–	0.02	0.09	6.63	77.14	6.27	1.09	0.61	8.14
6,630	B	–	–	0.18	0.26	6.91	75.46	4.96	2.11	10.12
1,032	CCC to C	–	–	–	0.19	1.45	16.86	46.03	23.55	11.92

Note: Corporate Finance includes both financial and nonfinancial issuers (%).
Source: Fitch (Fitch Ratings Global Corporate Finance 2020 Transition and Default Studies, March 31, 2021).

TABLE 14.2   Fitch Global Corporate Finance Average Five-Year Transition Rates: 1990–2020

Average Five-Year

No.	Rating	AAA	AA	A	BBB	BB	B	CCC to C	D	WD
788	AAA	52.54	13.96	2.79	0.76	–	–	–	0.63	29.31
5,453	AA	0.33	51.15	24.87	2.84	0.48	0.06	–	0.06	20.23
15,706	A	0.01	4.67	56.47	14.74	1.91	0.54	0.10	0.45	21.11
16,433	BBB	0.03	0.26	8.42	54.41	6.91	1.96	0.48	1.28	26.25
6,456	BB	–	0.05	0.79	20.24	31.66	8.44	1.39	4.85	32.57
4,852	B	–	–	0.43	3.54	14.22	29.18	2.49	10.28	39.84
805	CCC to C	–	–	0.25	4.10	3.23	21.37	7.58	36.77	26.71

Note: Corporate Finance includes both financial and nonfinancial issuers (%).
Source: Fitch (Fitch Ratings Global Corporate Finance 2020 Transition and Default Studies, March 31, 2021).

The five-year matrix shows more movement across ratings classes. For example, the same AA has only a 51.15 percent chance of remaining an AA, and a higher chance of defaulting after five years, based on historically observed migration. Thus, since time is a driver of credit variability—that is, credit risk—CVaRs for longer time horizons will be larger, all else being equal.

Firms will measure CVaR over multiple time horizons depending on the type of credit portfolio being monitored. For a loan portfolio, firms may calculate and monitor a one-year CVaR because default likelihoods may not be assessable over a shorter period; for a credit card portfolio, firms may calculate and monitor a one-month CVaR, since delinquencies and default likelihoods may be easier to assess in this time period.

Second, the time horizon chosen to measure losses matters because it will be a function of how quickly the firm is able to react to losses. Thus, it is a choice variable. If exposures can be unwound or mitigated quickly, then the loss horizon chosen is likely to be short to reflect this. If exposures are illiquid or difficult to hedge, then the horizon period is likely to be longer. Understanding the time frame helps in contingency planning. If capital needs to be raised or positions unwound, management needs to know how quickly it must act to stem losses.

The Loss Distribution

The second step is to calculate the probability of losses of a certain size occurring. In the section that follows, we will describe how to construct the loss distribution for the portfolio, but before doing so, we explore the properties of these distributions once constructed.

The loss distribution of a credit portfolio describes the relative frequency, or probability, associated with all possible loss levels that a portfolio could experience within a given time horizon. Figure 14.1 depicts a typical shape of a loss distribution for credit portfolios. The *x*-axis measures losses and the *y*-axis the relative frequencies of the losses.

In Figure 14.1, we see that its shape is not symmetric. Rather, there is a high probability of experiencing small losses and a low probability of having large losses. This gives rise to the asymmetric, or skewed, shape and the "fat tail," with the curve extending out to the right where these improbable but large losses are represented.

As explained, this picture corresponds to the default view of credit losses, meaning the portfolio of exposures is considered to have the extremes of either no defaults, at the leftmost point with zero losses, or some very large losses on the far right side, or other losses within the portfolio of varying amounts between the two points. It can be expected that the amount of losses will be small because the default probability of a company is, in

Probability

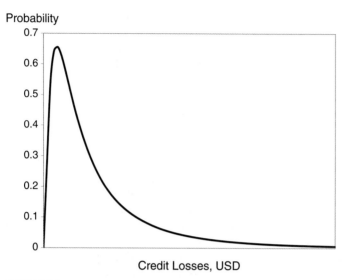

Credit Losses, USD

FIGURE 14.1   Loss Distribution, Default View

normal economic circumstances, fairly low, especially for investment-grade entities. Any single firm is unlikely to default or even be downgraded in a limited period. Returning to Table 14.1, one can read that the default probability of a BBB rated entity is only 0.12 percent for one year. This explains that the risk of losing money is small to start with if a portfolio is composed of a diversified collection of investment-grade credits. However, defaults do happen and losses are experienced, which explains the shape of the curve in Figure 14.1: a high probability of credit losses of small amounts.

In contrast, large losses are rarely experienced but will have a very big impact. One scenario is the default of a large exposure, which may also trigger the default of correlated exposures. This scenario is uncommon because large exposures are closely monitored and are typically reduced when clear signs of deterioration emerge. The other likely scenario is an unforeseen event occurring that triggers a cascade of defaults. Recent examples include the COVID-19 pandemic or the 2007 crisis. Before these events, many firms had accumulated exposures they thought were reasonable and in line with their normal risk appetite. All of a sudden, one or a series of events occurred and many companies defaulted, some directly affected by the pandemic and some not.

It is impossible to imagine all types of events that may happen, but major unforeseen events have happened with some regularity. On the loss distribution, this corresponds to the extreme right tail of the curve, where frequency is low and severity is high. The curve is very close to the x-axis but not on it. The probability of a large loss is close to zero but not exactly zero. The corresponding losses are, however, extremely high.

Under the default view, there are only two scenarios for each exposure: either it defaults or it doesn't. In contrast, under the MTM view, credit quality can go up as well as down. The movement in credit quality is visible in Tables 14.1 and 14.2 and is known as credit migration. As a consequence, a credit portfolio has an entire value distribution showing not just the losses but also the gains. Take the BBB credit: while it has a 0.12 percent chance of being downgraded, it also has a 2.84 percent of being upgraded. Credit migration forms the basis for most MTM approaches. Thus, instead of estimating a loss distribution based on the frequency and severity of default, in the MTM case we consider a loss distribution based on the probability of an obligor's rating migration and the corresponding expected market value. It stands to reason that if a BB exposure is riskier and worth less than the A exposure, if an A exposure slips in rating to a BB, its obligation has not defaulted but is now worth less. As a consequence, the credit portfolio's value will change.

Note that MTM techniques are broader than incorporating ratings migration. Because credit prices change, often daily, reflecting investor information globally, which casts a wider information gathering net than ratings agencies are able to cast, credit price volatility is also incorporated into MTM calculations. Credit prices change frequently and ratings change infrequently. Therefore, these broader MTM techniques may have finer-tuned estimates of credit risk.

The Confidence Level

How certain do we want to be that the firm has enough capital to withstand a very large loss? We answer this question with a confidence level. Deciding what level of confidence the firm wishes to have in withstanding losses is the remaining piece of the CVaR three-step framework and ties directly to the firm's risk appetite.

A higher confidence level goes hand-in-hand with a lower risk appetite, and vice versa. It is a choice variable, meaning, the organization must decide if it wishes to withstand losses that are so infrequent as to occur only 5 percent of the time (a 95 percent confidence level), 1 percent of the time (a 99 percent confidence level), 0.1 percent of the time (a 99.9 percent confidence level), or less than that.

There are various considerations in setting the confidence interval. Often, it is set to align with an actual or target rating. Suppose an institution wishes to maintain its BBB/Baa/BBB rating. If rating agencies' historical data show that a BBB/Baa/BBB-rated entity has a one-year 0.25 percent default probability, the company may set its confidence interval at 99.75 percent.

Note that the rating agencies will both review firms' internal risk quantification processes, including VaR calculations, and also employ their own similar capital models.

In Figure 14.2, we duplicate Figure 14.1, with some points added. The area under the curve sums to one (100 percent). The expected loss (EL) of the portfolio is defined as the probability-weighted average loss and is denoted EL in the figure. The confidence interval, a choice variable, corresponds to a loss amount beyond which the company is not prepared to withstand. Suppose the firm chooses a confidence interval consistent with point R. At point R, the area under the curve is 99.9 percent, with only 0.1 percent to the right. If this point corresponds to losses of $100 million, then the firm will hold capital to withstand losses up to this point.

In this example, the CVaR is $90 million, which is equal to the loss amount of the $100 million corresponding to the 99.9 percent confidence level, less the expected loss, EL, which is $10 million, that the firm has already collected in its pricing. The CVaR is the economic capital.

In the example that we have been using, we looked at the one-year default probabilities as the basis for the loss distributions. Sometimes the confidence interval is expressed as a return period, which means that the loss value corresponding to a 99 percent confidence interval, for example, can be interpreted as the 1-in-100-year loss event, and a 99.9 percent confidence interval can be interpreted as a 1-in-1,000-year loss event.

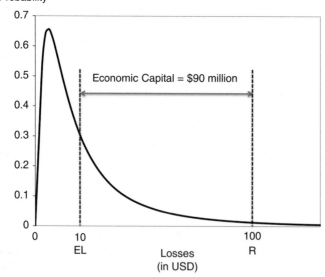

FIGURE 14.2 Loss Distribution, Default View, with Selected Points

In practice, firms with a large credit portfolios set their confidence intervals to be quite high and will calculate CVaR with a 99.5 percent or 99.9 percent confidence interval, suggesting that, for reasons easy to understand, they almost never want to face losses that can completely deplete their capital dedicated to credit.

Tail CVaR

Given that our estimate of a loss distribution is unlikely to perfectly reflect the true underlying loss distribution of a portfolio, the difference in losses between say 99.5 percent and 99.9 percent is somewhat of an arbitrary distinction. Thus, another supplemental metric used to capture extreme occurrences in the tail of the loss distribution is what's known as tail-VaR, or TVaR, and it is calculated as the average of the amount of losses that may occur in excess of some already extreme level, such as beyond the 0.5 percent (99.5 percent) level. This just enables us to summarize what the average loss is likely to be if, indeed, the losses experienced are in excess of the 0.5 percent level. The value will be higher than economic capital and is sometimes referred to as shortfall.

Caveats

What we just described is a basic CVaR framework. Implementation difficulties arise from various sources, including uncertainty and information gaps in: (1) any one exposure's probability of loss, (2) the correlation across exposures, and (3) recovery rates. However, even if Figure 14.2 perfectly described the probabilities associated with all loss values, we still face uncertainty because actual losses could happen anywhere along the distribution. They are most likely to fall around point EL, but there's always the chance that they will fall at other points and we don't know beforehand where the losses will end up. A key point of any VaR approach is that it serves as a statistical guidepost only. Even if a firm is conservative and sets a high confidence level, it may still experience losses in excess of its confidence level. In addition, credit risk is not a risk that can be perfectly quantified, nor can it be completely eliminated. As discussed in Chapter 5, like other VaR measures, CVaR does not represent the worst-case scenario, and no model can fully anticipate all outcomes.

In this section, we explained how to interpret the loss distribution. We now turn to reviewing what is needed to generate the distribution. This exercise helps to understand how portfolio management can influence the shape of the distribution, thereby reducing capital requirements.

CREATING THE LOSS DISTRIBUTION

If a firm had access to a long and robust time series of loss data from portfolios that look similar to the portfolio under consideration, there would be no need to create a loss distribution. We could simply observe the loss experience to see how bad losses can actually get. However, few entities have complete data, and even if they did, a portfolio today will look different from any portfolio in the past. How losses develop is a function of the credit quality of the obligor, their industries, the state of the economy, the correlation of the exposures, the seniority of the exposure, as well as many other elements we have discussed throughout the book, none of which is static.

Therefore, we instead use information on the drivers of loss, such as the credit quality of the obligor, recovery rates, and correlation across obligors, and we build or create a loss distribution by considering all these drivers taken together.

There are three main building blocks that we will consider here in creating a loss distribution.

1. The probability of default for a single exposure.
2. Value of the loss upon default, including recovery.
3. Portfolio effects: the joint loss distribution which reflects relationships across exposures.

The first two components are used to derive the loss distribution for a single exposure. The third component considers how all exposures interact in the aggregate. We will discuss each of these in turn and will make some simplifying assumptions. First, we ignore time value of money. Second, we treat each exposure as a single payment due at maturity. Third, we treat recovery as a certain amount.

Step 1: Assessing the Probability of Default for a Single Exposure

To arrive at the probability of default for a single exposure, under the default view, we use only the rightmost column of information in Table 14.1 (unlike an MTM approach, which uses information on migration for all intermediate credit quality points). In Table 14.3 we reconstruct Table 14.1, showing only the probability of default. For example, an A-rated credit will have a 0.09 percent chance of default within a year. This step is relatively straightforward and requires having access to data. If the exposures are large corporate credits, then these data are available from rating agencies and from other sources such as Moody's Analytics, an affiliate of Moody's Investor Services that provides ratings. If the entity has exposures of counterparties

TABLE 14.3 Fitch Global Corporate Finance Average Annual One-Year Default Rates: 1990–2020

	D
AAA	0.12
AA	0.05
A	0.05
BBB	0.12
BB	0.61
B	2.11
CCC/C	23.55

Source: Fitch (Fitch Ratings Global Corporate Finance 2020 Transition and Default Studies, March 31, 2021).

that are not rated by the agencies, then the firm must either develop and use its own internal ratings or, if these are insufficient, it would need to buy the information from a vendor.

Step 2: Assessing the Value of the Loss upon Default, Including Recovery

Here, we need to know the value of the gross exposure and the expected recovery should the counterparty default. If a $30 million loan has an expected recovery upon default of 30 percent, then the value of the loss given default is $21 million ($30 × (1 − 0.3)). Furthermore, if the probability of default is 0.05 percent the expected loss is $10,500 (which is the loss given default multiplied by the probability of default).

Step 3: Portfolio Effects: The Joint Default Probability

We begin here with an illustration of a portfolio made up of three loans, as shown below in Table 14.4. For each of these loans, we measure exposure as the amount outstanding, or GE.

Calculating the expected loss and the loss given default for each individual loan is straightforward enough. We also know the potential range of losses associated with the loss distribution—from zero (no defaults) to $41 million. However, knowing the probabilities associated with the points between $0 and $41 million for the loans combined together in a portfolio requires knowing the joint probability distribution of default. Without this, we cannot calculate the probability of default of the three loans simultaneously or the expected loss of the portfolio as a whole, as indicated by the question marks in Table 14.4. Nor can we calculate the intermediate loss outcomes for the portfolio as a whole.

TABLE 14.4 Illustrative Portfolio of Three Loans: Loss Given Default

	Exposure	Probability of Default	Recovery Rate	Loss Given Default	Expected Loss
Loan 1, AA rated	$20 mil	0.05%	40%	$12 mil	$0.006 mil
Loan 2, A rated	$30 mil	0.05%	30%	$21 mil	$0.011 mil
Loan 3, BBB rated	$10 mil	0.12%	20%	$8 mil	$0.010 mil
Total Portfolio	$60 mil	?	32%	$41 mil	?

The joint probability distribution tells us the probability of all possible combinations of default/no default across all the loans in the portfolio. That is, the probabilities associated with loans 1, 2, and 3 all defaulting together, all loans not defaulting, only loans 1 and 2 defaulting, only loans 1 and 3 defaulting, only loans 2 and 3 defaulting, and only one loan defaulting at a time. For each of these eight possible outcomes, there is an associated probability and the sum of all the joint probabilities adds to one. What we really want to know is the relative frequency of the various loss amounts associated with all possible outcomes. That is, we want to know the relationship between portfolio loss amounts and the probability of experiencing those loss amounts—namely, the loss distribution.

There are two real-life challenges with building the loss distribution. First, with more loans in the portfolio, the number of possible combinations rises exponentially. A portfolio of 10 loans has 1,024 joint probabilities (for the two states of default and nondefault and 10 loans, or 2^{10}); a portfolio of 100 loans has 2^{100} joint probabilities. As one can see, the computational requirements become challenging. Thus, just keeping track of all outcomes and the associated losses quickly becomes unwieldy (and in addition, an analytical solution for calculating descriptive statistics such as the variance of the portfolio, becomes intractable). This is true even if all of the loans are uncorrelated with one another.

Second, we know that loans are correlated, and the actual joint default probabilities of the loans are a function of their correlations. If for example, loans 1 and 2 are independent, the joint probability of default is straightforward, or (0.05% × 0.05%) or 0.000025%. However, this is not realistic because default probabilities across loans are not independent. When one loan defaults, the chance of other loans defaulting also rises to some degree.

This interdependence must be factored in. Typically, interdependence is modeled as linear, meaning the degree of interdependence does not vary with the amount of losses. This linear dependence is simply correlation.

Two companies are positively correlated if they exhibit the same behavior when faced with similar external events. At the simplest level, think of companies in the same industry that tend to react to the same economic factors. For instance, when the global economy is in recession, industrial investments are reduced. As a result, the construction, building materials, commodities, and heavy machinery sectors are struggling together. Companies deriving a large proportion of their revenues from these industries are all under stress at the same time. Just think of the construction industry in a broad sense in the United States in the aftermath of the 2007 crisis. There were so many homes for sale and so few lenders willing to finance new projects that the number of new constructions declined strongly. As a result, all companies involved in the construction business, from raw materials to builders, lost revenues and their creditworthiness declined.

The profitability of an entire industry or geographic sector can be impacted by a single event, which causes systematic risk, and this risk is reflected in high correlation across exposures, in contrast to risk introduced by the individual credit characteristics of companies, known as idiosyncratic risk.

As a consequence of these two real-life challenges, the actual calculation of the loss distribution for a portfolio is handled by way of a simulation, such as a Monte Carlo technique. In the simulation, the computer, with the probability of default for each exposure and correlations across exposures specified in advance, generates possible outcomes of loans defaulting in various combinations and the losses corresponding to these outcomes. If the computer is given instructions to generate 10,000 possible loss outcomes (trials), the loss outcomes are then ranked from low to high and grouped into bins to form a histogram. Plotting a histogram in the traditional fashion, with the relative frequency of the outcomes on the vertical axis and the loss outcomes on the horizontal axis, gives us the loss distribution. Note that a relative frequency, with enough trials, is in fact a probability.

In Tables 14.5 and 14.6 and Figure 14.3, we show these three components. Table 14.5 shows the simulated outcomes of losses for 10,000 trials generated by a Monte Carlo simulation. Table 14.6 shows the grouping of the loss outcomes into bins, chosen by the user, with a tabulated relative frequency (actual frequency divided by the 10,000 trials). Note that we could narrow the size of the bins (say from $300 to $100 amounts) and increase the number of trials and we'd get a finer and more continuous-looking distribution. Figure 14.3 shows the plotting of these two elements—the loss amounts and their associated relative frequency, in a histogram.

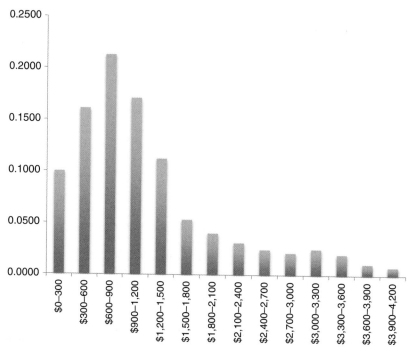

FIGURE 14.3   Histogram of Simulated Loss Outcomes

TABLE 14.5   Simulated Loss Outcomes for 10,000 Trials

Trial #	Losses
1	$2,145
2	$2,040
3	$4,038
4	$1,105
5	$789
6	$2,464
7	$2,063
8	$1,666
9,995	$1,171
9,996	$1,987
9,997	$929
9,998	$991
9,999	$1,004
10,000	$2,138

TABLE 14.6 Simulated Loss Outcomes for 10,000 Trials Sorted into Histogram Bins

Trial #	Losses	Groupings: Losses between	Frequency	Relative Frequency	Cumulative Frequency
1	$2,145	$0–300	1,001	0.1001	0.1001
2	$2,040	$300–600	1,612	0.1612	0.2613
3	$4,038	$600–900	2,129	0.2129	0.4742
4	$1,105	$900–1,200	1,711	0.1711	0.6453
5	$789	$1,200–1,500	1,123	0.1123	0.7576
6	$2,464	$1,500–1,800	533	0.0533	0.8109
7	$2,063	$1,800–2,100	402	0.0402	0.8511
8	$1,666	$2,100–2,400	311	0.0311	0.8822
		$2,400–2,700	247	0.0247	0.9069
		$2,700–3,000	215	0.0215	0.9284
9,995	$1,171	$3,000–3,300	251	0.0251	0.9535
9,996	$1,987	$3,300–3,600	201	0.0201	0.9736
9,997	$929	$3,600–3,900	110	0.0110	0.9846
9,998	$991	$3,900–4,200	80	0.0080	0.9926
9,999	$1,004	$4,200–4,500	40	0.0040	0.9966
10,000	$2,138	$4,500–4,800	34	0.0034	1.0000
		Total	10,000	1.0000	

Now we can simply read either from Table 14.6 or the chart in Figure 14.3 to see the CVaR at a chosen level of confidence. We have other useful information at our fingertips as well. For example, no loss exceeds $4,800, and 99.7 percent of the losses are less than or equal to $4,500. Losses associated with a 99 percent confidence interval are between $3,900 and $4,200. The expected loss is $1,204 (not shown), and the median loss is slightly more than $900. For precise loss amounts associated with a confidence level, we would simply read from the table of trial outcomes. We would sort the trial outcomes from lowest to highest and for the loss amount at, for example, the 99.9 percent confidence level, we'd observe the 9,990th largest loss outcome.

There are significant benefits to constructing a loss distribution using a simulation technique. Correlations across exposures and default probabilities can be modified. In this way, the calculation can be forward looking, meaning that, for example, if a correlation between two credit types were historically low but is expected to rise in the future, a higher correlation can be inputted into the simulation model. Similarly, historical default probabilities can be overwritten with estimates of what these probabilities might be in the future, or default probabilities based on current market data (e.g., Moody's Analytics approach) can be utilized. In addition, in a simulation, recoveries can be allowed to vary (that is, themselves treated as random variables), since we know that treating them as static is an oversimplification because recoveries tend to fall as the frequency of defaults rises.

While numerous software packages provide Monte Carlo simulation engines that generate distributions, credit analysis often integrates forecasted paths of financial market and economic variables into the simulation. Because credit analysis is best performed within a current and forecasted economic context, some simulation engines are now paired with an economic scenario generator (ESG). The ESG will generate simulated paths of the joint behavior of market variables. One such ESG is Barrie & Hibbert (part of Moody's Analytics), which takes an MTM approach to credit risk. On an exposure-by-exposure basis within a portfolio, the ESG considers credit transition probabilities, credit spreads, the risk-free yield curve, correlations across credit markets globally, correlations with equity market paths, and other variables. With simulated paths for each variable, the ESG will generate a return (or loss) distribution.

Data Requirements

The well-known garbage in, garbage out (GIGO) adage is relevant for credit portfolio management. Having sophisticated models and high-skilled people to run them is of limited use if the data that feeds them are incomplete.

For either the default or MTM approach to measuring credit risk, the management information system should capture all relevant data, such as counterparty, country, industry, rating, exposure, tenor, prepayment options, interest or coupon rate, collateral, and other credit enhancements. If a firm is exposed to the same counterparty across several transactions, each transaction's characteristics must be captured.

As explained earlier, with a default view, for each exposure composing the portfolio, four types of data are necessary: exposure, default probability, expected recovery, and joint default probabilities. These four data requirements are as follows:

- Exposure: The exposure is the GE, NE, or AE (see Chapter 4) and according to each firm's choice.
- Default Probability: Few firms have enough internal data to extract default probabilities from their own portfolio. It would necessitate a large portfolio and reliable data over a long period of time. As a result, the industry standard is to rely on external vendors who analyze the performance of a large universe of companies over a long period of time. S&P, Moody's, and Fitch regularly publish the evolution of their ratings, similar to those in Tables 14.1 and 14.2.

- Expected Recovery: For each transaction, an assumption of recovery upon default must be made, and each firm may have specialized terms that will affect its own loss, net of recovery. To simplify, firms may adopt a uniform recovery rate for exposures of the same nature—for instance, 40 percent for all senior unsecured transactions.
- Joint Default Probability: Next, we turn to correlation and to estimating joint default probabilities, which is not a simple task, especially given that in certain years there are actually few default observations. Firms that have enough historical data may use their own values, but in many cases, firms will not have enough internal data and will use estimates provided by vendors.

  Because the number of actual cases of joint default occurrences is not very high, a common methodology is to use other indicators of a company's financial strength as a proxy for likely default or migration. The two main proxies used in the marketplace are the market value of assets and equity prices. The main benefit is that their values change often, reflecting the sentiment of the investors vis-à-vis their future performance. It is, therefore, possible to develop a statistical model capturing the way they evolve, and to use the outcome as a proxy for joint default or joint migration.

For joint default probabilities, Moody's Analytics Global Correlation Model (GCorr™) provides numbers derived from the market value of assets, calculated with their version of the Merton Model, which we describe in Chapter 7.

For the MTM approach, it is necessary to obtain rating migration probabilities as well as correlations. Here again, S&P, Moody's, and Fitch are the main sources of data for firms that do not have their own model or data.

ACTIVE PORTFOLIO MANAGEMENT AND CVaR

CVaR can be lowered with active portfolio management, as illustrated in the loss distribution of Figure 14.4. In that, the curve approximated by the dark bars has a high and narrow hump indicating that there is a relatively high probability of experiencing a low level of losses. Also, the curve converges toward zero relatively quickly, so the likelihood of a high level of losses is remote. All in all, this loss distribution reflects a healthy portfolio. The curve approximated by the light colored bars is much flatter. The probability of experiencing only small losses is much less than with the portfolio represented by the dark bars. Also, there is a higher chance to experience medium-sized losses. Furthermore, this loss distribution stays well above the *x*-axis for a while, showing that the probability to be hit by large losses is

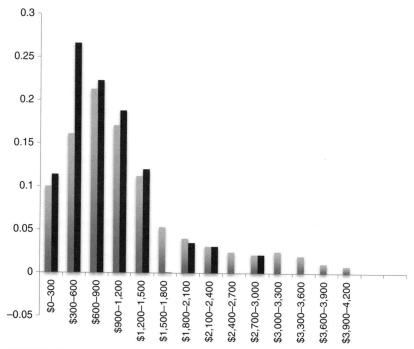

FIGURE 14.4 Histogram of Simulated Loss Outcomes before and after Active Portfolio Management

not insignificant. It has a "fat tail" that reveals undesirable portfolio characteristics. The light-colored distribution is the portfolio before active portfolio management, and the dark-colored distribution is the portfolio after active portfolio management.

The portfolio responsible for the light-colored bars may have been originated without care or it may have experienced deterioration of counterparties over time. It requires much more capital than the one attached to the distribution represented by the dark bars: The 99.5 percent confidence level associated with the dark bars is closer to $2,700 versus $3,900 under the light bars. Thus, it is a good candidate for an active portfolio rebalancing exercise that aims at moving the light-colored bars closer to the dark ones. The result will be that the capital needed to support the portfolio will be much less after than before rebalancing, or alternatively, for a given amount of capital, more business can be generated, thus improving the return on risk-adjusted capital.

Portfolio-management steps that can be taken to tighten the loss distribution include:

1. Elimination of weak names.

This is easier said than done, and it can be hard and costly to execute, but in the end, eliminating weak names may help cut future losses.

For example, assuming no recovery and no correlation across obligors, a $15 million portfolio of 100 BBB obligors and 50 single B obligors with $100,000 each in notional exposure has, at the 95 percent confidence level, a one-year CVaR of $390,000 under the default view using the data from Table 14.3. If the 50 single-B obligors were replaced with BBB credits, the CVaR would be reduced by about two-thirds to $136,000. Note that these CVar values are in addition to expected losses of $272,000 and $118,000, respectively.

2. Reduction of peak exposures.

Peak exposures are counterparties or assets in a portfolio that stand out due their large size relative to the rest of the portfolio. They are sometimes called tall trees. Reducing them will have a material impact on the shape of the loss distribution. For example, assuming no recovery and no correlation across obligors, a portfolio of 10 BBB obligors with $1,000,000 each in notional exposure at the 95 percent confidence level has over three times the CVaR as the same-sized portfolio of 100 BBB obligors with $100,000 each. Note that the expected loss is the same in both cases.

3. Diversification.

Having many correlated counterparties in a portfolio is not favorable. If something that has the power to influence the performance of many companies at the same time occurs, large losses could affect the portfolio. One of the goals of portfolio managers is, therefore, to avoid concentration of correlated exposures. Everything else being equal, a well-diversified portfolio necessitates less capital than one containing a lot of correlated obligors.

Bringing diversification to a credit portfolio is one of the most powerful tools to reduce capital needs. For example, assuming no recovery, a portfolio of 100 BBB credits each with a 0.5 correlation has a one-year 95 percent CVaR—twice that of a portfolio of same-sized credits having a 0.25 correlation.

PRICING

Pricing is a complex topic beyond the scope of credit risk management. We simply reiterate some basic concepts:

- Expected losses have to be priced-in for each and every transaction. As the name indicates, it is known that, on a portfolio basis, companies will default and cause some losses. What is not known is which company will default. Some have a higher chance than others, but even companies with a higher rating can default. The portfolio should, therefore, at least generate enough revenue to compensate for the expected losses.

- Covering expected losses with revenues is not enough, however. A company cannot make money if it merely covers expected losses with margins collected from performing transactions. A profit margin has to be added to the aggregated amount of expected losses to pay for other expenses like general administration and also to provide a profit to the shareholders, covering their opportunity cost of equity capital.
- In targeting profit, return expected by shareholders is taken into account. Capital is provided by shareholders and put at risk by the credit activities of the company. If shareholders expect a 12 percent return, then a company with $500 million of shareholder capital must integrate an additional $60 million of revenue in its pricing strategy to compensate the shareholders.

FINAL WORDS

In his well-known book, *The Black Swan*, Nassim Nicholas Taleb describes the general unpreparedness of most institutions to face highly unexpected events. As he put it, having never seen a black swan does not enable us to conclude they do not exist. In other words, it is not always possible to envisage extreme scenarios but it is not a reason to ignore that they exist. It is a strong message for risk managers, who have to always be on the lookout.

VaR approaches have been criticized for failing, and the crisis of 2007 is a testament to the failure of risk-bearing firms to properly assess their risks. We reiterate that VaR is a tool, only one of many in the risk manager's toolbox, and it serves as a guidepost alongside stress tests and other considerations to help size capital requirements. It will be only as effective as the quality of the data and the robustness of the analysis permit and, importantly, knowing its limitations in capturing extreme, unforeseen events.

VaR also has been criticized for assuming normal probability distributions. Losses and credit returns as presented throughout this chapter are far from being normally distributed. VaR is also criticized for having a backward-looking approach. Although credit ratings, which are historical, are widely used, this is only one contributor to the loss-probability distribution. Portfolio composition can reflect a forward-looking business plan, and defaults and correlations can be derived from forward-looking market prices and linked to economic forecasts, to name a few.

To summarize, CVaR—and VaR, more generally—is a statistical approach for evaluating how much capital a firm needs to hold to be viable. Many factors influence the ultimate size of credit losses, and these factors are largely under the control of the firm in its portfolio construction—the quality of the obligor, the seniority of the obligation, the correlation across obligors, and the size of the exposures. Because these elements are under the control of the firm, the probability distribution for either losses or returns that results is a product of a portfolio construction process versus something that a firm is passively subjected to. Thus, in addition to providing a guidepost, CVaR is an important tool in the portfolio-management process.

One final comment is that some institutions, such as pension funds and bond mutual funds, that are exposed to an enormous amount of credit risk may not interpret the CVaR as indicative of a capital need since they do not manage their funds using a return on capital framework. In this case, CVaR is simply a way for these institutions to size the amount of potential losses and to manage their portfolios accordingly.

CHAPTER 15

Regulation

We have explained how financial institutions calculate the economic capital they need to support their credit operations and described their primary goals as meeting self-imposed solvency requirements and also measuring and optimizing the profitability of their business. In this chapter, we survey how regulation affects credit risk management practices and in particular what regulators require of financial institutions as minimal amounts of capital. This is known as regulatory capital, and its size is influenced by a number of parameters, including the content of the credit portfolio.

Governments and their agencies around the world regulate financial institutions to ensure the safety and soundness of the financial system, which protects consumers, businesses, and economies overall. In particular, regulators provide considerable oversight to those firms that take funds from individuals with the promise to repay or make these funds available on demand or at a later time. This includes depository financial institutions (such as commercial banks, credit unions, and thrifts), insurance companies, and securities brokers, among others. The mission of financial regulation ranges from keeping financial systems safe and sound by instilling confidence in the financial system and ensuring solvency of financial institutions, to leveling the playing field for investors, to preventing fraud, and to promoting ethical market practices. Regulations for banks, insurers, and other financial institutions around the world are currently undergoing a transformational overhaul. Although much of the activity took root before the 2007 crisis, that crisis gave regulators resolution authority to step up their oversight, tighten rules, close loopholes, and expand their scope to work cooperatively toward bringing more entities under regulatory supervision. Much of their focus, particularly the regulatory arms of central banks, is on large, complex, and systemically important financial institutions since the unraveling of just one of these could make global financial markets collapse.

Globally, the Financial Stability Board (FSB) "coordinates at the international level the work of national financial authorities and international standard-setting bodies in order to develop and promote the implementation of effective regulatory, supervisory, and other financial sector policies. Its mandate is set out in the FSB Charter, which governs the policymaking and related activities of the FSB. These activities, including any decisions reached in their context, shall not be binding or give rise to any legal rights or obligations."[1] The 19 countries in the G20, plus Spain, plus four more of the most industrialized economies Hong Kong, Netherlands, Singapore, and Switzerland, participate in the FSB and have adopted the regulatory, risk management, capital requirement, and resolution standards for banking, derivatives, money market funds, and securitization.

The Bank for International Settlements has implemented Basel III rulemakings for central banks, which, in turn, must implement these rules across banks in their home countries. Note that the FSB envelops the implementation of Basel III, so these are not two competing regulatory frameworks; rather, Basel III is part of the standards package being implemented via the FSB.

In Europe, insurers and pension plans are regulated by Solvency II, which is the EU's rulemaking directive for these institutions. In the United States, the Dodd-Frank Wall Street Reform and Consumer Protection Act of 2010 affects not only the rules, oversight, and supervision of all financial institutions, but also reforms the regulation of credit rating agencies and goes so far as to implement changes to corporate governance and executive compensation practices. We describe various regulators and their jurisdictions later in this chapter.

In this chapter, we will explore various facets of regulation. First, we cover why regulation matters for the credit risk manager of a company doing business with a regulated entity. Next, we explore why regulation matters for the credit risk manager of a company doing business as a regulated entity. Finally, we discuss how regulation matters, with a survey of the key regulators and the major directives affecting the financial industries in the United States, Europe, Canada, and Asia Pacific, where much of the industry's activity occurs.

DOING BUSINESS WITH A REGULATED ENTITY

Doing business with a regulated entity, whether it's a utility company, pharmaceutical, food-processing company, or bank means that the credit profile

---

[1]*Source:* FSB, November 2020.

of that entity will be materially affected by the regulation. The credit profile can benefit from regulation, or alternatively, create pitfalls for the creditor, as we explore next.

Benefits from Regulation

Alignment of Interests   In addition to their other, closely related missions, regulators act on behalf of the customers of financial institutions who, as depositors, policyholders, and customers, having prepaid for services, are often, in fact, creditors to these institutions. The regulator, working on behalf of the customer, provides an ancillary benefit to all creditors, such as bondholders, by keeping the regulated entity on sound footing, and to monitor, and potentially limit, its risk-taking. Thus, there is an alignment of the creditors' interests with the objective of the regulator, with the creditor getting a benefit from the regulator's oversight and enforcement activity.

Solvency   In some instances, regulation makes companies stronger financially, and this is true for financial institutions. In particular, the regulators have strict requirements on the level of capital that these institutions need to hold. This is true not just in the aggregate, but also on a business line or even a transaction-level basis. For example, each time that a life insurer wishes to shift invested assets out of government bonds and into riskier assets such as equities, the regulatory rules are there to require an increase in regulatory capital to reflect the heightened risk from the reallocation. Because capital is expensive, the capital rules provide an effective constraint on the level of risk taking.

Oversight and Governance   Regulation provides an additional layer of governance, and this is good for the creditor because the governance is being conducted by an entity whose mission aligns with the creditor's objectives, under normal circumstances. The regulatory oversight thus raises the burden of proof for management to engage in M&A activity, make expensive and/or unnecessary capital expenditures, or take on too much debt, which ultimately protects the creditor.

A large part of the oversight is disclosure. Regulators require companies to disclose information about their operations, including detailed financial information. Although not all information disclosed becomes available to the public, the disclosure helps to correct a natural information asymmetry between a creditor and obligor. The obligor would rather disclose less information, and the credit analyst would like access to more information. Thus the regulator provides a public good through its information gathering and dissemination. Often accompanying the information disclosure and the increased transparency is a system of early warning signs that trigger various enforcement actions, again, to keep the entity on sound footing.

Systemic Risk and Contagion   Finally, to the extent that the regulated entity is a financial institution, the curtailment of risk appetite by the regulator coupled with the information disclosure requirements creates a public good and should benefit all creditors insofar as the potential for systemic risk (contagion) is lower in a regulated environment. Although this benefit may not be tangible to any one particular creditor, it does help to make credit markets operate more effectively. The ability to lower systemic risk is a primary objective of the G-20 and Dodd-Frank.

Pitfalls from Regulation

Not All Creditors Are Treated Equally by the Regulator   We noted earlier that the regulator's and creditor's interests are aligned, with the solvency of the entity important to both, and that creditors get to free ride on the regulated entity's oversight. Although this is often true, it is not in all instances because, from the regulator's point of view, not all creditors are equal. The regulator's constituency is usually the retail customer, not an investor or business counterparty. Thus, when a regulator gets involved with an entity's operations, it is likely to give preferential treatment to customers. We caution that this is a general statement, and there are instances in which the regulator subordinates the claims of the customers to other business counterparties or to other creditors. However, these cases are usually the exception, not the rule.

Seizure and Lack of Orderly Disposition   Regulators can intervene with a regulated entity's business operations to varying degrees. There is usually a schedule of events that triggers an intervention, such as a breach of minimum capital. The most extreme form of intervention is conservatorship (receivership), in which a regulator takes over the entity and either manages its rehabilitation or, if not viable, its liquidation. In these instances, the regulator will interfere with the transfer of proceeds, and an orderly disposition of the assets by a bankruptcy judge may not occur. When regulators step in and seize the entity's assets, all contractual rights of the creditors may be subordinated to other stakeholders, and creditors' claims will fall in value and even become worthless. This can happen with or without *force majeure* clauses in the contracts (*force majeure* clauses are used by obligors to expunge their liability in the event of governmental or regulatory intervention, or for acts-of-God events).

For this reason, creditors must evaluate the pros and cons of lending to a regulated subsidiary instead of a parent company. The subsidiary produces the cash flows and likely has a higher rating, but it is regulated. The parent has the benefit of not being regulated, but also has no operations, is dependent on upstream dividends, and may have a lower credit rating.

Note that doing business with an unregulated entity can still have exposure to this risk of governmental seizure. Take the case of General Motors' (GM's) creditors in 2008. GM, a largely unregulated entity, was insolvent and could have entered bankruptcy to move forward with an orderly and dispassionate disposition of assets. Instead, the U.S. federal government, by fiat, took control of GM, put over $30 billion of financing into the company, and gave the bondholders shares of a newly organized company worth only a small fraction of their investment, subordinating their interests to the United Auto Workers (UAW) union. The concurrent seizure of Chrysler had an outcome for its creditors that was not dissimilar. For instances in which the government deems a company too big or too important to fail, as that company approaches insolvency, there is political risk that jeopardizes the creditor's rights.

In the case of regulated entities, this political risk is just a form of regulatory risk that can cause credit losses, and it is a fact of life of doing business with them. The regulator can and does step in and take control over the company's assets, which could render the creditor's claims meaningless.

Moral Hazard   Moral hazard manifests itself in various ways. First, regulated entities, knowing that there is a guarantee fund or insurance in place (such as FDIC, SIPC, or PBGC in the United States) to protect their customers should the risks that they take result in losses, have an incentive to take on more risk. Most managers would never knowingly assume more risk on account of insurance or a guarantee fund being in place, yet many behavioral finance studies find that risk-taking is seldom a product of a deliberate decision-making process. A notable exception occurred in 2003, when, as both housing prices and subprime lending were escalating, U.S. Representative Barney Frank now infamously commented on Freddie Mac and Fannie Mae, "I do think I do not want the same kind of focus on safety and soundness that we have in OCC and OTS. I want to roll the dice a little bit more in this situation towards subsidized housing."[2] It is not difficult to infer that allowing the federal housing agencies to roll the dice was a decision made more palatable knowing Congress was standing by with a bailout should it be needed.

---

[2]U.S. House of Representatives Financial Services Committee hearing, September 25, 2003.

Second, the creditor can rely too heavily on the regulator's work and not perform enough of its own due diligence. Again, we go back to the 2007 crisis, when, as data suggested, the housing bubble was ready to burst, some analysts, investors, and observers naively figured that all was well since these entities were overseen by regulators with access to their operations, management, and data, and were in a position to stop irresponsible lending and investment activities should they occur. The regulator's oversight may not be granular enough, nor adaptable to the innovations that the regulated companies experience, positioning the regulator one or two steps behind the supervised company.

Finally, owing to a safety net, customers may be more willing to do business with a regulated entity, which allows the entity to grow faster. In most financial institutions, fast growth is synonymous with unwitting and excessive risk-taking, with unfavorable outcomes. Although regulators recognize the danger that fast growth poses, their presence may be somewhat of an enabler.

Gamesmanship Regulation imposes many operational constraints that impede an entity's operations, financing, and strategic and organizational decisions. Thus, many of the decisions made by management will be affected by the regulatory presence. As a consequence, management will seek to organize itself to give it the most discretion as possible. For lack of a better term, we call this gamesmanship, and it can take various forms.

Organizational Arbitrage

First is organizational arbitrage, in which management (and shareholders) place key personnel, financing, strategy, and even some operations outside of regulatory supervision. For example, nonregulated parent companies will issue shares, which keeps the equity financing out of the regulatory domain. A nonregulated management company may sit alongside the regulated entity and, via service contracts, extract excess cash from the regulated company, which can then be sent upstream to the parent company. In other cases, SPVs will be formed to assume risks, issue securities, and manage cash outside of regulatory supervision. These activities allow the organizations more flexibility in running their businesses.

Although the regulator may be overseeing how its constituents are treated, the company's business will be increasingly managed outside of this oversight.

Regulatory Arbitrage

Second, there is regulatory arbitrage in which an entity bases it decisions for operations, financing, or strategy on where it will get the most favorable regulatory treatment. It will have set up various legal entities and will pick and choose which to engage based on the most beneficial regulatory treatment. A popular misconception is that insurers and SPVs used offshore havens such as Bermuda and the Cayman Islands for the tax-purposes benefits. As important, and perhaps even more so, is a regulatory climate that is more favorable than that in the United States or Europe.

Ratings Arbitrage

Another common form of gamesmanship is ratings arbitrage. For many financial institutions, regulators use ratings to assess the credit risk of assets held and to set regulatory capital requirements. A company may decide to take a credit risk exposure to gain a favorable regulatory treatment. One excellent example of this prior to the 2007 crisis was the investment in collateralized debt obligations (CDOs), which were structured in order to secure AAA ratings for the buyers. Financial institutions liked these instruments because they minimized regulatory capital requirements. As we now know, the fundamentals of these securities did not perform as intended. During the financial meltdown, institutions that purchased these instruments suffered and their creditors were affected as a consequence.

Uneconomic Decision Making

More generally, the gamesmanship can take the form of simple uneconomic decision making in which regulated companies may enter into transactions that are favorable from a regulatory capital standpoint—that is, they use less regulatory capital, yet may have lower risk-adjusted returns or use more economic capital. For example, an insurance company may choose to transfer risk to a U.S. licensed reinsurer whose credit profile is not that strong in lieu of transferring the risk to a financially stronger offshore company because of the incremental cost associated with using an offshore reinsurer that the regulator imposes, such as requiring a letter of credit. Or, in the case of regulatory arbitrage as described earlier, the decision to engage a particular legal entity may be uneconomical, but is preferable for the regulatory advantages.

DOING BUSINESS AS A REGULATED ENTITY

In this section, we summarize why regulation matters for the regulated financial entity. We will not cover the regulatory aspects of nonfinancial firms, such as utility companies, since there is little overlap with this form of regulation and the credit risk management function.

The day-to-day business activities of a regulated entity will be influenced by regulatory rules. This includes its customer-facing activities such as marketing, communications, and new-product development. It also includes internal management activities, such as investment decisions and particular duties of the company's officers. The regulator's presence will be felt throughout the organization, and the credit risk manager will work closely with the chief compliance or chief legal officer to keep from running afoul of regulatory directives.

For the credit risk management function in particular, the regulator will supervise the entity's many exposures to credit risk, such as aging receivables, large balances due from particular counterparties, the valuation of collateral securing an asset, derivatives usage, specific terms and conditions in agreements with counterparties, ratings of tradable securities on the balance sheet, and many more. The supervision will range from monitoring some of these areas, to absolute restrictions, to valuation adjustments based on a quantitative assessment of the risk, to requiring more capital to be allocated to particular risk-bearing activities.

The credit risk manager must know at all times how the firm's internal assessment of risk and capital lines up with the regulator's assessment. Why? First, the company never wishes to breach regulatory limits on exposure or violate any other restrictions. Not only do rule violations put the entity on the wrong side of the regulator, including fines, sanctions, or greater reporting burdens, but some violations can be made public, which can damage the entity's reputation in the marketplace. Second, all else equal, firms will want to have as much capital in excess of the regulatory minimum as possible, since a large margin puts distance between the regulator's reach and the entity. Regulated entities like to point out that the regulatory assessment of credit risk lacks precision, overlooks transaction details that mitigate loss exposure, and suffers from other shortfalls that end up overstating the risks faced by the entity. Despite these protests, most highly rated entities hold capital well in excess of the regulatory minimum, largely in anticipation of the stresses placed on the excess capital margin during economic downturns.

The regulator's assessment of the amount of credit risk exposure taken and the amount of capital required is often based on a formula, which we will discuss in some detail later. At a high level, there are two basic approaches.

In one, the regulator evaluates how much capital is needed based on the riskiness of positions. This amount (regulatory capital) must then be exceeded by the capital the entity actually holds. In the second, the regulator revalues the entity's assets (in a downward direction; i.e., it applies haircuts) and then recalculates actual capital held (revalued assets minus liabilities) and then compares this amount to a regulatory minimum. Both techniques are subject to various modifications, including what forms of hybrid capital are admissible, ad hoc charges for counterparty credit risk, and other asset and liability valuation adjustments.

In the next section on "how" regulation matters, we summarize how the various regulators assess and charge for credit risk.

HOW REGULATION MATTERS: KEY REGULATION DIRECTIVES

In the sections that follow, we describe how regulation affects financial entities with an overview of the key regulators and regulatory directives that they must contend with.

Many international institutions coordinate efforts to set standards and harmonize regulation to close loopholes. The Financial Stability Board ("FSB") and the G-20 are two such international bodies. The Bank for International Settlements is a banker for central banks, organized as a consortium of the member central banks. Although not a regulator itself, it has formed the Basel Committee on Banking Supervision that seeks to harmonize the regulation of banks globally, with a particular emphasis on risk recognition and capital adequacy. In addition, supranational organizations such as the World Bank Group and the International Monetary Fund, both members of the FSB although not regulators, provide oversight to both financial institutions and to sovereign nationals where the financial institutions are domiciled. They exert their oversight through their lending programs via the terms and conditions of the lending agreements, which are not dissimilar to a regulator's rules. They further exert influence by being situated with stand-by lending facilities. The International Swaps and Derivatives Association (ISDA) is a global trade association for the swap market and is actively participating in the G-20 and other undertakings around the globe as they relate to swaps regulation.

In the United States, numerous agencies are responsible for regulating financial institutions. The Dodd-Frank Act recognizes this and, in response, has created the Financial Stability Oversight Council (FSOC) to oversee financial institutions. The regulation attempts to coordinate efforts across products types, such as banking, insurance, and securities, and also to harmonize the patchwork approach to the regulation of these entities that currently involve both state-by-state and federal oversight.

In Europe, the three most important agencies are the European Banking Authority (EBA), the European Insurance and Occupational Pension Authority (EIOPA), and the European Securities Markets Authority (ESMA), which also recognize that they must work in concert with each other to close regulatory loopholes.

In Canada, the Office of the Superintendent of Financial Institutions, (OSFI) regulates commercial banks, insurance, pensions, lending institutions, and credit unions (cooperatives). These institutions, with the exception of the banks, also have provincial regulation. Securities are regulated at the provincial level only. Next, we discuss key regulatory directives in more detail as they affect financial entities.

Dodd-Frank Act of 2010

The Dodd-Frank Act was passed in response to the financial crisis in an attempt to prevent another financial crisis. The law's scope was broad, and mandated the creation of a new agency responsible for implementing and enforcing compliance with consumer financial laws, introduction of more stringent regulatory capital requirements, better oversight and regulation of over-the-counter derivatives, more regulatory scrutiny of ratings agencies by the SEC, initiating changes to corporate governance and executive compensation practices, incorporation of the Volcker Rule, requiring registration for advisers to certain private equity funds, and making significant changes in the securitization market. Many areas of the law have been successfully implemented, including stress testing of banks and adequate capitalization. Stress testing by the Federal Reserve system of member banks occurs on an annual basis and the last test, whose results were released in April 2021, show that all large member banks were adequately capitalized. This is a notable result since in 2020, economies around the globe severely contracted.

In 2018, U.S. Congress passed the Economic Growth, Regulatory Relief, and Consumer Protection Act, which rolled back portions of the Dodd-Frank Act. The rollbacks related in large part to allowing smaller financial institutions to not have to comply with various directives, such as the Volcker Rule. Another feature of the new Act required the consumer credit bureaus to allow individuals to freeze their credit reports at no cost to them.

Although Dodd-Frank's major emphasis is on closing regulatory gaps and reducing the country's exposure to systemic risk, there are many initiatives that address a financial institution's credit risk management activity.

The Financial Stability Oversight Council is charged with identifying threats to the financial stability of the United States, promoting market discipline, and responding to emerging risks to the stability of the United States financial system. It directs various existing agencies, such as the Federal Reserve, to implement and enforce various requirements for financial institutions, including lower leverage, stronger risk-based capital, and greater liquidity. It is chaired by the U.S. Treasury, and is comprised of the following additional voting member agencies: the Federal Reserve, Office of the Comptroller of the Currency (OCC), Securities and Exchange Commission (SEC), Commodities and Futures Trading Commission (CFTC), Federal Deposit Insurance Corp (FDIC), Federal Housing Finance Agency (FHFA), National Credit Union Administration (NCUA), the Bureau of Consumer Financial Protection, and an independent member with insurance expertise appointed by the president and confirmed by the Senate. Notably, Dodd-Frank dissolved the Office of Thrift Supervision and allocated its oversight responsibilities to other agencies.

Among FSOC's 10 voting members, there are eight agencies that impose regulatory rules, and each of these has a myriad of rules affecting the recognition, measurement, and curtailment of credit risk and capital allocation as it relates to its assumption, with some of the rules preceding Dodd-Frank and some rules being enacted as a result of Dodd-Frank. The interested reader can find all of the regulatory rules on www.regulations.gov, which has a search function by regulator and date. Rules as they relate to Dodd-Frank can be found on the U.S. Treasury's website at www.treasury.gov.

Basel III

The Basel Committee on Banking Supervision,[3] under the aegis of the Bank for International Settlements, has enacted a comprehensive set of reform measures developed to strengthen the regulation, supervision, and risk management of the banking sector. These measures are commonly known as Basel III. Note that Basel III is the current directive, having superseded Basel II. These measures are highly similar to Dodd-Frank's in that they aim to (1) improve the banking sector's ability to absorb shocks arising from financial and economic stress; (2) improve risk management and governance; and (3) strengthen banks' transparency and disclosures, which are designed to help raise the resilience of banks to periods of stress, called microprudential regulation. Also like Dodd-Frank, the reform measures target systemic risk, which they call macroprudential regulation.

---

[3]BIS, "Basel III: International Framework for Liquidity Risk Measurement, Standards and Monitoring," December 2010.

Rule-making from Basel III, as implemented by the U.S. Federal Reserve, must coordinate with the Dodd-Frank regulatory reform legislation. This is easier said than done, because there are many inconsistencies across the two rule-making bodies. For one, Dodd-Frank requires that regulators decouple any requirements they impose from referencing the ratings of external ratings agencies, whereas Basel III permits this.

In Europe, banks must comply with Basel III as supervised by the EBA, and the EBA, as the regulator, may make additional capital assessments on banks in the EU, as it is considering doing now with the European debt sovereign crisis and its fallout on European banks.

Basel III sets minimum capital requirements, minimum liquidity, and maximum leverage for banks. Capital is assessed using the approach of evaluating the risk in the assets (a risk-weighted-assets formula), assigning a capital charge, and then comparing this to actual capital held. There are then layers of capital that need to be held relative to the risk assessment. Larger banks need to hold additional buffers, on top of several layers of required capital that are assessed. Entities may elect to use an internally developed (own) model that would allow a more granular approach to measuring credit and other risks. The internal model results require comparison against the formulaic approach, and basic guidelines in recognizing and measuring risk are required, including an approval of the model and the economic scenario generator that underlies it.

Banking rules have been largely implemented by the G20 via the FSB. As of 2021, the rollout of the regulation implementation has moved to derivatives, securitization, money market funds, and resolution planning.

Solvency II

Solvency II is the directive for supervision of insurance and pensions in the EU by the European Insurers and Occupational Pension Agency (EIOPA). Solvency II supersedes the earlier Solvency I directive. Also, similar to Basel III, Solvency II lays out specific requirements for supervised institutions to recognize, measure, curtail, and allocate capital for credit risk exposure. These range from allocating capital based on credit rating and concentration thresholds, to allocating capital for structured credit products based on the quantifiable amount of credit enhancement with which the securities are supported.

As with Basel III, regulated entities may use EIOPA's formulaic model for determining required capital or they may use an internally developed (own) model. There is of course some opportunity for gamesmanship in the usage of an internal model. However, the methodological approaches that companies are ultimately able to adopt will have been reviewed by EIOPA in the commentary periods prior to the full implementation, and, thus, model arbitrage should be minimized.

U.S. Insurance Regulation

Currently, there are 50 regulators across the United States, each supervising insurance companies licensed (or otherwise permitted) to do business in their respective state. Regulators across states coordinate some efforts in terms of rule setting, capital adequacy, disclosure, and marketing practices under the National Association of Insurance Commissioners (the NAIC). The NAIC seeks to harmonize rules and reporting. It is generally effective, but many rules are not adopted universally. States are not required to adopt NAIC model legislation.

However, since regulators know their state's insurance companies very well, they are able to pay significant attention to what goes on in their backyards and are effective watchdogs. Although seemingly disparate and decentralized, these regulators did their job in keeping most licensed insurers out of trouble during the 2007 crisis (AIG's troubles emanated from its noninsurance operations). In 2010, the NAIC took a bold step and rejected the use of Acceptable Ratings Organizations (e.g., Moody's and S&P) ratings for residential mortgage-backed securities (RMBS) assets, and hired PIMCO, the world's largest independent bond manager, to review and rerate these securities for credit risk and Blackrock for CMBS.

That said, as the complexity of transactions increases, particularly with respect to embedded options in life-insurance policies (such as minimum investment return guarantees), and as the use of offshore vehicles continues to grow, the need for trained and highly specialized supervisors is on the increase, which may suggest that there are economies of scale that centralization could foster. Prior to Dodd-Frank, there was momentum building for the federalization of insurance regulation.

With Dodd-Frank and the goals of closing loopholes in regulatory arbitrage, the Federal Insurance Office (FIO) was created. Note that the FIO has a mission to coordinate and gather information and to consult with the FSOC on insurance matters. The FIO is not a regulator, not a voting member of FSOC, and the 50 states in the United States still have their full supervisory powers.

States take a formulaic approach to risk measurement and capital assessment, using the second type of methodology, as described earlier, in which assets are revalued and the resulting recalculated capital (called surplus) is compared against various thresholds.

U.S. Pension Regulation

Defined benefit pensions of the private sector are regulated by the Pension Benefit Guaranty Corporation (PBGC), an agency of the U.S. government founded to provide insurance for underfunded, terminated plans; assist with the bankruptcy process; and to ensure timely and uninterrupted payments to retirees. Concerned about the credit risk posed by pension plans to workers and retirees, the Pension Protection Act of 2006 strengthened contribution and funding rules and required increased transparency to liability recognition and asset valuation.

The PBGC walks a fine line, because forming and keeping the plans open to new hires is optional on the part of corporate sponsors and something that the government wishes to promote. Thus, refraining from placing regulatory burdens on corporate sponsors is part of the PBGC's mission. Notably, there is no risk-weighted asset concept for a pension plan, and no capital requirement as there is with a bank or insurer. Plan sponsors must simply abide by "prudent-investor" rules as defined by ERISA (Employee Retirement Income Security Act), which give the plan sponsor significant leeway in managing the plan's assets.

From an institutional creditor's perspective, a corporation's pension plan represents a large and typically underfunded liability with the potential to grow, not just because actual liabilities could surpass current projections but also because asset performance that is expected may not materialize. Not only does the pension plan stress the finances of the corporate obligor, if and when the corporation (plan sponsor) enters bankruptcy, the PBGC will be exercising its control to represent the interests of workers and retirees, which puts the creditor's claims at risk.

Derivatives Regulation

Derivative regulation around the globe is in the midst of being implemented via the FSB for the 24 countries in its jurisdiction. Since much derivative activity has been conducted on an over-the-counter (OTC) basis—meaning bilateral agreements between two parties—regulation of millions of individual transactions would have been impossible. Transactions have, to date, been conducted on an ad hoc basis, often using a standardized contractual form known as an ISDA, with counterparties negotiating how much collateral needs to be initially posted and subsequently topped up, based on price movements of the underlying asset or on downgrades to the counterparty's credit rating. Regulators globally witnessed the weakness in these agreements due to the systemic risks posed; since the institutions engaged in the transactions are leveraged, if one's counterparty cannot make good on an agreement, that threatens one's own ability to make good on other agreements.

The movement has been toward moving derivatives transactions into exchanges and clearinghouses, where the rules are consistent, collateral requirements are systematic, and in which participants' exposures to various assets can be monitored.

The undertakings are being spearheaded by the FSB overall, ESMA in the EU, and the SEC and the CFTC (Commodities Future Trading Commission) in the United States. Asia, Japan, Australia, Hong Kong, and Singapore have taken steps to implement G20 commitments.

Regulation of Broker-Dealers

In the United States, security broker-dealers are regulated by the Financial Industry Regulatory Authority (FINRA), which is a nongovernmental regulator that serves as a watchdog for all stock exchanges in the United States and has a mission to protect the investing public. Broker-dealers must be licensed with FINRA in order to operate in the securities business. FINRA does not regulate firms from the standpoint of credit risk recognition and management.

In contrast, the SEC does impose capital rules on broker-dealers to reflect the credit and other risks in their operations. The SEC's Net Capital Rule (Rule 15c3-1) works similarly to U.S. regulated insurance capital rules, by which the entity's statutory net worth is adjusted downward to reflect credit and other risks embedded in its assets. Similar to the Basel III and Solvency II capital calculations based on an internal model versus a regulator's formula, in 2004 the SEC began allowing the largest broker-dealers to use an internal model consistent with Basel guidelines.

Also noteworthy is that, under the Securities Reform Act of 1934, the SEC regulates Nationally Recognized Statistical Ratings Organizations (NRSROs) such as S&P and Moody's since their ratings are the primary and most heavily relied on credit risk indicator to most investors, both institutional and individual; integral to the functioning of the capital markets; and what Congress describes as "of National Interest." The regulation has been amended and strengthened at various points in time, notably 2002 (Sarbanes-Oxley), 2006 (Credit Reform Act of 2006), and, most recently, Dodd-Frank. Ironically, the use of ratings is inadmissible for quantifying regulatory capital requirements under Dodd-Frank.

In the EU, in response to the financial crisis and the contribution of the ratings agencies to the crisis, the recently created European Securities and Markets Authority was appointed supervisor of the credit rating agencies.

In Table 15.1, we summarize the key financial regulators and their territories and industries.

TABLE 15.1   Selected Financial Regulators

Regulator	Industry Domain	Territory	Selected Credit Risk Management Directives
EBA	Banks	EU	Basel III, including risk recognition and measurement; capital setting; liquidity management
EIOPA	Insurers and pension funds	EU	Solvency II, including risk recognition and measurement; capital setting; liquidity management
ESMA	Securities ratings agencies	EU	Risk recognition and measurement; capital setting
Federal Reserve	Banks, bank holding companies, and large complex financial institutions such as securities holding companies	United States	Basel III, including risk recognition and measurement; capital setting; liquidity management
FDIC	Commercial banks	United States	Risk recognition and measurement; capital setting
NCUA	Credit unions	United States	Risk recognition and measurement; capital setting; liquidity management
FHFA	Freddie Mac; Fannie Mae; Federal Home Loan Banks	United States	Capital setting; framework for post-conservatorship functioning (for Freddie and Fannie)
SEC	Securities firms; broker-dealers; investment advisors; ratings agencies (NRSROs)	United States	Net capital rules and associated variations to this market conduct governance, transparency, methodology
U.S. Treasury	Coordination of other regulators	United States	Implementation of Dodd-Frank directives
FINRA	Broker-dealers	United States	None
PBGC	Private defined benefit pensions	United States	Prudent investor and required plan contributions triggered by an underfunded status threshold
CFTC	Options, futures, swaps	United States	Capital requirements based on admitted assets

TABLE 15.1   (*continued*)

Regulator	Industry Domain	Territory	Selected Credit Risk Management Directives
States (50)	Insurance	United States	Risk recognition, measurement and reporting; capital requirements; liquidity management
FCSO	Insurance, pensions, lenders, credit unions	Ontario, Canada	Risk recognition and measurement; capital setting; liquidity management
OSFI	Banks, insurers, private pensions, trusts and loan companies	Canada (Federal)	Risk recognition and measurement; capital setting; liquidity management
Provinces and Territories (13)	Securities	Canada	Capital, bonding and insurance requirements; other financial and operational disclosure requirements
Hong Kong Monetary Authority	Banks and depository institutions; Securities/swaps	Hong Kong	Basel III, including risk recognition and measurement, capital setting
Australian Prudential Regulation Authority (APRA)	Banks and deposit taking institutions	Australia	Basel III, risk recognition and measurement, capital requirements, liquidity management

FINAL WORDS

For financial institutions around the globe, there is increased harmonization of regulation. Capital and regulatory standards are more aligned and based on the real world economic shock experienced in 2020; financial institutions, thanks to enhanced capital adequacy imposed by regulators, are safer and sounder. Countries are also becoming better at preparing for and managing the fallout from a systemic risk event should it occur. Finally, although the methodological approaches between industry and regulators may converge, regulators will always add in a safety margin that industry participants will object to, and the fundamental conflicts between the regulator's desired level of capital and the regulated entity are unlikely to dissipate.

CHAPTER 16

Accounting Implications of Credit Risk

The objective of this chapter is to highlight some current accounting issues as they relate to credit risk management. In Chapter 6, "Fundamental Credit Analysis," we approach accounting from the point of view of evaluating the creditworthiness of a prospective or existing counterparty. Understanding basics of how assets, liabilities, contingencies, revenue, and costs are accounted for by a counterparty is integral to understanding that company's credit profile. In this chapter, we instead approach accounting from the point of view of the originator in understanding the accounting implications of originating, holding, or transferring credit risk exposures.

We review accounting guidance from both the Financial Accounting Standards Board (FASB) for U.S. Generally Accepted Accounting Principles (GAAP) and from the International Accounting Standards Board (IASB) for International Financial Reporting Standards (IFRS). Since accounting guidelines in general are continually being updated as they adapt to current business practices and needs, any guidelines that exist at a given time may be amended or superseded by others.

As of July 2021, most countries have adopted IFRS. In the United States, the Securities and Exchange Commission (SEC) is still determining whether to adopt IRFS to replace U.S. GAAP; there does not appear to be momentum towards this outcome though the SEC has stated the value of a uniform set of accounting standards and reporting globally. In 2009, FASB instituted a new codification system to streamline its guidelines into one authoritative set of standards that can be logically followed by any user, not just a certified public accountant (CPA) and years of auditing experience. Thus, what were known in the past as Financial Accounting Statement (FAS), Financial Interpretation Number (FIN), Accounting Principles Board (APB) opinion, or emerging issues task force (EITF), and the like have been mapped to a new and consistent naming convention, the Accounting Standards Codification (ASC) system. International Accounting Standards also has two classification naming systems. Before 2001, standards were classified under IAS; from 2001 onward, standards were issued under IFRS.

We underscore that any accounting topics that we describe are not comprehensive and may not be reflective of the current accounting guidance at any time in the future since guidance is continually being updated. Our discussion is aimed at giving readers a high-level overview of issues that they need to be aware of. In all cases, what we cover below should not be construed as accounting advice.

We cover a nonexhaustive list of topics that we feel are most central in the context of credit-exposed businesses under U.S. GAAP and IFRS. We begin with an overview of accounting for impaired loans and leases, and then follow with the basics of loan-loss accounting and then the joint regulator's (U.S.) policy statement on the Allowance for Loan and Lease Losses, developed to comply with FASB's guidelines. We briefly cover the accounting treatment for other credit instruments, such as corporate bonds, as they relate to impairment.

Next, we cover derecognition and consolidation because these accounting issues relate directly to the accounting treatment of special purpose entities that are a key mechanism in asset securitization. Here again, regulators amended their directives in response to FASB and the IASB.

Then we cover netting, followed by accounting for hedges, and, finally, we touch on credit valuation adjustments (CVA) and debit valuation adjustments (DVA), including the accounting for what's known as "own credit risk."

LOAN IMPAIRMENT

General principles a creditor should apply to account for impairment in a loan portfolio under U.S. GAAP are ASC 450, "Accounting for Contingencies," and ASC 310, which addresses disclosure and detail around loan and trade receivables but not securities, leases, and certain other assets that may have become impaired. Under IASB, the treatment of loan impairment is roughly similar, so we will not go into detail here. An estimated loss from a loss contingency, including uncollectable receivables or loans, is needed because a fundamental accounting goal is to match revenues and expenses. If a loan portfolio generates revenues, there will doubtlessly be credit losses, and setting up a provision for losses as revenues are recognized permits this matching. The estimated loss is thus accrued by a charge to income if it is probable that an asset had been impaired and that the amount of loss can be reasonably estimated. ASC 310 provides further clarity that the uncollectability of both interest and principal should be considered when evaluating impairment (that is, credit losses include late payment) in addition to non-payment, and that measuring the amount of impairment can be done either from an observed market price or from estimating the discounted value of the impaired loans' future cash flows, including collateral.

A loan is impaired when, based on current information and events, it is probable that a creditor will be unable to collect all amounts due according to the contractual terms of the loan agreement. FASB allows for impairment to be recognized both for specific loans known to have problems and more generally for a portfolio of loans known to have problems in the aggregate but without knowing which particular loans in the portfolio are troublesome.

Neither ASC 450 nor ASC 310 specifies how a creditor should: (1) determine that it is probable that it will be unable to collect all amounts due, (2) identify loans that are to be evaluated for collectability, (3) record a direct write-down of an impaired loan, and (4) assess the overall adequacy of the allowance for credit losses. These important decisions are left for the creditor to undertake in its normal loan review procedures. As a consequence of the creditor's judgment, the creditor creates a loan-loss reserve, which we discuss next.

LOAN-LOSS ACCOUNTING

When a bank originates a loan portfolio, it creates a loan-loss reserve for impairments as a contra asset for losses it expects from the portfolio. As described earlier, reserves for impairments are established only for losses that are expected. Again, expected losses include those that are specifically identified and those that are expected in the aggregate. The bank will perform its own internal analysis for why losses are expected to occur, and many of the techniques described in the preceding chapters, such as using expected default frequencies (EDFs™) or rating agency credit migrations, are used for this purpose.

We provide an illustration for loan-loss reserving in Table 16.1.

TABLE 16.1 Loan-Loss Reserving on the Balance Sheet

USD Millions	Jan 2020	Mar 2020	Sep 2020	Dec 2020
Loan Assets	10,000	9,980	9,950	9,950
Loan-Loss Reserve, Contra Asset	200	180	150	195
Net Loans	9,800	9,800	9,800	9,755

In January, the bank has $10 billion in loans, and against these loans, has reserved $200 million for expected losses, which creates an expense of $200 million on the income statement (the P&L) and a net asset of $9.8 billion on the balance sheet. At the next quarter, the bank acknowledges that $20 million of its uncollectable loans are total losses after all recovery is factored in. The bank writes off the $20 million from its gross loans and takes the reserve down by $20 million. The reserve goes down because the bank has figured that the loss was within its expectations as represented by its reserves. Net loans are still $9.8 billion and essentially, nothing has changed. All performance was within expectations and had already been factored into the bank's calculation of its net loans. There is no change to net assets and no change to income since the bank had previously recorded a $200 million charge.

In September, the same situation happens but now with a write-off of $30 million. The bank takes down both its gross loan holdings and its reserves as well, and net assets do not change. Again, the loss materialized but the bank had already expected it, so there is no change on its total net asset line and no change to income.

Between September and December, the economy takes a turn for the worse and delinquencies rise unexpectedly across the loan portfolio. The bank's CRO and CFO fear that losses will exceed what was originally estimated to be $200 million, and the new estimate for total losses associated with the original portfolio of $10 billion is now $245 million (the $200 million in original reserves plus the $45 million of additional reserve relating to changed conditions), or $45 million higher than originally estimated. Loan-loss reserves are now increased by $45 million. Gross loans don't change, since there are no new originations or write-offs, so now net loans fall by $45 million. The reduction in net assets, which is a bad debt expense, is reflected in income, so pre-tax income—all else being equal—falls by $45 million.

This is a highly simplified example. In reality, it is difficult to decompose observed delinquencies and losses into what was anticipated versus what was unanticipated. If losses are somewhat larger than expected, is it timing, seasonality, or a geographic aberration as opposed to absolute loss amounts, when all is said and done? Even with a long time series of data on credit migration and expert analysis, the reserves that will ultimately be needed are still an estimate that is subject to error. If it were determined that a portion of the additional $45 million reserve was attributed to some of the $50 million already written off in the first three quarters—for example, $20 million—then net income would fall by the remainder,

$30 million in the example given. Stated another way, the CRO needs to assess what reserves are appropriate for the $9,950 million of gross loans outstanding and any change to existing reserves that this entails would affect income.

Note that how often and how significantly loss reserves are reset will affect income volatility. Thus, loan-loss reserves are a key balance sheet item for management. Because there is ambiguity as well as discretion in establishing loss reserves, a topic that we expand upon later, establishing a new reserve or changing a reserve once established is, within broadly defined parameters, at the financial institution's discretion. Thus, the institution has some leeway in establishing these provisions and in recognizing income.

REGULATORY REQUIREMENTS FOR LOAN-LOSS RESERVES

Income recognition worries the SEC and public accounting firms registered with the Public Company Accounting Oversight Board (PCAOB, the auditors of publicly traded firms), since the opportunity for managing earnings is present, and inadequate reserves worries regulators. For accounting issues as they relate to banks, such as reserving and the impact on earnings, there is a dialogue maintained between the FASB and the banking regulators (known as banking "agencies" by the FASB), namely, the Federal Deposit Insurance Company (FDIC), the Federal Reserve Bank, National Credit Union Administration (NCUA), and the Office of the Comptroller of the Currency (OCC).

This dialogue resulted in an Interagency Policy Statement on the Allowance for Loan and Lease Losses first released in 1993, then amended in 2003 and again in 2020.[1] In the statement, there are numerous directives regarding application of FASB guidelines on disclosure and accounting for loan losses. The directives include not only measurement of estimated credit losses and the estimation process, but also the governance of the process itself. Outlined are responsibilities of the reporting entity's board of directors and of management, the process for independent review of the methodology employed, and the qualifications and independence of loan review personnel, among others.

The credit risk management function may be involved in the reserve setting either directly or in the capacity of an independent reviewer. If

---

[1] Federal Deposit Insurance Corp, "5000 Statements of Policy: Interagency Policy Statement on the Allowance for Loan and Lease Losses," www.fdic.gov.

independent from the business unit, credit risk management can be assigned to review the methodology employed or to perform the credit review of loans. As per the banking agencies' directive, the review functions need to report directly to the Board of Directors.

IMPAIRMENT OF DEBT SECURITIES

Recognizing bond impairment depends on how the debt instruments are classified upon purchase, namely under ACS 320 in U.S. GAAP, "Accounting for Investments in Debt Securities," and under a similar classification under IASB guidelines (IAS 39). Debt securities can be classified as held to maturity, available for sale, or as trading securities. The classification drives the accounting treatment and, thus, how impairment is treated.

For bonds designated as available for sale (AFS), valuation changes are to be assessed as either credit related (nontemporary) or temporary, such as from yield curve movements. Valuation changes due to temporary, noncredit events are recognized on the income statement as other comprehensive income, an entry below the earnings line. The corresponding recognition on the balance sheet is through accumulated other comprehensive income, which is a component of shareholders' equity. Thus, when valuation changes for noncredit events—such as the yield curve increasing—and the reporting entity intends to hold the bond until the price recovers, the change in market value attributable to this factor is recorded in other comprehensive income on the income statement and correspondingly affects accumulated other comprehensive income on the balance sheet. Note that if the reporting entity is more likely than not to sell the bond before price recovery, the change in value is recognized directly in income.

For changes in value that are credit related, the amount of the value change attributable to the credit quality change is recognized in income, and this is known as other-than-temporary impairment (OTTI). This treatment is followed regardless of whether the reporting entity intends to hold onto or sell the asset. However, the described treatment of accounting for noncredit valuation changes prevails—for the element of the value change attributable to yield curve and other noncredit related factors, regardless of whether these changes are recognized in accumulated other comprehensive income or income directly, is a function of how long the owner intends to hold the bond. While reversals to impairments are not permitted for any future recoveries, under ACS 320 the difference between the new amortized cost basis and the cash flows expected to be collected is accreted as interest income.

Under IASB, for bonds that are available for sale, an impairment is recognized directly in income only if there's evidence of credit default. Reversals to impairments are permitted for any future recoveries.

Under FASB, for bonds designated as held-to-maturity, total impairment is the amortized cost basis less the bond's fair value. The portion of the impairment attributable to credit loss is recognized in income. All other sources that the value change can be attributed to (such as interest rates) are recognized in accumulated other comprehensive income. Then the part of the impairment attributable to all noncredit sources is accreted to the carrying amount of the bond through accumulated other comprehensive income over the remaining life of the bond. Under IASB, the impairment is measured as the carrying amount of the bond less the present value of estimated future cash flows discounted at the instrument's original effective interest rate. This method may not be equivalent to a fair-value estimate under FASB. Impairment is recognized in the income statement. Under IASB, the impairment calculation is unlikely to reflect credit deterioration unless it is to the point of default.

DERECOGNITION OF ASSETS

Derecognition of assets, which allows originated transactions and some or all of their associated assets and liabilities to become off-balance-sheet, and consolidation of the special purposes entities and vehicles (SPEs and SPVs, respectively) that house them are integrally related. Under IFRS 9, "Financial Instruments, Recognition and Measurement," which governs derecognition under IAS, the SPE must first be consolidated. Then a flowchart test is followed to see if derecognition is allowed. If the originator has no rights or no remaining rights to the cash flows of the SPE, or has no control over the SPE and no substantial risk or reward from its relationship with the SPE, then it can derecognize. The originator's continued involvement with the transaction (for example, as a servicer) does not preclude it from derecognition, provided that certain conditions are met, which are essentially that it acts only in a pass-through capacity, just collecting cash from one place and passing it through to another.

Under U.S. GAAP, the treatment for structured finance transactions involving an SPE was governed by derecognition guidelines in ASC 860, "Accounting for Transfers and Servicing of Financial Assets and Extinguishments of Liabilities" until 2008, when they were updated with ASC 810. Originators (or other participants involved in an SPE) may derecognize an asset and achieve sale accounting if they have no control over the asset upon transfer or thereafter, if the transferor is legally isolated from the transferee (originator) and all of its affiliates, and if there are no constraints on the transferor's sale of the assets. The derecognition step is taken first or in conjunction with the consolidation test, as described next.

CONSOLIDATION OF VARIABLE INTEREST ENTITIES (VIEs)

Consolidation of SPVs and SPEs (hereafter referred to as SPEs) and other entities set up for the purpose of facilitating securitization transactions has been at the forefront of accounting issues in the last decade because, up until 2003, SPEs did not need to be consolidated by any other entity. As discussed in Chapter 8, dedicated to securitization, a primary driver behind an originator's setting up an SPE was to keep the assets and liabilities off its balance sheet while still retaining some economic benefit from the transactions. Keeping the assets off-balance-sheet is desired because otherwise capital requirements would be far higher. Under current banking rules in many jurisdictions, capital is determined, in large part, as a factor of risk-weighted assets; the greater the assets, the greater the capital, all else equal. Thus, bigger balance sheets are more capital intensive.

However, the proliferation of securitizations created large amounts of assets and liabilities that were orphans—recognized on no one's balance sheet. Recall Enron and its exploitation of the off-balance-sheet treatment of its business dealings, in which billions of liabilities went unrecognized. As a consequence of Enron, Sarbanes-Oxley was passed in 2003, and the FASB, in concert with the legislation, created guidance, known as Financial Interpretation Number (FIN) 46R. FIN 46R required that the entity with the largest variable interest and, more distinctly, with the most to lose in the SPE (for example the originator or the servicer) needed to consolidate the SPE. Guidelines were promulgated to determine which participant held the largest variable interest with the most downside. Note that FIN 46R and subsequent directives consider a whole class of entities, of which an SPE is a special case, called variable interest entities (VIEs). VIEs include not only SPEs and SPVs, but also joint ventures between two companies and other arrangements in which participants have variable stakes. Qualified SPEs (QSPEs), which were widely employed in asset-backed commercial-paper conduits, loan securitizations, and other types of securitizations, were exempt from FIN 46R.

Then, in 2009, Financial Accounting Statement (FAS) 166 and FAS 167 amended FIN46R (now ASC 810 captures all consolidation issues). FAS 166 removed the exemption for QSPEs and under FAS 167 a qualitative approach to identify which party has the power to direct the entity's activities, rather than a downside risk approach, is used as the primary determinant of which entity must consolidate. Thus, for many banks, the implementation of FAS 166 and FAS 167, and subsequently ACS 810, increased the amount of assets and liabilities reported on the balance sheet, with a corresponding impact on regulatory capital requirements.

Under IASB's IFRS 10, the test for consolidation relies more heavily on who controls the VIE. However, by and large, the two bodies have succeeded in adopting a reasonably similar approach. That said, the IASB and FASB have not concluded their efforts regarding consolidation.

At the time, this accounting change had such a material impact on banks that originate these securitizations and other structured finance transactions that the FDIC, one of several U.S. banking regulators, actually allowed banks to delay their compliance with regulatory capital requirements, during which time, banks rebuilt their capital bases as they brought assets back on the balance sheet.

ACCOUNTING FOR NETTING

In Chapter 17, we cover netting of derivative asset and liability positions across counterparties as a form of mitigation. As we recall, offsetting, or netting, is the act by which two counterparties owe each other money, and under a legally enforceable agreement, they are allowed to net the two sums, resulting in just one counterparty remitting a payment to the other. In the following discussion, we cover netting of derivative positions. However, netting is not limited to derivatives; for example, it is practiced in the insurance industry with claims receivable against premiums payable, in the securities lending markets (borrowings against lending), and in other markets.

Under U.S. GAAP ASC 210-20, provided there is an unconditional legally enforceable right to offset, netting on the balance sheet is permitted but not required. However, although presenting net positions is optional, almost all industry participants choose to make use of it. If the right of offset is conditional, then amounts must be shown on a gross basis. Under IASB, provided there is an unconditional legally enforceable right to offset, netting is *required*. A master netting agreement (MNA) is the legal contract used by most participants that gives them the legally enforceable right to offset.

The key word is unconditional. Under IASB's IFRS 32, if the MNA's terms are that offset is allowed only if one of the companies defaults or goes into bankruptcy, then amounts due and owed must be presented on a gross basis (until such time that there is a default or bankruptcy, if ever). Under current U.S. GAAP, netting in this circumstance is both permitted and widely practiced.

Bank A	Bank B	Bank A	Bank B
Unconditional Right of Offset		Conditional Right of Offset, No Netting (Gross amounts)	
Assets			
$US 400 million		$US 1,000 million	$US 600 million
Liabilities			
	$US 400 million	$US 600 million	$US 1,000 million

FIGURE 16.1   Netting Illustration, U.S. GAAP and IFRS

Figure 16.1 shows an illustration of positions on a net and gross basis. On the far right of the table, assets and liabilities are shown on a gross basis; Bank A has $1 billion of assets owed to it by Bank B, and $600 million of liabilities it owes to Bank A. If the MNA includes an unconditional right of offset, then the assets and liabilities are netted, which shrinks balances on the balance sheet (far left column).

HEDGE ACCOUNTING

Hedge accounting is important for the credit risk manager to understand, first, because a hedge may be employed to mitigate credit risk exposure, and second, the accounting treatment is partially dictated by the creditworthiness of the counterparty.

Accounting for hedges under U.S. GAAP is guided by ACS 815, "Derivatives and Hedging." If the derivative is used as a hedge and if the hedge is deemed effective, it is recognized as either an asset or liability and valued at fair value, and it may be classified as either a fair-value hedge or a cash-flow hedge.

Accounting for a Fair-Value Hedge

If a company uses a derivative to offset an exposure to changes in the fair value of an asset or liability or of an unrecognized commitment, this use would be classified as a fair-value hedge. If so, the accounting treatment of the asset or liability would change. For example, if a company wants to hedge an exposure to a bond that has been classified as available for sale, once the hedging transaction is entered, that bond's change in value will now be recognized in income, rather than in other comprehensive income (OCI), which would have been the case in the absence of the hedge. In this way, the change in the value of the bond, now reflected in income, offsets the change in the value of the fair-value hedge that also flows through income.

A reporting entity seeking to use fair-value hedge accounting for its derivatives must meet certain requirements including the effectiveness of hedge. Effectiveness is determined through a periodic assessment to confirm that the hedge is "highly" effective in offsetting changes in the fair value of the derivative with changes in the fair value of the hedged position.

Each derivative in an MNA is tested individually for effectiveness after considering rights of offset because offsetting amounts will affect the valuation of the hedges on a portfolio level. In addition, a counterparty's credit risk is considered in estimating the hedge's effectiveness, even if it is not eventually factored into the effectiveness test. Also, we will cover the treatment of counterparty credit risk in derivative valuation next, on credit and debit valuation adjustments.

Accounting for a Cash-Flow Hedge

Cash-flow hedges are used to hedge exposure to cash-flow volatility. The accounting for cash-flow hedges differs from that for fair-value hedges. Like fair-value hedges, cash-flow hedges are recognized at fair value on the balance sheet; however, changes in value of the hedges do not flow through income but rather to OCI.

For a hedge to qualify for a cash-flow hedge, certain conditions must be met, including effectiveness tests that, like a fair-value hedge, are highly prescriptive.

Accounting for Macro Hedges

In addition to hedging particular exposures, companies also enter into hedging transactions to hedge an aggregation of exposures, known as a macro hedge. Thus, the hedge is viewed on a portfolio basis. In this case, hedge accounting does not apply, and the change in value of the macro hedge is recognized in both equity and income, and it is subject to CVAs and DVAs, as discussed in the next section.

Hedge Accounting under IASB

The treatment of derivatives under IFRS 9 is similar on the surface to ASC 815 but many details and nuances differ between the two. Companies using IAS may elect to account for their hedges under IAS 39, which precedes

IFRS 9, in lieu of IFRS 9. IAS 39 has been criticized because it lacks principles, is strictly rules-based, and, as a consequence, there may be a mismatch between the application of hedge accounting and the entity's risk management objectives. For example, under IAS 39, an airline that hedges jet fuel with a forward contract for crude oil cannot use hedge accounting for the forward contract.

CREDIT VALUATION ADJUSTMENTS, DEBIT VALUATION ADJUSTMENTS, AND OWN CREDIT RISK ADJUSTMENT

In other parts of this book, such as Chapter 20, we touch upon the mark-to-market (MTM) value of derivative positions and outline why a position's value is different from a price paid (collected) to buy (sell) a derivative.

On top of this, the MTM value of the positions can be adjusted downward for the creditworthiness of one's counterparty. To illustrate, if an MTM position of a derivative is worth something with a highly creditworthy counterparty, the same position is worth less with a less creditworthy counterparty. Since no counterparty is truly free of credit risk, all positive MTM positions could be marked down by some amount. This is the essence of a credit valuation adjustment (CVA).

In symmetry with this concept, if one's MTM position becomes negative (goes in the favor of one's counterparty) and there is a net liability, this, too, can be marked down for one's own creditworthiness. This is a debit valuation adjustment (DVA). The DVA reflects one's own credit risk in valuing one's liabilities.

Credit and debit valuation adjustments (CVA and DVA, respectively) and own credit risk adjustments are being incorporated by financial and other institutions in response to fair-value measurement directives under both IFRS and U.S. GAAP.

Both IFRS and U.S. GAAP guide reporting entities on the measurement of fair value in allowing markdowns for the credit risk of assets held and for the mark downs on one's own liabilities for one's own credit risk that one's counterparty is exposed to.

Currently, most large financial institutions adjust the values of traded products using CVA and DVA to reflect the credit risk of one's counterparties and also for one's own credit risk. Neither FASB or IASB give specific guidance on how the adjustment should be calculated, and the various ways to calculate credit risk discussed throughout this book are used in practice.

The calculation of CVAs and DVAs are tied to the MTM position valuations and, thus, are not straightforward. In fact, the calculations are involved enough that many firms will outsource the function to specialist valuation firms that will remove the quantitative burdens for companies needing to perform these calculations. Valuation specialists also provide an independent third-party validation role for the values of these relatively illiquid instruments.

IFRS 7

IFRS 7 touches on some of the other accounting issues in this chapter, so we will mention it briefly. IFRS 7 requires disclosures on a reporting entity's financial instruments and how they affect the entity's financial position, performance, and cash flows. It also requires disclosures on the risks associated with those financial instruments and the processes for how an entity manages those risks.

IFRS 7 both combines and goes beyond the disclosure requirements previously set out in IAS 32 and IAS 30. Some examples of items requiring disclosure are the ineffectiveness of both cash-flow and net-investment hedges recognized in income, provisions against impaired assets, and a ratings analysis (internal or external) to reflect the credit quality of financial assets that are neither past due nor impaired.

FINAL WORDS

The purpose of the chapter is to give the reader a flavor of some of the most common accounting implications that the credit risk manager would come across and likely need to understand in performing a credit risk management function. That said, accounting guidelines are continually being updated to reflect both commercial realities and the FASB and IASB continuing improvements in harmonization of guidance for recognition, disclosure, and valuation. We reiterate that the preceding discussion is by no means sufficient in either the depth or breath of the issues at hand.

Mitigation and Transfer

CHAPTER 17

Mitigating Derivative Counterparty Credit Risk

Chapter 5 explains why certain transactions, such as derivative transactions or supply/purchase agreements of commodities, generate a type of credit risk called counterparty credit risk. The chapter also explains how to quantify it, which presents a challenge because the exposure amount changes constantly over the life of the contract. Recall that the exposure amount depends on the market value of the product underlying the transaction, such as a commodity, an interest rate, or a foreign-currency exchange rate, which can vary considerably over time. This is why it is a dynamic exposure and not a fixed one. The more volatile the underlying product, the more uncertain the counterparty credit risk exposure.

It is not surprising, then, that this uncertainty has led to the development of mitigating techniques to make transactions less risky for the parties involved. A firm can have an appetite for, say, interest-rate risk, but may not want to take the associated credit risk on the counterparty. Similarly, a company may need to lock in the price of a commodity over a long period of time but does not want to be exposed to the risk of loss from its counterparty defaulting prior to the termination date of the contract.

The mitigating techniques work to isolate the risk of default of the counterparty from the underlying contract. What they achieve is to reduce, transfer, or eliminate the credit risk and leave the participants exposed either to primarily market risk for derivative transactions or to the commitment to sell or buy a product for the supply/purchase agreements related to physical delivery of commodities like oil or sugar.

MEASUREMENT OF COUNTERPARTY CREDIT RISK

As a reminder, a dynamic exposure is measured with the concepts of mark-to-market (MTM) and value at risk (VaR):

- The MTM value of a derivative contract is a snapshot of the economic value of a transaction at a certain point in time, based on the value of the underlying product. If it is a positive number, what traders call an in-the-money position, it indicates credit risk exposure, meaning that the contract itself has value, so if the counterparty fails to live up to the contract, there is a loss. It fluctuates with the changes in the market value of the product underlying the transaction. As such, it can be a highly volatile number. The MTM value is, therefore, closely tracked and is the driver that triggers mitigation actions. Most large financial institutions calculate MTM for all transactions generating counterparty credit risk exposure on a daily basis.

- The value at risk (VaR) measure of counterparty credit risk for a dynamic exposure is a forward-looking measure of the exposure associated with a transaction. It aims at forecasting, with a chosen degree of confidence, a realistic value of the expected credit loss of a transaction over its lifetime should a counterparty default. It is sometimes called the future estimated exposure or potential future credit exposure. Its primary use is to set a credit limit and to calculate the amount of capital necessary to support a transaction. Thus, it has no impact on the relationship between the parties. It is an internal calculation, not shared with the other party. Note that the time horizon chosen can be much shorter than the final legal maturity of the contract, like a few days for certain highly traded products, as the credit risk is present just between the time to receive the confirmation that the original counterparty defaulted and to take action, such as replacing the counterparty with another in the same trade.

Much of what we present in what follows applies to both exchange-traded derivatives, which are standardized contracts that are traded on an exchange, and over–the-counter (OTC) derivatives, which are bilateral transactions between two counterparties that in many cases are not standard. In instances in which we describe the interaction between two counterparties, these are OTC transactions. We also introduce how the counterparty credit risk is affected by trading through a central clearinghouse and how the clearinghouses themselves mitigate their own exposure to this risk.

MITIGATION OF COUNTERPARTY CREDIT RISK THROUGH COLLATERALIZATION

The idea behind mitigation is to cap the counterparty credit risk exposure at some predetermined, acceptable level, known as a threshold. Mitigation is achieved thanks to a mechanism that kicks in whenever the value of the credit exposure (i.e., the MTM value) reaches or exceeds the threshold agreed upon between the two parties involved in a transaction. As long as the MTM is below the threshold, nothing happens.

How is this accomplished? The usual process is called collateral posting, collateralization, or margining. Collateral posting has been a feature of the derivatives market for almost as long as the market has existed. This is the way it works: The counterparty that creates the exposure provides to the other party an amount of money or securities equivalent to the difference between the value of the transaction and an agreed threshold of unsecured exposure. We illustrate the process in Figure 17.1.

Suppose that Company A enters into a derivative transaction with Company B and that each party has agreed to a $10 million threshold. As long as the MTM value of the deal remains below $10 million, nothing happens. If one day the deal is valued at $15 million in favor of Company A, Company B must post $5 million of collateral. If the following day the transaction is valued at $17 million, Company B must post an additional $2 million. If, on the next day, the value retreats to $16 million, Company A must give back $1 million to Company B. When the collateral exchange is settled, the exposure never exceeds the $10 million that Companies A and B have agreed to take on each other.

In derivatives markets, firms are not involved in only one but in multiple trades with the same counterparty. As a result, the threshold does not apply to each individual transaction but to the entire portfolio. The MTM value of each and every trade is calculated and then added up. Taking into account all portfolio transactions is known as netting all positions, and the mechanism is fully described in the ISDA (International Swaps and Derivatives Association) documentation presented later. Note that some deals create exposure to a counterparty and some deals give a counterparty one's own credit exposure. The result of all additions and subtractions is then compared to the threshold and to the amount of collateral already exchanged. Netting is conducted on a legal-entity basis. For example, if a firm has positive and negative exposures to two legal entities that have the same parent company, these exposures cannot be netted.

Another method of collateralizing derivative exposure that is commonly used with large corporates rated below investment grade is to cause derivatives to be secured together with loans under the counterparty's primary secured-bank-credit agreement. This is done because these corporates are generally prohibited by their credit agreements from posting separate collateral for derivatives. These highly specialized arrangements are heavily negotiated and require careful attention to the terms of the relevant credit documentation exposure.

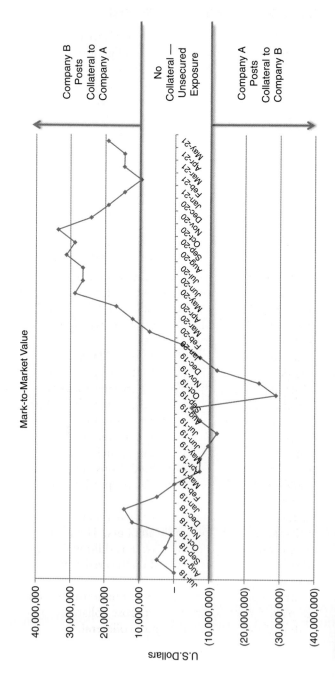

FIGURE 17.1 Collateral Posting

Analyzing the Counterparty and Setting the Threshold

An essential task of the credit risk assessment unit is to analyze the financial strength of a potential counterparty. Like all mitigation techniques, collateral posting is not a substitute for risk analysis. It does not improve the credit quality of a counterparty but simply limits losses in case of default.

The first decision to be made is whether to transact with a counterparty at all. Before setting a threshold, a firm must be comfortable with the creditworthiness of its counterparty and with its ability to post collateral when needed. If a firm is weak and has limited access to liquidity, setting a low threshold alone is not sufficient. If the MTM value increases, a weak counterparty may not have sufficient collateral to post, or it may be precluded from posting by restrictions in its loan documents and could default on its obligation to do so. This may translate into a straight loss for all its trading partners.

For example, the inability to post collateral caused the demise of the U.S. broker-dealer MF Global Holdings Ltd. in 2011. MF Global had entered into large transactions (primarily the purchase of sovereign bonds with the proceeds of repurchase agreements) whose value deteriorated quickly with the European sovereign debt crisis. As a result, MF Global's counterparties requested collateral that MF Global did not have, which led to its default and liquidation in a very short period of time.

The second decision is to set a threshold for collateral posting. In other words, two firms deciding to do business together agree on the amount of uncollateralized or unsecured counterparty exposure they are comfortable with. In practice, these thresholds are not negotiated. The largest financial institutions agree to set very low or even zero thresholds in order to make the transactions with each other as safe as possible. If the thresholds are not zero, they are normally based on rating agencies' ratings, or ratings-triggers. If a firm is downgraded, the threshold drops automatically and the firm must post additional collateral to its counterparties. Typical threshold amounts are shown in Table 17.1.

The standards also contain a minimum transfer amount (MTA) in order to avoid an exchange of cash for small amounts. The idea is that if the change between two valuations is immaterial, no additional cash is required. The MTA is either a fixed amount or based on the credit rating of the counterparty, also seen in Table 17.1.

Collateral relationships may be one-way relationships, meaning that only one of the parties may be required to post collateral. In a two-way relationship, both parties are required to post collateral.

TABLE 17.1 Illustrative Threshold Amounts

Debt Rating: Moody's	Debt Rating: S&P Global	Threshold Amount	Minimum Transfer Amount
Aaa	AAA	$35,000,000	$1,000,000
Aa2	AA	$25,000,000	$1,000,000
A2	A	$10,000,000	$1,000,000
Baa2	BBB	$5,000,000	$500,000
Ba1 or lower or unrated	BB+ or lower or unrated	0	0

Margin-call mechanisms are fairly standardized except for the frequency of margin calls and the manner in which collateral must be handled by the receiving party.

Negotiations also take place when a counterparty, because of its status or for other reasons, either is not allowed to or not willing to post collateral. These instances are infrequent, and most happen when a counterparty is anxious to do a one-off deal that is not collateralized together with others or if a deal has end users (which we will explain later). Credit analysts must then review the specifics of the transaction as it relates to counterparty credit risk exposure before providing an opinion on the deal.

Weak credits, including hedge funds, are also required to post additional funds (e.g., initial margin, "independant amount") for certain types of derivatives. This may be a fixed amount but it is more commonly determined on a transaction-by-transaction basis and returned as each transaction is closed out. Under the ISDA documentation architecture discussed later, these amounts legally secure all transactions between the parties, not only the transactions under which they are posted.

Collateral Posting: The Valuation Agents

For each bilateral collateral relationship, one party is legally responsible for the computation of the MTM values of each transaction in the portfolio and for the valuation of the collateral already posted. This party is called the valuation agent.

The computations of MTM values and the valuation of existing collateral start after market closing to take into account the most recent information available. The results are available to back offices when they arrive in the office the following morning. They then share the numbers with all their counterparties and ask for additional funds (if the MTM values have deteriorated and/or if the collateral assets have lost value) or announce a refund (when they have too many collateral assets). Asking for collateral is known as making a margin call.

If the process works well, the counterparty credit exposure will exceed the threshold only for a few hours, between the market closing and when the collateral assets are received. Thus, the uncollateralized exposure is of short-term nature and, absent strong volatility, does not pose much additional risk. Notices of margin calls have to be sent early, typically before 1:00 p.m., and the funds must be transferred the following business day. In practice, most firms endeavor to settle all margin calls the day they receive the notice. In rare cases when the market is very volatile, some counterparties even make intraday margin calls.

What happens if the counterparty fails to post collateral? It is considered to be a breach of the master agreement between the parties and the asking counterparty then has the right to terminate all transactions and liquidate the positions to reduce its losses. Assume, using the same prior example, that the aggregate MTM value of all trades goes one day from $12 million to $15 million and that the threshold is $10 million. Let's also assume that the counterparty had met its previous margin call and had posted $2 million. If it is unable to post the additional $3 million, the trades are liquidated. Absent more changes of MTM value, this leads to a gross loss of $15 million and a net loss of $13 million.

In exceptional cases, credit risk assessment teams of the counterparties can agree to exclude a particular trade from collateral posting requirements, meaning that no collateral is required, regardless of the MTM value of the trade. These rare and increasingly uncommon cases involve the largest and most creditworthy firms that have great bargaining power, and they may have short-term trades that are difficult to value. Also, in some instances, an entire derivatives relationship with a very creditworthy firm, typically a large corporate, may be uncollateralized.

Acceptable Collateral

Collateral assets must meet the following basic criteria to truly mitigate credit risk:

- Credit quality: Collateral must have high credit quality. The collateral received to mitigate counterparty credit risk cannot pose credit risk in its own right. For example, low-rated bonds posted as collateral may themselves default. Thus, usually only high-quality collateral is normally accepted, such as those with ratings of at least AA/Aa or even the increasingly rare AAA/Aaa bond.

- Liquidity: Collateral must be liquid; that is to say, it can be sold easily. If a counterparty defaults, the trades are liquidated and the collateral assets are sold to maximize the amount of money recovered. Instruments with deep markets like government bonds are preferred because they can be sold easily. Even high-quality corporate bonds can take time to sell or be subject to wide bid-ask spreads. Furthermore, highly liquid collateral assets are easy to value, which greatly facilitates the process.
- Price stability: Collateral must have price stability. If the collateral's price is volatile, the price movement between two valuation dates can cause losses. A sharp decline of MTM values can trigger a margin call that is, at best, settled the following day, which thereby exposes a firm to additional credit risk. Similarly, money can be lost between the time that the decision to sell collateral assets is made and that the proceeds of the sale are actually collected. Price stability is not an issue when cash is delivered, but it has to be taken into account for other forms of collateral. In practice, when the price of collateral is volatile, haircuts, as described further on, are applied.
- Correlation: Collateral must be uncorrelated with the transaction. To be effective, collateral must not be positively correlated either with the counterparty or with the underlying product. If the risk of the counterparty defaulting coincides with the loss of value, or even the default, of the collateral, the mitigating efforts are close to worthless. This is called wrong way collateral, which means that, instead of providing security to a transaction, the value of the collateral assets declines when the exposure increases.
- Security interest: The party must have a perfected security interest in the collateral. The right to truly own and liquidate the collateral in a default scenario must be conveyed to the party that receives it. In case of default, a third party must not claim the rights to the collateral. Bulletproofing this security interest is the domain of lawyers who specialize in these transactions.

Occasionally one or more of these requirements may not be met when a counterparty, typically a fund or similar entity, insists on posting only certain classes of assets that it is likely to have available. In this situation, normally an adjustment is made by requiring initial margin or overcollateralization in some form.

Haircuts

In a perfect world, collateral would always consist of cash, which is completely liquid, stable, and void of credit risk. However, in the real world,

TABLE 17.2   Collateral Haircuts

Eligible Credit Support	Valuation Percentage
Cash in eligible currency	100%
U.S. Treasury obligations having a remaining maturity as of the relevant valuation date of not more than 1 year	100%
U.S. Treasury obligations having a remaining maturity as of the relevant valuation date of more than 1 year but not more than 5 years	99%
U.S. Treasury obligations having a remaining maturity as of the relevant valuation date of more than 5 years but not more than 10 years	97%
U.S. Treasury obligations having a remaining maturity as of the relevant valuation date of more than 10 years	95%

companies often have to compromise and settle for assets other than cash. All financial assets have a specific risk profile, and some may score well for credit quality but less for liquidity or price stability, and vice versa. To address this issue, the industry has developed the usage of haircuts, or valuation percentages, that represent a discount applied to the face value of collateral, which is less attractive than cash. The haircut serves to adjust for the difference between the amount of money expected to be recovered and the actual proceeds of the liquidation. Small haircuts are applied to high-quality and liquid collateral with limited price volatility. Conversely, collateral assets presenting more credit risk, being less liquid and prone to price changes, bear larger haircuts. Note that longer U.S. Treasury obligations are subject to haircuts due to price volatility.

If collateral belongs to a family with a haircut of 2 percent, it means that 100/98 percent = 102.04 percent of the requested amount must be posted. In other words, $1 million of collateral can only cover $980,000 of margin requirements. The concept of haircuts is also central in the design of repurchase agreements, or repos, presented further on in this chapter.

In Table 17.2 we present examples of haircuts used in the industry.

Readers interested in accessing more detailed information on eligible credit support are encouraged to visit ISDA's website (www.isda.org).[1]

---

[1]ISDA, the International Swaps and Derivatives Association, Inc., is a global trade association of swaps and derivatives dealers who participate in the privately negotiated (OTC) derivatives industry.

Segregation of Money

In most jurisdictions, including the United States, entities that receive collateral from clients to secure derivatives transactions are supposed to segregate the money coming from other sources. That means that the funds received must not be used for purposes other than the derivatives transactions. In particular, they must not be commingled with the entity's own money and must not be used as a source of liquidity for operating expenses or to collateralize the entity's own derivatives transactions.

Imagine that the MTM value of trades move against the entity that received the funds. The entity must then give back some of the collateral assets to the other party. If the funds have been used and are not available, this party would not be able to receive back its own money.

The segregation of accounts is a fundamental principle, but it is also a big risk for all derivatives players because there is no easy way to verify that the counterparties are keeping the funds they deliver separate from other sources. There is a major risk of fraud, which was demonstrated when MF Global Holding filed for bankruptcy in 2011. It was widely reported that millions of dollars of assets belonging to MF Global's customers had been used by the company for its own purposes, that is, as collateral for its own, proprietary trading.

LEGAL DOCUMENTATION

Standardizing the legal documentation governing derivatives transactions is achieved thanks to the widespread use of documents published by ISDA. Legal documents between parties engaging in derivatives transactions are negotiated but have their foundations in the ISDA documents and, to the extent possible, deviate little from these, especially for the most liquid and simple trades. Customizing documentation creates risk since it invites opportunities for events not anticipated and, thus, creates additional exposure.

There are three fundamental documents related to derivatives transactions:

1. The ISDA master agreement: This is the cornerstone of the legal relationship between two entities. There is ordinarily only one for all over-the-counter (OTC) derivatives and similar transactions between two trading parties. However, if a firm operates through several subsidiaries, each legal entity is required to have its own master agreement in place. What ISDA proposes is a template (the most recent one was published in 2002) but companies are free to negotiate changes if they can agree. Once the master agreement is completed, it is rarely modified, except

to reflect major changes in the organization of one party. It does not normally contain any deal-specific information.

2. The credit support annex to the master agreement (CSA): This is the most important document for credit risk management purposes as it specifies key parameters such as the valuation process, thresholds, eligible collateral, and corresponding haircuts. In practice, it is the only document credit analysts review. Specialized legal-staff members negotiate the other documents. The CSA also contains a dispute resolution mechanism in case of disagreement over valuations of MTM or collateral assets. It is placed as an annex to the master agreement.

3. The confirmation: This document spells out the economic terms of each individual trade.

DEALERS VERSUS END USERS

In the derivatives market, a distinction is made between dealers and end users. A dealer is a financial institution that enters into a derivatives transaction either for its own trading book of business or to intermediate transactions across clients. The largest U.S.-based derivatives dealers are Bank of America, Citigroup, Goldman Sachs, J.P. Morgan and Morgan Stanley. An end user is a party that enters into a derivative transaction in order to hedge risk associated with its business operations. The idea is to offer different services to dealers who act for their own account or as intermediaries, and to firms for which financial products are not their main business but a support to their core activities.

Differences in treatment arise mainly in the collateral posting requirements and also in the clearing process, which we cover next. Generosity is extended to end users, who may have less access to collateral than a financial institution and, therefore, may be unable to post collateral when needed. Credit analysts have to carefully study the creditworthiness of these potential counterparties and the nature of the trades that are envisaged with them. As a result, the volume of business can be limited and the type of transactions restricted to deals presenting less risk.

BILATERAL TRANSACTIONS VERSUS CENTRAL COUNTERPARTY CLEARING

Let's start by describing the two main families of derivatives products:

1. Exchange-traded derivatives are very transparent transactions where participants transact via a regulated exchange like the CME Group in the United States or ICE Futures Europe in the U.K. This category

mainly involves futures and options on commodities (e.g., soy beans, natural gas) or foreign exchange. Like other listed products, buyers and sellers have access to the current price for the product they are interested in buying or selling, if it matches their needs. Execution of the trades follows well-established rules and the participants' counterparty is the exchange itself. To reduce the default risk of the exchange, deals are collateralized with all the methodology explained above.

2. Over-the-counter (OTC) derivatives are agreements between two parties that are bilaterally negotiated. Pretrade, no one else is involved, although indicative conditions are shown on trading systems for some products. When the two parties agree on a deal, they can either execute it bilaterally or involve a third-party central clearing counterparty (CCP). Depending on the underlying product, settlement may be their choice between settling bilaterally or voluntarily through a CCP, or settlement via a CCP may be a requirement imposed by authorities and regulators.

Once again, the mitigation of credit risk for transactions involving exchange-traded derivatives has been explained in the previous paragraphs. What follows relates to OTC derivatives and explains the pros and cons of bilateral versus centrally cleared transactions from a credit risk perspective.

The margin requirement used in bilateral transactions is a long-standing risk mitigation technique. It has served its purpose and has been tested with success in a large number of bankruptcies where it proved to be an efficient tool in reducing losses after a counterparty's collapse. Over time, market participants became comfortable with taking a level of credit risk that spawned the fast development of the derivatives markets.

However, for all institutions involved in business that is generating dynamic credit exposures, collateral posting creates some issues. We summarize the three most significant ones:

1. Margin requirements are highly inefficient as each and every bilateral trade must be collateralized, which leads to many exchanges of collateral for related trades. Consider the case of an interest-rate swap between Company A and Company B.

   In this instance, given the MTM value of the swap, Company A has posted collateral. At a point in time, Company B may wish to exit the position, but Company A may not wish to terminate. Thus, to accomplish the same objective, Company B enters into a similar swap with Company C, only this time it takes the other side of the trade. The MTM values of the two swaps are close in value, so Company B has to post collateral to Company C. As a result, in this simple example, twice the collateral is being posted for the same positions taken. It is easy to imagine that in a world in which so many related transactions are closed every day, many firms across the globe have to post collateral to each other. This is inefficient, costly, and leads to operational errors. In very large relationships involving many thousands of trades, significant errors may occur frequently because the parties have not agreed on the universe of trades they have in place, a process called portfolio reconciliation, or simply "port rec."

2. Margin requirements have systemic risk. The entire financial industry is exposed to the default of even a single counterparty. As firms have business relations with up to thousands of counterparties, if one company defaults, it exposes the whole industry to potential losses. If the collateral assets in place are properly valued and all the assets deposited with the defaulted party are accounted for, losses will be limited to the unsecured exposure (i.e., the threshold for margin requirement). In reality, it is not unusual that in the case of a large-scale bankruptcy, the liquidation process is not very smooth. Volatile prices may prevail, causing the positions to be closed out at levels causing losses far in excess of the collateral. Deposited assets may be lost or frozen as part of the bankruptcy procedures. In short, with even only bilateral relationships between trading counterparties, the default of a single entity can have a devastating effect on the entire industry and trigger consequences difficult to forecast. These were precisely the circumstances in 2008 when the U.S. government took over AIG. AIG was involved in hundreds of billions of dollars of derivative transactions and the government feared that its failure would trigger a domino effect, that is, other major bankruptcies. The ultimate consequence remains unknown, had the U.S. government not stepped in.

3. Margin requirements are resource intensive. In addition to the IT platform necessary to compute MTM positions and collateral requirements, back offices must handle the collateral assets they receive from counterparties and transfer assets to counterparties when required to do so. For large institutions, the numbers are big and the process cumbersome and prone to operational errors. The largest financial institutions can hold more than $100 billion of collateral assets and employ hundreds of people to manage the entire process, which is complex and costly.

An alternative to a bilateral transaction is to trade with a central clearing counterparty. Although, they both specialize in intermediating derivatives transactions, there is a major difference between a CCP and a clearinghouse: the CCP guarantees the trade against the default risk whereas the traditional clearinghouse does not. For OTC trades, CCPs are not involved in the negotiations of the trades, but when two parties agree on terms, the parties inform the CCP, which intermediates trades between two parties. In the United States, futures contracts, options on futures contracts and off-exchange foreign exchange futures and swaps are intermediated by the Futures Commission Merchants (FCM), which are regulated by the CFTC, a government regulator. Instead of facing the credit risk of the trading partners, each party ultimately faces the credit risk of the CCP. Collateral assets are no longer posted to the party that is actually on the other side of the trade but to the CCP, which is also responsible for the MTM of transactions and the calculation of the margin requirements. These functions are called clearing. The biggest advantage is that instead of bearing credit risk of multiple counterparties, all firms are ultimately facing only one party. If the CCP is properly capitalized and managed, it should not default because it does not take any risk itself. It is just an intermediary and is exposed only to the risks associated with intermediation.

When one firm defaults, only the CCP is involved in the bankruptcy proceedings. If its risk management process was efficient, it should have sufficient collateral assets in hand. In case of shortfall, there is a whole "waterfall" describing where the missing funds will come from. The CCP has access to its own capital (called the skin-in-the-game participation) and also, if needed, to a guarantee fund supplied by its members.

CCPs for OTC trades are sometimes the same entities involved in the exchange-traded derivatives but play a different role. They are usually publicly traded or privately owned companies. Examples in the United States are ICE or DTCC (www.dtcc.com) and, in the U.K., LCH owned by London Stock Exchange. In all cases, the word "member" is used to describe a financial institution authorized to clear its deals via a CCP, even when the CCP is an independent company in which members do not own any capital.

CCPs are active in all major financial markets, and large global financial institutions are members of multiple CCPs around the world, sometimes more than 50. The CCP12 (www.ccp12.org) is an industry association with, as of 2021, 37 major CCPs as members.

Generally speaking, CCPs have no tolerance for credit risk and are very strict and consistent in asking for a high level of collateralization pursuant to their official rules. They carefully select which entities they accept as clearing members. They may require an initial margin to allow a counterparty the right to conduct trading, before any clearing actually occurs. The initial margin provides the CCP with a cushion against the market volatility in case a counterparty defaults.

Historically, most OTC derivatives transactions were bilateral. With the meltdown following the 2007 crisis, regulators around the globe have scrambled to move all standardized OTC derivatives trading into the highly capitalized central counterparties. The absence of central clearing for credit-default swaps and other OTC derivatives has been frequently cited as a major contributor to the 2007 crisis in the United States that quickly transformed into a major banking crisis.

Although clearing of single-name credit derivatives through a CCP remains voluntary, few trades remain bilateral, with the exception of end-user and one-off transactions. It is estimated that more than 70 percent of all credit derivatives transactions are cleared thought a CCP. For those transactions that remain bilateral, other features to expect are additional and possibly more frequent margin requirements, such as posting a multiple of regular margin calls, or the need to have the collateral assets held by third-party custodians. Furthermore, for derivatives that remain traded on an uncleared basis, regulators will require financial institutions to hold a large amount of capital for these, which may make them uneconomical.

The biggest question is what would happen if a CCP fails. Central counterparties are supposed to provide stability to the financial system yet they concentrates the exposure of all market participants (and possibly the world economy) to a handful of CCPs. The amount of collateral assets deposited at major CCPs is astronomical. It is not hard to imagine that a failure of a single CCP could cause a chain reaction of a larger magnitude than the default of single bankruptcy. As usual, in the realm of credit risk management, risk can be reduced but neither completely anticipated nor completely eliminated.

PRIME BROKERS

When large international financial institutions dominated the derivatives market, it was relatively simple to assess the credit quality of the trading partners and to make informed decisions. As more and more firms entered the trading world, the task became much harder. For instance, risk analysts now have to review the financial situations of a myriad of privately held hedge funds with short histories, few employees, and limited funds. Despite uncertain credit quality and sometimes untested business models, because hedge funds are major players in certain financial markets, financial institutions would be at a competitive disadvantage not to do business with them. Conversely, hedge funds do not want to limit their business to a small number of counterparties, because their business model is to exploit opportunities wherever they arise. As such, they are interested in giving confidence to potential partners.

This situation led to the rapid development in the early 2000s of prime brokers. Major banks like Goldman Sachs, J. P. Morgan, or Morgan Stanley specialize in dealing with hedge funds and have prime brokerage operations. One of the major roles of a prime broker is to act as an intermediary between a hedge fund and its ultimate counterparties. When hedge funds place trades, they negotiate directly with their counterparties, which in prime brokerage terms are called executing dealers. However, upon execution, a transaction, is given up to their prime broker, so that the prime broker is the entity the counterparty faces. The prime broker executes back-to-back transactions with both the hedge fund and the executing dealer. The executing dealer, therefore, does not take any credit risk on the hedge fund but, instead, only on the prime broker. Collateral requests are met by the prime broker and not by the hedge fund. It is up to the prime broker to analyze the creditworthiness of the hedge funds they want to do business with and to provide them with liquidity. They are specialized in such a function, so they can employ specialized staff.

Prime brokerage has been around the financial services industry for a long time, but it was not very active until recently. With the recent proliferation of hedge funds, it became a major business unit and massive source of revenue for the major players. The difference between prime brokerage and clearing is that prime brokerage includes other services such as securities lending and repo, so, unlike a clearinghouse, the prime brokerage seeks to make money by extending credit to its customers. In addition, prime brokerage provides customers a wide array of financial services including crediting customer accounts with proceeds from short sales. In a prime brokerage relationship, normally all the products furnished by the prime broker are cross-collateralized, so that the customer receives netting benefit. The prime brokers themselves use clearinghouses to conduct trading including trading on behalf of their customers.

REPURCHASE AGREEMENTS

Repurchase agreements, known as repos, are a type of transaction that generates counterparty risk. Repos are a commonly used financing technique involving two parties. One party, the borrower, sells a security and commits to buy it back at a predetermined price and at a certain date. The other party, the lender, temporarily purchases the security against cash and sells it back at the agreed date. The risk taken by the lenders is that the securities are not repurchased due to the inability of the borrower, thus repos can be characterized as presenting counterparty risk.

As a convention, the expression *repo* is used to describe the viewpoint of the borrower and *reverse repo* refers to the same transaction but described from the point of view of the lender.

Repos involve collateral management, in a way similar to what has just been described. Repos are legally purchases and sales but are in economic effect a form of secured lending. The main difference with other forms of secured loans is that the value of the collateral asset has to be maintained at an agreed level during the lifetime of a transaction. In order to strengthen credit risk mitigation, repos are overcollateralized. This means that, in order to receive, say, $10 million of cash, the borrower must provide more than $10 million worth of collateral. If the collateral assets' value declines, the borrower receives a margin call and must provide additional collateral. If it fails to do so, the agreement is terminated and the collateral liquidated by the lender.

Institutions utilize repos to raise cash, and, during the period when the money is borrowed, the ownership of the security is in fact transferred. Money can be raised for general purposes. Another usage is to finance the purchase of securities. By pledging them immediately as part of a repo agreement, the buyer of the securities has just to fund the overcollateralization amount.

Conversely, reverse repos are a way for institutions with cash available to lend money, taking limited credit risk on the borrower, and being well paid to do so. The repo agreement states the repurchasing price of the security, which is higher than the original purchase price, which provides a fixed-rate interest payment to the lender. Therefore, it is viewed as a cash investment.

From a risk management perspective, the credit analysis is very similar to the process described earlier. The first step is to become comfortable with the creditworthiness of the counterparty. The presence of collateral is a strong mitigant but not a sufficient condition to lend money to weak companies. Once a counterparty has been accepted, transactions are structured in a way to almost eliminate the credit risk via overcollateralization.

The overcollateralization is achieved via haircuts, as described earlier. Haircuts are based on the type of security temporarily purchased, including corporate bonds, government bonds, and a broad array of other types of securities. The more volatile, the less creditworthy, and the less liquid the asset is, the larger the haircut.

Transactions are typically of short-term nature, normally less than one year. Some involving U.S. Treasuries have a lifetime of one day and are called overnight repos. Repos are documented with standard documents. In the United States, the master repurchase agreement published by the

Securities Industry and Financial Markets Association–SIFMA (www.sifma .org) is utilized, and outside the United States the global master repurchase agreement published by SIFMA and the International Capital Market Association–ICMA (www.icmagroup.org) is utilized.

Finally, let us mention that one of the largest repo markets involves central banks that provide funding to private banks against collateral. In the aftermath of the 2007–2009 crisis, central banks were actively providing liquidity to banks in their jurisdictions via repo transactions.

FINAL WORDS

Standardization in mitigating counterparty credit risk for derivatives transactions has promoted the usage of these markets and made them more efficient. The involvement of CCPs for OTC trades significantly changed how counterparty credit is managed. Central clearing has advantages by having operational efficiencies, standardized collateral management, and risk pooling. In reality, there is debate about the ability of CCPs to prevent a collapse of the financial system. There is now a huge concentration of risk in a few entities at the center of many financial markets. The risk of the failure of a CCP cannot be ignored.

CHAPTER 18

Structural Mitigation

In this chapter, we present structural techniques used to mitigate the default risk of a debt instrument and to reduce the impact of a default by increasing the recovery rate.

When we review how to analyze the creditworthiness of a corporate, of individuals, of asset-backed securities, and of CLOs in earlier chapters, we focus on the cash-flow-generating ability of a counterparty. What is different in this chapter is that we examine how the debt instruments can be structured up front to protect investors when the financial performance of the issuing entity is deteriorating. The two topics are closely related and complementary. Before considering investing, credit analysts must thoroughly analyze the issuing entity. Then, in a second step, they must focus on the debt itself and the way it is structured. All details regarding the structural elements are found in the various legal documents prepared at the time of the originating transaction.

The techniques we will review are structural insofar as they are either embedded in the way the financial instrument is engineered and documented or they utilize the support of third parties. There is a large variety of ways to strengthen a transaction to reduce its credit risk or to increase the recovery in case of default. There is no limit to creativity. Investors benefit from a steady evolution of structural features, which gradually become market standards.

For credit analysts, supporting the structuring of a transaction is an enriching experience. Rather than rejecting a transaction considered too weak, a good professional can add value by helping design mechanisms aimed at making deals stronger. The main objectives to good structuring are to protect creditors against a deterioration of the financial performance of the counterparty during the lifetime of the transaction and to enable transactions with weak counterparties.

We will also cover ways to offer investors a chance to trade risk versus return in securitization schemes. This is accomplished primarily by tranching, which creates senior and junior obligations of debt issued by special purpose vehicles.

The counterparty credit risk generated by derivatives transactions is covered in the previous chapter.

TRANSACTIONS WITH CORPORATES

Corporate borrowers primarily use loans and bonds as their preferred funding instruments, and these, with letters of credit (LoCs), all generate default risk. Since the structural mitigation techniques used for loans are similar to those used for bonds and LoCs, we will focus our attention on loans in this section.

Commercial loans are old and simple products, whose technology has been well tested through numerous economic cycles. There has been little innovation over the years and all market participants know well how to make a loan stronger or weaker. Competition in the marketplace will dictate to some degree the strength of the structural mitigants. During credit crunches, banks lend reluctantly, and borrowers have strict conditions imposed on them, in addition to paying a high interest rate. The lower their credit quality the tougher the terms are. Conversely, when the economy is growing, banks want to increase their revenues and chase business. Competition leads to softer conditions in favor of the borrowers.

The loan documentation is the set of legal documents agreed on by lenders and borrowers. The most important one in the set is the "credit agreement," which contains all the details of the loan. From a credit risk management perspective, the most relevant loan details in the credit agreement are related to four main topics: the priority of payments, the security package, the covenants, and the definition of the "events of default." We will review these four aspects in the following sections, but before that, we present an overview of the loan market.

Segmentation of the Commercial Loan Market

The main parameter that dictates the lending conditions offered to a borrower is its credit rating. Loans to investment-grade companies are treated completely differently from loans to noninvestment-grade companies. Furthermore, markets for these loans are not the same. Table 18.1 is a high-level presentation of the two markets. New terminology is introduced in Table 18.1, which we explain in the following sections.

TABLE 18.1   Segmentation of Commercial Loan Borrowers

Investment-Grade Borrowers	Noninvestment-Grade Borrowers
Borrowers are well-established companies.	Borrowers are low performing and/or very leveraged companies. Some companies that have been acquired by private equity firms (as part of a leveraged buyout scheme) are in this category.
All loans are *pari passu*, that is, all lenders are treated the same way and have the same level of seniority.	
Loans are typically unsecured.	
Loans are syndicated and purchased by large commercial banks, in order to anchor a relationship.	Loans with different priorities of payments are created, placing some creditors ahead of others in case of liquidation of the borrower.
Covenants are simple and not very restrictive, except for borrowers with a rating close to noninvestment grade.	Loans are structured by large investment banks but distributed to specialized investors like hedge funds or structured finance vehicles (primarily collateralized loan obligations or CLOs—see Chapter 12).
Many facilities are unfunded because borrowers want to have the option to borrow but do not necessarily need the cash all the time. They are called revolvers.	All loans are secured by some of the borrower's assets.
	Covenants are very strict.
	Loans are fully funded at inception.
	They are called leveraged loans or high-yield loans, a reference to the high interest rate paid by the borrowers.

Senior versus Junior Debt

In case of default or liquidation of a company, all creditors are not treated equally. In most cases, the liabilities of the defaulted company exceed its assets, so a decision has to be made about who is paid and when. The court in charge of the bankruptcy procedure or—if the company cannot be reorganized—the liquidation process ultimately decides which creditors receive the available funds in priority. The priority order is the result of a number of factors:

■ The legal environment. For example, the company is legally required to pay outstanding taxes or workers compensation insurance for employees. The tax authorities and the workers compensation insurer typically do not participate in the negotiations among creditors. They can demand payment because, if they are unpaid, the rights of a company to operate during a bankruptcy procedure or reorganization are forfeited.

- The judgment of the court. For example, key suppliers are paid before lenders to keep the business afloat and avoid immediate liquidation. It is not uncommon to try to maintain a company's operations in order to try to recover as much as possible for all creditors. If suppliers are not paid, they stop delivering their goods or services, which accelerates the demise of the firm. Suppliers are, therefore, typically paid before lenders. Note that to provide liquidity in order to maintain operations of a bankrupt company, banks sometimes provide debtor-in-possession (DIP) loans, which become the most senior obligation.
- The terms of the legal agreements with the creditors. We focus on this aspect later.

When issuing debt, companies can create instruments that have various priorities of payments. This technique is known as subordination, and the products that are created are senior and junior debt. The debt can be loans or bonds. Senior means that the lenders are paid back first. Junior means that they are paid back if money is left after all senior debt has been repaid. Junior debt, therefore, stands between the senior debt and the equity. Junior debt holders and equity investors have a residual claim on the assets on the firm, in that order. They have a chance to be repaid only after senior creditors have been fully paid back. As a consequence, junior debt is, for the issuer, more expensive than senior debt. In case of financial stress, the expected recovery rate of junior debt is, by definition, lower than that of senior debt. It is a riskier investment, which warrants a higher interest rate for loans and a higher coupon for bonds.

Financial institutions will issue hybrid capital, which is a form of junior debt. As the name suggests, it contains some debt-like and also some equity-like features. It offers a way to strengthen a capital base and meet ratios demanded by regulators. Under Basel III, the global regulatory risk and capital framework for banks, hybrid capital issued by banks will count as either Additional Tier 1 (AT1) capital, or Tier 2 capital up to a limit. Some hybrid instruments include preferred stocks, perpetual preferred securities, and mandatory convertible securities, all of which are deeply subordinated to senior unsecured debt. From an AT1 and Tier 2 capital perspective, a hybrid security would qualify only if it has no claim on a banks' assets if the bank fails, meaning it would require a feature that makes it become fully subordinated to depositors and general creditors. In addition, a hybrid security would qualify for AT1, in addition to all other requirements, if it does not have a maturity date.

Secured versus Unsecured Loans

A secured loan is a financing instrument that first relies on the cash flow generated by the borrower to pay interest and principal, and second on a lien on some assets (the collateral) to reduce the loss in case of default. As long as the borrower is able to make the scheduled interest and principal payments on the loan, the assets taken as collateral remain in the possession of the borrower. However, if the borrower misses a payment, the lender has the right to seize the assets and sell them to recover its losses.

The easiest example of a secured loan is a mortgage, be it a residential mortgage to an individual or a commercial mortgage to a developer. Lenders have a lien on the property, that is to say, the right to repossess it if certain conditions are met. When the borrower honors all payments legally due, the real estate assets stay with the borrower, but when the borrower defaults, the lender can foreclose the property.

All types of assets can be taken as collateral to a loan. The general rule is that short-term assets (e.g., receivables) secure short-term loans and long-term assets (e.g., building or equipment) secure long-term loans.

Pledging assets to secure a loan does not increase the credit quality of a borrower because the probability of default is not affected by the security package of the loan. The credit analyst's job remains unchanged: to thoroughly assess the financial strength of the borrower in order to make a lending recommendation.

The security package comes into play when forecasting the expected recovery in case of default. When a secured loan defaults, it is expected that the recovery will be higher than the recovery of an unsecured loan of similar seniority. The secured lenders have access to the pledged assets and the unsecured lenders have to share the residual assets with all other creditors.

Forecasting the recovery value of an unsecured instrument is difficult. Among other things, one has to estimate future values of balance sheet items, which is particularly challenging when dealing with intangible assets like goodwill or R&D expenses. In contrast, assets taken as security of a loan agreement are normally tangible and well delimited. As such, their valuation is a manageable and meaningful exercise.

For a credit analyst, there is a big difference between the assessment of an unsecured loan to a high-quality borrower and a secured loan to a weak one. For the former, the analyst thoroughly analyzes the cash-flow generation ability of the borrower and must be convinced that the cash flow will be around until the maturity of the investment. Little consideration is given to the residual value of the assets. As described in Chapter 4, financial institutions make recovery assumptions for pricing and for modeling their portfolio. They typically use 40 percent for all senior unsecured facilities, a conservative proxy since the historical average is somewhat above this.

The analysis of a secured loan follows a similar process as far as the credit assessment of the borrower is concerned. However, lenders recognize that a borrower's ability to repay a loan could be impacted by the occurrence of even mild economic events or operational issues and that, on a stand-alone basis, it would be risky to extend the credit, that is, fund the loan. This is why a pledge on assets is required. Credit analysts therefore also must become comfortable with the value of the collateral being proposed. They must thoroughly assess what the recovered value could be in case of bankruptcy. To do this, the support of experts like property assessors is often necessary.

Covenants

Covenants are conditions imposed on the borrower as part of a loan or financing facility, such as an LoC. Their objective is to maintain the risk profile of the borrower by keeping the borrower from deviating too much operationally, financially, or strategically from its current path. Lenders impose a list of things that a borrower can or cannot do in order to maintain its credit quality as long as the loan is outstanding.

For credit analysts, negotiating tight covenants represents a guarantee that the borrower will endeavor to maintain its creditworthiness regardless of the evolution of its economic and operating environments. Failure to maintain the conditions of the covenants is a default event and the loan becomes immediately due. In the real world, breaching covenants does not necessarily translate into a forced default by the creditors. If the parties agree, covenants can be waived or reset against compromises from the borrowers, like a price increase or, in the case of a secured loan, the provision of additional collateral.

Solid companies are able to benefit from generous covenants. Their market power combined with competition among banks enables them to obtain favorable covenants. Thus, the covenants would not constrain them unless their situation became dire in a short period of time. As long as they perform at a level close to where they were at the inception of the loan facility, covenants will not prevent them from operating normally.

In contrast, weak companies face tight covenants that limit their financial flexibility. Lenders want to control the activities of the borrowers, which are prevented from making any decision that could significantly change their financial profile.

The market standards revolve around three types of covenants:

1. Affirmative covenants list what a company must do to maintain its business in good shape, for example, keep a legal existence, maintain its building, and preserve trademarks. Also, borrowers commit to provide financial information on a regular basis to lenders.
2. Negative covenants limit what a company cannot do as long as the loan is outstanding. The main elements are (1) the limitation on taking on other secured debt, which prevents other creditors from accessing the borrower's assets; (2) the limitation on sale and leaseback transaction, for the same reason as above in point 1; and (3) an interdiction to merge with another firm, to sell itself (change of control), or to sell significant assets. A good example of a negative covenant was reported by the *Wall Street Journal* in March 2014. At the time the electronic retailer RadioShack was struggling and intended to close 1,100 stores. However, the newspaper reported that it would breach one of the covenants of its $835 million facility, which required that the company maintain at least 4,278 stores.
3. Financial covenants are a subcategory of the negative covenants. They come in different forms: Maintenance covenants require an issuer to meet certain financial tests every reporting period. Incurrence covenants require that the borrower remains in compliance when it takes an action like paying a dividend, entering into a merger or an acquisition, or issuing more debt.

The most common examples of financial covenants are a minimum coverage ratio (cash flow or EBITDA over specified expenses like interest payments), leverage (level of debt relative to assets or equity), current ratio, tangible net worth, and maximum capital expenditures.

To recap, the stronger the borrower, the less restrictive the covenants are. Additionally, as with other lending terms, the economy and competition between lenders influences the rigidity of the covenants. As such, loans originated during tough economic times will have restrictive covenants, and when the economy improves, loans even to the same borrower will have looser covenants. Loose covenants give way to what is called covenant-lite, or simply cov-lite, loans. When lenders accept incurrence instead of maintenance covenants, this is a favorable period for borrowers. Requiring a company to meet solvability and liquidity criteria in only a particular instance enables it to deviate from its path and perform worse than if it had to abide to maintenance covenants, which must be respected at all times.

Events of Default

The definitions of *events of defaults* are fairly standard, but credit analysts must, with the assistance of their lawyers, review them carefully to avoid surprises. The focus must be on what constitutes a default, what kind of grace period is granted, and the relationship with the other debt facilities of the borrower. Events of defaults also contain provisions about the consequences of false representations and inability to enforce a parental guaranty. A misrepresentation or problem with a parental guaranty typically would trigger a default in the same way as a missed payment.

The consequences of all events of default are similar: All sums, including principal, accrued interests, and fees owed to the lenders become due immediately.

Impact of Structural Mitigants on Default Probability

Let's mention an important point: the default probability of a corporate borrower is not modified by the creditor's position in the priority of payment chain or by the loan's security. Rating agencies primarily assign credit ratings to corporate issuers, what S&P Global Ratings call "issuer credit rating" (ICR). Senior and subordinated debt have the same likelihood of default. If a borrower does not generate enough cash to finance its operations and service its debt, it defaults. All financing agreements include a cross-default clause, which means that the default on one facility automatically triggers the default on all facilities. Borrowers cannot pick and choose what they want to pay if they run out of cash. It is the responsibility of the bankruptcy judge to decide how the available money is disbursed.

As far as covenants are concerned, restrictive covenants can increase the default probability for a given time horizon because a borrower may default if it breaches a covenant, even it has some cash left to service its debt for a few more weeks or months. Lenient covenants can extend the time before default is triggered; the company that will ultimately default operates above default thresholds only because the thresholds are low. Operations continue even though the financial situation of the company deteriorates.

Impact of Structural Mitigants on Recovery Rates

In theory, covenants have no impact on the recovery rate because they do not give access to more or less collateral. However, covenants that contribute to a delayed default, like incurrence covenants, have the potential to lower a recovery rate. When a borrower ultimately defaults, its assets may have lost considerable value and the creditors, especially the subordinated

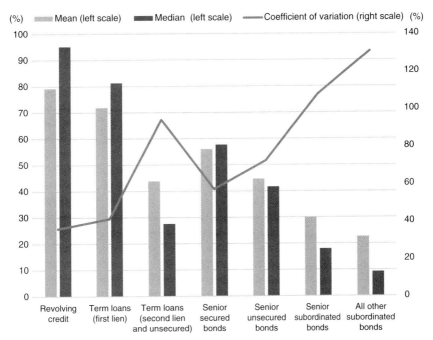

FIGURE 18.1 Discounted Recovery Rates by Instrument Type, 1987–2019
Sources: S&P Global Ratings, "Default, Transition, and Recovery: U.S. Recovery Study: Distressed Exchanges Have Boosted Recent Bond Recoveries," December 12, 2019, Table 1.

ones, recover much less money than if the default would have occurred earlier with the existence of more restrictive maintenance covenants.

The seniority of the loans and the existence or not of a security package have a major impact on the ultimate amount lost by lenders in case of default. As explained earlier, this is actually the very reason why loans are secured. Without collateral, lenders would be reluctant to provide funds. With collateral, they know that their losses will be reduced or even eliminated.

There are multiple sources of historical data for recovery rates of defaulted financial obligations. One example is S&P, which publishes statistics like the ones presented in Figure 18.1.

In the mid-2000s, S&P went one step further and began assigning "corporate recovery ratings" to leveraged loans that enabled bank loans to be rated for recovery expectations. It is reserved to bank loans issued by borrowers with an issuer rated in S&P's speculative-grade—at or below the BB+ category. Note that it is not a broadly based rating but applies only to

TABLE 18.2   S&P Recovery Ratings Scale

Recovery Rating	Recovery Description	Recovery Expectations	Issue Rating Notches Relative to Corporate Credit Rating
1+	Highest expectation, full recovery*	100%	+ 3 notches
1	Very high recovery	90%–100%	+ 2 notches
2	Substantial recovery	70%–90%	+ 1 notch
3	Meaningful recovery	50%–70%	0 notches
4	Average recovery	30%–50%	0 notches
5	Modest recovery	10%–30%	– 1 notch
6	Negligible recovery	0%–10%	– 2 notches

*Recovery ratings are capped in certain countries to adjust for reduced creditor recovery prospects in these jurisdictions.
Source: Standard & Poor's Recovery Rating Criteria for Speculative-Grade Corporate Issuers published on December 7, 2016, and republished with revisions and updates on February 4, 2020.

a specific loan to take into account the way it is structured. S&P describes its recovery ratings as an estimation of "the percentage of principal and accrued interest due at the point of hypothetical default on a company's debt instruments that can be recovered following its emergence from a hypothetical bankruptcy."

In Table 18.2, such a rating starts with the borrower's issuer credit rating (ICR), which is then modified by an expected recovery rate. In the event of a high recovery rate, there can be an uptick to the rating. We remind readers that *notch* means a + or – ratings step. For instance, a loan issued by a corporation rated B+ could be rated up to BB+ with a recovery rating of RR1+. However, it is important to understand that issue-level ratings, contrary to issuer credit ratings, are not meant to indicate a probability of default but the expected recovery on a specific issue given a default by the issuer.

Similarly, Fitch assigns recovery ratings ranging from RR1 "outstanding recovery rating prospect given default" between 91% and 100% to RR6 "poor recovery rating prospect given default" between 0% and 10%.

There are two main applications for the loan specific recovery rating. First, it can influence the risk appetite of an investor. As explained in Chapter 4, the expected recovery rate is one of the key features of a credit exposure and investors may decide to deploy more capital in a debt instrument if they expect a higher recovery in case of default. Second, recovery rate is an essential component of analytical models, for instance to calculate the capital necessary to support a portfolio (Chapter 13) or the default probability of a CLO tranche (Chapters 11 and 12).

TRANSACTIONS WITH SPECIAL PURPOSE VEHICLES

Chapter 11 provides an introduction to asset securitizations. We explain that SPVs issue asset-backed securities whose repayment depends on the cash flow generated by a pool of assets.

Investors in ABSs benefit from many protection mechanisms. Whereas a company has many types of creditors (e.g., suppliers, professional services providers, governmental agencies), SPVs primarily owe money to their investors, and use structural techniques to strengthen their ability to pay off their investors. Unlike a loan or other funding facility, the mitigants are not always part of the documentation but may result from the way that the SPV is organized.

Senior/Subordinated Structures

In Chapter 11, we explain the structure of ABS transactions. In summary, several tranches are created in order to offer securities with different risk/return profiles. Investors with a limited risk appetite choose highly rated securities, positioned on top of the waterfall in which cash is distributed to investors. Risk is low, and so is the return. Investors looking for high returns purchase deeply subordinated securities, which benefit from a distribution of cash only once all more senior securities have been serviced. These securities are typically rated at the lowest limit of the investment grade or even noninvestment grade scale, and their default probability is relatively high.

The level of subordination is the most influential driver, but not always the only one, of the rating. Very senior tranches sometimes benefit from other structural enhancements that support their ratings. The following graph (Figure 18.2) summarizes the average default rate per rating category of all structured finance securities rated by S&P between 1979 and 2019. It clearly illustrates that the higher the rating, owing to more subordination, the lower the probability of default. Let's point out that contrary to a corporate issuer, different tranches issued by the same special purpose vehicle can have different ratings. The rationale is that due to the waterfall, if a tranche with little subordination defaults, the transaction will go into early amortization (see the later section in this chapter) and tranches with higher subordination levels may not default and investors may be made whole.

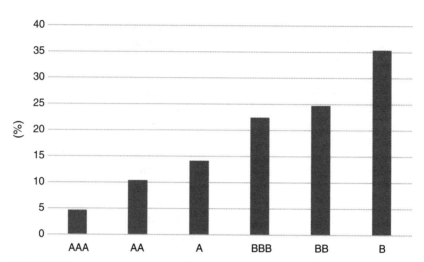

FIGURE 18.2   Global Structured Finance Cumulative Default Rates, Conditional on Survival (1976–2019, Five-Year Horizon)
Source: S&P Global Ratings, 2019 Annual Global Structured Finance Default and Rating Transition Study, June 9, 2020, Table 2.

Credit Enhancement

The ABS market has witnessed a tremendous evolution over the years primarily to diversify the asset classes being securitized and to strengthen the transactions in order to attract more investors.

In summary, a strong structure cannot compensate for weak collateral. Financial engineers and rating agencies can imagine innovative ways to make the transactions stronger but securitizations backed by fundamentally weak assets are doomed to fail. During the 2007 crisis, no or few defaults stemmed from weak structures. All were generated by bad collateral, for which no structural mitigation can help.

Let us now review the most common techniques used to strengthen a securitization scheme.

Credit Enhancement of Assets   In Chapter 11, we explain that it was essential to fully understand and assess the credit quality of each individual asset that is securitized.

To further strengthen the quality of each asset, a third-party guaranty can be purchased. This is a form of credit enhancement as, in addition to the credit quality of the borrower, investors in the ABS scheme benefit from the credit strength of the guarantor.

The way it works is that, if a borrower defaults, the party that guaranteed it indemnifies the SPV for all or part of the unpaid amounts. There are two main things to pay attention to:

1. In some cases, the full amount is guaranteed, in some cases only a partial amount. If there is a full loss but the guarante is only partial, the recovery on the defaulted asset will not be 100 percent.
2. The credit quality of the guarantor must be studied carefully. Before giving any sort of credit to the guarantor when estimating the risk of loss, the analyst has to be comfortable with the claims-paying ability of the guarantor. In case of doubt, only partial credit can be given, or no credit at all. Some concentration limits can also be put in place. Full credit is granted if one single company does not guarantee more than, say, 30 percent of the total collateral value.

The largest market with transactions benefiting from collateral-level credit enhancement is residential mortgages. The mortgages can benefit from public or private guaranties:

- Public: In many countries, the government tries to encourage home ownership by offering full or partial guaranties to private lenders. In the United States, several major entities, organized as government-sponsored enterprises or GSEs, buy qualifying mortgages from private lenders and securitize them. They are the Federal National Mortgage Association (Fannie Mae), the Federal Home Loan Mortgage Association (Freddie Mac), the Government National Mortgage Association (Ginnie Mae), the Federal Housing Administration (FHA), and the National Credit Union Administration (NCUA). Although the U.S. government had never guaranteed the financial obligations of Fannie Mae and Freddie Mac, it seized them in 2008 and, operating under the government's conservatorship, recapitalized them and made good on their obligations. This act confirmed to investors that all GSEs had the backing of the government, not just the explicitly guaranteed Ginnie Mae, NCUA, and the government-owned FHA, which was a long held presumption in the capital markets, and that MBS issued by those GSEs were safe from default.
- Private: Specialized insurance companies also sell insurance to lenders. These in turn benefit investors in MBS, both those that are backed by the federal agencies and also those without agency guarantees. In the United States, the largest mortgage insurers are Genworth Financial, MGIC, Arch Capital Group, and Radian Group. Their original business model was to insure losses between 10 percent and 20 percent of

agency-backed mortgages. Since the agencies would back only mortgages with a 20 percent down payment, if a borrower did not put the full 20 percent down, these private mortgage insurers would insure the amounts between 10 percent and 20 percent to make the mortgages eligible for the agency guaranty programs. During the housing boom, the private mortgage insurers got more deeply involved in nonagency-backed mortgages and mortgage securitizations both in volume and in the amount of risk assumed, to their demise. All private mortgage insurers were hit hard by the mortgage crisis. The most notable casualty was the PMI Group, a market leader that filed for bankruptcy protection in November 2011 because it anticipated that it would be unable to honor all existing and future claims on the policies it had issued.

Excess Spread and Cash Reserves   In normal market circumstances, the SPV enjoys a positive cash flow because the sum of the coupons paid to the investors in the securities is typically less than the interest payments it collects from the borrowers, since interest rates charged to borrowers are higher than the coupons paid to investors. This is good news for the investors because it provides an additional source of funds that can be used to strengthen the transaction.

Many structures use the excess cash flow, known as excess spread, to constitute a reserve for rainy days. If the SPV experiences a shortfall of revenues, due to a higher-than-expected level of collateral default, the cash reserve is tapped to pay the bondholders. If and when payments resume at a more normal level, the cash reserve is replenished.

The cash reserve is designed to compensate for a temporary cash shortfall but not to excessively protect bondholders. Most SPVs sell tranched securities representing various risk/return options. The investors holding the lowest tranches—the equity-like securities—take a lot of risk and expect to be compensated accordingly. Thus, they resist the creation of large cash reserves that benefit the higher tranches, just as investors in corporate equity can resist the build-up of retained earnings that bolster the security of the corporation's debt investors. The size of the cash reserve is, therefore, capped, as is the proportion of excess spread that goes to the cash reserve. When one of the two ceilings is reached, cash is released to the equity investors.

When analyzing debt issued by an SPV, the mechanism around the cash reserve has to be thoroughly understood. If it is weak, it may indicate that the transaction is structured to please the equity investors to the detriment of the bondholders. It is not unusual that equity investors expect a quick payout.

Rating agencies play a big role in the sizing of the cash reserve. The larger it is, the higher the securities' ratings.

Overcollateralization Overcollateralization, or simply OC, means that the special purpose vehicle obtains more assets than the aggregate amount of all securities issued. For instance, a transaction with a 5 percent overcollateralization sells, say, $100 million worth of securities but the sponsor must provide $105 million worth of collateral (principal only, future interest payments not taken into account) to receive the full amount of cash. It means that the sponsor must have access to other sources of funding for the $5 million it originates and transfers to the SPV.

Another way of creating overcollateralization is to use the excess spread, as defined in the previous section, at the beginning of the transaction to repay a portion of the most senior tranches. As the level of debt is gradually reduced, OC is being created. An OC target is set so when the desired level of OC is reached, the distribution of cash flow can resume according to plan, for instance to pay all residual cash to the equity investors.

Investors benefit from OC because they are more likely to receive the payments they expect even if some collateral assets default. Without overcollateralization, the first default translates into an immediate dent in the most subordinated security. As long as less than the overcollateralization amount (5 percent in our example) defaults, all securities are repaid in full. The same applies to the regular interest payments.

Early Amortization Early amortization refers to an acceleration of the repayment of principal upon occurrence of predefined amounts. The idea is relatively similar to the concept of covenants we reviewed earlier for the loans. Certain conditions are imposed, for instance, to the collateral pool and to the servicer. If they breach the conditions, the deal enters into "early amortization" in order to protect the investors.

There are two main consequences of early amortization:

1. If the transaction includes the reinvestment of repaid collateral assets, as is the case for short-term assets like credit-card receivables (Chapter 8), it stops. All the funds collected from the collateral are used to repay the securities and no new assets are purchased.
2. The available cash is used in priority to pay back senior debt. The distribution of money to junior investors is interrupted and resumes only

when senior investors are fully repaid. This means that investors in the second-highest tranche and below do not receive any payment until the most senior tranche is repaid in full. If there is money left, the second highest starts being repaid, then the third one, and so on.

Let's examine the most common events that can trigger early amortization:

- A higher level of default than expected. The transaction documentation contains a threshold and a clear definition of the way to measure default.
- The excess spread level is below the desired level. The reasons can be a high level of default, which means less collateral to make interest payments, or, in case of transactions with reinvestments, the market conditions have changed and the newly originated collateral is not priced as well as the original collateral.
- A breach of an OC test. Each tranche of an ABS can have its own OC test. It is measured as a ratio between some collateral value and the size of the tranche. If a tranche-level OC threshold is breached, early amortization ensues.
- The financial distress of the sponsor and/or servicer.

Financial Guaranty: Insurance for Securities   Once sizeable, the financial guaranty industry has almost completely disappeared. The business model was straightforward: specialized companies with AAA ratings guaranteed the timely payments of interest and principle of securities issued by third parties. As a result, securities with a natural, that is, pre-guaranty rating of say, A/A2 were upgraded to the same rating as the financial guarantor, typically the AAA/Aaa. This form of credit enhancement was widely used throughout the capital markets.

The investors could, therefore, rely on the credit quality of the guarantor and be less concerned by the quality of the securities themselves. The industry was dominated by four U.S.-based monoline (meaning that it was their only line of business) insurance companies: Ambac, FGIC, FSA, and MBIA. These companies were active globally, with a focus on the United States and Europe, and a small presence in Japan. Besides them, multiline insurers were occasionally providing similar policies. Monolines sprang up in the 1970s to support the municipal bond market, which is characterized by issuers too numerous (think school districts, cities, and towns) for even large teams of credit analysts to master. Their value was to provide confidence to investors and, therefore, to help the distribution of municipal bonds.

Thanks to their success in the municipal market, they extended their reach to the ABS (MBS and CDO) market(s). Issuance was growing at a fast pace and here again the AAA guaranties helped to facilitate the distribution of securities.

Then, starting in the early 2000s, monolines became important players of the growing CDO market (Chapter 12). The rationale was that CDO collateral was well understood to them, since it consisted of ABSs. Thus, the monolines felt comfortable taking the CDO credit risk. One of the major differences though was the size of the transactions. It was not unusual for these firms to guarantee issues in excess of $1 billion of a CDO tranche backed by thousands of mortgages, which was far greater than most ABS transactions that they had been underwriting.

When the mortgage crisis started, monolines were hit on several fronts: the "regular" MBS (residential and commercial) portfolios they had guaranteed and the CDOs as well. The amount of losses they accumulated was very large compared to their claim-paying capacity. As a result, Ambac and FGIC filed for bankruptcy protection, FSA was acquired by a smaller monoline, Assured Guaranty, and MBIA split itself into several entities; one of them, National Public Finance Guarantee, is still active guaranteeing municipal bonds.

CHAPTER 19

Credit Insurance, Surety Bonds, and Letters of Credit

In this chapter, we introduce three long-standing and traditional products that protect firms against losses triggered by the default of a counterparty. Although they differ in technique, all the products enable companies to transfer credit risk to banks and insurance companies that provide the products. They are, therefore, useful to corporate risk managers anxious to reduce the amount of credit risk exposure on their own books. Most users of the products consider that the credit risk has been completely or nearly completely eliminated since losses are experienced only when a counterparty *and* the protection seller default simultaneously, which is highly unlikely.

Each product has its own characteristics, some imposed by regulators, some engineered over time by the main market participants, some reflecting the risk appetite of the providers. They are either bought for one's own needs or for the benefit of a third party that demands that they be provided. The buyer of the product may or may not be the beneficiary of the product; the beneficiary is the entity that seeks to transfer its credit risk exposure. Some variations of the products may have an exclusive application, and others compete with each other as substitutes. Credit risk managers' purchasing decisions are driven by what is available, what the objectives are, what they can afford, or what the situation they face requires. Table 19.1 provides a quick overview of the main participants and uses of these products.

For much of the chapter, we take the point of view of the company looking to transfer (alternatively known as "distribute") its credit risk, that is, the ultimate protection user, since we believe that this approach helps to better understand the products. We discuss features and options of the products that may be of interest to anyone seeking credit protection. In the last section, we cover these products as they relate to the risk-assuming company, and we discuss both their credit risk management challenges and how their behavior shapes the products they sell.

TABLE 19.1   Participants and Products

	Providers	Main Uses	Purchasers	Beneficiary
Credit insurance	Insurers	Trade receivables Loans Trade finance	Corporates Banks	Policyholder
Surety bond	Insurers	Construction contracts; legal obligations	Construction companies; various commercial enterprises	Client (third party to the contract)
Letter of credit	Banks	All kinds of performance, physical or financial; transactions; trade finance	Corporates and banks	Client (third party to the contract)

CREDIT INSURANCE

The Product

Trade credit insurance or simply credit insurance, was originally designed exclusively to protect trade receivables. Simply, it protects a company against the risk of not being paid by its customers after a sale. Coverage is available almost everywhere, is most popular in Europe, and is gaining acceptance in the United States. One of the reasons for its popularity is that, unless cash is requested prior to or upon delivery of a physical good, sellers have no other mitigants available, contrary to all other transactions generating credit risk, as reviewed in earlier chapters.

The product is relatively simple and an efficient way to avoid credit losses stemming from unpaid receivables. The company purchases a credit insurance policy from an insurer. The company's customers or clients, that is, those from whom the company has receivables, are called buyers. The insurance policy pays a certain percentage of real losses incurred after a buyer fails to pay an invoice within the terms that had been agreed upon.

For most companies, the largest single current asset is trade receivables; so losses from these, in excess of what's expected, could dwarf earnings and deplete equity. Thus, for many businesses, controlling this exposure is a critical task.

In the last couple of years, insurers have started underwriting modified trade credit insurance policies to protect banks not against payments of sales of their own goods, a business they are obviously not involved in, but against other financial obligations. Credit insurers have been creative and adapted their policies to accommodate their banking clients. The product is known as non-payment insurance (NPI). In doing so, insurers have to be careful to remain within the limits of what insurance regulators authorize them to underwrite as such policies could be considered to be "financial guaranties," a product prohibited for multiline insurance companies by U.S. insurance regulators. The policies are designed to offer not only credit risk transfer but also regulatory capital relief.

Market Participants

Three European insurance companies primarily providing only trade credit insurance dominate the global credit insurance market: Euler-Hermes (France, a subsidiary of Allianz), Atradius (Spain and the Netherlands), and Coface (France a subsidiary of Arch). They offer very similar products and have a faithful customer base. The International Credit Insurance & Surety Association (ICISA) (www.icisa.org) is a trade group representing most major credit insurers in the world. In 2019, they wrote a total of nearly €7 billion of premium and paid more than €3 billion of claims to their policy-holders. It is often mentioned that the relatively large size of the European market can be explained by the high volume of transactions between neighboring countries with different legal systems, different languages, and, until 2002, many different currencies. Assessing the credit quality of a French customer is a challenging task for a German company, so the easiest way not to worry about payment is to buy insurance. The success in the local markets led to a global expansion, and branches and subsidiaries of the three leaders can be found in the United States, in Latin America, and in Asia. Ready access to the financials of privately owned European companies is also cited as one of the reasons for such high-coverage penetration in Europe.

In the United States, apart from the local branches or subsidiaries of the European credit insurers, the market participants are specialty-underwriting units of large property and casualty insurance companies such as AIG, Chubb, or Liberty Mutual. However, the United States market has been stagnant for a while. American companies are more concerned about protecting against default by their foreign customers rather than against default by their domestic customers. In other parts of the world, credit insurance has only a marginal presence despite huge commercial efforts by large insurance companies.

The three European insurers have their direct-sales forces, but the largest distribution channel is through insurance brokers. There is a multitude of brokers involved in the credit-insurance business. Large companies tend to work with the largest brokers like Aon and Marsh McLennan, but there are a host of smaller specialty brokers like BPL Global or One Source with a substantial customer base. Some InsurTech companies are starting to offer online distribution.

Coverage Types

Ground-Up Coverage Most policies issued by the three European insurers provide ground-up coverage, meaning coverage begins to take effect as losses start to occur, in excess of a small deductible retained by the insured party. Such policies provide an efficient protection against the frequency risk (i.e., the risk that many small- and medium-sized clients default) and the severity risk (i.e., the default of one large client), because even small losses are indemnified.

Excess of Loss/Stop-Loss Coverage Instead, corporations can secure coverage on an excess of loss (XoL) or stop-loss basis. For example, a policy is structured with a large deductible of $10 million, and covers aggregate losses up to $200 million in excess of the $10 million. The policyholder receives up to $200 million of indemnity, once its own accumulated losses during the policy period reach the deductible amount of $10 million.

Insurers like AIG or Chubb offer XoL policies that protect against the more severe losses stemming either from an accumulation of small losses or a large default in excess of a large deductible. The former scenario might arise from a sharp economic slowdown; the latter scenario might happen due to the bankruptcy of a client with a large payable. However, insurers normally control concentration with policy sublimits and grant large limits parsimoniously.

Credit Limits

Credit insurance is no different from other insurance products, and insurers want to both understand and control the losses they agree to cover. During the underwriting process, the insurer wants to know the policyholder's receivables exposures to its counterparties (or buyers, in the jargon of credit insurance as mentioned above), meaning the breakdown of what's owed and by whom and any loss history available. Based on this and other data and criteria, the policy will cover losses in the aggregate based on this pool of receivables. During the lifetime of a contract, policyholders are required to update the insurer on the status of the receivables. However, since business is dynamic, the pool will change, and policyholders are given some discretion to file claims against the policy for new buyers, or for receivables on existing buyers in excess of the amount reported at an earlier time. Thus, these claims will be filed under the discretionary credit limit, the DCL, which allows the policyholder to file a claim without explicit review.

Policyholders must secure approval for credit limits in excess of the DLs. If a policy has a discretionary limit of $2 million and the policyholder did not receive the explicit approval for claims in excess of this, then indemnity would be limited to $2 million. The insurers, however, agree to indemnify losses below the $2 million threshold.

Discretionary limits are typically relatively small, say, a few million dollars. When entering or renewing a credit insurance policy, a company can have its buyer list preapproved so that business transactions are not interrupted by insurance coverage negotiations. It is not unusual for insurers to preapprove limits for only part of the policy period, giving them a chance to control their exposures on companies they are unfamiliar or uncomfortable with.

Larger discretionary limits are reserved for the largest and most sophisticated policyholders that have solid credit risk management processes in place and a demonstrated track record of limited credit losses. By giving policyholders more flexibility in deciding with whom to transact business (more freedom with larger DCLs), the insurers are, in essence, outsourcing a large part of their underwriting responsibilities to the policyholders. Not all insurers grant these large DCLs.

Pre-approved limits may be set by country (e.g., maximum claims for all Italian buyers at $200 million), by industry (e.g., maximum claims for construction businesses of $50 million), by counterparty (e.g., maximum claims for General Electric at $10 million), or by other dimensions. Granting limits is a nice source of revenue for the credit insurers because policyholders need to pay a fee to get limits approved or renewed, and they are valid for only a short period of time. For a company with a large portfolio of buyers, getting them approved can, therefore, be rather costly.

Regardless of the discretionary limit, the insurer typically indemnifies only 90 percent of the incurred loss for all claims on a pro rata basis, meaning if the policy limit were $200 million in excess of $50 million, losses would have to be at least $222 in excess of $50 million ($272 million in total) for the policyholder to collect the full $200 million from the insurer. The insurer's goal with the loss-sharing mechanism is to maintain an alignment of interest with the insured, that is, to give the insured an incentive to manage its credit book professionally. This is a good illustration of one principle we present in Chapter 3, namely, "Does the seller keep an interest in the deal?"

Strengths and Weaknesses of Trade Credit Insurance

To recap, credit insurance is a simple and efficient tool. The insurance format provides certainty of coverage and, contrary to some capital markets products like credit derivatives, it is a good match with the nature of exposures. The documentation is straightforward and, thanks to the competition between insurers, prices are reasonable.

The product is not without weaknesses. The product's technical features and overall inflexibility are sometimes mentioned as reasons that the product is not more widely adopted. Yet one can understand why insurers impose certain rules that are essential to managing their credit exposures.

Key weaknesses that are commonly cited:

- Rigidity: Most insurers have a very strict underwriting model and rarely accept changes to the product they sell.
- Only receivables: As we have seen so far, corporates are exposed to credit risk from a large and growing variety of sources. Credit insurance applies only to trade receivables and strictly excludes other activities generating credit risk. Credit insurance is, therefore, only a partial solution for a corporate risk manager anxious to protect their entire book.
- Short-term policies: The coverage period within a policy is limited to three to six months, which represents the typical term of payments to customers. This does not match the needs of some companies that frequently extend payments for longer periods. Think of a heavy-equipment manufacturer where production can take several years. Whereas the policyholders would like to be covered until the final product is delivered and they are paid in full, the credit insurer may offer only a renewable six-month policy.
- Whole turnover policy: European insurers originally covered only the entire trade receivables portfolio and did not accept subportfolios of their clients. They did not want to be adversely selected against and needed to receive revenues associated with the strongest segments of the portfolio in order to be able to cover the weaker names at a reasonable price. Over the years, especially in the North American markets and under pressure from multiline insurers, the commercial behavior has evolved, and it is now possible to avoid insuring the entire portfolio but a selection of buyers.
- Cancellation/reduction of credit lines: This is probably the most serious deterrent for many potential buyers of credit insurance. Some policies offered by European insurers have typically the unilateral right to reduce or cancel coverage with as little as one day's notice. The insurer

will typically honor the outstanding receivables but can stop coverage of new invoices. They use their ability to reduce or cancel a credit line when buyers start showing signs of financial stress or in case of economic crisis, which is precisely the time when the demand for credit insurance grows. This is what happened in the spring of 2020 during the COVID pandemic when thousands of credit limits were reduced or cancelled. Some insurers, especially multiline insurance companies in the United States, differentiate themselves by offering noncancellable credit lines, which is a strong selling point.

Besides credit insurance, nonrecourse factoring is another product enabling a company to transfer the risk of nonpayment of a customer to a third party. Factoring is the sale of accounts receivable to a third party, usually a specialized company or a bank (the *factor*), in exchange for cash. By selling its receivables, a company can receive the cash associated with the sale of a product before the end of the payment term agreed upon with the customer. The factor acquires the receivables from, and pays cash to, the company. The factor then collects the payment from the ultimate customer. As it relates to credit risk, there are two types of factoring. In recourse receivables financing, the risk of nonpayment remains with the company. This means that in case of a default, the factor will collect back some of the cash amount it advanced to the company. In nonrecourse receivables financing, the risk of nonpayment is transferred to the factor. This is also known as "true sale." In case of default, the factor assumes the loss. Nonrecourse factoring can therefore be viewed as a combination of a short-term loan and credit insurance. There are many factors in the United States: large commercial banks and specialty finance companies.

Political-Risk Insurance

Political-risk insurance policies are often bundled with credit insurance policies since they both involve receivables collection problems. In addition to financial stress, nonpayments from foreign clients can occur as a result of their home governments banning currency conversions. This happens in emerging economies during times of economic stress when hard-currency (e.g., euro and U.S. dollar) reserves of a country are depleted. Foreign governments restrict conversion to keep what hard currencies are available to pay for essential commodities like oil. Even if a buyer is able and willing to pay its foreign suppliers, it is prevented from doing so by the ban on currency convertibility. Political-risk insurance policies thus combine credit insurance with the risk of nonconvertibility of the currency. They are offered both by private insurers and by public entities (e.g., the Export-Import Bank of the

United States, www.exim.gov, or the Export Credits Guarantee Department in the U.K., www.ecdg.gov.uk) as a way to support exports.

SURETY BONDS

There are a large variety of surety bonds but their technology is fairly similar. Surety bonds are most common in the construction and real estate industries and in doing business with government entities. Commercial surety bonds, which are a special type of surety bond, also are used by virtually all industry sectors to guarantee legal or fiscal obligations.

The Product

A surety bond is a three-party arrangement in which the fulfillment of a contract, a future payment, or the meeting of a legal obligation is guaranteed by a surety provider, known as a surety. The surety provides a beneficiary (the obligee, a second party) with a monetary indemnification in case the bond purchaser who has the obligation to perform (the principal) does not perform as contracted. To illustrate, the obligee, such as a governmental entity, requests the product; the principal is a contractor with the obligation to perform who purchases the bond; and the surety is the insurance company that issues the bonds. A commonly used surety bond is a construction completion bond—a municipality contracts with an excavation company to build a parking lot and requires that the excavation company post a bond from a surety equal to the value of the contract. The bond protects the municipality in the event that the company does not complete the job. If the company fails to complete the job, the municipality would then receive funds from the surety to complete a partially built parking lot.

A legitimate question is what does performance under the terms of a contract have to do with credit risk because, in most cases, the underlying contract or obligation is not financial? Experience shows that the main reason why companies do not perform and, consequently, why surety bond payments are triggered, is that they are unable to due to finances. The technical ability or willingness to complete a contract is rarely the problem, but financial troubles prevent the execution.

Thus, requiring a surety bond is a way to protect against a credit risk. The beneficiary or obligee loses money only if two entities fail at the same time: the principal and the surety. Because surety bond providers are large insurance companies that are heavily regulated and have strong credit quality, the chance that the surety bond is not honored is remote. (Note that even if the surety were to fail, state insurance regulators in the United States have guarantee funds that may cover the obligations.)

An important feature of the bond is how payments are triggered. Some bonds are on demand, meaning that the surety commits to pay if the principal or the obligee requests it. Other bonds leave room for negotiation prior to payment, and, therefore, these provide less credit protection. Needless to say, obligees prefer on-demand bonds, but principals and insurers push for less rigid conditions of payment.

Surety bonds are primarily offered by large multiline insurance companies: CNA and Liberty Mutual or Travelers in the United States and Tokio Marine & Fire in Japan, and there are few companies whose business is limited to surety bonds. Bonds are bought and sold through insurance brokers.

Principal Families of Bonds

The surety market is split into two subcategories: contract surety bonds, primarily used in the construction industry, and commercial surety bonds, typically required by government agencies. In most countries, contract surety is a much bigger and homogeneous market than commercial surety, which is highly fragmented in terms of products.

Contract Bonds Contract surety covers various types of bonds required at different stages of a construction project. They are used both in the public construction market, where the client—and beneficiary of the bond—is a public entity, and in the private market where the beneficiary is, for example, a real estate developer. In all cases, they cover an obligation of a construction company. There are variations in each country but we describe the three main types:

1. Bid bonds are requested by developers from construction companies that are bidding on contract work for new projects. Although many companies are anxious to be involved on new, large-scale projects, public and private developers invite only a limited number of contractors to bid in order to simplify what could be an unwieldy process involving numerous contenders. To screen out contenders who are not serious, they require contractors to post a bid bond in order to participate in the selection process. If a contractor wins the bid and then reneges on the project, the bond is drawn. The bond amount is generally set at about 10 or 20 percent of the project cost. Note that these bonds may not always cover credit risk per se. A contractor who walks away may not be

doing so for financial reasons, but rather because of a change of strategy, doubt about the financial strength of the client, or work overload.

2. Performance bonds figure prominently in the project cycle. Also known as completion bonds, contractors are required to post these bonds with the developer as the beneficiary. They are drawn if the contractor fails to complete the project according to the contract's terms, including the timetable and quality criteria. In most countries, the amount of the performance bond is set at 10 percent of the contract amount. However, in the United States, performance bonds will cover 100 percent of the contract amount. In surety contracts, there is often a replacement provision allowing the surety provider the right to replace the defaulted contractor with a new contractor to complete the work. This provision keeps the surety provider from making a large cash outlay to the beneficiary and helps to control the costs associated with the surety bond.

3. Advance payment bonds involve the credit risk exposure that the developer has to the contractor throughout the project life. Usually, the developer makes advance payments to the contractor to provide liquidity to cover ongoing expenses. The risk for the developer is that the contractor defaults on the contract and the advance payments are not refunded. Contractors are, therefore, required to post a bond for an amount roughly equal to the advance payment received.

Commercial Bonds   Companies in virtually all industries require commercial bonds in certain circumstances. The main use of the bonds is to guarantee a legal or financial obligation. The public entity requesting the bond requires access to an additional source of payment in case the company it is engaged with fails to meet its obligation.

Court bonds are a form of commercial bond. Within this category, appeal bonds are a product used in the United States. If a defendant loses a case and appeals the decision, the court will require an appeal bond. The court's goal is to deter defendants from appealing and to cover some legal costs. The bond amount is normally the same amount as the defendant's payment required by the court's decision. This amount can be in the hundreds of millions of dollars. If the defendant loses again and is unable to pay, the bond is drawn to compensate the plaintiffs. Defendants' appeal bonds usually require collateral, since the exposure that the surety faces can be substantial.

Commercial bonds are highly varied and can be customized for various transactions and types of obligations. In another example, bonds are used by importers to accelerate customs clearance. Because the exact calculation of import duties can be time consuming and delay the release of imports, importers post bonds that allow them to access their products immediately and to pay their import duties later. The tax authorities are comfortable with bonds issued by strong insurers that give them assurance that they will ultimately collect what's owed. Foreign car manufacturers are, for instance, heavy users of surety bonds since having cars in the dealer showroom is preferable to having them sitting in a port waiting for customs clearance. In this instance, the credit risk that the tax authorities would face, were imports allowed to enter before collecting duties, is now mitigated by the posting of the bond.

LETTERS OF CREDIT OR LoCs

The Product

A letter of credit (LoC or simply LC) is a written commitment by a bank to make a payment to a third party when the bank's client requests it or when the third party requests it. It is, therefore, particularly well adapted for a company or a government entity that wants protection in the event that a counterparty does not perform something it has committed to do.

Similar to surety bonds, LoCs may not be a financial guaranty per se but effectively protect against default risk because financial problems are the most common cause of why a company does not perform. Letters of credit can explicitly cover risks of nonpayment, that is, a default risk, which we cover further on.

The concept behind LoCs is that they provide a financial backstop. They enhance the credit quality of a counterparty by having a strong financial institution behind the counterparty should it fail to perform. Letters of credit, therefore, offer an additional protection because an entity would lose money only if its counterparty and the issuing bank were to default at the same time.

In LoCs, contract wording is clear, standardized, and well tested. Little room is left open for negotiation once payment is requested, thereby minimizing legal risk. As such, they are considered to provide the best protection against the nonperformance of a company.

Below are two examples of wording used in LoCs in which the LoC is requested by Company A to cover the commitment of Company B and issued by Bank ABC:

1. We hereby authorize Company A to draw on us, Bank ABC, for the account of Company B up to an aggregate amount of $10 million . . .
2. We hereby establish our irrevocable letter of credit in favor of Company A for the account of Company B for the amount of $10 million available at sight, drawn on Bank ABC, by your request for payment at sight. . . .

The objective of requiring an LoC is to avoid taking any kind of credit risk, including having to monitor the credit quality of counterparties and their guarantors. Standard market practice is to require the bank issuing the LoC to have a minimum financial rating of, for example, A/A2, and at least, for example, $3 billion of assets. Standard contracts also require the replacement of the issuing bank should its rating or assets fall beneath these criteria. Standard market practice also treats an LoC issued by a strong bank as the equivalent of cash. Thus, when LoCs stand behind credit exposures, the notional exposure is reduced by the amount of the LoC, without haircut.

We conclude this section by explaining three common features of LoCs:

1. *Irrevocable:* The issuing bank cannot cancel the LoC before its stated expiration date. If the financial condition of its client deteriorates, the bank must handle the consequences.
2. *Stand-by:* An LoC is a contingent obligation of a bank; it is not a loan, nor is it funded. That is why LoCs are often referred to as stand-by letters of credit, to underscore the fact that they are contingent.
3. *Evergreen:* If the LoC is evergreen, although the contract wording contains a termination date, the LoC will automatically be renewed unless the issuing bank informs its client and the beneficiary that it will nonrenew.

Illustration of LoC

In the following section, we present examples in which LoCs are used. One of the most common applications is trade finance, and it is hard to imagine trade finance operating without LoCs. Another usage area of LoCs is in the reinsurance industry, and most transactions involving foreign or offshore reinsurers make use of LoCs.

Trade Finance   Trade finance refers to the financial arrangement developed by banks to facilitate the exchange of goods between two companies located in different countries. This represents a major activity for large commercial banks across the globe to support their corporate clients.

One of the main challenges faced by exporters is to get paid by clients operating in a different legal environment. The rewards of selling goods outside its own country can be big, but so is the credit risk. At issue is getting comfortable with the ability of a remotely located client to honor an invoice. The risks can be acceptable in developed economies in which reliable recordkeeping and legal systems are in place but more problematic in emerging economies.

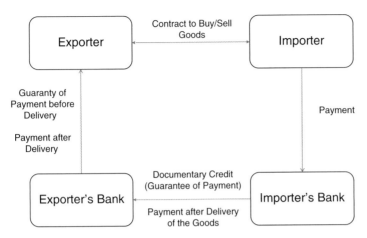

FIGURE 19.1 Trade Finance LoC

This is where LoCs come into play. It is common for a company selling its product abroad (the exporter) to request the assistance of its bank to secure payments from its client (the importer). The goal is to transfer the credit risk of the importer to the bank. This is achieved in several steps, listed here (and see also Figure 19.1):

■ A contract is made between the importer and the exporter that stipulates the rights and obligations of each party, such as the nature of the products to be delivered, the price, and the payment terms granted to the importer.
■ The exporter's bank agrees to relieve its client from the importer's credit risk but requires that a local bank, whose credit risk is considered to be stronger than the importer's, guarantee the payment of the importer in an irrevocable way. The exporter makes this request to the importer.
■ The importer then asks its bank to issue a specific form of LoC called "documentary credit" to the exporter's bank. This guarantees payment upon successful completion of the trade. The LoC is then sent to the exporter's bank.
■ The exporter's bank notifies its client that the LoC has been received. This means that the bank has obtained the documents it needs to guarantee the payments and that the sale can take place. The bank, therefore, takes credit risk on the importer's bank.
■ After delivery of the goods, the exporter receives payments from its bank. From its point of view, the transaction is completed and there is

no credit risk remaining. However, its bank still has to collect the funds from the importer's bank and, therefore, carries a credit risk on it.

■ The exporter's bank then requires payment from the importer's bank, which transfers the funds.

■ The importer's bank requires payment from the importer and receives the funds, which completes the transaction.

The LoC provided by the importer's bank is the cornerstone of the entire process. Its issuance triggers the chain of events, which makes the transaction possible. Without it, the exporter's bank would not agree to guarantee the payment, and the exporter would not sell.

If the exporter's bank is confident that its client can deliver what it promised and that the importer's bank can pay, it may elect to prefinance the exports. This means than the exporter can actually receive cash from its bank even before delivering its goods. In other words, the strong language of the LoC is a security that most banks feel so comfortable with that they will advance money against them, giving exporters a source of working capital.

Letter of Credit in the Insurance Industry   The insurance industry is also a large consumer of LoCs. Why? Credit risk is a by-product of insurance contracts and insurance companies are not prepared to take this risk, thus, they demand LoCs to secure these contracts.

A common example is with reinsurance contracts, which are insurance contracts purchased by insurance companies to cover the exposures they accumulate in their normal course of business. When one insurer buys a policy from a reinsurer, premium payment is often made up front, and it can be sizeable, in the hundreds of millions of dollars. The reinsurer promises to pay claims given certain events under the terms of the reinsurance contract. The credit risk arises because the reinsurer could fail to pay if claims payments were to become due. Unless the reinsurer's credit rating is very high or unless there are offsets that can be used to mitigate the exposure (similar to the offsets used in derivatives netting, which we cover in Chapter 17), the insurer may require the reinsurer to post an LoC. The amount of the LoC can be variably defined in the LoC itself, for example, varying with the size of the premium or with the loss experience of the insurer's underlying policies.

Letters of Credit versus Surety Bonds   Virtually all uses of surety bonds also can be fulfilled by LoCs. Whenever a private or public entity requires a bond, an LoC can be provided instead. Risk managers of developers and of public entities, therefore, can choose between asking for a bond or an LoC. When the beneficiary is indifferent between the two, companies (principals) have a choice. There are many instances in which banks, proposing an LoC, and insurance companies, pushing for a bond, are competing to support their clients.

Letters of credit utilize language that is clearer, more standard, and stronger than a surety bond, and beneficiaries often feel more secure with an LoC versus a bond. Why, then, are bonds still prevalent?

For instances in which the beneficiary is indifferent between a surety bond and an LoC, the principal will prefer to use a surety bond. There are three main reasons for this:

1. Banks have limited credit capacity, and, internally, LoCs compete with loans for this limited capacity. As we discuss further on in the chapter, LoCs and loans are commonly part of a same credit facility so, from a user's perspective (principal), using an LoC limits the amount it can borrow.
2. Letters of credit are expensive. Insurance companies have a different profitability model than banks, and they may be able to offer credit risk capacity at prices banks would not accept.
3. Letters of credit are easily drawn by beneficiaries, whereas the softer language of most surety bonds leaves the door open to negotiation. Principals may believe that they have the chance to avoid a surety bond being drawn, whereas that chance is virtually impossible with an LoC.

Finally, the surety bond industry has, generally speaking, a good track record in most countries. Market participants are accustomed to quickly and efficiently handle large volumes of bonds and, when necessary, claims. Bond issuers provide value to the beneficiary that helps maintain and develop the acceptance of their products.

THE PROVIDERS' POINT OF VIEW

Credit Insurance

For insurers, credit insurance generates large portfolios characterized by a very large number of buyers (all the insured's clients) and peak exposures on the largest companies in the world. Just think of how many companies sell to large retailers like Walmart in the United States, Carrefour in France, or Tesco in the United Kingdom. When a supplier to these large companies purchases credit insurance, this generates additional exposure to the insurer that adds to what it already has in its portfolio from other policyholders.

Credit insurance portfolios have primarily short-term credit risk exposure because most sales carry 30-day or 60-day payment terms. The exposures are direct (as opposed to contingent) but unfunded, meaning the insurer has not made any cash outlay when the policies incept. In case of default of a buyer, the insurer indemnifies its policyholders and is granted the right to collect money from the buyer. The legal term allowing the insurer the right to do this is subrogation. In these instances, credit insurers are treated as senior unsecured creditors when trying to collect.

The main challenge of the credit insurers is, therefore, to manage their accumulation on peak names. There are three main techniques used to shape the portfolio:

1. First, the insurer will limit the capacity it offers to their clients at the point of origination. When a policy is sold, the insured knows that its indemnity on some names is capped at a certain amount, whereas the rest of the portfolio may benefit from full coverage. Exposures of related companies (e.g., subsidiaries of a parent company) are aggregated under one limit to avoid concentration. Capacity will be more limited for instances in which the buyer's industry has fewer players, such as large retail.

2. Second, the insurer will reinsure its exposures to third parties, such as to Hannover Re, Munich Re, or Swiss Re. Each year, credit insurers and reinsurers sign a treaty in which a portion of the originated exposures is transferred from the insurer to the reinsurer, thereby reducing the credit insurers' exposure to peak risks.

3. Finally, after origination, some insurers can reduce the capacity originally made available during the lifetime of the policy. This is, of course, not popular with clients. When a buyer's credit deteriorates, policyholders are informed that the existing exposure is covered but that future receivables may not be. This method may work to reduce the insurer's losses in certain cases but not always. When the buyer's circumstances become so dire that it needs to restructure its liabilities, banks may ask the insurer to maintain coverage to help the buyer stay afloat. If the company subsequently defaults, insurers may lose money alongside the banks.

Credit insurers, thanks to their activities, have come to own a very valuable database capturing payment histories of tens of millions of companies around the world. The competitive advantage of a credit insurer does not come from a superior quality of information but rather from the way it analyzes the data. Some credit insurers sell their analysis. The rating service of Coface (www.coface.com) is one such provider.

Surety Bonds

Insurers will request an indemnity agreement from their clients (the principals). This means that, if the beneficiary of the bond triggers a payment, the insurer provides funds but subsequently requests reimbursement from its clients (the principals). The indemnity agreement is the legal way that insurers get exposed to the principal's credit risk. The exposures are either contingent on their clients' failure to fulfill an obligation or direct when the bond has been triggered. In case of bankruptcy, insurers are considered to be senior unsecured creditors.

When underwriting a surety bond, insurers primarily focus on the credit quality of their client. If they are comfortable with it, they issue the bond without collateral. With less strong companies, insurers can request security such as liquid collateral assets or even an LoC. A secondary analysis focuses on the purpose of the surety bond and the wording of the legal document. Naturally, since insurers want to avoid disbursing cash to the beneficiaries, they focus on types of surety bonds they are comfortable with. For example, on-demand bonds are thought to be too risky by many insurers. Favorable wording does not reduce the credit risk for the insurer, it merely contributes to the avoidance or delay of a contingent credit risk being transformed into a direct funded risk.

From a credit risk management point of view, managing the accumulation of single-name exposures is a challenge. Insurers can limit their exposure on certain names by simply ceasing to issue new bonds. This tactic is not the best way to manage long-term client relationships, so sureties will often secure more capacity by reinsuring their portfolio.

The other big challenge is lack of diversification from industry concentration. Because surety bonds are primarily used in construction projects, construction companies dominate surety providers' portfolios. The construction industry is cyclical, and most companies' fortunes rise and fall at the same time (i.e., they contribute systematic risk to the insurer's portfolio). To achieve some diversification, sureties write commercial bonds that provide exposure to a variety of sectors.

Letters of Credit

Letters of credit are a basic product of a commercial bank and one that banks must offer to anchor a commercial relationship. Letters of credit contribute to the credit risk portfolio generated by bank activities. A few items of note:

- Companies that need LoCs from time to time arrange a generic facility that enables quick execution at known conditions. Commercial banks provide capacity either on a stand-alone basis or, more frequently, as part of a credit facility. As the risk is similar to loans, the credit facility covers various types of loans (e.g., revolver, swing line) and LoCs at the same time. The legal conditions, which are contained in the credit agreement, have certain sections that are common to all kinds of facilities and some are specific to LoCs. From a credit risk management standpoint, the most important sections relate to covenants and pricing, as we discuss in Chapter 8. If the amount is large, the entire facility is syndicated among several banks, that is to say, that a bank takes the lead in the negotiations and then distributes the risk to other banks that wish to participate.
- Requests in trade finance across clients tend to involve transactions with the same countries and within these countries, involving the same local banks. For instance, there are only a handful of Chinese banks with which Western banks are comfortable. A company that sells to a Chinese company will request an LoC posted by a bank from this short list. This creates a concentration issue that must be managed carefully because an accumulation of large exposures on certain names and countries (e.g., China, Russia, Brazil) can happen quickly.
- Trade finance is competitive and exporters typically contact several banks when shopping for an LoC, which sets off a competitive round of offers. The exporter is working on sales and simultaneously negotiating with various banks on the LoC. Thus, the terms offered are competitive, such as low fees and high cash advances. This can put pressure on the risk analyst working for the bank to accept less-than-desirable conditions.

FINAL WORDS

In this chapter we present readers with an overview of traditional markets for credit risk transfer. Credit insurance, surety, and LoCs are traditional products that work well and which pose little basis risk, meaning that the coverage is more or less fitted to the exposure. For most companies, the largest single current asset is trade receivables, and credit insurance is a relatively simple and efficient way to manage losses with this asset, including small losses. Surety bonds are commonplace in the construction industry, allowing that market to function. Trade credit is an established market with many banks competing for the business.

Although not without weaknesses, these traditional markets benefit from having well-established and standardized contracts and regulatory infrastructure that, on balance, helps to protect users from counterparty risk. The market also is accessible to traditional corporate risk managers, including those of smaller companies, and brokers help to facilitate the transactions.

From the providers' point of view, the challenge common to all these products lies in managing the accumulation of peak credit exposures and to reduce their exposures when the economic look is negative without alienating their customers.

CHAPTER 20

Credit Derivatives

Few financial products enjoy a reputation as negative as credit derivatives. Warren Buffett's comment in his 2002 annual shareholder letter that "in my view, derivatives are financial weapons of mass destruction" helped to foster this reputation, even though his comment did not specifically address credit derivatives. The role that some highly specialized forms of credit derivatives subsequently played during the 2007 crisis reinforced the negative perception they carry. Before rendering an opinion on the virtue of credit derivatives, it helps to understand the mechanics of the product and the legitimate role that it can play in the risk manager's toolbox.

The product has not evolved much in the last decade but the volume traded declined significantly as gross notional outstanding was more than $60 trillion in 2007 compared to around $11 trillion in June 2021. The main changes involve definitions in the legal documentation, to make sure that CDs stay true to their objectives and reflect always evolving market practices.

THE PRODUCT

Credit derivative is a generic term that captures all derivative products related to the transfer or assumption of credit risk only. There are a few products that can be included in this category but one of them, the credit default swap (CDS), constitutes the overwhelming majority of all transactions. Another type of credit derivative is a credit-linked note (CLN), which we review in Chapter 11. The expressions *credit derivative* and *credit default swap* are almost interchangeable, and in this chapter we will focus only on the most common form of credit derivative, the CDS. The CDS market plays a critical role in credit risk transfer and credit risk trading. It is also used to build synthetic balance sheet CLOs, as we learn in Chapter 12. As of June 4, 2021, the total gross notional amount of CDSs outstanding was $11.3 trillion generated by 598,000 trades.[1]

A CDS is not an insurance product per se, even though it feels like one. It is fundamentally an option, rather than either a swap or an insurance policy. There is a protection buyer, who wants to transfer the credit risk that may be faced on an entity, and a protection seller, who is ready to accept the credit risk on the same entity. The contract is between the protection buyer and the protection seller. The entity whose credit risk is transferred via the CDS is called the reference entity and is neither involved nor even aware that a transaction is taking place. In exchange for protection against the default of the reference entity, the protection buyer pays a fee, technically called a fixed amount but generally referred to as a spread or premium, to the protection seller. In case of default of the reference entity, the protection seller pays the protection buyer according to a mechanism that we describe later. In these respects, a CDS feels very much like a credit insurance policy.

However, one of the reasons that CDSs are not insurance products is that protection buyers can receive money even though they do not suffer a loss, that is, unlike insurance policies, a CDS does not indemnify the protection buyer. As a matter of fact, any person can buy protection and be paid, regardless of whether they are exposed to the credit. In terms of insurance, the buyer is not required to have an insurable interest. The expression *protection* is a bit of a misnomer because protection may be irrelevant to the transaction.

Figure 20.1 presents a schematic of the entities involved in a transaction. A contract occurs between buyer and seller. A third party, the reference entity, has no involvement with the transaction. The buyers pay a periodic or up-front premium (fee) to the seller and the seller, should a credit event occur, pays a sum to the buyer.

The reference entity can be a corporation (e.g., General Electric), a country (e.g., France), or an asset-backed security (e.g., a residential mortgage-backed security). Although conceptually they work in the same way, the legal contracts will differ among the three. For instance, the definition of a credit event for a corporation is different from that of a sovereign entity.

The legal contract documenting a CDS is, to the extent possible, standardized, primarily to facilitate the execution between the parties. Like other derivative contracts, market participants use the standard forms developed by the International Swaps and Derivatives Association (ISDA). There will be regional adaptations, for example, like the specific definition for

---

[1]*Source:* ISDA Swapsinfo, www.swapsinfo.org.

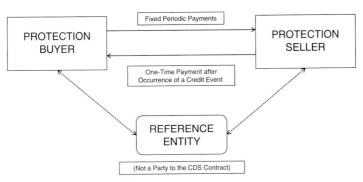

FIGURE 20.1 Basic CDS Structure

bankruptcy of Japanese reference entities. We invite readers to visit the ISDA website, www.isda.org, and see Chapter 17 for some more detail on these contracts.

Credit default swap contracts are denominated by what is called the floating rate payer calculation amount, more commonly known as the notional amount. This is the largest payment that could occur should a default occur, with the relevant obligations of the reference entity being valued at zero. Notional amounts are normally round numbers such as $5 million or $10 million.

The premium, often called spread, is a percentage of the notional amount. It is expressed on an annual basis, even though payments occur quarterly, and in basis points or bps (1 basis point = 0.01 percent; e.g., 100 bps = 1 percent). Often the rate itself may be low, often less than 1 percent for creditworthy entities. Utilizing basis point terminology is more convenient than percentages, for example, 85 basis points per annum is more understandable than 0.85 percent per annum.

For example, on May 4, 2021, the five-year CDS price for IBM Corp., according to Bloomberg, was 38.494 bps p.a., meaning, for a contract offering protection up to five years, the buyer would pay 0.38 percent on $10 million per year, or $38,494 per year. Most CDS contracts provide protection for tenors of one, three, five, or seven years. Longer tenors are possible but rare. The majority of CDSs have five-year tenors.

CDS spreads were traditionally paid quarterly, more or less one fourth of the yearly spread. However, in April 2009 things changed dramatically with what is known as the "Big Bang." An upfront payment and a fixed coupon for the lifetime of the derivative contract were introduced. Now, for CDSs such as North American single-name corporate CDSs, part of the premium is paid up front at the inception of the contract, then a standard

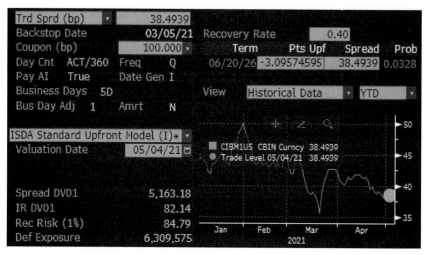

FIGURE 20.2   Price Indication for Five-Year CDS for IBM Corp.
Source: Bloomberg.

running spread of either 100 bps per annum (p.a.) (for investment grade reference entities) or 500 bps p.a. for speculative grade reference entities is paid quarterly.

The upfront payment is essentially the present value of the difference between the actual CDS spread and the standard running spread. Such a CDS might be priced at 10 percent + 500 bps, meaning that the protection buyer would pay 10 percent of the notional amount at inception, plus 500 bps per annum, paid quarterly. The up-front payment can, therefore, be very substantial, particularly if the reference entity is distressed.

For investment grade entities trading with a 100 bps p.a. coupon, the convention among market participants is to present conventional spreads, that is, the actual spread paid, irrespective of the fact that payments occur up front (from buyer to seller when the spread is over 100 bps p.a. and from seller to buyer when the spread is below 100 bps p.a.) and on a quarterly basis for the 100 bps coupon.

Figure 20.2 shows data for a five-year CDS on IBM Corp on May 4, 2021:

"Coupon (bp): 100" means that the protection buyer will pay the notional amount of the contract multiplied by 100 bps p.a. quarterly for 5 years.

"Pts Upf: –3.0957" ("points upfront") means that the seller (not the buyer, as there is a minus sign before the number 3) will pay notional amount of the contract multiplied by 3.0957 percent at the inception of the contract. This amount was calculated by Bloomberg and may differ from what market participants agree with each other.

"Spread: 38.4939" means that buyer and seller agreed to trade at a spread of 38.4939 bps p.a. or 0.38 percent of notional transacted. The rough math, ignoring time value of money, is 100 bps + (– 3.0957% × 10,000 (to convert to bps) / 5 years) = 100 – 61.9 = 38.49 bps of spread.

Corporates, insurance companies, hedge funds, and banks are the biggest buyers of CDS. On the other side, banks and hedge funds sell protection. The largest market participants in volume are investment banks such as Deutsche Bank, J.P. Morgan, and UBS. Risk managers anxious to get a sense of the availability and prices can find indications of pricing of CDSs from IHS Markit, Bloomberg, or by calling their banks who act as market makers.

THE SETTLEMENT PROCESS

One of the fundamental features of a CDS is that the payment to the protection buyer in the event of default of the reference entity is not triggered by any actual loss experienced by the protection buyer but by the occurrence of publicly observable events called credit events. In addition, a feature of the CDS market is that, in all but the most customized CDSs, the amount of payment is the same for all buyers of CDSs on the same reference entity and is set as the result of a credit event auction.

Credit Events

The payment process, called the settlement process, starts with the occurrence of credit events, which are specified in the transaction documents. Their definitions are intended to capture circumstances in which most creditors may lose money. The list and definitions are standardized and all participants rely on the ISDA wording. Credit events are adapted to each family of reference entities (REs) such as a corporate, a sovereign entity, or an ABS. We outline next the two events that are standard credit events for a corporate entity, and two others that apply in some circumstances.

1. Bankruptcy: The reference entity (RE) or its creditors petition for bankruptcy protection or any equivalent law. In the United States, this corresponds to Chapter 11 or Chapter 7.

2. Failure to pay: The RE misses an interest or principal payment on borrowed money in a specified amount, after any grace period expires (some CDSs do not grant any grace period and are triggered immediately after a missed payment).

3. Debt restructuring: The RE renegotiates the terms of its debt with the banks and the result is that debt holders are worse off after the restructuring than before. Typical examples include an extension of maturity (e.g., the repayment date of a loan is extended by two years) or an increase of the interest rate, itself not undesirable but reflective of the maturity extension, worsening of other terms, and general credit deterioration.

4. Obligation default, obligation acceleration, repudiation/moratorium: ISDA defines these events in its documentation (the 2003 ISDA Credit Derivatives Definitions) but they do not apply to most CDSs and are rare, so we will not detail them further.

The list appears redundant, but it protects the CDS buyer from the situation in which a reference entity's financial stress causes losses and yet the CDS would not be triggered. Thus, the likely situations are covered, and only one event needs to happen to trigger payment. Two parties may agree that some credit events are irrelevant, in which case they can decide to enter a CDS with a shortened list of credit events. These instances are rare and not recommended for the CDS buyer.

In most cases, the credit event is black and white, for instance, filing for bankruptcy protection. In some cases, though, events fall into a grey area. An example is the restructuring of Greece's sovereign debt during the summer of 2011. The restructuring was engineered partially with the intention to avoid triggering a credit event on all outstanding CDS, as it was feared that it would lead to large losses for many banks! The ambiguity of what defines a credit event and the possibility for multiple opinions about their occurrence led ISDA to create five regional credit derivatives determinations committees, or simply DCs, to decide on credit events and ensuing cash settlements. The members of the DCs are investment bankers and institutional investors. In nearly all cases, the process is smooth, but there have been a few instances in which DC members disagreed and sought the opinion of external parties. More information can be found on the DCs website, www .cdsdeterminationcommittees.org.

The occurrence of a credit event also means the early termination of the CDS prior to maturity. The protection is no longer available after a credit event, even if the defaulted entity keeps operating and defaults again, which happens from time to time.

All legal terms used by market participants are updated from time to time by ISDA members to reflect the evolution of the capital markets. The most recent definitions were published by ISDA in 2014. However, a few years later, it was noticed that some financial institutions were abusing these definitions and were engineering bankruptcies primarily in order to trigger a CDS settlement rather than properly reorganizing a struggling company. As a result, ISDA published in 2019 a "Narrowly Tailored Credit Event Supplement" to address the shortcomings of previous definitions. The main change was the introduction of a Credit Deterioration Requirement in the Failure to Pay definition, essentially to make sure that companies would not voluntarily fail to pay back their debt but do so only in case of real financial stress. This is a good example of efforts made by ISDA to maintain the integrity of the CDS market.

Cash versus Physical Settlement

At the risk of repeating ourselves, upon a credit event, the seller pays the buyer regardless of whether the buyer has suffered a loss. The amount paid is now primarily determined by a cash settlement process, which is in contrast to a physical settlement that prevailed up until the early 2000s. We will still review briefly, as understanding the physical settlement process helps to understand the mechanics of the cash settlement process that has become the norm over the last decades.

Physical settlement was prevalent in early credit derivatives because it was presumed that buyers would use CDS contracts to protect actual investments in corporate bonds and instruments of similar seniority like loans and sought to be made whole if an issuer defaulted. To achieve this, they would deliver the bond or loan they held to the CDS seller, who would pay them par value. The expression *physical settlement* reflects the physical delivery of the obligation itself from the buyer to the seller. At that point, the seller, as the new owner of the obligation, would become a creditor of the defaulted entity and would recover whatever was available from the sale of the issuer's assets. More frequently, protection sellers would simply sell the bonds and other obligations at deep discounts to third-party investors who specialize in distressed securities.

The physical settlement process worked efficiently as long as CDS buyers owned bonds or loans that they could deliver. When speculators and other types of buyers entered the market, physical settlement showed its shortcomings. If a CDS buyer did not own the bond, the buyer had to purchase the bond in the market. The buyer would always strive to obtain and deliver the particular bond that was cheapest to deliver. Bonds were often difficult to buy, and the rush to buy them after a credit event led to inflated prices, which reduced the net amount that a CDS buyer would ultimately net after having bought the bond at the inflated price. This phenomenon, called a bond squeeze, was formidable for many CDS buyers after major bankruptcies such as Enron in the early 2000s. As the market continued to develop with more buyers not owning deliverable bonds, the disconnect between protection being bought and sold in the CDS market and the value of the outstanding bonds widened. In fact, for many CDSs, the aggregate outstanding notional is usually a multiple of the deliverable bonds issued.

The bond squeeze and other technical difficulties, such as buyers delivering long-dated bonds to sellers of short-term protection, led to the gradual marginalization of physical settlement and the advent of cash settlement. Although cash settlement prevails now, physical settlement is still an option in CDS contracts.

Cash Settlement and Credit Event Auction

In cash settlement, upon a credit event, the CDS seller pays the CDS buyer a portion of the notional amount of the CDS, which completes the transaction between the two parties. The portion of the notional is intended to reflect the amount that a senior unsecured creditor would lose after recovery, that is (1 − recovery rate) × (notional CDS amount). The working assumption behind a CDS contract is that buyers are senior unsecured creditors and will realize a recovery rate of a senior unsecured creditor.

The objective of the cash settlement is to make investors, who will experience some recovery, whole when the entity defaults. The issue then becomes what the recovery is likely to be. After a credit event, buyers seek to be paid right away, but the actual recovery rates on bonds or loans remain unknown for quite some time as bankruptcy proceedings ensue. Thus, the technique to work around this logistical hurdle is for CDS dealers to participate in a credit event auction, a valuation method devised by ISDA, controlled by regional ISDA determinations committees (DCs), and administered by DC Administration Services (DCAS) and two private companies, IHS Markit (www.ihsmarkit.com) and Creditex (www.creditex.com), a subsidiary of IntercontinentalExchange-ICE. The auction establishes a price for the distressed reference security, which becomes the recovery rate used for the cash settlement of CDS contracts. The market price is disseminated quickly after a credit event, usually well within a few weeks. This establishes the net payment from seller to buyer. Dealers that desire to buy bonds, and thus have the equivalent of physical settlement, may participate in the auction.

TABLE 20.1 Auction Prices of Reference Securities Following Credit Events

Reference Entity	Date	Result
Selecta Group BV	October 20, 2020	51.625
Chesapeake Energy Corporation	August 4, 2020	3.5
Hertz Corp.	June 24, 2020	26.375
Argentine Republic	June 12, 2020	31.5

Source: Creditex and IHS Markit, www.creditfixings.com.

The auction process makes the assets' value transparent and allows for quick settlement, both of which have helped foster more usage and innovation in the CDS market. Technical information about the way the auction is conducted can be found at www.cdsdeterminationcommittee.org. Results of auctions can be found at www.creditfixings.com, a website run jointly by IHS Markit and Creditex. Table 20.1 shows examples of recent auctions following credit events.

For example, on May 22, 2020, the car rental company Hertz filed for bankruptcy protection as a result of the COVID-19 pandemic. On May 24 the determination committee confirmed that a credit event had taken place. The auction was held on June 24 and settlement occurred on June 26. Protection sellers were obliged to pay buyers the notional amount of the CDS less the recovery value. The final price was 26.375 cents on the dollar for the senior unsecured debt. In the case of a $10 million CDS, protection sellers settled with buyers by paying them $7.36 million, which was the $10 million of notional protection less the market's price of the recovery value, which was $2.64 million. At the same time, the list of deliverable obligations was published for participants opting for physical settlement. For instance, one was a 4.125 percent Senior Note due 2021 with final maturity October 15, 2021. Instead of the seller paying the buyer $7.36 million, some sellers accepted the note and paid buyers par value in exchange.

Some buyers may have credit exposure to the entity but may have a different recovery expectation than most senior unsecured creditors. These buyers would need to simply scale the amount of notional they buy based on whether they expect to receive, upon default, more or less than the cash settlement of the reference bond. For buyers who do not actually have any credit exposure on the reference entity, and who, instead, are simply taking a view on an entity's creditworthiness, the amount of notional purchased would be a function of the buyer's desired level of exposure and allocation of capital toward CDS fees, that, upon no credit event, is money never seen again.

VALUATION AND ACCOUNTING TREATMENT

The U.S. GAAP and IFRS require that CDSs, like other derivatives products, be marked-to-market (MTM) with changes in their values recognized in income of both the protection seller and the protection buyer. Because CDS prices often have significant volatility, they generate large swings in income. Figure 20.3 shows the CDS price over time of Walmart Inc., the giant retailer. As one can see, there is tremendous price volatility. The volatility may reflect general market uneasiness, which is not necessarily related to the fundamental credit quality of the reference entity. The volatility is one reason why corporations, particularly public ones, are reluctant to purchase CDSs to protect their credit exposures. Even if having the protection is attractive, corporate executives believe that their main stakeholders both shun and misunderstand swings in income, especially from noncore, derivatives activities. This feature restrains corporates from buying CDSs, even if doing so would help to remove credit exposures from their balance sheets.

As with other financial instruments, if the prevailing market price of a CDS, adjusted for the remaining tenor of the contract, is higher than the price that the buyer paid for the contract, the buyer benefits. The MTM is,

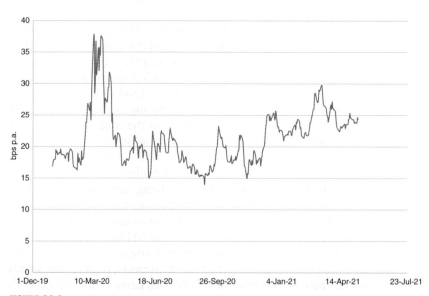

FIGURE 20.3   Price of Five-Year CDS for Walmart Inc.
Source: IHS Markit.

therefore, positive. If the price decreased, it would be the other way around: the protection buyer records a loss. In this sense, the MTM calculation is similar to other instruments.

However, the precise MTM calculation is more involved than for other financial instruments. Although the CDS itself may have an observable price, the position associated with having bought or sold the CDS has to be valued. At a high level, the MTM value of a CDS is the present value of the difference between the prevailing market price the day of the valuation and the transaction price. For instance, if a CDS contract was concluded at 100 bps p.a. and the current market price (for the remaining tenor) is 150 bps p.a., the MTM is the present value of 150 − 100 = 50 bps p.a. for the notional amount over the remaining tenor. In this case, the protection buyer records a profit (which makes sense intuitively because the protection buyer purchased for 100 something that is worth 150) and the protection buyer records a loss (because the protection seller sold for 100 something that is worth 150).

What complicates the MTM valuation for a CDS position is a two-way cash flow that transpires over time. Since buyers pay both up front and over time, the buyer's valuation of its position is the current price of the CDS less the present value of the cash outflows it expects to make under the contract. Similarly, the seller's valuation of its position is the present value of the cash inflows it expects to receive less the present value of the payment it would make given a default event.

The time dimension itself is not complicated. The complication arises from the fact that there may be a credit event, and if so, the buyer no longer has to make (and the seller no longer receives) the quarterly payments, other than what has accrued from the previous quarter's payment to the point in time of the credit event. Thus, the cash outflows (and inflows) are uncertain based on the chance of a credit event happening at any point over the tenor of the contract. This uncertainty throughout the contract's life is what complicates the math needed for the valuation, which must consider the conditional probabilities in calculating expected values for the MTM. For example, the chance that the reference entity defaults in the eighth quarter of the contract's term is predicated on not having defaulted in the prior seven quarters. The chance that default happens in the twelfth quarter is predicated on not having defaulted in the first eleven quarters, and so forth.

In addition, both buyers and sellers adjust the MTM valuations of their CDS positions for the creditworthiness of their counterparties and themselves, known as credit and debit valuation adjustments, respectively, which we discuss in Chapter 16. Because there is counterparty credit risk on both sides, buyers and sellers are permitted under accounting guidelines to mark down the values of what's owed to them to reflect the creditworthiness of their counterparty (credit valuation adjustment, or CVA), and also to mark down their obligations owed to their counterparties for their own credit risk (debit value adjustment, or DVA).

The principles just described constitute the fundamental basis underlying the methodologies employed in the industry. Given the mathematical complexity in calculating MTM positions, the valuation function is handled by a firm's quantitative specialists or it is outsourced to valuation specialists, and each industry participant will develop its own view about the most accurate and practical MTM methodology. We invite readers interested in knowing more about this topic to refer to the many publications on this topic.

USES OF CDSs

There are three predominant uses of CDSs in the market. The first is to secure credit protection. Market participants with credit exposures, such as bonds or loans, may buy a CDS. A second use is an investment in credit by selling the CDS and earning a fee which is essentially a credit spread, similar to a credit spread earned on a bond of the same reference entity. This gives the investor an exposure to the credit of the reference entity without funding a bond and without exposure to interest rate risk. Third, an investor can short a reference entity's credit by buying a CDS without having an underlying exposure to protect. In this case, market participants gain when the reference entity defaults. We discuss each strategy next.

Protection of a Credit Exposure

Credit-default swaps were originally created to protect or hedge credit exposures owned by commercial and investment banks, primarily stemming from bonds and loans. In fact, the creation of CDSs is usually attributed to portfolio managers from J.P. Morgan and other banks, anxious to manage their peak exposures without alienating customer relationships.

Today, simply hedging an exposure remains one frequent motivation of protection buyers. Corporates and financial institutions purchase CDSs as part of the active management of their credit portfolios. Needs arise when origination success leads to proportionally high exposures or when the financial situation of a counterparty deteriorates. Credit-default swaps provide a convenient way to quickly execute a transaction without being in the undesirable position of informing the client or customer that its credit is not well regarded.

Many credit managers, however, are not seduced by CDSs as a hedging option. In addition to income statement volatility, one big issue is basis, which is the difference between the actual loss and the compensation received from the settlement. Since all CDS buyers receive the same amount relative to the notional as a result of the credit-event-auction process, the settlement amount may not cover any single protection buyer's exposure after recovery. Or, the settlement amount could surpass one's net exposure, resulting in a profit being made. Either way, there is uncertainty about the amount that may be received. This is basis *risk*, that is, the chance that there is a difference between the actual loss and the compensation received from the settlement. The simple existence of basis risk is a strong deterrent for some companies that prefer pure insurance solutions that provide a clear indemnification of the actual losses suffered.

Investment in Credit: Long Credit

The motivation of most protection sellers is to make money by taking an exposure to credit risk, that is, to invest in credit risk. Their credit analysis process is similar to that of a bond buyer or a lending institution. After a thorough credit analysis, if the seller is comfortable with the creditworthiness of the reference entity and if the pricing is adequate for the risk taken, the seller puts its capital at risk in exchange for the CDS premium. Note that, in principle, selling a CDS and simultaneously buying a U.S. Treasury bond is the financial equivalent, meaning it has the same cash payoff as investing in a corporate bond. In the former case, one invests cash into a Treasury bond and earns a risk-free return, which is supplemented by the CDS premium that captures incremental return for assuming the credit risk of the reference entity (the corporate in question). In the latter case, one invests cash into a corporate bond and earns a return that is comprised of two pieces—a risk-free return plus a spread for assuming the corporate's credit risk. Thus, both strategies have the same return. If the corporate defaults, both strategies have the same downside: The CDS seller loses the notional less the recovery value (must pay the protection buyer) and the corporate bond investor loses the amount of the bond less recovery.

There are two main advantages to selling CDSs over buying a bond or other ways of taking views on credit. First, CDSs offer the possibility to take credit risk on a stand-alone basis, that is, isolated from the other types of risks typically present in bonds and other products. In the preceding example, we described the financial equivalence of two investment strategies, but the CDS investor need not purchase the Treasury bond. The CDS can be bought a la carte, allowing the investor to take a position only on an entity's credit. Unlike a corporate bond or loan, the CDS is immune from interest-rate risk, for the most part. Credit quality is somewhat related to interest rates since both are affected by the macroeconomic environment and CDS values are discounted for time value of money. However, by and large, the evolution of interest rates does not affect the value of a CDS. What drives the CDS prices is the perceived credit quality of the reference entity, and the general price of credit risk in the marketplace.

Second, taking a position on credit risk does not require cash. Unlike buying a corporate bond, which requires funding, selling a CDS does not require a cash investment, which is attractive for companies (banks) for whom cash and liquidity are deployed parsimoniously. Even for entities with access to large amounts of cash, taking a credit risk position without using cash may be preferable to taking one requiring cash because it increases financial flexibility. However, while financial flexibility may be achieved, note that selling the CDS is fundamentally a leveraged bet. In many cases, very little or even no cash has been fronted, so if the default event occurs, the seller may not have the cash available to make good. The CDS seller can be selling multiple CDSs with an aggregate notional far in excess of the cash and liquid resources it possesses. This is why central counterparties clearinghouses (refer to Chapter 17) and buy-side counterparties require sellers to post collateral against the CDS contract, especially if the seller is not highly rated.

Speculation in Credit: Shorting Credit

Although CDSs were not designed for speculation, their simplicity enables it. In particular, hedge funds often monetize a view on the credit trend of a company or of a country. Often, the view is a negative one and the hedge fund will "short the credit," that is, buy protection via a CDS without having any exposure. The transaction delivers a profit in case the reference entity deteriorates or defaults. The accumulation of short positions can result in a run on a company or a run on a country. Often, the presence of the large short positions calls into question the reference entity's creditworthiness, and thereby restricts its sources of liquidity and capital that might otherwise have been available in the lending markets. On top of this, speculators can easily accumulate large and costly positions such that they have an incentive to take whatever measures are available to trigger a default. Without judging these transactions, we present how they work:

- Step 1: The fund manager believes that the credit quality of Company A will deteriorate over time and that the market disagrees or has not yet figured this out. The CDS price is low compared to what it could be when the deterioration materializes. Let us assume 100 bps p.a. for a five-year trade.

- Step 2: The fund manager buys protection with a five-year CDS on Company A from several counterparties. Let's assume it buys $100 million of notional. It costs the fund manager $1 million per year. The transaction is called a naked short, "naked" because the fund manager has no exposure to protect and "short" because the fund will profit if the value of the reference entity falls.
- Step 3: What the fund manager forecasted to happen actually occurs: after two years, the financial situation of Company A deteriorates and the CDS price jumps to 300 bps p.a. The fund manager wants to take profits off the table and decides to collect (or crystallize) them, which can be done in one of two ways. First, the fund manager can negotiate with the protection sellers for an early termination (unwinding) of the contracts. Most broker-dealers routinely agree to unwind a trade, as they commit to maintain a two-way market to provide liquidity. Thus, the unwind would realize the MTM value of the position, which would be approximately 200 bps × $100 million × 3 remaining years, or $6 million, for the fund manager. We remind readers that one reason why the calculation above is only an approximation is that the actual MTM valuation takes into account the probability of default of counterparty (i.e., the CVA). If unwinding is not possible, the fund manager can sell protection at current market prices, which will cancel out the short position. For example, the fund manager could sell three-year protection on $100 million at 300 bps p.a., thus receiving $9 million over time. After making remaining payments on the original CDS, the net economic result is the same—$6 million net for the fund manager, which will approximate its MTM position gain. Some disadvantages of the multiple positions are greater credit exposure to counterparties, use of credit lines, and the possible cost of posting collateral.

Regulators and government officials dislike naked short CDS because they could accelerate the demise of a company or of a country. For precisely this reason, in 2011 certain European countries forbade naked short positions on sovereign credits such as Greece and Italy. The impact of such measures is hard to assess; some observers believe the restrictions are useless at best and counterproductive at worst.

In 2020, media reported the naked short strategy employed by hedge fund Pershing Square. Its founder Bill Ackman felt in early 2020 that the COVID-19 pandemic could have a devastating effect on the worldwide economy. At the time, the financial markets had not yet integrated this possibility and CDS prices were low and he bought a lot of them. In its letter to investors dated April 6, 2020 (www.pershingsquareholdings.com), the fund confirmed its activities: "Our hedges were in the form of the purchase of credit default swaps (CDS) on the U.S. investment grade and high yield credit indices, and the European investment grade credit index." The *Financial Times* reported that the overall position was roughly $70 billion and generated a realized gain of $2.6 billion in a few weeks.

CREDIT DEFAULT SWAPS FOR CREDIT AND PRICE DISCOVERY

In Chapter 7, we discuss how CDS prices are a source of information regarding an obligor's credit quality. Since the CDS market promotes credit risk transfer and trades, the ensuing prices reflect all the market's information about the credit quality of an obligor and tend to react quickly to changes in circumstances. Thus, apart from entering into a contract to actually hedge a risk, invest in credit, or speculate on an entity's creditworthiness, the CDS market is a valuable resource for the credit risk manager needing to have early warning signs about an obligor, or to use for pricing a transaction in which credit risk is present. That being said, there are caveats in using CDS prices and those we discuss in Chapter 7 are as relevant here in understanding the limitations of CDSs as a form of credit protection and credit investment.

CREDIT DEFAULT SWAPS AND INSURANCE

To recap the beginning of this chapter, CDSs are not an insurance product because they do not indemnify the protection buyer according to their actual losses. Any qualified investor can buy a CDS protection regardless of any existing risk and can receive money regardless of whether losses are suffered. That said, insurance companies were among the largest sellers of CDSs prior to the 2007 crisis. They used their financial strength to sell protection to banks on structured finance instruments like residential mortgage-backed securities (Chapter 11) and collateralized-debt obligations (Chapter 12). They generated significant revenues but also took significant amounts of credit risk, and in turn they experienced huge losses when the mortgage market collapsed.

Today, most insurers have ceased selling CDSs. Their activities are limited to buying protection to hedge the corporate bonds they own as part of the investment portfolio. Most U.S. insurance regulators frown on licensed insurance carriers from engaging in derivative transactions and require disclosure and/or approval and steep capital charges. As a result, the larger insurers established wholly owned broker-dealer subsidiaries with a parental guaranty, which ring-fenced their insurance businesses, securing a high credit rating and thus securing better terms in dealing with counterparties.

INDEXES, LOAN CDSs, MCDSs, AND ABS CDSs

To conclude this chapter, we will summarize some other varieties of CDSs.

Indexes

Credit-default swap indexes have developed over time, and are owned today by IHS Markit. However, they can be traded by anyone. The three main families of corporate CDS indices are CDX, referencing North American corporate reference entities, iTraxx Europe, and iTraxx Asia-Pacific. Sub-families include indices dedicated to North American investment-grade names (e.g., CDX.NA.IG) and noninvestment-grade names (e.g., CDX .NA.HY). For instance, CDX.NA.IG index contains 125 names rated from AA to BBB, equally weighted, representing various industry sectors, available in tenors of 3, 5, 7, and 10 years. The index price reflects the average of the spread of each reference company in the index. Every six months, a new series is launched, and the list of constituents revised. Of the $11.3 trillion CDS notional outstanding as of June 4, 2021, $7.8 trillion were comprised of multiname indices.[2]

For the credit risk manager, indices are of limited interest because they do not enable hedging a precise exposure but only a basket of exposures and the risk manager cannot change the contents of the basket. Credit traders utilize indices, and they can build positions by combining indices and single name CDSs. They are also useful to hedge the systematic MTM risk associated with single name CDSs. For instance, a risk manager who has purchased protection on a large number of entities via several CDSs can be concerned with MTM losses stemming from a general tightening (i.e., decline) of the credit spreads. The risk manager can sell protection on an index because the tightening would result in an MTM gain, which would partially offset the losses on the single-name positions.

Loan CDSs

Loan CDSs or loan-only CDSs are known as LCDSs. Whereas CDSs are designed to mirror the credit risk of a bond, a senior unsecured loan, and, in general, any senior unsecured exposure, LCDSs are meant to cover

---

[2]*Source:* ISDA Swapsinfo, www.swapsinfo.org.

leveraged, syndicated, secured credit exposures. As such, the only reference obligation that can be physically delivered in case of default is a secured loan. Therefore, LCDS can be of interest for risk managers anxious to protect exposures on noninvestment-grade names.

Municipal Obligation CDSs (MCDSs)

Municipal obligations CDSs (MCDs) are CDS contracts designed to reference municipal obligations. Prior to April 2012, MCDSs were nonstandardized, especially as they related to credit events and settlement, in part because of the variation in legal environments across municipal issuers. As of April 2012, ISDA changed the protocol for MCDSs to align with credit and sovereign CDSs, including the use of credit event auctions and granting the Americas, DC committees binding authority over determining credit events. Overall, volume of MCDS contracts is very low and very illiquid as only a handful of banks are active in the market. Only the largest issuers like State of New York or State of Illinois trade, and are traded infrequently.

ABS CDS

Similarly, ABS CDS are related to asset-backed securities. They were widely used in the mid-2000s to build synthetic collateral debt obligations as we will see in the next chapter. Today, they almost belong in the museum of credit history!

CHAPTER 21

Bankruptcy

Throughout this book we have attempted to provide help on how to avoid credit losses. Alas, even the best analysts and the most clever portfolio managers will at times face bankruptcies in their portfolio. In this chapter, after defining bankruptcy, we outline the common characteristics of companies that end up in bankruptcy proceedings and some early warning signals of the soon-to-declare bankruptcy companies. We conclude with some examples of high-profile cases.

Some companies default due to their own problems, not as a result of the entire economy, nor even the industry they are in. The risk manager community calls this type of exposure an "idiosyncratic risk." If fraud is not involved and sound risk management principles as described earlier in this book are followed, most creditors have time to analyze their positions, to reduce their exposures, to strengthen their transactions, and to diversify their portfolios, which will minimize idiosyncratic risk, and credit losses should be minimal.

However, if a major and unexpected event occurs and leads to a major economic crisis, many counterparties will default. The magnitude of the credit losses will depend on the quality and efficiency of the portfolio management efforts. A company able to reduce industry and single name concentration and to hedge its exposures with credit derivatives or credit insurance should suffer less than those companies that have neglected their portfolio management activities, but all credit portfolios will feel some impact.

The 2007 crisis is one example that led to the default of many companies, although the largest ones were in the financial industry, due to involvement in the residential mortgage sector. Another example is the COVID-19 pandemic, which accelerated the demise of numerous companies in various industry sectors affected by the lockdowns and the restrictions imposed on businesses and consumers. In 2020, S&P Global recorded 226 defaults globally among the companies they rate, compared to 118 the year before. These companies represented many different industry sectors and the four largest were oil and gas (50 companies), consumer products (35), media/entertainment (31), and retail (24).

WHAT IS BANKRUPTCY?

What is bankruptcy exactly and how is it related to default? An obligor's default is defined as its failure to live up to the terms and conditions of the contract between it and its counterparty. This is, most noticeably, failure to make timely interest, principal, or other payments under the contract. When the obligor defaults, its counterparty has various contractual rights to take action against the obligor, such as to claim assets or to take control of the organization and replace management. Usually when failure to make a payment occurs, the counterparty will immediately exercise its contractual rights. Most firms have multiple counterparties, and a default of one contract often means actual or imminent default of other contracts. Therefore, creditors will work fast and furiously to capture what assets they believe are rightfully due to them. The obligor, to protect itself from the onslaught of creditors, files for protection under bankruptcy laws. As soon as bankruptcy is filed, the creditors must subsume their claims to a bankruptcy proceeding. In the United States, these are administered by the debtor-in-possession or a Chapter 11 trustee.

Although each country has its own bankruptcy law, the laws function in more or less the same way around the globe, and in this chapter we focus only on United States bankruptcies. In the United States, there are two main chapters of U.S. federal bankruptcy law for commercial enterprises. Chapter 11 is a bankruptcy law for reorganization that allows the obligor to work out and restructure its obligations for the purposes of a fresh start such that it emerges from the bankruptcy proceedings as a viable entity. Chapter 7 is a bankruptcy law for liquidation in which the obligor is assumed to be unlikely to survive, even with a restructuring, thus it undergoes liquidation.

At bankruptcy proceedings, all creditors are represented. At the table are lenders (banks and bondholders), suppliers, shareholders, and institutions such as the Pension Benefit Guaranty Corp., which has to take over the defined benefit pension liabilities if the company defaults. Chapter 11 status provides an opportunity to renegotiate all contracts, and nothing is off the table. The amount of debt can be reduced, labor contracts with employees renegotiated, and pension obligations cancelled. Ultimately, the reorganization plan must be approved by the court and by the creditors. Pursuant to a plan of reorganization, a debtor is able to repay only a portion of its debt to its creditors, hence the plan proposed is often unpalatable to the creditors.

Difficult negotiations occur, as the interests of all parties are not aligned. For instance, lenders want shareholders to abandon all their rights. On the contrary, shareholders want lenders to absorb losses on the money they lent in the past. Among lenders, all parties try to secure as many assets as possible to provide new financing.

Often, obligors file for protection under Chapter 11 only to discover that creditors do not approve the reorganization plan or that the plan doesn't work out. If so, the assets would then be liquidated and proceeds used to pay off the creditors, who would, in most instances, receive less than 100 percent of the debt.

For Chapter 11, one of the priorities is to maintain access to liquidity during the bankruptcy process. Specialized institutions provide debtor-in-possession or DIP financing that enables a company to keep operating. Credit analysts involved in DIP have to decide what level of collateral to require. The DIP lender has priority against almost all cash collected as a result of the sale of assets and liquidation or upon reorganization with new financing, until DIP is repaid.

Most bankruptcy proceedings are lengthy. In rare cases, prepackaged bankruptcies are presented to a judge. In such cases, negotiations between all stakeholders are concluded prior to the filing and the company. All parties agree so that the company can start operating in a new context right after the filing.

PATTERNS OF BANKRUPT COMPANIES

In Chapter 6 of this book, we present the two pillars underlying the traditional credit analysis of a company. As a reminder, they are the qualitative analysis, such as the quality of management and the competitiveness of the products, and the quantitative analysis, which consists of an extensive review of the financial statements. In this chapter, we instead describe high-level patterns among companies that ultimately declare bankruptcy.

Many companies that default on their obligations suffer from fundamental flaws in their business models, cost structures, or financial structures. Often the flaws are not obvious to management and wishful thinking keeps them from making needed, and sometimes radical, changes to keep the business afloat. When management cannot turn things around, ultimately the company runs out of cash and defaults on its financial obligations.

Well-informed credit analysts are usually aware of an obligor's flaws. This does not mean that they won't approve of extending credit to the obligor, but rather, they might recommend a low notional, short-term exposure, sufficient collateral, strong covenants, or a combination of these mitigating techniques.

Flaws in the Business Model

Flaws in business models can involve overly optimistic assumptions about the demand for a product or the ability of the company to cross-sell across its product line. Many mergers and acquisitions deals involve overly optimistic assumptions about business synergies that ultimately result in a diminution of value for shareholders and bondholders alike, such as the infamous AOL Time Warner merger. Examples in the manufacturing industry include the products themselves, which are no longer adapted to consumer needs. They may be too complicated, obsolete, too expensive, or simply useless. Think of a company like Kodak which at one point dominated its industry. As technological innovations and the changing shape of customer needs continue at a rapid pace, obsolescence will prevail and bankruptcies will follow.

In the service industry, changes in consumer habits, such as the growth in online shopping at the expense of the brick-and-mortar model, have been behind recent bankruptcies of many companies too slow to recognize a change in consumer behavior. When a new generation of consumers emerges and does not want to shop the way their parents did, established companies had better adapt themselves to their new customers' habits. Otherwise, new entrants will emerge and jeopardize the very existence of the incumbents. One example in the United States is Pier 1 Imports, a retailer of home furnishings, which was liquidated in May 2020. Gradually, consumers preferred to order their products online and companies like Wayfair grew very quickly in the United States and in Europe at the expense of Pier 1 and similar companies.

The airline industry is thought to be operating under a flawed business model; a huge capital investment (the cost of the aircraft) can never be fully recouped in the pricing, since airlines have huge pressure to cover their operating costs, and thus they compete with each other on a marginal cost, rather than average cost, basis. It is not surprising that companies in the airline industry are frequently in bankruptcy court.

Flaw in the Cost Structure

Credit analysts pay close attention to the cost structure of a company, including following key ratios and other financial metrics that we outline in Chapter 6 of this book. At a higher level, many companies default because their cost structure is out of synch with their market and competitors. When competition prevents sellers from transferring some costs onto their customers, operating margins become thin or even turn negative, debt becomes unserviceable, and ultimately they default. A cost problem can happen anywhere in the operations, investment, or financing of a company, but we discuss three areas where we have seen most problems occur.

The first area is in operating costs, and within this, labor costs. Wages and other compensation costs such as health insurance, payroll tax, pension costs, and worker's compensation insurance premiums present a formidable hurdle for many companies. In many developed countries, media and the politicians lament the loss of manufacturing jobs by the hundreds of thousands, but the reality is that many companies cannot survive if they keep their production in their home markets. Some companies that waited or were too late to send their production overseas paid a high price.

High-cost structures also involve the firm's financial structure. High leverage can pose a problem because of the costs of servicing this debt load, namely high interest payments and large principal payments. Although principal can often be refinanced, most situations involving high leverage are designed to be temporary, with the debt amortizing over time. Vulnerable companies include those purchased by private equity companies, where the acquisition costs are primarily financed by additional debt. There are many examples of leveraged companies that defaulted, one being the car rental company Hertz in May 2020 with $17 billion worth of debt on its balance sheet, partially due to a high growth strategy and partially due to a high level of debt going back to its acquisition by private equity firms.

Finally, we mention the problem of defined-benefit pension-fund costs. Although most companies no longer offer a defined-benefit pension to new employees, the accumulated promises that they have made to existing employees over the years have amassed into a large liability that, for most corporate sponsors, is not fully funded. Unlike a defined-contribution plan, a defined-benefit plan puts the onus on the pension sponsor (i.e., the corporation) to make contractual payments to retirees and in some cases, to their dependents, until death. Companies need to set aside funds to pay for these obligations, but most have set aside inadequate amounts. First, most companies fund at minimum amounts from both a legal (via the PBGC-required premium payments) and accounting-treatment perspective. Second, rates of return generally have fallen short of expectations. Third, people are living significantly longer that what companies assumed when they originally made the promises, thus extending their obligations further out into the future (presenting sponsors with longevity risk, which is the risk that people live longer than expected). Finally, many companies also offered other postretirement benefits such as health care, whose inflation has outpaced that of any other sector, again amplifying the corporate sponsor's future obligations.

Pensions have placed significant burdens on some companies. Many companies will not experience a cash crunch until the retirement spike hits their workforce. Increasingly, companies are proactively de-risking their pension plans with plan freezes, restructurings, buying asset and longevity risk protections, and fully de-risking by transferring their plans' assets and liabilities, with usually a sizeable cash top-up, to a third-party. However, many firms have been less proactive, and are poised for stress and the potential for insolvency due in part or in whole from pensions, in the future.

Flaws in the Financial Structure

Credit analysts have to pay more attention now than in the past to the refinancing risk of a company's debt. Being dependent on refinancing is a precarious situation to be in. No one can take for granted the readiness of existing lenders to extend their loans or new lenders to replace maturing debt with new loans. For industrial companies, the maturity of the loans should be spread out over time, so that no single large amount needs refinancing at any point in time.

Since banks and lending institutions rely on short-term financing, refinancing risk is more pronounced. Large institutions that sell commercial paper every day face the risk that one day investors turn their backs. High-profile examples of banks unable to refinance their obligations in the past include Dexia, a French and Belgian bank, with close to $100 billion of short-term debt, that was bailed out by the two governments in 2011, and MF Global, which we will discuss later on in this chapter.

SIGNALING ACTIONS

When financial difficulties become overwhelming, management commences taking radical actions to save their companies. These actions, which become publicly known, confirm to the credit analyst that the situation is dire.

Following is an incomplete list of actions that companies fighting to survive commonly use. Note that these actions are also used during a reorganization phase after a filing for bankruptcy protection.

- Healthy companies have large lines of credit available but typically do not draw on them. They are in place just in case a need arises in the future. As seen in Chapter 18, bank loans and bond indentures contain covenants that, when breached, prevent the borrower from having access to liquidity. Therefore, companies in need of cash tend to draw the full amount of the facility just prior to breaching some covenants. We will review the case of Kodak later on, which ultimately filed for bankruptcy protection. The first visible sign that their situation was dire was when it became known, in September 2011, that it had tapped its credit line. Kodak's stock price lost 25 percent of its value the following day as observers awakened to the tough times that lay ahead and they filed for bankruptcy protection a few months later in January 2012.
- Although there are good reasons to sell assets, when a firm decides to sell strategic properties or subsidiaries, it is usually a signal that it needs to raise cash quickly.
- Companies that raise capital in the absence of large acquisitions or planned investments may be doing so to simply raise cash to meet operational or financing obligations. Existing shareholders, either directly or via the company's directors, may approve this plan, knowing that dilution is preferable to having nothing if the firm is unable to raise the cash it needs and the firm heads to bankruptcy court.
- Hiring bankruptcy lawyers, investment banks, or specialized advisers to review strategic options is almost always a sign that a company is preparing itself for a default. The role of these advisors is to try to find a solution outside the bankruptcy courts whenever possible. They start discussions with the various stakeholders and quickly define options, such as finding a suitor to help the company stay alive. If no alternative to a bankruptcy filing is found, they typically stay involved during the reorganization process.

EXAMPLES OF BANKRUPTCIES

Eastman Kodak

Kodak's bankruptcy is a classic example of a company whose success was linked to a technology that gradually became obsolete and that was unable to reinvent itself to compete in a new environment. When Kodak filed for bankruptcy protection in January 2012, few people were surprised. Rumors about the filing had been circling the company for some time. A few months earlier, the media reported that Kodak drew on its bank lines, which was a sign that the company was running out of cash and drawing on its lines before it was too late. The management had naturally dismissed the filing rumors, but by mid-January 2012, the bankruptcy made the headlines of the global media.

Kodak was no ordinary company, and there was an aspect of nostalgia in the articles written and the comments made on TV. For many people, the little yellow boxes were synonymous with happy family vacations. Before the advent of digital cameras, souvenirs were immortalized in pictures taken on Kodak film. Kodak film was available all over the world, dominating the global market, with Fujifilm of Japan being a distant second.

In 1881, George Eastman had created The Eastman Dry Plate Company and two years later moved it to Rochester, in the northern part of New York State, close to the Canadian border. The company specialized in cameras and films for the general public, such as the Kodachrome series of films, introduced in 1935. In the early 1990s, Kodak employed more than 130,000 staff and made $16 billion in sales.

Kodak quickly understood the threat of the digital technology to their main business of films and film processing. Kodak invested early in digital cameras that directly competed with film. Rather than seeing competing products gradually making its film obsolete, Kodak decided to occupy the territory and not let the camera makers, primarily Japanese companies like Olympus or Canon, take away its business. The move was successful, and Kodak's digital cameras were one of the first to hit the market in the late 1990s.

Unfortunately, the competition quickly caught up, and Japanese and Korean competitors surpassed Kodak's sales of digital cameras. To make things worse, smartphones with high-quality built-in cameras reduced the demand for digital cameras altogether. One of the first decisions made after the bankruptcy filing was to shut the digital-camera unit, a move made to save precious cash. Kodak's other attempt to diversify away from film also was not successful. It entered the printer market, but its market share was small compared to leaders like Hewlett-Packard and Lexmark.

Early in 2012, Kodak was running out of options, and, burdened by high costs, filed for bankruptcy. Management and debtors worked hard to evaluate options and imagine a future for Kodak and 18 months later, a more focused company emerged from bankruptcy protection. Today, the company is still in business but much smaller. They focus on print, advanced materials and chemicals. In 2020 their revenue was $1.03 billion and their net income negative $541 million.

TABLE 21.1   Ten Largest Public Company U.S. Bankruptcy Filings since 1980

Company	Bankruptcy Date	Description	Assets
Lehman Brothers Holdings Inc.	09/15/08	Investment Bank	$691,063
Washington Mutual, Inc.	09/26/08	Savings & Loan Holding Co.	$327,913
WorldCom, Inc.	07/21/02	Telecommunications	$103,914
General Motors Corporation	06/01/09	Manufactures and Sells Cars	$82,290
CIT Group Inc.	11/01/09	Banking Holding Company	$71,000
Pacific Gas & Electric Co.	01/14/19	Energy	$71,000
Enron Corp.	12/02/01	Energy Trading, Natural Gas	$65,503
Conseco, Inc.	12/17/02	Financial Services Holding Co.	$61,390
MF Global Holdings Ltd.	10/31/11	Commodities and Derivatives Broker	$41,000
Chrysler LLC	04/30/09	Manufactures and Sells Cars	$39,300

Note: Listed in descending order by pre-petition assets (assets in $ millions).
Source: visualcapitalist.com.

MF Global

MF Global (MF) was by no means a household name. However, when it filed for bankruptcy protection in October 2011, it became the eighth largest bankruptcy in U.S. history in terms of assets, just ahead of Chrysler (Table 21.1). Large bankruptcies fortunately remain relatively rare. Since the publishing of the first edition of this book in 2012, only PG&E, the Californian electric utility that filed for bankruptcy in January 2019, joined the Top 10 list. This is why we are using the example of MF Global, a little dated but providing many lessons to learn from.

The failure of MF is a good example of a financial company dependent on short-term funding. Less than one week went by between the time it was downgraded and when it defaulted. Equally impressive was that it was liquidated shortly after its Chapter 11 filing because no company showed interest for any part of the business.

MF Global was a broker-dealer, heavily involved in some futures markets. Its clients were primarily institutional investors but also traders and end users such as farmers who were MF Global's customers, due to its big presence in agriculture derivatives products.

The problems of MF Global started when it was revealed that, in order to increase profitability, it had made massive purchases of European sovereign bonds. When European economic troubles increased, the bonds lost value. Because MF Global had financed them with borrowed money, it had to provide additional collateral to compensate for the loss of value. Then, in mid-October, rating agencies realized that the size of the bond holdings was too large compared to its balance sheet. As a result they downgraded the company and it took less than a week before all stakeholders lost complete confidence in MF Global. Clients that had deposited money with the firm took it back, and derivatives counterparties requested more collateral. MF Global was unable to supply the amount of cash requested.

The company filed for bankruptcy protection a week after the first downgrade. Soon thereafter, media reported that another firm had considered a takeover up until a couple of hours before the Chapter 11 filing, but the suspicion of fraud deterred the suitor. Large sums of customer funds were missing, and the suspicion was that these funds had been used to meet collateral calls from counterparties, an illegal action in the United States.

The lessons learned from the demise of MF Global are multiple. First, financial institutions depend on borrowed money and it does not take much for investors to lose confidence, which triggers a run on the bank that quickly leads to bankruptcy. In contrast to industrial companies like Kodak, the demise of a financial institution happens quickly. Other examples include Lehman Brothers and Bear Stearns, whose fates were sealed over a weekend. Another lesson is the danger of fraud or alleged fraud. There is not much that a credit analyst can do when the company is involved in illegal transactions or presents inaccurate financial statements. Without the discovery that MF Global had misappropriated customers' funds, the company might have been taken over, to the likely benefit of all creditors. Its client base was attractive, and several competitors considered purchasing the firm. All attempts fell apart after MF Global's management was unable to explain the missing customer funds.

FINAL WORDS

In this chapter we provide some context and color around bankruptcies. Recall that a key variable in loss-given-default, MTM valuation, CVaR, and other measures of credit risk exposure is the recovery value should an obligor default. The recovery value is determined in large part by the bankruptcy proceeding. How the negotiation, restructuring, or liquidation unfolds, as well as the actions of the obligor, its constituents, and the trustee immediately before, during, and post reorganization, will be key drivers of the ultimate recovery.

About the Authors

Sylvain Bouteillé is Head of Trade Credit for the Americas at AIG, the global insurance company. Prior to AIG, Sylvain worked more than 20 years at Swiss Re, one of the world's leading providers of reinsurance and insurance. In his last role, Sylvain was a Managing Director and a Member of the Global Business Management Committee of Swiss Re Corporate Solutions. Sylvain held various leadership positions at Swiss Re, including Head of Credit Risk Management NA and Head of Structured Credit Underwriting NA. Sylvain holds a MSc degree in Civil Engineering from ENTPE (France) and an MBA from INSEAD (France). He has been teaching Financial Statement Analysis and Credit Risk Management to graduate students at Queens College, City University of New York, since 2011.

Diane Coogan-Pushner is a financial economist who has held the positions of Chief Risk Officer of The Navigators Group, Inc., a publicly traded commercial insurer, and Managing Director for structured reinsurance solutions at Swiss Re. During the financial crisis, Diane founded the Risk Management program for the Queens College, City University of New York, where she was Director, Associate Dean, and a full-time faculty member. Earlier in her career, Diane headed the Market Analysis and Forecasting Division for AT&T's consumer markets and was a portfolio manager for insurance-focused funds. Diane has served on Standard & Poor's Insurance Advisory Council and on the board of a privately held insurance company. Diane received her PhD from Boston University and began her career at the World Bank working with the financial institutions of East Africa. She is a CFA® charterholder.

Index